1 MONTH OF FREE READING

at
www.ForgottenBooks.com

By purchasing this book you are eligible for one month membership to ForgottenBooks.com, giving you unlimited access to our entire collection of over 1,000,000 titles via our web site and mobile apps.

To claim your free month visit:
www.forgottenbooks.com/free212612

* Offer is valid for 45 days from date of purchase. Terms and conditions apply.

ISBN 978-0-266-39754-0
PIBN 10212612

This book is a reproduction of an important historical work. Forgotten Books uses state-of-the-art technology to digitally reconstruct the work, preserving the original format whilst repairing imperfections present in the aged copy. In rare cases, an imperfection in the original, such as a blemish or missing page, may be replicated in our edition. We do, however, repair the vast majority of imperfections successfully; any imperfections that remain are intentionally left to preserve the state of such historical works.

Forgotten Books is a registered trademark of FB &c Ltd.
Copyright © 2018 FB &c Ltd.
FB &c Ltd, Dalton House, 60 Windsor Avenue, London, SW19 2RR.
Company number 08720141. Registered in England and Wales.

For support please visit www.forgottenbooks.com

THE JOURNALS OF
LADY KNIGHTLEY OF FAWSLEY

"A PERFECT woman—nobly plann'd,
To warn, to comfort and command,
And yet a creature still and bright
With something of angelic light."

      WILLIAM WORDSWORTH.

"A Diary need not be a dreary chronicle of one's movements, it should aim rather at giving a salient account of some particular episode, a walk, a book, a conversation. It is a practice which brings its own reward; it is a singularly delightful thing to look at old diaries, to see how one was occupied ten years ago, what one was reading; the people one was meeting, one's earlier point of view."

      ARTHUR CHRISTOPHER BENSON.

Louisa M Knightley

THE JOURNALS OF
LADY KNIGHTLEY
OF FAWSLEY

Edited by JULIA CARTWRIGHT
(Mrs. ADY)

1856–1884

ILLUSTRATED

LONDON
JOHN MURRAY, ALBEMARLE STREET, W.
1915

All rights reserved

PREFACE

THESE selections from the private Journals of the late Lady Knightley are given to the world in obedience to her own wishes. Some years ago, she expressed a hope that it might be possible to publish some portions of her Journals, and asked me to undertake the task. This request was confirmed in a letter found among her papers after her death. "Not," the writer added modestly, "that the story of my life is worth telling, but because, I think, some of the things that it contains may interest and amuse my friends, and possibly appeal to a wider public." The present volume begins with the Journal first started by Lady Knightley in 1856, and carries the story down to the year 1884. This period includes the whole of her childhood and youth, as well as fifteen years of her married life, and ends with the death of the Duke of Albany, with whom she had been closely connected in the lifetime of her father, Sir Edward Bowater. Some parts of the Journal, relating to important public events or family affairs, have been supplemented by passages from Lady Knightley's weekly letters to her mother, Lady Bowater, who lived to an advanced age and only died, at her home in Richmond Park, in the year 1892.

This correspondence has also been placed in my hands, in accordance with Lady Knightley's last wishes, and has enabled me to add several characteristic touches to the picture of her life and surroundings that is so vividly set forth in these Journals.

JULIA CARTWRIGHT.

CONTENTS

CHAP.		PAGE
	LADY KNIGHTLEY OF FAWSLEY	xi
I.	CHILDHOOD AND EARLY YOUTH (1842–1860)	1
II.	LONDON AND CANNES (1861–1862)	19
III.	RICHMOND PARK, DUNWICH, AND ARBURY (1862)	36
IV.	THE ROYAL WEDDING (1863)	47
V.	RICHMOND PARK, DUNWICH, AND OSBORNE (1863–1864)	60
VI.	A GAY SEASON (1864)	73
VII.	A VISIT TO BALMORAL (MAY–JUNE 1865)	89
VIII.	BALLS AND WEDDINGS (1865–1866)	104
IX.	WINDSOR AND CLIVEDEN (1866)	113
X.	POLITICS AND SOCIETY (1866–1867)	121
XI.	LONDON, SUFFOLK, AND FROGMORE (1867–1868)	133
XII.	A VISIT TO SILESIA (1868)	145
XIII.	SIR RAINALD KNIGHTLEY (1869)	160
XIV.	MARRIAGE (1869)	171
XV.	HATFIELD AND BROOK STREET (1870)	185
XVI.	HARROGATE, SCOTLAND, OSBORNE, AND BURGHLEY (1870–1871)	204
XVII.	A LONDON SEASON AND A FOREIGN TOUR (1871–1872)	215
XVIII.	POLITICAL PARTIES AND CABINET MINISTERS (1872–1873)	226
XIX.	ROYALTIES—ENGLISH AND FOREIGN (1873)	242
XX.	A CONSERVATIVE MINISTRY (1874)	255
XXI.	LONDON AND HOMBURG (1875)	273
XXII.	THE GIRLS' FRIENDLY SOCIETY (1876–1880)	287
XXIII.	THE ROYAL TITLES BILL AND THE EASTERN QUESTION (1876–1877)	296

CHAP.		PAGE
XXIV.	THE BALKAN WAR AND CONGRESS OF BERLIN (1877–1878)	312
XXV.	AGRICULTURAL DEPRESSION AND CONSERVATIVE DEFEATS (1878–1880)	326
XXVI.	LORD BEACONSFIELD'S DEATH—THE DUKE OF ALBANY'S MARRIAGE (1881–1883)	344
XXVII.	CARLTON HOUSE TERRACE AND CLAREMONT (1883–1884)	363
	INDEX	381

LIST OF ILLUSTRATIONS

LADY KNIGHTLEY (Photogravure) . . . *Frontispiece*
(From Mezzotint, after G. B. Black, 1869.)

FACING PAGE

LADY BOWATER, H.R.H. PRINCE LEOPOLD, AND MISS BOWATER. DRAWING-ROOM, CHÂTEAU LEADER, CANNES, 1862 . 30

LORD CHARLES FITZROY, DR. GÜNTHER, H.R.H. PRINCE LEOPOLD, AND MISS BOWATER. CHÂTEAU LEADER, CANNES, 1862 32

LADY BOWATER 42

SOTTERLEY HALL, SUFFOLK 74

SIR RAINALD KNIGHTLEY, BART., 1869 . . . 160

SIR CHARLES KNIGHTLEY, BART., 1813 . . . 184

FIRLE PLACE, SUSSEX 192

FAWSLEY 204

ORIEL WINDOW, GREAT HALL, FAWSLEY . . . 248

PLAN OF FAWSLEY 290

FAWSLEY CHURCH 344

LADY KNIGHTLEY OF FAWSLEY, 1904 . . . 374

These illustrations are chiefly taken from miniatures and photographs in the possession of Sir Charles Knightley, Bart., and Lady Knightley, to whom both the publisher and editor of these journals are greatly indebted for their help and courtesy.

The photograph of the Oriel Window is reproduced by kind permission of the proprietors of *Country Life*.

LADY KNIGHTLEY OF FAWSLEY

1842–1913

THE girls of the present day sometimes forget how much they owe to the women of the last generation. They hardly realise how many of the privileges and opportunities which they enjoy were won for them by their mothers and grandmothers, those despised women of the Victorian era. By clinging steadfastly to their high ideals, by patient and untiring endeavour, these valiant pioneers fought their way, through difficulties and opposition, into the larger and freer life, and made all future progress possible.

Such a woman was Louisa, Lady Knightley, whose death, two years ago, was recognised on all sides as a loss, not only to her own family and friends, but to the whole British Empire. A typical Early Victorian by birth and education, Lady Knightley stands midway between the Evelinas and Emmas of the last century and the independent damsels of the present day. But in many ways she was in advance of her age. Born and bred in the narrowest of court circles, married into one of the oldest and most exclusive of county families, she naturally inherited the strong prejudices and prepossessions of her class. But her receptive mind was always ready to take in new ideas, and prepared to assimilate them. She was never harsh and censorious in her judgments, or needlessly severe on the more advanced views of the rising generation. From early youth she had never wavered in her fixed resolve to lead a life of active usefulness and devote all her powers to the service of God and man. All manner of social reforms appealed to her. Schemes for the improvement of housing and domestic economy, for the spread of education, thrift, and temperance, for village clubs and Reading Unions, model dwellings and penny banks, alike claimed her support. Above all, the condition of women and girls in every rank of life was the object of her keenest interest. She was one of the founders of the Girls' Friendly Society and of the Working Ladies' Guild, and afterwards took an active part in the work of Imperial emigration. Into this great movement she threw herself heart and soul, realising its importance both as the means of bettering the lives of women at home and of building up our Empire beyond the seas. In 1901 she was elected the first President of the South African Colonisation Society, and in 1908 she succeeded Mrs. Joyce as President of the British Women's Emigration Association. A strong supporter of women's suffrage, but no less strongly opposed to militant methods, she became the first President of the Conservative and Unionist Association for the Franchise of Women, and lent her powerful influence both as speaker and writer to the advocacy of the cause. Lady Knightley was also a member of the National Union of Women Workers, and took a leading part in its Congresses and Conferences. When, a few weeks after her death, in October 1913, the National Union held its Congress at Hull, and the loss which womanhood had sustained by this sad event was publicly announced, the whole assembly rose at the mention of Lady Knightley's name and paid silent and reverent homage to her memory. Her interest in hospitals and ambulance work was also keen. She was a Lady of Grace of the Order of St. John of Jerusalem, and passed the examination which qualified her for admission to this Order. As a member of the Committee of Management of St. George's Hospital and of the Northampton Infirmary, she took an active and enlightened share in the work of these larger institutions, and was a liberal supporter of cottage hospitals and other local charities in the country district round Fawsley. An ardent churchwoman herself, she was always ready to help the bishops and clergy in building schools and churches, and constantly visited Northampton to lay foundation stones and open bazaars and fêtes in aid of Church extension in this populous town. After taking a prominent part in the struggle to preserve religion in our schools, she became a member of the Northamptonshire Education Committee, and won golden opinions from her political opponents in this capacity.

From her girlhood, politics had been one of Lady Knightley's chief interests, and her marriage to Sir Rainald Knightley, who sat as Conservative member for South Northamptonshire during forty years, introduced her to the highest political circles. She played an active part in electoral contests, speaking and canvassing vigorously for her husband and his colleagues, and during the fierce struggles of the eighties it was no secret that Sir Rainald owed his seat to his wife's eloquence and popularity. Lady Knightley was one of the original members of the Primrose League and was present at the inauguration of this now famous association, in Lady Glenesk's house in Piccadilly. The rapid growth and excellent organisation of the League owed much to her practical abilities, and to the end of her life she remained a member of the Grand Council and Ruling Councillor of the Knightley Habitation.

In all of these varied departments of public life Lady Knightley's remarkable gifts of body and mind were conspicuously revealed. Her fine bearing, clear musical voice, and deep convictions made her an admirable speaker, while her statesman-like qualities, unfailing tact and courtesy, and generous appreciation of worth in others, rendered her invaluable as a chairman. She often said laughingly that her vocation in life was to sit on committees, and no one who has worked with her on councils and boards can fail to do justice to the rare powers which she displayed on these occasions. The most delicate and difficult negotiations were entrusted to her care and were successfully carried through by her tact and skill. When in 1905 she went to South Africa as President of the newly formed Colonisation Society, Lord Rosebery is said to have remarked at a meeting of the Rhodes Trustees, " If Lady Knightley is able to compose the differences between our two ladies' committees, I shall be prepared to rise in the House of Lords and propose her appointment as Ambassador to Paris, or anywhere else ! " Of the charm and distinction of her presence, of her finely cut features and frank blue eyes with their winning gaze, of the sweetness and humility of her nature, it is hard to say too much. At her death, political opponents joined with friends in extolling her talents and virtues, and a Liberal member for Northamptonshire, who was one of her colleagues on the Education Committee, did not hesitate to call her " one of the noblest of English-women."

From the age of fourteen, Lady Knightley kept a Journal in which every evening she noted down the chief incidents of the past day, together with anything she had seen and heard which she felt to be worthy of notice. These records fill sixty volumes and cover a period of fifty-seven years, from April 1856 to September 1913, when she breaks off her narrative in the middle of a visit paid by the Duchess of Albany to Fawsley, only a fortnight before her own death. It is clear from many passages in these Journals that they were written with a view to publication. Lady Knightley speaks of studying other letters and diaries, the *Reminiscences of Sir Mountstuart Grant Duff*, the *Recollections of Mr. Leveson Gower*, the *Journal de Marie Bashkirtseff*, and the privately printed *Letters of Lady Lyttelton*, with the object of " improving her own Journal, and making it more interesting." She herself had a genuine literary instinct, besides possessing a wide knowledge of English, French, and German literature. From childhood, to be an author had been one of her greatest ambitions, and after her marriage she wrote an article on the county of Suffolk in the *Quarterly Review* and contributed several papers to the *Nineteenth Century* and other magazines, besides writing a variety of pamphlets on social and political questions. As the Duke of Argyll prophesied, when he met Miss Bowater at Balmoral in 1865, the Journal which she was in the habit of keeping with such regularity cannot fail to prove an invaluable document for the use of future historians of the nineteenth century.

Lady Knightley's close connection with the Royal Family lends especial interest to the record. Miss Bowater accompanied her parents and Prince Leopold to Cannes in the winter of 1862, and was there when Sir Edward Bowater, in whose charge the little Prince had been placed, died on the same day as the Prince Consort. The task of consoling and cheering the orphan boy fell to his youthful daughter, and on their return to England Miss Bowater paid frequent visits to Osborne, Windsor, and Balmoral. Her picture of the widowed Queen surrounded by her fatherless children at this sorrowful time is most touchingly drawn, while her lively account of life at Balmoral, in its freedom and joyousness, forms one of the pleasantest parts of the Journal. Queen Victoria honoured Lady Knightley with many tokens of her confidence and regard, and expressed her high opinion of her to others in the warmest terms, while her intimacy with Princess Christian lasted to the end of her life. On the Duke of Albany's marriage to Princess Hélène of Waldeck, Lady Knightley was appointed Extra Lady-in-Waiting to Her Royal Highness, with whom she formed a close friendship, which was deepened by the premature death of the Prince to whom she had been so long and deeply attached. The Duchess of Albany, in fact, was staying at Fawsley in September 1913 when Lady Knightley contracted the fatal chill which brought her life to a sudden close. Her gracious Majesty, Queen Mary, who had known Lady Knightley from her childhood, was in Northamptonshire with the King for the army manœuvres at the same time, and paid her a visit only a few days before she died.

Another feature of these Journals is the sidelight which they throw on political controversies and parties, and the graphic portraits which they give of the leading statesmen of the day, with whom the writer was brought into contact by her husband's position. Visits to Hatfield and Burghley, to Euston and Chevening, dinners with the party leaders in Arlington Street and Downing Street, Foreign Office and Admiralty receptions, evening parties at Dorchester or Londonderry House, breakfasts at Chiswick and Buckingham Palace, garden-parties at Sion and Holland House, all find a place in these pages. Conversations with

Lord Salisbury and Lord Carnarvon, with Sir Stafford Northcote, Mr. Hardy, and Mr. Goschen, with Lady Dorothy Nevill and Lady Cork, with Sir William Harcourt and Mr. Disraeli, with Mr. Gladstone, Mr. Balfour, and Lord Hartington, are recorded in the same lively and animated style. A dinner with Lord Wolseley and Robert Browning for neighbours, a talk with Mr. Motley or Mr. Froude, a ride with Lord Stanhope or Mr. Lowe, a week-end with the old Duchess of Cleveland at Osterley or an evening party at the Speaker's with the full moon shining on the Terrace and the lights reflected in the river, were red-letter days in Lady Knightley's annals.

On the one hand, we have a vivid picture of the London season, with its bewildering whirl of dinners and parties, of concerts and balls, its friendships and flirtations, its court functions and parliamentary debates, its glimpses of distinguished personages and foreign royalties, of great poets and painters, of historians and travellers, Shahs and Sultans; on the other, we are introduced to the interior of a country house in the heart of the Midlands and learn to realise the thousand occupations and duties, the vast accumulation of business and trifles which go to make up the life of the mistress of a large country house. With all her love of London society, Lady Knightley was passionately fond of her country home. She threw herself with as much zest and enthusiasm into this life as into the other, and rode to hounds, galloped across country, canvassed and spoke at Primrose League and Girls' Friendly Society meetings, and planted trees and trudged over farms, as she often said, " like the true country bumpkin that I am ! "

Whatever she did was done with all her might. No one was a greater lady in Northamptonshire or was more careful of the welfare of the tenants and labourers on the Fawsley estate than Lady Knightley, both during her husband's lifetime and when his death left her the sole mistress of this beautiful home.

Lady Knightley's Journal, we repeat, is a work of genuine historic value, but this is far from being its only merit. As a human document, it has a still deeper interest. It is the frankest, most guileless and natural of records. The writer hides nothing and excuses nothing. She confesses her own mistakes and faults as freely as she does those of her neighbours. She makes no secret of her ambitions and desires, of her love of admiration and wish to make a good marriage from the worldly point of view, while at the same time she insists that nothing shall ever induce her to marry a man whom she cannot love and respect. She has many amusing tales to tell of her own preferences and hesitations, of the discarded suitors who hung on her glances and wooed her hand in vain. When at last the right man appeared she discussed his qualifications and analysed his personality in the most judicial manner, before finally accepting his proposals. But once her choice was made, she never faltered, and the gay and lively girl proved the best and most devoted of wives.

The strong prejudices of her caste, as might be expected, are apparent on every page. Her horror of democracy and innate belief in the feudal system and the governing power of the few were as firmly rooted as her dislike of smoking for women or of bad manners in men. No less decided were her personal likes and dislikes, her antipathy to Mr. Gladstone and her distrust of Mr. Disraeli—both of which, however, became modified on closer acquaintance with these great party leaders. But the nobility and beauty of her character shine forth on every page. Nature had endowed her with many gifts and graces. She possessed that fortunate union of quick intelligence and ready sympathy which makes a woman at once the best of listeners and the most delightful of companions. She was never too busy to listen to your story, never too much absorbed in her own affairs to be unable to give you her full attention. Every face lighted up when she entered a room, everyone missed her when she was gone. To the last she kept her powers of enjoyment, her love of travel and delight in congenial society. " Oh, how I love entertaining ! " she would exclaim, not only when she received her friends in the ancestral halls of Fawsley or the saloons of Carlton House Terrace, but in the small London house where much of her later years was spent.

As we read the pages of these Journals, it is intensely interesting to watch the development of this fine character, ever eager to learn new lessons, to scale fresh heights, and find more worlds to conquer. Above all we admire the strength of purpose, the undaunted courage with which Lady Knightley met and overcame the difficulties in her way. It was no easy task to disarm Sir Rainald's opposition to his wife's appearance on public platforms and to the expenditure of her time and strength on objects for which he cared not a straw. His old-fashioned notions and fastidious tastes were shocked by many of her proceedings. But, by the exercise of unfailing tact and patience, she frequently succeeded not only in overcoming his opposition but in converting him to her way of thinking, and in the end Sir Rainald actually became a strong champion of women's suffrage.

Lady Knightley's life, we rejoice to think, was a singularly happy one. A brilliant girlhood was followed by an exceptionally fortunate marriage, which satisfied her highest aspirations, and gave her the work for which she had always longed. That this union was doomed to be childless was indeed a bitter drop in her cup, but even this disappointment was turned to good account, since it enabled her to devote her time and energies more exclusively to the service of others.

All through life she possessed a remarkable power of inspiring affection, while she herself was the most loyal and faithful of friends. What wonder that she was beloved by men and women of every age and class? The mothers and girls who listened to her addresses often exclaimed, " Oh, it was lovely! We would rather hear Lady Knightley speak than anyone else!" After her death, testimonies to the wonderful effect produced by chance words that fell from her lips came from all sides. " The influence of Lady Knightley's life and work," wrote her great friend, Princess Christian, " will never die." She has not lived and worked in vain. The note of high courage and hopefulness which was her message to the world still speaks through the earth-born mists of doubt and sorrow, bidding us be of good cheer and calling us on to follow the gleam.

> " Through such souls alone,
> God, stooping, shows sufficient of His light
> For us i' the dark to rise by. And I rise."

THE JOURNAL OF LADY KNIGHTLEY OF FAWSLEY

CHAPTER I

Childhood and Early Youth

1842–1860

LOUISA MARY BOWATER, afterwards Lady Knightley, was born in London on April 25, 1842. In a sketch, entitled " Memories of Happy Days," which she began to write at Rowfant on January 1, 1908, but unfortunately left unfinished, she gives the following account of her father and family :

" My father, General Sir Edward Bowater, was born as far back as 1787, which forms a curiously long link with this year of grace 1908. He was educated at Harrow, where he had five Prime Ministers, including Lord Palmerston, for schoolfellows, as well as Lord Byron. The poet, who was nicknamed ' Hopping Dick,' on account of his lameness, by the other boys, was very intimate with him, and used often to write his exercises. After my father left school, he never saw Byron again, but he knew his friends Moore and Rogers, and once, when a discussion arose as to which was the poet's lame foot, I remember hearing him say that it was certainly the right one. My grandfather, Admiral Bowater, was a friend of Lady Byron's parents, and I have still in my possession a letter written from Seaham on December 31, 1814, in which Lady Milbanke informs him of her daughter Annabella's marriage to Lord Byron, which took place two days later.

"In 1804, while still a Harrow boy, my father was gazetted into the 3rd Regiment, now the Scots Guards, and promptly refused to do any more lessons. He was present at the siege of Copenhagen and went through all the Peninsular War, being present at Talavera and passing the night inside a big French drum. He also served at Waterloo as aide-de-camp to General Turner, and early in the day, at Hougomont, received a wound in the foot, of which he felt the effects to the end of his life. His parents, Admiral and Mrs. Bowater, lived at Hampton Court, in a house on the Green, looking into Bushey Park. Hence arose a close friendship with the Duke of Clarence, who then lived at Bushey House; and when, in 1830, this Prince ascended the throne as William IV., he immediately made my father one of his equerries. On Queen Victoria's marriage, he was appointed Equerry to Prince Albert, and when advancing age made it difficult for him to ride, the Queen, with her usual kindness, transferred him to her own household as Groom-in-Waiting, a post which he held till his death in 1861. In 1843, a year after my birth, Her Majesty gave him the Thatched House Lodge, Richmond Park, for his residence, and when, after he died, Colonel Augustus Liddell declined the offer of the house, the Queen granted its use to my mother for her life.

"In 1839, my father married Emilia Mary, only daughter of Colonel Michael Barne of Sotterley and Dunwich, in the county of Suffolk, by Mary, daughter of Ayscoghe Boucherett of Willingham, Lincolnshire. My mother dearly loved her Suffolk home, and we spent all our winters at Sotterley during my grandmother's lifetime, moving to Richmond Park for the spring and summer. There I learnt to live the happiest life in the world, that of an English country gentlewoman, an excellent preparation for my future life in Northamptonshire. 'I think my beau-ideal,' I exclaimed, when I rode over to Henham with my father, to visit his old comrade, Lord Stradbroke, 'is to live in the country and manage my estate to perfection.'

"My grandmother, Mrs. Barne, *née* Boucherett, was a remarkable old lady. Very pretty she must have been, if her portrait by Downman at all resembled her, and greatly was she admired. In 1792, she went to Toulouse for the winter with Mrs. Stewart Mackenzie of Seaforth and her daughter, and was there during the stirring times of the French Revolution; but neither in her journal nor in her letter-book, which are still in existence, does she make any reference to political events excepting that on one occasion she remarks there were shouts of ' A bas la cocarde blanche !' at the Opera. Did no echo of what was passing in Paris reach the provinces ? or was pretty Miss Boucherett too much taken up with her admirers ? One of these, the Marquis de Senneau, actually followed her to the wilds of Lincolnshire and spent the whole winter hunting there. However, she did not smile upon him, and he eventually returned to France and was guillotined.

"In those days, besides the fine old Adams house at Willingham, which has only lately passed out of the family, the Boucheretts had a house at Stallingborough, near the Humber. One evening, my great-grandfather and his wife were sitting by the fire, when he rose and went to look for a book in the library. Presently he returned, saying he could not find it. His wife went to look for the book, but also came back without it, and Mr. Boucherett asked her, ' Did you see anything ? ' ' Yes,' she replied, ' I saw your father's face between the folding doors.' ' That was what I saw,' said Mr. Boucherett, ' and I asked you to go there on purpose to hear if you had seen him too.' Shortly afterwards he pulled the old house down.

"On my birthday of fourteen—April 25, 1856—I began to write the Journal which has been my faithful companion ever since. It was a memorable epoch in my life, and I well remember a day of intense pleasure. We spent the day in London. I was taken to the Pantheon and the Soho bazaar; my health was drunk at dinner, and in the evening we went to a child's ball at Buckingham Palace. My frock was white tarlatan over silk with a silver band and a streamer of flowers on the upper skirt, and I wore a white acacia wreath in my hair. It was great fun. I danced all night, chiefly with the Farquharson boys, and in one quadrille had the Prince of Wales for my partner. The Queen and Prince Consort both shook hands with me, and the Duchess of Kent sent for me to speak to her. When the time came, I went in to supper with my partner, a young De Celto, and sat down where we could find room, not in the least realising that we were breaking into the Royal circle. The Queen made us welcome in the kindest way and called us to her table, but I can still see my father's face of dismay as he watched our proceedings.

"My next birthday was, I remark, a less exciting one, but I record with satisfaction that I sat up very late and was for the first time promoted to go upstairs alone, without a maid being sent to fetch me from the drawing-room.

"On looking over the pages of my old Journals, I am surprised to see what a quiet life I led, compared with children of the present day. One party at Christmas, or at the most two, and day after day of regular lessons and exercise, walks to Kingston and Ham Common, varied by occasional drives with my mother to Hampton Court and the Old Palace at Richmond, and expeditions to town for dancing and drawing lessons. My greatest pleasure was the rides which I took with my father, when he was not in waiting, and many were the pleasant canters I enjoyed in Richmond Park and on Ham Common on 'Princess,' his gentle but still spirited old mare. My chief companion was a young German governess, Agnes Lentz, to whom I owe not only the knowledge of German, which has been so useful to me all through my life, but the strong moral and religious principles which she never ceased to impress upon my youthful mind. She came to us in 1855, when I was thirteen, and remained my governess for the next five years. After she left my mother's service, she remained in England for some time, and I saw her frequently, and when, in 1885, she retired to her home in Germany, I still kept up a constant correspondence with her. In 1907, I went to stay with the Landgraf of Hesse, at his country seat in Holstein, and took this opportunity to pay Agnes Lentz a visit at Hamburg.[1]

"In this same year, 1855, we spent a delightful fortnight in France, and visited Paris, Rouen, and Dieppe. I have never forgotten these places and the sights we saw on this occasion, although I have never visited many of them again. I think I must have been an observant child, although I fear, from lack of childish companions, a somewhat priggish one, for I remember so well what I saw at that age, and the Crystal Palace, with its courts new and fresh, was a perfect revelation. Although an only child, I was strictly brought up, as I think my readers will agree when I relate the following incident, which recalls the similar experiences of Harry and Laura in one of my favourite story-books, *Holiday House*. My cousin Edith and I had been asked to an outdoor party by some kind neighbours, the Miss Fishers, one day in June 1856; but as it rained, we were not allowed to go, and were sent out in a close carriage to do some errands for my mother. On our way back the weather cleared up, and we persuaded my French governess, who was with us that afternoon, to let us go, just as we were, to the Miss Fishers. These kind old ladies were delighted to see us. We had great fun, and played games and danced country dances after tea, and were just starting a quadrille when the following note from my mother was handed to me by a servant:

"'Louisa, you will come away directly you receive this. You ought not to have gone, and if you are at tea, you will come away all the same.—EMILIA BOWATER.'

"My dismay on reading these words was great. 'Fortunately for my countenance,' I write in that day's Journal, 'I did not at first notice the want of affectionate expressions; however, I saw this order was not to be

[1] Agnes Lentz died in July 1909, two years after I went to see her at Hamburg. Our friendship had lasted more than half a century —L K

trifled with, and collecting my party, I rushed into the carriage. There I read my note again, and forthwith burst into tears. Edith kept me company, and we got home in a dreadful state. Papa sent us a message, desiring us not to appear at dessert; but soon afterwards Agnes came and heard our story, and comforted us, and took us down with her. When we said good-night to Papa, he told us that he would talk to us to-morrow.' Fortunately, by morning milder counsels prevailed, and the next day I was able to record that, ' after another slight ebullition, yesterday's storm passed away.'

" In spite of occasional displays of severity, my father was the kindest of men, and my happiest hours were spent in his company. He was never tired of recalling his military experiences and telling me stories of Wellington's campaigns. On the 18th of June we always drank in solemn silence to the memory of the Great Duke and the heroes of Waterloo, and old Peninsular generals often dropped in and sat for hours, fighting their battles over again.

" On the 9th of July, 1856, I was taken to Buckingham Palace to see the Guards march past, on their return from the Crimea. I can never forget the cheers which the men gave for the Queen, or the proud, pleased, and delighted gaze which they raised up to the balcony where Her Majesty stood, with the young Princes and Princesses, the King of the Belgians, and the Count of Flanders. I remember, too, their worn, haggard faces, some of them perfectly black from exposure. ' What memories the sight recalled! The parting from wife and child, the march through the streets in the dense morning fog, the long sea-voyage, the blood-stained heights of Alma, the flank march on that misty Sunday morning, and then the long, dreary winter, the fatal work in the trenches, the weary days in hospital! And now the same Guards were marching in triumph through London, amid the cheers of their countrymen and the smiles of their Sovereign and her children. But oh! what a contrast to the proud band who left these shores! How many gaps we see in the ranks! how many thousands are sleeping to-day under the green sod on Cathcart hill!'

"In the following June, I was present at the Review in Hyde Park, when the Queen conferred the Victoria Cross on some of her gallant soldiers.

"*Friday, June* 26, 1857.—We started for town at 8 a.m. in the chariot, with post-horses, and made our way easily to our seats, in a pavilion draped with red cloth, where sat the Dukes of Nemours and Montpensier, the Indian princes resplendent with pearls and emeralds, the Duchess of Wellington, Sir Charles Napier, Lord Ernest Paget, and many others. The sixty-two Crimean heroes were drawn up below in an immense open space, surrounded by troops and dotted with officers galloping about. By the time we had puzzled out the different regiments the salute was fired, and in a few minutes the Royal cortège appeared. The Queen, mounted on horseback and wearing a scarlet jacket with a Field-Marshal's sash and the ribbon of the Garter over a dark blue habit, and a wide-awake hat with an officer's feather, rode along the line and then took up a position exactly in front of our stand, but with her back to us. The heroes were marshalled opposite, and came up one by one. The Quartermaster-General read each name, and Lord Panmure handed the Cross to the Queen, who bent forward and with her own hands hooked it on to each man's coat. The Princes were in Highland dress, the little Princesses in white; the Princess Royal wore a white bonnet and looked remarkably well, and I had a good look at the Prince of Prussia, who is fair, very young-looking, and certainly handsome. When the ceremony was over, the troops marched past—Life Guards, Enniskillings, 11th Hussars, horse and foot artillery, the Royal Marines,—the finest body of men on the ground,—the 79th Highlanders, and two companies of Blue-jackets, who doffed their caps by way of salute. Having passed in slow time, they came round again in quick time; the cavalry and artillery cantered past, with bands playing. After this the Queen rode down the line of heroes—a graceful action which charmed us all. The Royal cortège then re-formed and departed amidst the thunders of a royal salute. The scene now became very animated. Great congratulations were going on below us, officers were galloping about, and the Guards' band playing ' God save the Queen ' in front of us. Among the distinguished personages pointed out to me were Lord Lucan, Lord Cardigan, Sir Colin Campbell, who was in command of the troops, Lord and Lady Palmerston, and Sir Benjamin Hall. I saw my cousin, Charles Ridley, at the head of the regiment, and his son Billy was keeping the ground.

" Another event of this same year, which made a profound impression upon me, was my visit, which I paid in company with a large party of cousins, to the Princess Theatre to see Kean in *Richard II.* We occupied the Queen's box, and were dressed in mourning for the Duchess of Gloucester. I enjoyed it more than I can say, even more than I expected. The scenery and dresses were gorgeous, and the acting first-rate. I was greatly delighted at seeing knights in armour, squires and men-at-arms. Of all the scenes, the one I liked best was the historical procession. But we were not destined to see the play to the end. The curtain was being drawn up for the fourth act, when I suddenly saw a gas light blaze up, and in another moment the curtain was in flames. The scene which ensued was beyond all description. Papa turned round and said to us, ' Sit perfectly still,' and many voices in the pit shouted the same to those around. The curtain was quickly dragged down, some fifty persons having rushed on the stage, and water was instantly brought to bear upon the flames. Mrs. Kean, with the most admirable presence of mind, came forward and said, ' Let me entreat of you all to sit still, only sit still.' Again and again she repeated her injunctions, refusing, amidst vociferous cheers, to be led away. Meanwhile curtain after curtain was dragged down, and it became alarming when a burning beam fell upon the stage. A few minutes afterwards the flames were subdued, the cheers redoubled, and Kean was loudly called for. When he appeared, the huzzas became deafening; the motley crowd upon the stage—where men-at-arms, fools, and half-dressed actors were mixed up with coachmen in their shirt-sleeves—surrounded him, all cheering at the top of their voices. Silence being at length restored, he was about to speak, when a voice from the pit exclaimed, ' One more cheer for Mrs. Kean,' and the house rang again. As soon as he could make himself heard, Mr. Kean addressed the audience as nearly as I can remember in these terms : ' Ladies and gentlemen, on such an occasion I scarcely know what to say to you. By a merciful Providence we have all of us been preserved, and beyond what you see, no damage has been done. I thank you heartily for your sympathy.' This little speech was greeted with loud cries of ' Hear, hear,' and more cheering. We now began to think of retiring, which we did without any inconvenience by the Queen's private entrance, and reached home by 1 a.m. Of my own feelings throughout this exciting scene I can scarcely speak. My first instinct was to grasp the things on the shelf before me, in readiness for the flight. Then accounts which I had read of the burning of Covent Garden rushed into my head. But I did think of God, and asked His help. The cheering excited me very much, scenes of that kind always do, and when it was all over I felt very grateful."

If the nearness of London to her Richmond home was a great advantage to Louisa Bowater, in some ways she was happier still at Sotterley Hall. Here she gave herself up to the pleasures of a free country life—milked the cows, fed the horses, planted shrubs, and trimmed laurels with her father and uncle. And she went for long walks in the woods with her cousins, gathering berries and moss, and watching the tomtits and woodpeckers. But even in these rural haunts, General Bowater's connection with the Court, as we see from Louisa's Journal, kept her in close touch with public life.

"*Sotterley, January* 25, 1858.—The wedding of H.R.H. Victoria, Princess Royal, to H.R.H. Prince

Frederick William of Prussia. At dessert we attacked the wedding cake sent us by their Royal Highnesses and drank the health of the royal bride and bridegroom. May they be happy!

"*February* 14.—After dessert this evening I read aloud to Papa and Mamma Captain Edgell and Isabella's most interesting accounts of their five months' siege in Lucknow, written partly on the spot and partly after they had reached Allahabad. Thrilling indeed are these hurried, unvarnished notes which tell of their terrible experiences, of death and starvation staring them in the face."

When, a few months later, these friends returned from India, her joy at seeing her friend Mrs. Edgell was sadly damped by the sight of her shattered frame and the melancholy condition of her baby, Louisa's godson, who hovered for many months between life and death.

"*Sotterley, February* 23.—A general muddle, fuss, and hash l I may as well explain the cause of all this disturbance. In consequence of all the late attempts to murder the Emperor of the French having been hatched in England by foreign refugees, His Imperial Majesty has written to Lord Clarendon, representing that both he and the French nation thought that some change should be made in our laws on this point. Lord Palmerston accordingly brought in a Bill on the 'Conspiracy and Murder' question. The debates were long and animated, Radicals and Conservatives combined to vote against the Government, and the consequence was that the Ministers were defeated by an immense majority on Friday night. Lord Palmerston resigned the next day, and Lord Derby takes his place. The result of all this is that the Queen remains in London, and that Papa was obliged to start for town at 8.15 a.m. this morning. No one knows when he will return, so our journey to Richmond and my Confirmation are all placed in abeyance, and we are left in the most uncomfortable state of uncertainty. Altogether it is a horrid bore!"

After the death of her grandmother in December,

1858, Sotterley ceased to be the home of Sir Edward and Lady Bowater, much to Louisa's regret. It cost her a pang to leave this beloved place, where so large a part of her childhood had been spent, and which looked more beautiful than ever in these days of early spring.

"*March* 3, 1859.—I never saw anything like the rapidity with which spring seems to advance. To-day there are no less than six blossoms on the apricot tree, the elm is in full leaf and looks purple in the setting sun. The wood-pigeons are building in every old trunk, the rooks are as busy as possible, a pair of robins have made their nest in one of the farm-stacks, and every morning I see two beautiful little pied wagtails pecking up moss and grass on the lawn. The thrushes are relentless in the pursuit of worms, and the woods ring with the song of the blackbirds. The other evening I noticed a laurustinus bush so thick with bees that it reminded me of the mignonette bed at Richmond Park last June. The starlings still congregate in small flocks, but I see they have mated already. The air is as soft and balmy as it is in May, the stars shine out clear and bright every evening, and I hear the owls hooting in the barn. To-day the sky is a clear blue, the warm sunshine lies mildly on the hills and flickers through the fir-wood, lighting up the old church tower and playing lovingly over the flowers. The wind is laden with sweet odours. Blackbirds and thrushes, yellow-hammers and robins fill the air with delicious music, and the gentle cooing of the wood-pigeon is heard from each ivy-clad tree. In every nook and corner some form of vegetable life is stirring, and every day sees us—or at least myself!— welcoming some pet plant with a shout of joy. Oh, this spring weather! Was there ever anything so lovely, or was any place in the world so beautiful as this dear old Sotterley!"

But although Louisa shed bitter tears and wrote touching elegies of farewell to Sotterley, she found herself back in her Suffolk home before many months were past. Her parents paid frequent visits to her uncle and aunt, Mr. and Mrs. Frederick Barne, who now owned Sotterley, and Louisa greatly enjoyed the companionship of her three cousins, St. John, Philip, and Edith. The doings of the two boys, their life at Eton and in the army, are chronicled at length in her Journal, while their sister Edith, a charming but very delicate girl two years younger than herself, became Louisa's adopted sister and inseparable companion. During the years between 1856 and 1864, when her cousin died, there is scarcely a page of the Journal on which Edith's name does not appear. The two girls paid long visits to their respective homes, and wrote daily letters to each other when they were apart. They read the same books and discussed the same questions. And after the manner of girls, they exchanged ideas on whatever subject was uppermost in their minds at the moment—whether it were Byron's poems or Charlotte Brontë's novels, the works of Goethe and Schiller, of Heine or Chateaubriand, Kingsley's sermons or Tennyson's *In Memoriam*, *Picciola* or *The Daisy Chain*.

From early youth Lady Knightley's love of letters was apparent. She not only read every book she could lay hands on, but she wrote critical essays, formed judgments, and expressed her opinion on all manner of topics—literary and political. As she grew up she naturally derived the keenest pleasure from intellectual conversation, and enjoyed nothing better than the society of literary celebrities.

" One of my earliest recollections," she writes, in the autobiographical fragment quoted above, " is that of being taken to see Miss Langton, the daughter of Dr. Johnson's friend, Bennet Langton, who was then living in great poverty over a toy-shop in Richmond. I well remember standing on the sofa to read a letter addressed to her by Dr. Johnson, her godfather, of which she was extremely proud. Miss Fanshawe, the author of the famous riddle on the letter H which has often been ascribed to Byron, was also an inhabitant of Richmond whom I often saw. There were our kind neighbours, the Miss Fishers, two delightful old ladies full of life and intelligence, who knew Dr. Wolff the traveller, and Mrs. Alfred Gatty, and Leslie the popular Academician, at whose house interesting people were always to be found. One day, early in 1861, Miss Jane Fisher told me a romantic story of a young Spanish refugee whom she had once prepared for Confirmation, and then lost sight of completely. Last summer, to her surprise, some strange ladies called, and apologised for their intrusion by saying that the distinguished Spanish General Savaria had charged them with a message to his former benefactress. He wished her to know how much he had owed all through his career to the religious principles which she had implanted in his mind, and sent her word that during his recent campaign in Morocco he had read the last prayers over the dying soldiers from the English Prayer Book which she had given him. Miss Jane forthwith wrote to her old friend through the Spanish Embassy, and soon afterwards received an album containing portraits of the General, his mother, and the chief personages of the Court and Army, with a graceful Spanish dedication to herself on the title-page.

"Another literary friend whose kindness I can never forget was Miss Agnes Strickland, whose home was at Reydon Hall, near Southwold. We saw a good deal of her when we lived in Suffolk, and visits to Reydon were red-letter days in my girlhood. She was generally to be found surrounded by books and historical portraits, engaged on some new work, and I was never tired of looking at her lovely little painting of Mary Queen of Scots. I remember one day in the autumn of 1860 finding her busily engaged on a new book, *Bachelor Kings*. A few weeks later I called again and found her studying a bundle of precious manuscripts—the themes composed by Mary Queen of Scots when she was a child at the French Court, in the form of letters addressed to the Dauphin's sister, Madame Elisabeth, afterwards wife of Philip II. They were first written in French, and then translated into Latin. As usual, Miss Strickland fired up over Mary Queen of Scots, and I got a rise out of her over Froude's *History*, which she proclaimed 'A most false book.' In the following June, Miss Strickland, being in London, called on us at Richmond Park. She would not come in, but left a copy of her *Bachelor Kings* with my name on the flyleaf and a most kind inscription—altogether a gift of which I was not a little proud."

In 1859, Louisa left the schoolroom and went to her first ball at Norwich with a large party from Burlingham.

"*October* 19.—I wore white tarlatan, with lilies of the valley, and danced ten dances, never sitting down once. My partners were Mr. Robert Gurdon, Sir Robert Buxton, Messrs. Henniker, Wodehouse, Astley, Gurney, Burroughes, and Martin Smith, my cousin. Mr. Gurney danced best, but Martin Smith was the most interesting, from the good-natured, cousinly way in which he took me in hand, and also more particularly because he was able to give me the latest news of his sister, dear Louisa White, with whom we stayed at Peper Harow last year. She is abroad now at Mentone for the winter, which he trusts will set her health up entirely, but he added: 'I hope so, at least—it is in God's hands.'[1] That was the gem of the evening for me. And now for myself. Of course I know that I am a little goose for being flattered by the attentions that were paid me, and for being gratified at the success which I certainly had—for I suppose it is a success to dance all night at one's first ball! It is always pleasant to be good-natured, and of course I had every advantage, in point of going with a party, and being all but in one's own county of Suffolk. But it has shown me one thing clearly—that I am vain. How will it be at my next ball, I wonder? We are no less than eighteen in the house, including a nice Mr. and Mrs. Ricardo and Colonel Charlton, with whom I had a lively discussion at dinner to-night over modern poetry, which

[1] Louisa Smith, the wife of Colonel Dalrymple White, died at Lyons on her way home in the following April, and was buried at Peper Harow, Surrey.

he pronounced to be trash! I defended my favourites —Byron, Sir Walter, Longfellow—vigorously!"

Mr. Martin Smith and his sister, whose early death was a real sorrow to Miss Bowater, were related to her through their mother, a daughter of Sir Matthew Ridley. Her grandmother, Admiral Bowater's wife, originally Miss Louisa Lane,[1] had been previously married to a barrister named George Hawkins, by whom she had a handsome daughter, who in 1803 became the wife of Sir Matthew Ridley, and lived till 1864. Laura, Lady Ridley, was much attached to her half-brother, General Bowater, and proved a very kind friend to her niece, and we find frequent allusions to this aunt, as well as to her ten children and numerous grandchildren, in Louisa's Journals. She was on friendly terms with all her Ridley cousins, whose intellectual tastes made them especially congenial companions, and was particularly fond of Sir Matthew's sons, Matthew and Edward,[2] and of the painter Ridley Corbet and his sisters.

"*Richmond Park, July* 14, 1860.—To-day, soon after luncheon, Aunt Laura's son, Sir Matthew Ridley, arrived with his children, all grown, of course, out of knowledge. St. John soon followed, and Arthur Birch and Mr. Broughton called, so that we had quite a party on the lawn. Afterwards we all took a walk in the Park, chaffing and joking away, and Matthew and I had some interesting talk about Tennyson. It is positively refreshing to find a schoolboy who has an idea beyond hunting, which, fond as I am of St. John, he never had!

"*July* 30.—I was in great luck this evening, for my cousins Charles and Harriet Ridley came down for the

[1] A charming portrait of this lady, painted by Romney, was left by Sir Edward Bowater to his half-sister's son, Sir Matthew Ridley, while another Romney, a portrait of Mrs. Bowater's father, Mr. Thomas Lane of Tettenhall, Staffordshire, was sold by Lady Knightley, shortly before she died, to her cousin, the present Viscount Ridley.

[2] Matthew, 1st Viscount Ridley, born 1842; married 1873, Hon. Mary Marjoribanks, daughter of Lord Tweedmouth; died 1904. Edward, Mr. Justice Ridley, M.P. for South Northumberland, 1878–80; Judge of King's Bench Division; born 1843; married 1882, Alice, daughter of Col. Bromley Davenport, M.P.

night, and at dinner I sat between Charles and Mr. Hough, the Vicar of our church at Ham, with Harriet on the other side. The two latter had not been together many minutes before they were deep in theology, and presently I contrived to get a word in. We discussed Kingsley first of all. Mr. Hough knows him intimately, and says he is a most extraordinary mixture, a rationalist and man of very unsound principles, an inveterate sportsman, greatly in earnest and at the same time undoubtedly attractive. The word 'earnest' made Mr. Hough remark that a great deal of mistaken homage is paid to earnestness without much regard to what the earnestness is about. I said, surely there was more hope of a man who was really in earnest about something, becoming earnest about the best things, than of a trifler. He disagreed, saying that the more firmly a man was wedded to wrong opinions the more difficult it was to turn him from these. Harriet upon this gave an ecstatic description of Mr. Spurgeon, to which Mr. Hough replied that as long as he is cool he is a most eloquent preacher, but the moment he gets excited he becomes familiar, and often lapses into positive blasphemy. We next discussed Tennyson. Neither Harriet nor Mr. Hough like him, and both call him wild and incomprehensible. I confessed that I liked him. Mr. Hough prefers Longfellow, but none of us like *Evangeline*. Harriet and I both think *Hyperion* charming. I suppose that too is incomprehensible and very German, although that in my eyes, I remarked, was no objection, whereupon Mr. Hough accused me of mysticism! Keble's *Christian Year* was next pronounced to be also incomprehensible—Bishop Blomfield is said to have called it his Sunday puzzle. The Bishop of Oxford was declared to be a most eloquent but most untruthful man, and Mr. Gladstone and Sidney Herbert were roundly abused, called impostors and I don't know what all! What a heretic I seem to be! Certainly I admire them all! But altogether it was a most agreeable evening."

In that same July, Louisa was present at the first

meeting of the National Rifle Association on Wimbledon Common, an event which kindled a wave of widespread enthusiasm throughout the country.

"*July* 2, 1860.—We all set out about half-past one in the Irish car for Wimbledon Common, which had assumed a very different appearance from its usual wild and desolate beauty of aspect. Leaving the carriage, we made our way through the vast encampment to the enclosure where the Royal tent was pitched with the Guards' band posted before it. It was a picturesque scene, the gay uniforms of the Regulars contrasting with the sober grey suits of the Volunteers, and these again with the bright colours of the ladies' dresses. There was a goodly sprinkling of Riflemen, and several splendid specimens of that fine corps the Duke of Manchester's Mounted Rifles. Soon a sort of general buzz and stir proclaimed the Queen's coming, the band struck up the National Anthem, the Royal Standard floated from the top of the tent, and off went every hat as she appeared, accompanied by Prince Albert, the Prince of Wales, Princess Alice, the Duke of Saxe-Coburg, and the little Princesses. Amid the cheer of the spectators, she walked down to the tent by Lord Elcho's side, fired the first shot and proclaimed this the first meeting of the National Rifle Association to be open. A salute of twenty-one guns followed and a tremendous burst of cheering, and the rush to see the Queen was so great that the crowd could only be kept back by a hastily formed cordon of gentlemen, who surrounded the dais occupied by the Royal party."

A week later, Louisa accompanied her parents to the Crystal Palace, where she witnessed the grand conclusion of the meetings so brilliantly inaugurated by the Queen.

"*July* 9.—We sat in the centre of the Great Transept, directly facing the orchestra, which was filled with dense masses of Riflemen. Lord De Grey and Ripon occupied the chair as Mr. Sidney Herbert's representative, and was supported by Lord Elcho, the President of the Association, Colonel Kennedy, Lord Grosvenor, etc.

Near him sat four celebrated beauties, the Duchess of Wellington, Lady Elcho, Miss Seymour, and Lady Spencer, the latter of whom was decidedly my favourite. After an all but inaudible speech from Lord De Grey, during which the mob struggled to force its way into the galleries, which were already densely crowded, Lord Elcho—the admired of all beholders—came forward in a Rifleman's uniform, and in a clear, ringing voice proceeded to read out the names of the successful competitors. These heroes ascended the steps to the platform one by one, and received their prizes from Lord De Grey, while Lord Elcho's comments, delivered in the most racy, good-humoured manner, were the life of the whole affair. Young Ross—the fortunate winner of the Queen's Prize, £250, and of the Gold Medal of the Association—was loudly cheered, and the Guards' bands struck up 'See the conquering hero comes!' Lord Elcho then came forward and announced that the young man was a native of Scotland, who, at the age of seventeen, had joined a Yorkshire corps, because he was at a private tutor's in this county. Truly, to be the champion rifleman of England at eighteen is something to be proud of! The much-coveted prize was then delivered to him, amidst the enthusiastic plaudits of the whole assembly and the congratulations of the veterans on the platform, who crowded round him to shake hands, after which he was called upon to exhibit his medals to the crowds below—and mighty cool he seemed about it all. Lord Elcho made an appeal on behalf of the newly formed Association, and the meeting ended with three hearty cheers for Her Majesty. If Monday was the Royal day of the meeting, this was essentially the popular day, and it was in truth a fine thing to see twenty thousand English men and women assembled in that glass palace, to take their share in this truly national undertaking. May the blessing of God rest upon our Volunteers, for they have come forward nobly to defend their native land, and may their arms never be used in any more bloody contest than those which we have seen this week!"

CHAPTER II

London and Cannes

1861–1862

THE year 1861 was a memorable one in Louisa's life. In February she was present at a series of balls and festivities in honour of Lord Rendlesham's coming of age. For the first time she became pleasantly conscious of the admiration which she excited. She confesses guiltily that it is impossible to deny the fact that flirtations are great fun, and asks herself with alarm, " Am I growing very vain and frivolous ? " But she was just as happy discussing Froude and Henry VIII. with Sir Thomas Fowell Buxton, or dining alone with her father in a lodging at Woodbridge, where the two spent the snuggest and merriest of evenings after the Rendlesham ball. This power of enjoyment and delight in social intercourse of every description was a distinctive feature of Lady Knightley's character, which she retained to the last, and was no doubt one secret of her popularity.

Her first London season was a brilliant success. She rode in the Park, went to balls and concerts, and made many friends. Her handsome features and tall, graceful figure, her fair complexion and fine blue eyes, excited general admiration, while the perfect simplicity and engaging frankness of her manners, her eager and intelligent interest in every variety of topic, were additional attractions. On the 27th of June, Miss Bowater's presentation at Court, which had been delayed first by an attack of illness and then by the death of the Duchess of Kent, took place.

"At last the long-expected day is come and gone, and the presentation to my Sovereign, one of the last few relics of the age of chivalry, has taken place. All has gone off as well as possible, and I think Papa, the person I was most anxious to please, was really gratified at the reception I met with, and the way I got through it. The train of my Court dress was white silk, the petticoat white net, both trimmed with roses and lilies of the valley, and I wore a wreath to match, with feather and cut lappets, pearl-diamond earrings, pearl necklace and bracelets. I had quite a levee of maids in my bedroom before passing into the sitting-room, where a whole bevy of cousins—Wheatleys, Martin Smiths, Cooksons, Moncks, and Ridleys—awaited me. I confess I was rather glad to get into the carriage, and even then, in the streets, the staring seemed very strange. Once inside St. James's Palace, I was in a new world. Papa pointed out an immense number of people, of whom I can only remember a few—Madame de Flahault,[1] Lord and Lady Palmerston, Lord Combermere, Sir Thomas Troubridge, who lost his leg in the Crimea, etc. Soon after the doors opened, Papa left us to take up his station, and we began to make our way into the Presence—I beginning to feel very pit-a-pat. Down with our tails, and I found myself between a double file of men, who seemed at least seven feet apiece. I looked neither to the right nor to the left, but steadily at Mamma's long black train, and presently heard my name announced and found myself close to the Queen, who smiled most graciously upon me, as I made a deep curtsy and kissed hands. The Prince shook hands with me, and next to him stood the Crown Princess of Prussia, Princess Alice, and Princess Mary of Cambridge, whose handsome, good-natured face I hailed quite like an old friend, and who also shook hands with me. The Crown Prince of Prussia, the Prince of Wales, and

---

[1] Mercer Elphinstone, only child and heiress of Baron Keith, born 1788; married 1817, Auguste, Comte de Flahault, afterwards Ambassador to London and Vienna; died 1867. Her eldest daughter married, 1843, Henry, 4th Marquis of Lansdowne.

Prince Louis of Hesse were also there. By this time my train was swept up behind, and I turned to follow Mamma, and felt how quickly it was over. Papa rejoined us almost directly, saying, ' I'm as pleased as Punch ; you both behaved very well, and the Queen was *most* gracious to you ! ' Well — that, at least, was satisfactory. We were at home soon after four, and I at once equipped myself for riding, which we agreed would refresh us more than anything. The Park was very empty. We rode down the Row with the Duke of Wellington, and Papa pointed out Lord Stratford de Redcliffe and Lord Elgin, both remarkable men. I also saw Gladstone at the Drawing-room.

" *Friday, June* 28, 1861.—We dined early, and dressed for a concert at the Palace—the first entertainment of any kind that has been given since the Duchess of Kent's death. The performance was entirely composed of sacred music, to my surprise and delight. The singers were Mlle Titiens, Signor Giuglini, Signor Gardoni, Mr. Santley, and last, not least, Mlle Adelina Patti, the *prima donna* of seventeen, who has taken the town by storm this season. The first part consisted of selections from *St. Paul*. The air ' Jerusalem, Jerusalem ' was lovely, and also the final chorus, ' Happy are they who have endured.' The second part was composed of a miscellaneous selection, in which I most admired Haydn's ' With verdure clad,' splendidly rendered by Mlle Titiens, ' Cujus Animam ' from Rossini's *Stabat Mater*, and ' The heavens are telling,' which everyone seemed to enjoy. The Queen was not present, but the Princess Royal and Prince of Wales did their part extremely well ; the latter especially has inherited all his mother's grace.

" *Thursday, July* 4.—We drove down to Harrow Speeches, and went first to the Head Master's house, and then to the speech-room, or rather to the foot of the steps leading up to it, for to get in was a work of time and patience, so great was the crush. On our entry we were greeted by Matt and Edward Ridley, the heroes of the day, who insisted on our scrambling across their platform into our places immediately behind the

Head Master's chair, and among all the grandees. I had the good luck to be presented to Lord Palmerston and Lord Digby ; Sir John Lawrence, Lord Clarendon, the Archbishop of York, etc., being close by. At length the hall being completely filled, Matt sprang up and read some Latin Alcaics, and Edward spoke in a Latin play. Jeune,[1] who seems to be one of the cleverest boys, read part of his essay on Wallenstein. He does not know a word of German, but wrote his essay entirely from Coleridge's translation, and, begging his pardon, I think it was a great pity he chose that subject. It is easy to see that he is not in the least imbued with Schiller's spirit, although part of his essay, I must allow, was very good. Lord Strafford's defence was most beautifully spoken by Bernard. Every one of these pathetic words went to one's heart. Afterwards Matt took the part of Scapin in a scene from Molière's comedy, and did it capitally, though the accent of the whole party might have been improved. It was curious to look at the happy, intelligent faces of the speakers and wonder what their future careers may be. Which of these names which I then heard for the first time will ring in my ears through life and become household words ? Who can tell ? After a long wait, we succeeded in reaching Dr. Butler's house, and sat down to a magnificent luncheon in the refectory. Matt and Edward both came and talked to me most pleasantly, and very proud I felt of them both.

"*Saturday, July 6.*—After eating luncheon with Lady Huntingfield, we drove down to a breakfast at Cambridge Cottage, Kew. Nothing could be more good-natured than were both the Duchess and Princess Mary, and one saw a good many people one had heard of all one's life, and altogether it was very fine and very interesting. At dinner we met Lady Waterford, whom I was enchanted to see, having heard so much of her beauty, which is indeed very great, not only in

---

[1] Afterwards the Rt. Hon. Sir F. Jeune, created 1905 Lord St. Helier; married 1881, Susan Mary, daughter of Keith Stewart Mackenzie and widow of Lieut.-Colonel Hon. J. C. Stanley.

face, but in figure, shape of the head and neck, and above all in manner. My neighbour, Captain Keane, was a very agreeable and amusing person, when once we got off the beaten track of London conversation—the dullest of all dull things ! "

The following autumn found Louisa and her parents once more at Sotterley, which they finally left on September 5.

" *Sotterley Park, September* 4.—' My last day at Sotterley—harvest home—a fine morning,' such were the waking thoughts which rushed through my mind on the eventful day when we bade farewell *for ever as a home* to this home of nearly twenty years. At 11.30 we went to church. It was a pretty sight to see the labourers come in, wearing their different badges. Service over, they defiled to the park, to the music of the Wrentham Volunteer Band, while I rushed home to gobble up some lunch, and, hurrying after them, found them all seated in the very prettily decorated barn, and worked hard, distributing plum-pudding, etc. Pipes were produced, porter was handed out, and my uncle's health was drunk with three rounds of hearty cheering. Then he returned thanks, and proposed my own dear father's health, speaking in the most gratifying terms of his going away, and telling them what a good kind neighbour they would all lose in him. Papa really feels going away from the bottom of his heart, and nearly broke down in returning thanks, after the most enthusiastic cheering—and I made a goose of myself all the time ! Then came sports and tea, in the middle of which they insisted on cheering me, and I could not resist thanking them in a few short, broken sentences. Dear, dear Sotterley, may God bless and preserve all its inhabitants ! "

At this critical moment an unexpected event took place. Both the Queen and Prince Consort entertained a high regard for Sir Edward Bowater, whose health had been lately failing, and decided to ask him to take their delicate child, Prince Leopold, abroad for the winter. One May evening the Prince Consort paid a surprise visit to Thatched House Lodge, and, as he afterwards told her father, was very favourably impressed with Louisa herself.

"It was a cold, wet evening, and concluding that at 6.30 we were safe from visitors, Mamma had gone up to change her dress. I had already donned my old blue gown, and was kneeling in the window by Papa, coaxing him after my usual fashion, when the door opened and William in his most dignified manner announced, 'The Prince Consort and Major Du Plat.' 'Who? what!' exclaimed Papa, 'the Prince!'; and I bolted head foremost into the dining-room, and rushed upstairs, as soon as the coast was clear, to tell Mamma and change my frock. Never were toilets more quickly completed. In a few minutes we were down again. The Prince was exceedingly good-natured, but I thought him looking ill and much altered. He has a strong foreign accent. After talking to Mamma and me for some time, he departed; but it will be long before we forget the startle!"

Louisa was still more surprised when, three months later, the Queen's proposal reached her father at Sotterley.

"*Sunday, August* 11.—Flabbergasted! That is the only word by which I can possibly describe the state of amazement into which I have this day been thrown, and I am still doubtful whether the delightful plan which has been opened to us is not a dream of my own imagination. Sir Charles Phipps has written to Papa to the effect, that Prince Leopold being ordered to spend the winter in the South of France, and the Queen wishing someone to accompany him in whom she had implicit confidence, it had occurred to Sir Charles that the arrangement might suit us. The party is to consist of the little Prince and his tutor, who is also a medical man, and ourselves— all expenses defrayed by Her Majesty. Was there ever anything so delightful? Just at the moment when we are loosened from most of our ties and unsettled as to our future plans, that such a scheme should present itself to turn our minds from the sorrow of leaving Sotterley does seem really providential. But the delight of it! If it had fallen from the skies I could hardly be more astounded. My head is already full of the route, and I can only breathe it to my Journal, feeling I cannot sleep without doing this."

In due course the details of the journey were communicated to Sir Edward by Major Elphinstone, and one Sunday in October Lady and Miss Bowater, who had gone to town to prepare for their departure, received a sudden summons to Windsor.

"*Sunday, October* 27.—We had been to church, and in the afternoon St. John came in, pleasant and nice as he always is, and we sat down to chess, and were intent on our game, when Blandford arrived from Richmond, bringing a note to say that the Queen wished us to lunch with her the next day. Great was the consternation in the camp. We had made several engagements, which had to be cancelled *à la hâte*, and worst of all—I had no bonnet!

"*Monday, October* 28.—Off for Windsor about 10.30, met the coachman at Richmond—alas! with the wrong bonnet! Papa met us at Windsor station, and by great good luck we succeeded in finding a very becoming one in the town. Arrived at the Castle, we were taken to Lady Ely's room, she being out riding with the Queen, and had an interview with Lady Caroline Barrington, from whom we obtained much information about the little Prince. After lunching with the Household—*i.e.* Lady Augusta Bruce, Miss Stanley, Miss Macdonald, and Lord Harris—we went into the corridor. By and by came the Queen and Prince and the children, and very pretty it was to see them all together. They remained for about ten minutes talking to us, the Queen to Mamma, and Princess Alice, who is decidedly pretty and has very pleasing manners, to me. The little ones, including Prince Leo, played about and amused themselves by trying to make the dear little Princess Beatrice, who is evidently the pet of the whole family, say French words. The interview over, in which they were all most kind, we crossed the Holbein Gallery, St. George's Hall, and the Armoury, and climbed up to Papa's swallow's nest in the Star Tower, commanding the same lovely view as the North Terrace. After resting here some time, we went down to the Library, with which I was charmed, and leaving the Castle, returned home, tired but pleased with our day, which proved far less formidable than we had anticipated.

"*Thursday, October* 31.—We were busy preparing for the visit of the young Princes, Arthur and Leopold, who arrived with Major Elphinstone and Dr. Günther [1] about 1.30, and stayed till 4 p.m. Two such darling boys I have not seen for a long while. They were full of fun and merriment, and seemed greatly to enjoy croquet and hide-and-seek. Prince Arthur especially, with his handsome face and courteous manners, has carried all our hearts away."

The travellers set out on their journey on November 4, and travelled by slow stages, sleeping at Boulogne, Paris, Dijon, Avignon, and Toulon.

"*Paris, British Embassy, Rue du Faubourg St. Honoré, No.* 6.—Am I asleep or awake, or walking in a dream ? All seems so new and strange that I am really somewhat doubtful on the point. Nothing strikes me more on landing in this country than the hard labour done by the women. At Boulogne they claimed it as their privilege to carry the Prince's luggage from the boat to the hotel and thence to the station, and you constantly see them marching off under the heaviest loads. It was quite dark when we reached Paris, where an attaché awaited our arrival

---

[1] Dr. Albert Günther, Ph.D., came to England in 1860, after a distinguished career at the Universities of Bonn and Tübingen, and qualified himself as a physician and surgeon at St. Bartholomew's Hospital. He was selected by the Prince Consort to be medical attendant to Prince Leopold, and accompanied him to Cannes in this capacity. In 1864 he was appointed to the staff of the British Museum, and became Keeper of the Zoological Department. He resided chiefly at Surbiton, where he had a considerable practice, until his scientific researches absorbed his whole time. On his death in 1914, at the ripe age of eighty-four, the *Times* spoke in high terms of his attainments and attractive qualities, calling him a great personality whose position in the world of science would have been still greater but for his sincere modesty.

with two carriages, but I recognised several of my old haunts in our drive to the Embassy, a fine old-fashioned hotel *entre cour et jardin*, and therefore charmingly quiet. To our great relief there was no dinner-party, and Lady Cowley's kind manner soon set us at ease after our grand and somewhat intimidating reception; but great was my delight when she proposed taking us to the Opera. *Don Pasquale*, which we saw, is a lively little opera, with one lovely air—' Com' é gentil.' The house is very pretty and was quite full, M. de Persigny being among the audience. Nothing amused me more than to look at the people in the pit and observe the totally different cast of the faces. There, too, I made my first acquaintance with the genus attaché in a **Mr. Atlay**. It is curious to see ten years of Paris life grafted on to an Englishman. How tired he must be of doing the agreeable to all the people who come to the Embassy, and of flirting with all the young ladies—in both of which arts he appears to excel. . . . The Prince began to be much more sociable, and in the evening he came and laid his head on my shoulder, as we rushed along through the heart of *la belle France*. Nothing can be more good-natured than Dr. Günther, who is also exceedingly well-informed; and as to Canné, our invaluable courier, he is decidedly the eighth wonder of the world: he thinks of everything, knows everything, and generally appears to be in three places at once.

"*Hôtel d'Europe, Avignon, November* 10.—Papa was so unwell as to cause us a good deal of uneasiness. Mamma could not leave him, so I walked out with the Doctor and Prince, and drove in the afternoon across the Rhone and up the opposite heights. During our walk I was suddenly startled by hearing a deep, muffled voice behind me saying, ' Pour l'amour de Dieu, pour les pauvres prisonniers,' and at the same time the sound of money rattling in a box. On turning sharply round, I saw close to me a man with a large black cloth thrown completely over him, and only two black eyes looking at me through two slits in the cloth. The Prince shrank up to me, and even I felt glad when the Doctor dropped a few sous into his box, and so got rid of him. The coachman who drove us this afternoon was a Crimean soldier, with an English medal, which he showed us with pride, and great was his delight at seeing *le fils de la Reine d'Angleterre*. We visited the Cathedral and convent *Château des Papes*, now used as a barrack, but could not enter the latter, and had to content ourselves with gazing up at its solid masonry rising up stern and yellow—so different from our grey English towers. Nothing strikes us more than the total change in the character of the architecture, or reminds one more forcibly that we are near Italy. It was a brilliant day, and from the heights beyond the Rhone we had a magnificent view of Avignon lying in the rich valley, where the grey olives contrasted with the bright tints of the autumn woods, and the snowy heights of Mont Ventoux flushed with the rosy hues of sunset. Not a sound was to be heard save the distant tinkling of a bell, and the air had the still freshness that I have often felt in England at the same hour. All seemed like a dream, and I thought of Edith watching the same sunset behind the trees at Dunwich.

" *Hôtel de l'Eléphant, Vidauban, November* 13.—The railroad only goes as far as Toulon, so to-day we began posting, and watched with great glee the preparations for our start. A motley crowd assembled in the court-yard : Italian boys with monkeys and hurdy-gurdys, tall, well-made Provençals with dark hair, sparkling black eyes and pearly teeth, and postilions with jackets embroidered in red. At last we were *en route*—two carriages with four horses each, the first containing Mamma, the Doctor, and the Prince ; the second, Papa and myself. Anything so aboriginal as the harness I never saw, and it is still a mystery to me how the single postilion contrives to manage the leaders. But the whole thing was amusing to a degree ! You felt that you were passing *through*, not *over* the country. Then the picturesque figures that one saw : sometimes it would be a shepherd with a flock of goats and sheep, or an old woman with a gigantic hat perched upon a mule between loaded panniers, knitting as she went. Then we came upon a merry group of road-menders, who exchanged jokes with the postilion, or a donkey-cart laden with wine casks, and an old woman with a gay-coloured handkerchief tied round her head, peering out; or else we passed a great heavy, cumbersome diligence with three horses crawling along these abominable roads. But most amusing of all were the villages, with the women washing at the fountains, and mules being watered. The whole population turned out to see our change of horses, duly announced by the cracking of whips and jingle of bells. The dirt, however, equals the picturesqueness, and the first thing we did on arriving at Vidauban was to get out of the village as quickly as possible, and scramble up the rocky terraces of the olive gardens on the hillside.

"*Château Leader, Cannes, November* 14.—We left Vidauban at 9.30, and after passing the ruined arches of the Roman aqueduct at Fréjus, we had our first view of the deep blue Mediterranean, and began the ascent of the Esterelles. After slowly winding up a fine road for two hours, we reached the summit, and saw the snowy peaks of the Basses Alpes clearly defined against the deep blue sky, towering over the lower ranges of hills, while far below, basking in the Southern sun, lay the white houses of Cannes, leaning against the green hillside, close upon the Mediterranean waters. Changing horses at the solitary *poste* below the highest point, surrounded by a horde of children, we began a long descent through stone-pines and juniper and arbutus scrub, with only occasional glimpses of snow, mountains, and blue sea, until we reached Château Leader, one of the first villas on the Toulon road, and as far I can see, one of the nicest in Cannes. All the rooms are large and airy, and the drawing-room opens on to a terrace commanding a lovely view of the Mediterranean, the Iles Lérins, and the Esterelles jutting out into the sea. If only dear Papa were better, all would be perfect."

" A sad time followed," writes Lady Knightley in her Memoir. " My father grew daily weaker, and seldom went beyond the terraced garden. My mother could not bear to leave him, and most of my time was spent in the Prince's company. We played croquet and chess together ; I read to him, and did my best to amuse him and divert his thoughts when fits of home-sickness came over him, on receiving letters from Windsor. We took scrambling walks over the rocks or up the hills, and every fine morning rode our favourite donkeys, ' Jacques ' and ' Catherine,' among the olive groves and vineyards where now hotels and villas have sprung up. Sometimes we took longer expeditions on the mountains, and picnicked at some lovely spot, where I sketched while the Doctor and little Prince rambled about in search of lizards. We were not always welcome in these remote villages, and I well remember a woman shouting at us, ' Les Anglais ne sont faits que pour faire du mal ! ' Meanwhile my poor father grew daily weaker, and on December 14 the end came. For several days we had been hearing bad accounts of the Prince Consort's health, and that same morning I said to Mamma, ' I cannot help thinking that the Prince is more ill than we think—do you not remember that your father and the King died on the same day ? ' At 8 p.m., two hours after my dear father breathed his last, came a telegram from Windsor : ' Pray break to Prince Leopold that the Prince is very ill and that we are in great anxiety about him.' On Sunday morning, December 15, Lord Rokeby arrived from Nice with a telegram announcing that the Prince Consort had died tranquilly at ten minutes before eleven. I was busy all day writing letters, and had the poor little Prince with me. ' Poor child ! ' I wrote in my Journal, ' he is too young fully to realise all he has lost.'

" *Monday, December* 16.—Late in the evening, what really seemed the first ray of comfort came, in these telegrams from Windsor : ' Mamma hopes you are pretty well ; we are all heart-broken.—HELENA '; and, ' Dear Mamma wishes me to tell you how much she feels for you,

Lady Bowater, H.R.H. Prince Leopold, and Miss Bowater.
Drawing-Room, Château Leader, Cannes, 1862.

and how much she hopes you feel for her.—HELENA.'
Our answer was as follows : ' Lady Bowater's duty
to Princess Helena, and begs her humble duty to the
Queen, with the most heartfelt gratitude for the kind
telegrams, and the assurance of her deepest sympathy.'
On Friday, January 3, a still, grey, rainy day, strangely
in accordance with our feelings, my darling father's
mortal remains were laid to rest in the peaceful green
churchyard at Sotterley. It seemed too sad and strange
to think of him as dead and buried, with us far away in
a foreign land, and I sometimes felt as if it must
all be a dream from which we must soon awaken.
We were overwhelmed with kind letters, and my uncle
and aunt implored us to come to them at Dunwich,
Sotterley, whenever we liked ; but we at once offered to
remain with the Prince, if the Queen wished it, and
letters from Major Elphinstone and Sir Charles Phipps
showed us clearly that this was the case. Anything
that could comfort the Queen in her bitter trial seemed
to us a sacred duty, and I had the firm conviction that
this was what my dear father would have wished. In
the midst of her own overwhelming sorrow, the Queen
found time to write my mother the kindest and most
touching letter, expressing the deepest sympathy with
her loss and the highest regard for her dear husband.
Prince Leopold's pretty, winning ways greatly endeared him to us both, and during the next few weeks
he helped to cheer my poor mother, and would coax
her to go out when no one else could do this. Colonel
Cavendish was sent out first to take charge of the
Prince, in my father's place, but was soon succeeded
by Lord Charles Fitzroy,[1] now Duke of Grafton, whose
kindness I can never forget. I think he must have
had a fellow-feeling for my mother, having lost his own
wife at Cannes only a year or two before.

" We remained at Cannes till the end of March,
taking long excursions in the beautiful country round,
and enjoying the lovely weather. I particularly

[1] Charles Fitzroy, seventh Duke of Grafton, K.G., born 1821, succeeded his brother 1882.

remember a long drive to Napoule, where leaving the carriage we walked up a romantic gorge and I had my first view of Italy, lying like a small white cloud on the blue sea, beyond Nice and Mentone. Lord Dalhousie and Lord Rokeby were almost our only visitors, and a young Onslow sometimes came to play croquet with the Prince. But I always remember one day meeting old Lord Brougham,[1] in the queerest clothes—a very loud check pair of trousers and weather-beaten wide-awake. He stopped me, and held forth for a long time on the inconceivable folly, as he called it, of allowing the Prince to return to England in March. Of course I had no more to do with it than he had!

" We left Cannes with a pang of regret at the break-up of our pleasant party, after a last drive along the Happy Valley, a last visit to Mr. Woolfield's pretty garden, and a last game at croquet! Brought together on these Mediterranean shores for five months of intimate friendship, intensified by the scenes through which we had passed, we were now to be scattered to the winds—seldom, if ever, to meet again.

" Lord Charles, in his thoughtful kindness, tried as far as possible to avoid the places we had halted at on the way out. So we stayed at Marseilles, Lyons, Macon, Paris, and Amiens, and on the 3rd of April reached the 'Lord Warden' at Dover, where Prince Arthur and Major Elphinstone were awaiting us. The next day we travelled to Portsmouth, and landed in the *Victoria and Albert* barge at Osborne pier.

" *Friday, April* 4, 1862.—Prince Alfred was awaiting us, a fine handsome youth, darker than any of his brothers, and took us in a char-à-banc to the house. Here we were greeted most kindly by the three Princesses, who vanished with Prince Leopold, leaving Lady Augusta Bruce to take us to our rooms. Presently Princess Alice came and had a long, long talk with me. Sorrow has indeed made us know each other. How I

---

[1] Henry Brougham, born 1778; Attorney-General to Queen Caroline, 1820; Lord Chancellor, 1830–1834; created Baron Brougham, 1830; died at Cannes, May 1868.

LORD CHARLES FITZROY.   DR. GÜNTHER.
H.R.H. PRINCE LEOPOLD AND MISS BOWATER.
CHÂTEAU LEADER, CANNES, 1862.

grieve for her!—her young life crushed and blighted by a weight of care and responsibility of which few have any idea. They were all in and out of our room during tea, and when the Princes went to bed, Princesses Helena and Louise stayed with me a long time, talking sadly of all that has happened. At ten o'clock the Queen sent for Mamma, and had a long and deeply interesting interview with her—in Mamma's words, 'we talked like two old friends.'

"*Saturday, April* 5.—This morning Princess Helena was already in our sitting-room with Mamma when I went in there. Then came the Princes, Lady Augusta, and Miss Kerr. Before luncheon the Queen sent Princess Louise to bring me to her apartments at the other end of the house. She received me in the Prince's own room, and her first words were: 'Thank you for all you have done for little Leopold.' To me she does not look much altered; her manner was most kind although very dignified, and she asked innumerable questions about dear Papa's last illness and our future plans. I smile when I think how I told her of all the family arrangements, of the boys and Edith and Sotterley. I told her how blind I had been to Papa's danger, and she said with a deep sigh, ' Ah! one *is* blind '; and when I told her the doctors said he would have suffered if he had lived, she said, ' What *can* one wish, then ? ' After luncheon, Lady Caledon, Miss Kerr, Lady Augusta Bruce, and General Grey came to see us, and the Princes took us to their rooms, where Prince Alfred played to me on a self-acting piano given him by the Emperor Napoleon, and I had another long talk with Princess Alice and Princess Helena. Then I took a walk with Miss Kerr, and the soft wind, the green mossy turf, and the song of the birds made me feel I was in England again. The Princesses spent the evening with us. Princess Alice looked lovely, and Princess Helena struck me as *rayonnante de jeunesse et d'intelligence.*

"*Sunday, April* 6.—As usual, the younger Princes and Princesses breakfasted with us, and shortly before eleven we drove with Miss Kerr to service at Whippingham, a lovely little church lately restored under the Prince Consort's own direction, and indeed not yet finished. At the end of Morning Prayer there was a pause, and all the Royal children and most of the Household came in. Somehow, it all seemed very sad, the deep mourning, the seats draped with black, the vacant chair and name omitted in the prayers, and I thought of my own dear father, who we felt ought to be with us here. After luncheon, the Princesses took me to see the fort and the Swiss cottage and the museum, which is really beautiful. Princess Helena carried me off to her own room, where I spent some time looking at the pretty drawings which Princess Alice is making for Prince Louis. Mamma was with the Queen, so we went into Princess Alice's rooms, and she showed me a great treasure, a picture of her beloved father, taken after death, with the beautiful face looking so calm and peaceful. There we lingered on, talking in the twilight; Princess Alice lying on the sofa, while I sat in an arm-chair at her feet, and Princess Helena was on the floor at mine, and Prince Alfred perched on the table. We had quite a roomful at dinner, all talking and laughing together.

"*Monday, April 7.*—Our darling Prince Leo's ninth birthday. May God bless and keep that dear child and help him to be a comfort to his mother! I spent the morning with the Princesses, and saw the three Princes drive off in Prince Arthur's pretty little artillery waggon. In the afternoon we had an interminable game at croquet with all the Princes, and after tea had immense fun in the corridor playing with their little theatre. The Queen sent Mamma two beautiful prints of herself and the Prince, as well as a large photograph of herself and her children grouped round the Prince's bust, and gave me a lovely brooch with Prince Leo's hair. Sir Charles Phipps called on Mamma and told her that Thatched House Lodge was to be granted to Colonel Liddell. I spent the evening with Princess Helena, who was most kind and affectionate.

"*Tuesday, April 8.*—I took a last walk with Prince Leo and Dr. Günther, and bade an affectionate good-bye to the three Princesses. At the last moment the Queen sent for us, and was most kind but terribly overcome. Alas! poor Queen! The two Princes crossed with us in the *Fairy*. My darling boy cried bitterly at parting, and our journey home was very sad, the familiar form missing everywhere, and the dear place looking so pretty—and now we have to leave it!"

CHAPTER III

RICHMOND PARK, DUNWICH, AND ARBURY

1862–1863

THE next year of Louisa's life was a difficult one. The sad home-coming was followed by the dreary task of packing up and preparing to leave the Richmond house, which was now to pass into other hands. Their establishment was broken up, and she and her mother had already taken a long farewell of their beloved home, and were debating whether to settle in town or to accept Mr. Barne's offer of Sotterley as their temporary residence, when an unexpected intimation reached them to the effect that Colonel Liddell had declined to live at Thatched House Lodge, and that the Queen begged them to remain there. In the end Lady Bowater decided to accept this offer, and December found Louisa once more settled in the old home. For her these troubled days were brightened by the companionship of her devoted cousin Edith, who spent the summer at Richmond Park and to whom she paid a long and delightful visit in the following autumn at Dunwich. But this happy time was overshadowed by her cousin's rapidly failing health, and it was plain that this charming young girl's days were already numbered.

"*Friday, April* 25, 1862.—My twentieth birthday—alas ! it was a sad one !—that warm embrace and fervent blessing were missing. Yet he is safe with God, and one day we shall be together again. I woke at 3.30 a.m. and was rejoiced by the sight of a glorious sunrise and the concert of many birds. The post brought a budget from Osborne, a coral and gold locket from Prince Leo, with his portrait painted by Princess Alice, a gold locket with a pearl cross and their hair at the back from Princesses Helena and Louise, and charming letters from all three. The Queen's present to Mamma arrived early—a beautiful bracelet with Prince Leo's portrait and the following inscription: ' To Lady Bowater, in remembrance of her affectionate care of our little fatherless boy, Leopold.—VICTORIA R., April 1862.' This is the first birthday which Edith and I have ever spent together, but oh ! how things are changed with us both. It seems so sad and strange to see her on a couch of sickness and suffering, with little hope of recovery, and to hear how often she longs to die. Yet she is an immense comfort to me. We sat long together in the sunset, watching the beautiful light and talking of many things. What should I do without her ?

" *June 5.*—Philip, Madame, and I spent a long day at the International Exhibition. Everyone agrees that the *coup d'œil* is less fine than in '51, and certainly that is my own impression as far as I can remember. The nave is too crowded, and one misses the statues and flowers. We had just entered the picture gallery, and were standing lost in admiration before Gainsborough's ' Girl with a Pitcher,' when my attention was suddenly arrested by the courtly manner in which a stick which fell near me was picked up and restored to the owner, and great was my surprise to find myself close to Princess Alice. A little manœuvring enabled me to exchange greetings with Princess Helena, and then they passed on, a delightful example to the fine ladies who think it quite impossible to go on a shilling day. I recognised many old favourites among the pictures —Constable's ' Hay-Wain,' Turners and Morlands and Landseers—and what I admired most of all in the French section was Paul Delaroche's ' Martyr in the reign of Diocletian,' a young Christian virgin who had been drowned, floating down the stream, with a halo of radiant light round her head. The Belgian school is also very good, above all ' The Last Honours paid to Counts Egmont and Horn,' which quite startles one, so magnificently are these heads painted. Wandering among all these treasures occupied the whole morning. At two we proceeded to the American buffet for ' sandwiches and porter,' and then strolled about the numerous courts for the whole afternoon, devoting perhaps more attention to the harness and military department than to anything else.

"*June* 11.—A busy, bustling day, in preparation for our youthful Royalties, who arrived in a fly from Richmond station about four. Dear little Prince Leo looks so well, and we had a very merry afternoon with croquet and bagatelle. They paid Edith some nice little visits and were very dear to her, had tea, and then departed. Major Elphinstone of course came with them, and charmed everyone by his pleasing manners.

"*June* 22.—We drove over to Pembroke Lodge and had rather a good game of croquet. The Listers, Peels, etc., were there, also Lady Rose Fane and a Danish Captain de Falbe. Lord Amberley was very pleasant. He is a little shy man, and we rather herd together, like the two lost sheep of the party. I like his absence of pretension, not at all what you would expect of Lord Russell's eldest son.

"*July* 20.—To croquet at Pembroke Lodge—a small party. I continued the incipient flirtation with Lord Amberley. He seems a clever, well-read, ambitious little man, and called here last week, to my intense amusement.

"*July* 24.—My darling Edith's eighteenth birthday. Into Thy hands I commend her, O my God. I could not help hoping, as I watched the changes in the day, that it might be an emblem of her life, grey, overcast, and rainy early, later fine and bright. I saw the first harebells—her favourite flower—pale, alas ! and as colourless as herself.

"*July* 26.—We had a glorious drive in the early morning across the park to Barnes, the summer sun shining down on the rich green vales, the deer browsing in the plain, the woodpecker, with its lazy, undulating flight, scarcely fleeing at the sound of our wheels, the lake as still as a mirror, with the loveliest reflections of sky and banks undimmed by a single ripple. What a contrast to the bustle and turmoil of town, where the close of the season does not appear to exercise the slightest influence on the crowded streets! One feels daily more and more the pace at which most people of the present age are living. Can we wonder at the increase of insanity? There is a wild look in the eyes of half the men I meet on the railroad—not the fashionable swells, 'the men about town' of the *Saturday Review*—which makes me shudder. There is no rest, no repose for anyone in the present day; you are always on the go, for pleasure or for business. Is this preferable to the stagnation of former days? I do not know; it is difficult, almost impossible to decide. And for women in particular, is this restless, independent spirit good? This enfranchisement from prejudice, through which we all pass, in which I myself count so many stages, whither will it lead? I know it is a dangerous tendency, yet surely light, knowledge, truth, all these are worth striving for. God means that we *should* strive for them, in all humility, but in all earnestness. Neither the individual nor the generation can shut their eyes and say, 'I will see no more, I will go no farther.' We must all learn to unite the two lives—to live the one in its full extent as the best preparation for the other, which will be its glorious crown and completion, and where, as Monod so beautifully says, 'our eternal thirst for love, for light, for knowledge, for enjoyment, will be perfectly satisfied.'

"*Dunwich, Monday, September* 15.—I started after an early breakfast to drive our old maid Mellish and myself to Sotterley. We arrived at the Park about eleven, and walked to the churchyard, where now sleeps the best and fondest of fathers. Very calm and peaceful was that dear little churchyard, but bitter tears *will* fall, and bitterer were they when I entered the deserted house and visited his room. Alas! alas! it is all so very sad. Dear old Mother Cutler was glad enough to see me, and I went and saw a number of my old friends, who escorted me back to the house.

It all came so pleasantly and naturally that I could hardly realise the sad changes that have taken place since I was here last.

"*Grey Friars, Dunwich, Saturday, September* 20.— Mine eyes were rejoiced at breakfast by the sight of a letter from dear Prince Leo, announcing the Prince of Wales's engagement to Princess Alexandra of Denmark. He says he has seen her at Brussels, and that she is very pretty and amiable. The wedding is to take place next March at Windsor, but his mother, he adds, will not be present, which seems a great pity.

"*October* 10.—We were much concerned last evening at seeing in the paper an announcement that Her Majesty's journey from Reinhardtsbrunnen to Coburg was delayed in consequence of a slight accident to Prince Leopold, which proved more difficult to cure than was at first anticipated. Our anxiety, however, was not of long duration, for this morning's post brought a charming letter from Princess Helena, written by the Queen's desire, to tell us all about it. It seems that he ran a pen into the roof of his mouth, and the wound bled for a week, which, of course, reduced him very much, but he is really all right again. So like the Queen, this piece of thoughtful kindness. I wrote at once to thank Princess Helena.

"*Thatched House Lodge, Richmond Park, Monday, December* 8.—Home once more! Yes, it is home. Though it can never be what it once was, yet I do feel joyous and thankful to be here once more. Great was our surprise and delight on arriving to find that, by the indefatigable exertions of our good people, our *Lares* and *Penates* have all resumed their wonted places, and everything has an air of comfort, cleanliness, and good taste that charms my very being. Thanks be to God for this great blessing—for a *great* blessing we now feel it to be—and, under Him, to our good and gracious Queen.

"*Wednesday, December* 10.—Busy arranging books and letters. Wilhelm von Humboldt says, 'Old letters lose their vitality.' Mrs. Jameson remarks that this is

' untrue, and it is just because they retain their vitality that it is so dangerous to keep some letters, so wicked to burn others.' I think Mrs. Jameson is right : I have been tearing up some of Edith's letters to-night, and changed as she now is, still these letters have *life* in them—they bring her before me exactly as she was at that age, I fancy I hear her talk. Busy all day gardening and working in the schoolroom. It is such thorough enjoyment being at home, among all one's things, and feeling for the first time for a year that we have a settled home. This feeling is tiding us over these sad anniversaries better than I could have possibly hoped.

"*Sunday, December* 14.—A long, dreary day. A year—a whole year—has elapsed since my darling father was taken from us. I can scarcely believe it or realise that all these weary months have passed without him. The blank is just as great, the aching void in my heart which nothing can ever fill. Only the hope of the great Hereafter lives to cheer and strengthen. Where should we all be without this belief? But the thought of him recalls me to the present. He left me a sacred charge. ' Take care of Mamma,' were his last words, ' when I am gone, and do all she tells you ; she is your best friend.' My God, help me to fulfil it. How much my thoughts are at Windsor to-day. There all is united —the Prince's life, his death, his grave ; while our sad hearts must travel to the death-bed in a foreign land— to the grave in the quiet churchyard far away. Sweet, dear letters from Princess Helena and Prince Leopold brought with them a melancholy pleasure. Princess Louise and Edith also wrote later.

"*New Year's Eve*, 1862. *My own room*, 11.30.—Once more, Old Year, farewell. It is a grave thing standing thus between the Old and the New, looking back and looking forward. May God pardon my past errors and give strength for the future! His love alone can support me, that alone can never fail me. Oh that I might lose myself more and more in that love, that it might become more and more my very life and being! Three things mark this year : the visit to

Osborne, my long intercourse with dearest Edith, the departure from this place and our unexpected return. All more or less things to be thankful for. ' Look not mournfully into the Past,' said a wise man, ' it comes not again. Wisely improve the Present; it is thine. Go forth into the unknown Future without fear and with a manly heart.' "

Lady Bowater now made a determined effort for her daughter's sake to rouse herself from the torpor into which she had sunk after the shock of her husband's death. Louisa's own spirits revived with the buoyancy of youth, and she thoroughly enjoyed her return to society.

" *Monday, January* 5, 1863.—Last week Lord Amberley brought us an invitation to a party at Pembroke Lodge at which we assisted to-day. The guests consisted only of General Peel and his three daughters, and Professor and Mrs. Owen. The charade *Surprise* was acted with much spirit and cleverness, especially by Lord Amberley, who as Master Tom Sniffington ' taking off Dr. Switchem ' was inimitable. Very pretty, too, was little Agatha as ' Andromeda.' In short, the whole thing amused me immensely. Afterwards we had some pleasant chat, seasoned by Lord Amberley's mild attentions, and I was interested in meeting three such remarkable men as General Peel, Professor Owen, and Lord Russell."

The next day Louisa accompanied her mother on a visit to Arbury, the home of her cousin and guardian, Charles Newdegate, the well-known Member of Parliament for Warwickshire. This fine old house with its ancient conventual buildings and castellated façade added by Sir Roger Newdegate in the eighteenth century had lately acquired a new interest from the novels of George Eliot (Mary Anne Evans), whose father had formerly been a carpenter on the Arbury estate and whose brother was agent to the present owner. The scene of *Mr. Gilfil's Love Story* had been laid at Arbury, and the house itself described under the name of Cheverel Manor.

LADY BOWATER.
(From a miniature by Sir WILLIAM ROSS.)

"*Arbury, Wednesday, January* 7.—A fine winter's day, and I spent the morning wandering about these beautiful grounds under the cedars and Scotch firs, along the yew hedges and the moat, my thoughts going to the music of the falling waters tumbling over the rocks. After lunch we walked to the Home Farm, which is very snug and pretty, and coming home the reflection of the old grey house and mullioned windows and great beeches and cedars in the water were all most lovely.

"*Thursday, January* 8.—We drove to Leamington to an amateur concert given by fifty ladies and gentlemen, in aid of the North Warwickshire Relief Fund, a piece of rare enjoyment. I felt proud of my unmusical nation when I heard this exquisite performance given by my countrymen and women for the sake of the poor Coventry ribbon-weavers. A splendid air from *Jephthah* was superbly sung by Mr. Arthur Coleridge, and Haydn's canzonet, 'My mother bids me bind my hair,' was beautifully rendered by Mrs. Harvey. I cannot describe the entrancing effect of these delicious melodies or the way in which the audience hung upon the singers' lips, till in that great hall you might have heard a pin drop. In the twenty minutes' interval Charley Newdegate gave a speech about the distress, explaining that this was the third winter of suffering, and thanked the Ladies Feilding and others who had worked so hard in the good cause. It was a great pleasure to hear him speak—although, between me and my Journal, I do not think he speaks well nor do I like his action—and I felt proud of belonging to him, as his ward and cousin. Lord Denbigh held the plate at the door, and I took the opportunity of making myself known to this old friend of my father. The dear old gentleman seemed much pleased. He travelled back with us to Rugby, and much agreeable conversation passed between him and Mrs. Newdegate about the distress. The rate of mortality has actually decreased ! This is attributed not only to the children being better attended to by their mothers, but also to their being unable to purchase the cordials, largely composed of opium, with which they were in the habit of drugging them to a frightful extent. From Rugby we travelled with Mr. Clerk of Astley Castle, who is Counsel to the Crown, and talked much of Greece. Lord Palmerston, he says, had actually made up his mind that Prince Alfred should accept the crown, and only retracted in consequence of the general opposition abroad. I am very glad he has done this—England's moderation speaks volumes for her. As to the cession of the Ionian Islands, he says that the inhabitants are chiefly Roman Catholic and more Italian than Greek ; that they are largely a trading community, and that to take them from under the protection of the British flag and British Consuls would be doing them a poor service. All this was very interesting after my long months of seclusion.

" *January* 16.—A regular country-house day. Miss B—— and I walked in the morning. I cannot like that girl; there is no harm in her, but she does not suit me. The afternoon was spent playing billiards in the old gallery with Miss Montgomerie, who amuses me very much with her odd, independent ways. I sat next to Captain B——, who also begins to amuse me. He has plenty of fun and sense, and his profession of being a lady-hater piques me by its novelty.

" *January* 17.—Miss Montgomerie, Miss B——, and I had a charming drive to cover and saw the hounds meet, which I enjoyed very much, never having seen anything of the kind before. Afterwards Tina and I sat in the gallery in the firelight and twilight, with the old family portraits looking down upon us and the statues gleaming from either end. In the evening we had tremendous fun. Tina and I exchanged experiences after dinner, and when the gentlemen came in we found ourselves the centre of quite a brilliant circle —Captain B——, Mr. Clerk, Colonel Astley. We fell to talking of politics, and nearly demolished the latter, well backed by the other two.

" *Tuesday, January* 20.—Tina and I sat in the drawing-room all the morning, and I tried to sketch the great Gothic window. After luncheon we all played billiards in the gallery, and sat round the fire, telling the story of that other Tina who figures in *Scenes of Clerical Life* as pacing up and down this same gallery. I must say I like Captain B―― very much. He is good-natured, sensible, and honest. I only hope Hampton Court will not spoil him. And Tina is a darling—clever, sprightly, affectionate. Altogether I have enjoyed this visit very much, and so, I think, has Mamma. It has rubbed us both up and done us a world of good.

"*Richmond Park, February 7.*—Mamma and I had the usual London day — the bazaar, Roland's, my singing and music lessons. Pauer gave me greater praise than I expected. But why did he say, ' Werden Sie nur nicht eingebildet ! ' Has he remarked this grand failing in my character ? Yet I do not think I am conceited about my music. I have had too many home truths on the subject for that ! After the lesson Mamma and I had a charming walk across the Park to Mrs. Spiers, where we found a host of people assembled to admire Eliza's presents and trousseau and congratulate her on her approaching marriage. Among them were Mme Van de Weyer and her daughter, Sir Alexander Buchanan, the lately appointed Ambassador at Berlin, my old friend Constance Lennox, and Lord Leven and Lord Kirkcaldy, with whom we travelled down to Barnes. The latter can talk of nothing but the approaching Royal marriage and the preparations for the event at Windsor. Most delightful after all this bustle and turmoil was the drive home in the marvellously warm spring evening. It was nearly dark when we reached the Terrace, only a gleam of sunset still left in the sky was reflected in the river, swollen by an unusually high tide. Then came the Park, with its bare, leafless trees, a few distant lights sparkling between the stems, and the stars shining overhead—my friends Orion and the Pleiades were especially distinct as we climbed the hill to our hawk's nest. I felt the soothing influences of Nature, and contentment and thankfulness took possession of my heart—thankfulness more especially for the quiet home which it has pleased God to restore to us, and which I feel deeply is very much better for me than a life in town could have been. Politics are very interesting just now, and the more I read history, the more interest I must take in the history acting around me. Parliament met on the 5th, and the Prince of Wales took his seat in the House of Lords. Great are the discussions, especially upon foreign politics, the chief bone of contention being the cession of the Ionian Islands to Greece. They seem pretty unanimous as to the wisdom of non-intervention in America, and all seem to doubt the benefits to be conferred on the slaves by the success of the North—in short, Parliament echoes the *Times*; while, to the astonishment of everybody, an enormous meeting held at Exeter Hall declares, with the most overpowering enthusiasm, for Emancipation at all costs—the North and President Lincoln! And this in the teeth of the fact that black men are dying of starvation at New York by hundreds. Emancipation by all means, say I, but not, as I believe the Abolitionists would have it, at the price of the extermination of the coloured race. I am surprised to see Tom Hughes' name at that meeting. Then there is the Insurrection in Poland and the gallant resistance of the Prussian Chamber to the unconstitutional aggressions of King William. Party in England seems to be nowhere. The Government brings forward no measures, and the Opposition has no fault to find save with some of Lord Russell's dispatches to Denmark on that un-understandable question of Schleswig-Holstein, and to the Pope, proposing Malta as his residence."

CHAPTER IV

The Royal Wedding

1863

THE year 1863 opened gaily for Louisa, with the Royal wedding, which she attended in the pleasantest way, going with her kind neighbours, Lord and Lady Leven, to stay with their son, Lord Kirkcaldy, at the Bank at Windsor—" a piece of great good luck," as she remarks.

" *Windsor, Friday, March* 6.— We travelled to Windsor with Clare Thornton, and there found Lord and Lady Leven, Lord Kirkcaldy, Sophia and Florence Melville, Ronald and Julia, Madame Goldschmidt (Jenny Lind) and her boy. Everybody was rushing about, triumphal arches adorned the streets, and the town was as gay as a foreign place. We young people —Sophia, Florence, Ronald, and I—are in another house, opposite the Bank, and great fun we have !

" *Saturday, March* 7.—A long and exciting day. Clare and I were sitting writing after breakfast when Lord Leven rushed in. ' Come instantly, and the Dean will show us the chapel.' So off we flew, and saw the nave all fitted up with red cloth, and what I cared about most, the beautiful stained window and alabaster reredos erected in memory of the Prince Consort, and intended as a symbol of his public and private life. While we were there, the Crown Prince and Princess came in, and I had a good sight of them. She looked so fresh, so young and simple, with a bunch of spring flowers in her hand, and he is much handsomer and has a far more pleasing expression than I imagined. We also saw the temporary building at the end of the chapel, including the bride's room, which is all white and pink and loveliness. Then we walked down Eton, which also sports arches and decorations, and stood some time in the old school quadrangle. We spent most of the afternoon watching the crowds in the streets, and after tea took up our station near the bridge, and waited patiently for the bride. First we saw the four Princes—Frederick William, Louis, Arthur, and Leo—drive down. Gradually it grew dark, the lamps were lighted, and guns were fired to announce the arrival at Slough, each shot sending a little thrill through the crowd. At last General Seymour trotted past and the head of the escort appeared on the bridge. The carriage pulled up immediately opposite us, there was a rush and a cheer—a fair young girl in a white bonnet with pink rosebuds was seen at the window, bowing and smiling, and then on they passed, and all was over. I felt so glad to think that she knew the Queen and Princesses beforehand, and was not arriving among strangers !

" *Sunday, March* 8.—We drove to service at a lovely little church at Englefield Green, and after luncheon walked on the North Terrace, but came in soon, as it was bitterly cold, and Madame Goldschmidt began to sing to us, first German hymns, then ' O rest in the Lord ' and several airs from the *Messiah*, especially ' Behold and see if there be any sorrow like unto my sorrow.' The whole room was wrapt in deep attention. Opposite to me sat Dudley de Chair, his handsome features and remarkably beautiful expression contrasting finely with Florence's fair, spiritual face. Altogether I never spent a more delightful Sunday.

" *Monday, March* 9.—Started off early after breakfast with Florence and Walter Goldschmidt for the Castle, and saw some of the Royal party on their way to the chapel. This time I contrived to see that Princess Alexandra is of a very suitable height for the Prince; who is not so very short after all. I was watching them pass into the chapel when Walter suddenly exclaimed, ' There are the two little Princes on the Green,' and presently we came face to face with them. Major Elphinstone recognised me, and we stopped and had a talk. Both the boys looked well and grown, and great was the laughing and talking with me and my two little chaperons. Later in the day, we were amused by seeing the Lord Mayor and Aldermen in their fine coaches drive up to the Castle to present the Princess with a magnificent diamond necklace, and had a beautiful view of her as she went down to Eton. She is much prettier than her photographs, with just the modest, half-shy, half-pleased expression one likes to see as she bowed her acknowledgments right and left. We then marched up the Hundred Steps, meeting the lovely Lady Spencer with the Archbishop and Bishop of Oxford on our way, and proceeded to take Mr. Ruthven's very small rooms by storm. Great was the horror of his bachelor friends, as one by one they dropped in, to find him thus invaded, and very merry we made ourselves over the muffins and their discomfiture. Then back to find Lady Anna and Lady Emily Melville had arrived, and to enjoy another very merry tea-fight and a still merrier game of Silent Commerce, before starting to see the fireworks. I took my seat upon the box, and drove off under the starry sky and the old grey Castle walls, up to the chapel, where workmen were still busy, and through the cloisters to Canon Anson's house. From a terrace in front of this we looked down on the fireworks, which were exceedingly pretty, and I fell into a drowsy state, from which I was roused to return home, where a merry supper was very acceptable after the fatigues of the day. Sophia and I had a long talk about Papa and Edith and all kind of things. It is wonderful how sorrow brings people together. I feel that Sophia is now a real friend.

"*Tuesday, March* 10.—How glad we all were, when dressing and breakfasting on that cold, foggy Tuesday morning, not to be the plumed and trained dames of high degree, who, before we left our beds, were shivering in the train on their way from town! Cold enough we thought it when, soon after ten, Lady Leven, the Indian Princess Gourramma, Sophia, Florence, Ronald,

Clare, and myself marched up the Castle hill to the stand close to the guardroom gateway. The road was lined with Volunteers, whose grey uniforms contrasted well with the scarlet uniforms of the Coldstreams, Yeomen of the Guard, and royal officials swarming in all directions. Carriage after carriage came pouring up from the station containing duchesses resplendent with diamonds, cabinet ministers, generals covered with orders, bridesmaids, and bishops. Ronald and I did our best to put names to them, with various success. Soon the procession of the Danish Royal Family came down the hill; our own Princes and Princesses followed, and were received with loud cheers, Princess Helena looking very handsome. I heard afterwards that she was very much admired by all the foreigners. Great was our indignation at some of the people behind us refusing to stand up as they passed, and trying to bully us into a similar want of respect; but Ronald and I, on whom the brunt of their attack fell, as we chanced to be tall and conspicuous, stood our own and were loyal. Then came the bridegroom, who looked grave and handsome, though almost buried under his robes; and last of all, the bride, her classic profile well set off by the many folds of her white lace veil, but unrelieved by a single tinge of pink in her cheeks. We settled down, with what patience we could, to await the close of the ceremony. I employed myself pencilling a few lines to Mamma, and tried to realise the solemn scene going on within and to think of our widowed Queen looking down on her children. . . . Suddenly a mounted equerry rode rapidly past, guns boomed in the Long Walk, and bells rang out from every steeple. I would not for all the world have missed this outside glimpse of and share in the great event. It was worth anything to see the look of beaming happiness on the bridegroom's face as he stepped out of the gateway with his wife beside him. We hurried on to a crush luncheon at the Guards' barracks, where we met all the world and his wife, but came away early, and by favour of Captain Legge took up a very good position behind the sentries, to see the

Prince and Princess of Wales go away. After waiting patiently for three-quarters of an hour, down they drove in an open carriage, quite slowly, so that we had a good look at them. I am perfectly satisfied. She is all that is good, pure, innocent, and lovely, and both looked so supremely happy that it did one's heart good to look at them. Her excessive paleness of the morning had given way to a lovely pink colour, and amidst all the bowing right and left they found time to talk to each other. Once more, God bless them !

" Of course, as soon as the carriages had passed there was a rush-off started, little Lord Kirkcaldy, with the Indian Princess on one arm and me on the other, among all the Eton boys. In the iron gateway there was a jam. Lord Kirkcaldy shouted, ' Armitage, will you take a lady for me ? ' A tall individual sprang forward, and leaning on this stranger's arm, I walked between the ranks of the Volunteers amid the laughter and applause of the mob. But at the turn to the station the crush was really frightful, and we were almost swept off our legs. However, in time I got safely home, and spent the evening playing and dancing. Before Madame Goldschmidt left, I contrived to get a few words with her. I like her so much, and have seldom met so high-minded and charming a woman. She had been in the choir, and was most deeply touched with the whole ceremony. ' It was a blessed and holy scene,' she said. The Queen, in a widow's cap and deep mourning, wearing silk for the first time, witnessed the ceremony from a closet just above and to the left of the altar. She looked well, and although deeply affected when the bridegroom entered, as each pronounced the ' I will ' her whole face lit up with a smile. ' The Prince,' said Madame, ' bore himself nobly and with great dignity.' Very touching must it have been when all her children curtseyed to her. But amid all the tears, a happy diversion was created by a small scrimmage between Prince Leo and little Prince William of Prussia, who resented most vehemently his uncle's attempts at tutoring him.

" I sat next to Mr. De Chair at dinner, and must

mention him as one of the personages who have attracted me the most during this memorable week. Settled in Canada, and engaged to be married, he was pre-eminently safe, and I allowed myself to be drawn to him by peculiarly frank and pleasant manners, so unlike the blasé politeness of men of the world. We even went to the length of exchanging photos and autographs, and as we passed over to the other house by starlight, parted the best of friends—probably never to meet again in this world. But I am going on too fast, and forgetting the illuminations, which we drove out to see after dinner. Beautiful as fairyland was the Castle arch, its fiery lines standing out against the dark sky; and next to that, what I liked best was the Bank as seen from the bridge. Altogether, this was a pleasant ending to a never-to-be-forgotten day."

A month later, Louisa returned to Windsor again with a party from Roehampton, and was present at a children's dance given by Lord Kirkcaldy at the Bank. "It was great fun," she writes on April 8. "All the Hoods, Seymours, Van de Weyers, etc., were there, and we danced morris dances, Sir Roger, and a reel after the guests were all gone. Mrs. Grey introduced me to Sybil[1]—she *is* pretty. Lady Susan has been up to the Castle to see the Queen for the first time since the Duchess of Kent's death, and has had a beautiful bracelet very like Mamma's, with a miniature of the Duchess and lock of her hair, given her by the Queen."

"*Friday, April* 10.—This was a memorable day in my life. *Tagebuch, vertrauter Freund, nehme also dessen Schilderung auf!* The house being uninhabitable owing to preparations for the dance, I went out with Lady Susan and Florence, and walked on the North Terrace, where, in the soft spring air, it really felt as though one could see the leaves coming out. Returning to the Bank, I found Lord Kirkcaldy and Sophy going to drive to the nursery gardens at Slough. So I went with them, and a charming drive

[1] Sybil, eldest daughter of General Charles Grey, private secretary to Queen Victoria; married 1867, William, 10th Duke of St. Albans.

we had, and saw some lovely azaleas, which were one mass of blossom. In the middle of luncheon came a note from Miss Hildyard, asking me to be at the Castle at 3.30. So I walked up with Lord Kirkcaldy and Mellish, and went straight to Miss Hildyard's rooms, where I found her and both Princesses. We met the children in the corridor, and saw Princess Louis's new little baby, born on Sunday, or rather a bit of its cheek. Nothing could be more charming or affectionate than they all were. Princess Helena went to dress for walking, and Prince Leo was sent for to see me. Dear little fellow, it is such a treat to see him! Next appeared Prince Alfred, to show his lieutenant's uniform to his sisters, and very pleasant and good-natured he was in the few minutes' *tête-à-tête* I had with him. Then came little Princess Beatrice with her governess to see him, and after that Princess Helena and I sallied out by ourselves. It did seem so curious to see the sentries presenting arms as we two girls passed out under the great archway. Presently Prince Alfred and Prince Louis overtook us, driving together in a new Russian carriage. We had a long and very interesting talk during our hour-and-a-half's walk. The Princess struck me as having developed rapidly in the past year, no doubt the result of the new duties and responsibilities laid upon her since Princess Alice's marriage. She spoke much of her father and of his exalted conception of duty, which was the motive of his whole life. Both her sisters are very happy in their married life, but she herself is not impatient to follow their example, and hopes to remain in England when she marries. God bless and help her, and make me of real service to her! But the story of this day was not ended. I heard with dismay from Lord Kirkcaldy that Mr. E——, my all-too-attentive partner at the Rendlesham balls, had begged for an invitation to the dance to-night, and sure enough he met me on the threshold of the ballroom. I danced twice with him, but refused to give him a third dance, saying that I was never allowed to dance more than twice with anyone, and that I felt bound to be careful in my mother's absence. Then he made me promise to go to supper with him; but this did not come off, as I was dancing with Captain Seymour. So he claimed another dance, and as I said I was tired, took me to rest in a quiet nook. I sat down, and in a moment—all was over. I can only say that he has risen greatly in my estimation, but that I could never love him as he deserves to be loved, and I told him so plainly and firmly. I was deeply touched and yet a good deal relieved, and danced till two o'clock. I had never stayed till the end of all things before, and thoroughly I enjoyed it, as well as our merry supper afterwards. I chanced to say that I was sure I should never wake in time to catch the 12.25 train. Captain Seymour undertook that I should. I thought he was joking, but at 8.30 on the following morning there was a drumming and a piping in front of the Bank which would have startled the Seven Sleepers. Up I jumped, and was dressed in time to show Captain Seymour, by appearing at the hall window, that he had succeeded. Thanks to this early waking, Sophy and I were able to have a charming row up the river with Ronald and Mr. Ruthven before we joined the others at the station. I travelled with Lady Susan to Vauxhall, and in a few minutes was kneeling by my darling Edith's couch. Aunt Marian told me of Miss Stuart-Wortley's engagement to Mr. Welby. This will decide my fate."

The Princesses were very anxious at this time to have Miss Bowater for one of the maids of honour, and Louisa herself was much attracted by the idea. Unfortunately, not being the granddaughter of a peer, she was excluded from this post by Court etiquette, and Miss Seymour obtained the coveted post.

"*Richmond Park, Sunday, April* 19.—Somehow a disappointing day! I am not to be maid of honour and not to go to London! Well, it seems silly to care, and I don't care *now*, this lovely Sunday morning, sitting in my own snuggery, with the window wide open, and the song of the birds coming up all round, and the distant bells, and air laden with sweet smells, and the shadows sleeping on the grass, and the daisies looking up at the sun and blue sky, as if it were May. Yes, this is pure joy, and if I am not to have the other things I wish for no doubt it is because they are not good for me."

However, Mrs. Newdegate, who kept house for her son Charles, now proposed to take her young cousin out this season. Louisa spent much of her time in this lady's house in Arlington Street, and on her twenty-first birthday had the satisfaction of snapping her fingers at "Charley" and informing him that he was now no longer her guardian! Mr. Newdegate had already entered on his parliamentary career, and Louisa describes how, one day, on taking up the paper and turning to a most interesting debate on Italy, " to my utter amazement, I found the honourable member for Warwickshire dealing death and destruction from among the ranks of the Opposition, and being patted on the back by Lord Palmerston, to any extent. Who would have thought it ! "

" *Saturday, May* 16, *H.R.H. the Princess of Wales's first Drawing-room.*—My toilet began at eleven and was completed by 12.30, and between you and me, my dear Journal, was most successful. A train of white silk, the skirt a mass of white net, and the whole concern trimmed with white azaleas and maidenhair, a wreath of the same flowers in my hair. Mrs. Newdegate got into the carriage at one, thinking ourselves in capital time, but great was our horror on emerging into Piccadilly to find a string of carriages extending the whole way to St. George's Hospital. We resigned ourselves to our fate with what philosophy we might, the said fate proving to be to spend our time until 4.50 p.m. in regaining the point from which we set out. Three-quarters of an hour did we stand opposite Hamilton Place, and so on in proportion. Meanwhile the tide of *starers* flowed on, and Piccadilly was the fashionable promenade of the day. All our gentleman friends came and offered us buns, etc., and when at last we reached St. James's the Palace was comparatively empty, and the doors were closed to give the Princess time to rest. The throne-room, when we entered it, appeared much less full than usual. There was only a knot of officers opposite the Princess, of whom, not being the least alarmed, I had a good view as we walked up. She looked a bit of a thing, with a white gown and white face, two curls and a diamond tiara. The Lord Chamberlain discomposed me not a little by announcing me as ' Mrs. Bowater,' which, however, did not prevent Princess Alice from shaking hands with me most cordially ; Princess Mary followed her example, and to my amazement the Prince of Wales, which was the more gratifying as it is several years since I have met him. Next to him stood the Duke of Cambridge and the three foreigners, the Princes of Hesse, Orange, and Holstein. I made a low curtsy to Prince Louis, whereat he looked mightily astonished. *Soit mon succès, soit ma toilette*, Colonel Du Plat came trotting after me, and to my great amusement shook hands with Mrs. Newdegate, taking her for Mamma ! Then we made our way downstairs without any difficulty, and were at home by 6.30. I must not forget Mamma's kindness in herself going to buy my bouquet. I think even she was satisfied with my appearance, though it was a sad day for her—how much has happened since last the Prince of Wales and I stood face to face l

" 3 *Arlington Street, Monday, June* 8.—We dined early, and at 7 p.m. Mrs. Newdegate, Charley, and I were on our way to the city to meet the Prince and Princess of Wales at a grand ball given by the Lord Mayor and Corporation in the Guildhall. Winding our way along these unwonted streets under the shadow of St. Paul's, we descended in the Guildhall yard, and gazed through the long vista of columns at the gaily dressed crowds moving over the rich crimson carpet to the sound of inspiriting music. Having made our bow to the Lord Mayor, we stood in the narrow passage leading to the Hall, and soon the strains of the National Anthem announced the arrival of the Prince and Princess. They passed close to us and quite slowly, so that we had ample time to make up our minds that she is uncommonly pretty. Bowing gracefully though timidly, and closely followed by her handsome boy-husband, she looked like the princess of some fairy tale, and indeed the whole scene was very like fairyland. We naturally wanted to follow them into the Hall, which some foolish Common-Council men tried to prevent, and there was a most unseemly struggle, which actually ended in the police being sent for. Of course we got in at last, and very striking was the appearance of the grand old Hall, richly decorated with harmonious colours and crowded with people. The ceremony of presenting the freedom to the Prince was very soon over, and dancing began. Charley and I had a capital valse, which was most refreshing after the mauling I had undergone. Supper was the same miserable scramble, and then we watched the Royalties depart, and I had the pleasure of a very marked bow from Prince Alfred, after which I remember nothing more, for I was utterly tired out and turned quite faint from heat and fatigue.

"*Thursday, June* 11.—I went to a concert at Mrs. Monk's, the widow of the Bishop of Gloucester, and a capital one it was : a beautiful selection of Italian music sung by Carlotta Patti, Alboni, Gardoni, and Ciampi. Carlotta warbles like a bird, and goes higher than anyone ever did before, but I privately prefer Alboni's rich contralto. We hurried home that I might have my hair dressed by Cavallier and go with my aunt to the Opera, to hear the object of my ambition for years, *Don Juan*. Glorious indeed was the music; with Patti as Zerlina, and I fully enjoyed all the familiar airs, ' Vedrai carino,' ' La ci darem la mano,' ' Batti, batti ! ' etc. But as a whole I do not like the opera. The story is so wildly improbable that I could only regret such music being thrown away upon such a tale.

"*Friday, June* 12.—Mrs. Newdegate was laid up with a bad cold, so my day was spent with Charley, who talked politics over breakfast, rode with me in the Park till a deluge of rain sent us helter-skelter home, and went with me to a party at Lady Nugent's, where Mrs. Gurdon took charge of me, and I was as happy as a little queen, knowing everyone in the room, and regularly floating off on a tide of friends—Adairs, Custances, Buxtons, whom I had the pleasure of congratulating on Bell's marriage to Colonel Bulwer. I am to be her bridesmaid. Indeed, I do little but congratulate my friends on their marriages just now.

"*Friday, June* 19.—We went to Lady Gladstone's ball, an uncommonly good one, and for me a great *succès*, as I danced without intermission, which was much more than I expected at my first London ball after two years' absence.

"5 *Lowndes Square, Thursday, June* 25.—I came to stay with my cousin Jeanie Fenwick, and Mrs. Gurdon took me to a very nice ball at Mrs. Custance's, where I danced all the evening with Sir Robert Buxton, Mr. Charles Fremantle, Major Paynter, Mr. Gurdon, etc.

"*Friday, June* 26.—Jeanie and I sat out in the Park, where it was cool and shady. After a pleasant, sociable little dinner, the Mainwarings called for me at 9.30, and off we went to this long-talked-of Guards' ball, which was given to the Prince and Princess of Wales in the Exhibition galleries of last year. A more magnificent one has scarcely ever been given in this country. A picked guard in scarlet uniform extended all along the front of the building and up the stairs; even the cloak-room, with its dainty maidens in white muslin and Guards' ribbons, was exquisitely appointed. In a flutter of expectation up we went, and passed through a tapestried hall into a scene of Eastern magnificence. A lofty saloon was transformed into an enchanted garden of tall palms with fountains rising out of brilliant masses of flowers and fairy bowers of shells, ferns, and crystal basins, all reflected in mirrors along the walls. This paradise was enlivened by the flitting to and fro of our gallant hosts in that uniform which must ever be so dear to my heart. Lord Strathallan, who remembered my father, was very kind to me, and took me in to tea in a room between the ball and supper rooms. While we were there the Prince and Princess went in to supper. As they drew near, the curtain was withdrawn, and a magnificent trophy of armour with the star of the Brigade in the centre, above the gold-laden table, was seen down the whole length of the gallery. Supper was on the most sumptuous scale; the walls gleamed with arms, and champagne cup flowed from taps into gold and silver goblets. But in the ballroom the only ornament was a trophy of flags—the very same that were borne all through the Crimea—opposite the dais, above a bust of the old Duke. Oh! I felt thoroughly in my place among them all, and was pleased to find my claims recognised by Lord Strathallan. After this, I danced with Major Paynter and Arthur Birch, and was much amused by Sir Robert and his queer ways. Lord Kirkcaldy was also most kind—there is nothing like old friends."

CHAPTER V

RICHMOND PARK, DUNWICH, AND OSBORNE

1863–1864

LOUISA returned to Richmond Park after her gay season, to find plenty of society in this neighbourhood, and enjoy herself as much as ever with her old friends.

" *Friday, July* 17.—The Melvilles called to ask me to join their party to a camp meeting that evening, so after syringing fruit trees all the afternoon, I drove over late, had a merry schoolroom tea and croquet afterwards, and started about nine for Wimbledon, where the usual Volunteer meeting has been going on. We left the carriages at the Windmill and walked round between the lines of tents to a hollow in the south of that great duelling rendezvous of days gone by. There several thousands of spectators were ranged round the big fire, which flared up now and then, throwing a lurid glow on the sea of faces, and brought out the picturesque groups of the Victorias who, mingled with Guardsmen, were keeping up the fire. We all sat on the ground, a few chairs being the only distinction reserved for the ladies of Lord Elcho's party, which included the Duchess of Sutherland. There was nothing to keep order but Lord Elcho's word and the good feeling of the people, but there was not a single disturbance. We had some capital singing from Lord Feilding, Lord Bury, Mr. Harris, etc. ' Scots wha hae wi' Wallace bled,' ' Villikins and his Dinah,' ' The young man from the country,' and the choruses, taken up by the mass of people, were really grand. We also had some niggers and some beautiful glees from the Artists' Corps—in short, the bonhomie of the whole thing was delightful, and the punch which was handed round made it still more of a jollification.

"*Monday, July* 20.—Lady Leven and Madame Goldschmidt came to pay a long-promised visit. The latter is certainly one of the most charmingly suggestive people I know. We talked a great deal of the characteristics of various nations. She says one great failing in the German character is want of *Scheue*, which I translate *reserve* ; also that the elaborate education of German women, far more thorough as it is than that of English girls, avails them little, because it is never carried into practical life, but is swamped in household cares. In short, while feeling with me the indefinable, irresistible charm of German thought, she declares it is much better felt at a distance, and that German women are most unsatisfactory to live with, in spite of their large funds of intellect and knowledge. As to the Americans, she confirms Mrs. Trollope's opinion that they simply have not an idea how to behave. With all this licence, she believes the morals of the upper classes are pure, and a separation is almost unheard of. Her own people, she thinks, in many things resemble us, and possess in common with us that reserve which she calls ' the crown of life.' For the rest, the childlike simplicity and undeveloped character of the Swedish women, which I can fancy being very charming, is the result of a life of less high-pressure than ours. Of their scenery, too, she spoke with enthusiasm : of the long winters with the sparkling snow and dark pine-woods under the glorious moon, the rushing spring and the summer nights when it is never dark—all the wondrous poetry, in short, of those stern, sad Northern climes. She spoke of Frederica Bremer as a most remarkable person, infinitely superior to her works. My whole conversation with her was indeed most interesting.

"*Friday, August* 21.—A wonderfully long day. I was awake and *on the go* from 7 a.m. to 5 a.m. this morning. We started early for town, and in spite of the dreariness and desertion of the great city were rather amused by our wanderings. We sat some time with my aunt, Lady Ridley, who was most kind and affectionate, and—O joy!—presented me with twenty pounds. This will set me right for a long time. We came down by 4.50, dined with Mr. and Mrs. Mainwaring, and went to a dance at Hampton Court given by Lady Isabella St. John. Seldom, if ever, have I enjoyed anything so much. We were just the right number of people and a nice set—pretty girls, gentleman-like men, and capital valsers. I danced every dance but one, which I sat out as I was so tired, and for that might have had four or five partners. And then—O joy of joys!—we stayed for the cotillon, which I had never danced before. What a charming dance it is! There is so much variety, and so many opportunities of doing good-natured, unselfish things. I went dancing on in a perfectly frantic manner with Sir Malcolm MacGregor, who was remarkably pleasant, finished the cotillon with me, and saw us into the carriage."

A few days after this, Louisa joined her now invalid cousin Edith at Dunwich, and to use her own expression, " dropped into Dunwich ways as if I had left it only yesterday."

"*Saturday, September* 5.—Dear St. John's twenty-second birthday. How we are all growing up! I ran down to the sea, and watched the breakers that were coming in grandly under a grey sky. Quite late I had a few minutes' talk with dear Edith. I confessed my wrong feelings of impatience at her illness. She told me that she too had them to contend with, but that now God's purpose was very clear to her. Oh! she looked so lovely as she lay there under the shaded light, speaking these solemn words quite simply and gravely. God's ways are indeed blessed to her. It makes me feel very small—me the spoilt child of the world—to hear and watch her. . . . Dear child, I can see so plainly that God is leading her with His own hand away from this world and all connected with it— her interest in it all has so palpably diminished.

"*Wednesday, September* 30.—Dear Edith has been

warning me again of an old fault—looking down upon people who are not quite equal to me in refinement and intellect. I know I do, and I know I ought not. I wonder whether there is any use in struggling against a growing sense of one's own mental superiority? (What an ass I shall think myself for writing this, ten years hence!) I suppose one remedy would be a course of study, which would show one how very little one really knows. I am sure my essay upon Marie Antoinette ought to put me down a peg! Anything so crude and ill-digested I never read. I long for intercourse with someone infinitely superior to myself—not exactly what I had last week at Stanmore [a country house where she had lately been staying and where she had received another proposal], because a man who is making up to a woman necessarily flatters her vanity and self-love by the mere fact of doing so, but someone even more superior than Edith."

This last-named suitor was in many respects an eligible *parti*, and the renewal of his proposal soon compelled her to make a final decision. The worldly advantages of the marriage and the high regard which she felt for him and his family naturally made her hesitate, but mature reflection satisfied her that her feeling for him, considered apart from his position, was not such as to justify her in accepting his hand and heart, and she held firmly by her original resolve. She had hardly done with this suitor before a third presented himself.

"Well, Miss Loo," she writes in her Journal of December 6, "what and who next? Three offers in one year—this is really too bad. But I must be serious. God knows it is no light thing to refuse a man's true and honest love. Mamma and I drove over to luncheon with some friends at Southwell, and took a walk on the cliffs with them afterwards, and then and there Sir J—— R—— told me what he had long felt and desired. I was not altogether unprepared, as some months ago his mother had a regular maternal-matrimonial interview with my mother, asking if I were engaged and if her son had any chance. Since then I have carefully avoided the gentleman in question, but at least the matter is settled now, and we parted good friends, agreeing to meet in the future as friends and nothing more. I am sorry for his mother, who had evidently set her heart upon it ; but he, I trust, will soon be consoled."

An invitation to Osborne from Princess Helena was Louisa's next excitement, and early in the New Year she started gaily on her journey to the Isle of Wight, only grieving to leave the dear-loved cousin who was fading slowly out of life.

"*Dunwich, New Year's Eve*, 1863.—I rushed down to the cliff for a last look at the rolling sea, and saw the breakers rolling in grandly before an east wind, and then came home to Edith. I have just been reading Tennyson's lines to her, ' Ring out the old, ring in the new,' but as I gazed on Edith's altered face I asked myself whether it will please the Almighty Father to spare her to another New Year's Eve. He knows, and He knows best.

"*Osborne House, Tuesday, January* 5, 1864.—I found the Queen's messenger at Waterloo Station, and waited about an hour at Southampton till Prince Leiningen arrived in the *Elfin* and took me across to Cowes, where a carriage was awaiting me and took me to Osborne in a few minutes. The housekeeper showed me to my room, whither one by one came Princesses Helena and Louise, Prince Arthur and Prince Leopold—the latter delighted to see me, and not a bit shy. At six we went down to the Council-room to hear a lecture on the ' Origin of Language ' by Professor Max Müller. Lady Caroline Barrington, Lady Churchill, Countess Blücher, Mrs. Bruce, Miss Cathcart, Sir Charles and Mrs Phipps Sir Thomas Biddulph, Sir James Clarke, Major Elphinstone, and Dr. Holzmann were all present. The Queen with her half-sister, Princess Hohenlohe, and the children soon appeared. She shook hands with me, and sat down to hear the lecture. It began with an endeavour to trace the primeval language by observing the first utterances of children secluded from human companions. Then followed a recapitulation of much that one has read, tracing back all the European and Indian languages to a common source—the Aryan language, which was spoken, the Professor thinks, four thousand years ago in the heart of Asia. Of course the lecture was adapted to the children's comprehension, and he certainly has a very pleasant, clever face and a charming delivery. The lecture over, I was talking to Princess Louise in her room, when the door opened and one of my terrors, the pages, appeared: 'Miss Bowater, you are invited to dine with the Queen.' I rushed off to dress, and by the Princess's advice, put on my 'christening robe,' with white flowers and plain gold ornaments, and went with Princess Helena to the empty drawing-room in the other house, where the two Princes and Lady Churchill joined me. About a quarter before nine the Queen came down with Princess Hohenlohe and Princess Helena, and we followed her into a large dining-room, where our small round table seemed nearly lost. She looks well, and still wears her widow's cap, with the hair turned back, which suits her. The servants are in red liveries with crape round their arms, and the hatchment is still up here although it has been taken down at St. James's. Nothing could be kinder than she was, asking after Mamma and Edith, and not talking much to me herself, but encouraging the boys to do so. They were very droll, especially Prince Arthur, and made her laugh very much. After dinner, Lady Churchill and I joined the Household, and poor Major Elphinstone on his crutches hooked himself into the seat next me for the rest of the evening, but gained little by that, as I was awfully heavy in hand. Colonel Ponsonby was added to the party, and most agreeable he was, talking of Canada and St. John, whom he said they were all proud of, because he beat the Indians in running!

"*Wednesday, January* 6.—I walked with Princess Helena, joined in the Princes' dancing-lesson, and spent the afternoon sitting with Princess Louise, Princess Hohenlohe, Lady Caroline, and Countess Blücher, a dear old soul. After tea I played duets with Princess Helena, and dined with the Household. Lady Granville was there, and I sat between the Major and Professor, both very agreeable neighbours. The others struck me as cold and stiff. ' Ecouter et se taire, observer et laisser faire' is the motto here. We had another lecture, and a game at snapdragon with the boys, which was great fun.

"*Thursday, January 7.*—I played duets with Princess Helena, and shared the dancing-lesson, after which I had darling Prince Leo to myself, and found him quite unchanged. But I am forgetting the great event. There was a Privy Council, attended by Sir George Grey, Mr. Villiers (the Great Unwashed), and Lord Granville, and they all came to luncheon. A little man glided into the seat next me and entered into conversation with me, asking me about the ladies of the Household, whom I preferred, etc., and finally we found ourselves discussing the peculiarities, superiorities, and inferiorities, etc., of women. When the Cabinet had departed, I inquired who was my neighbour. ' Helps,' was the answer. I was *electrified*! To think I had been talking to a man in whose works I so delight, without knowing it! It was just a chance I did not quote *Friends in Council* to him. But on thinking over what he said it quite confirms the idea I gleaned from his book that he *despises* women. Professor Max Müller, Major Elphinstone, and Prince Arthur left, and I dined with the Household. Lord Granville was most amusing about spirit-rapping and Sir Bulwer Lytton, etc. I was especially tickled by the coolness with which he said, ' I bet anything Derby puts the Duke of Richmond into the next Cabinet.' He seems to think it very likely that King George of Greece will come to grief, and hears that he only accepted the throne to get away from a disagreeable captain!

"*Friday, January* 8.—I played with Princess Helena, and had a great dancing-lesson from the two nice Miss Lowes. Alter luncheon I took an hour's solitary constitutional in the kitchen garden. Later on we had the usual social tea in Princess Louise's room, and Fräulein Bauer read *Perthes* to Princess Helena and me. The Princesses are *quite* charming, as usual. Prince Leo assisted at my toilet, after which we had a grand ball, and the Queen was present for a short time. She was very kind, talking to me, and calling me 'Louisa.' Sir Thomas and Lady Biddulph and myself dined with the Queen, and in the middle Her Majesty received a telegram. After dinner, Princess Helena whispered to me, ' Alix is unwell.' About eleven o'clock Mrs. Bruce and Sir Thomas were suddenly summoned, and at the end of a few minutes the latter walked into the drawing-room and announced in a loud voice, ' The Princess of Wales has a fine boy ! ' Great, of course, was the excitement and delight. The following telegram from the Prince of Wales to the Queen was handed round : ' Dearest Alix was safely delivered of a fine boy at nine o'clock this evening. Both mother and child are doing well; her pulse is excellent, and there is not a single unfavourable symptom.' The whole house was in a bustle, preparing for Her Majesty's departure, while everybody speculated as to what had or had not been done, under these unforeseen circumstances. The event had not been expected till March, and the Princess, who was in the best of health, had been out walking in the grounds at Frogmore that afternoon, watching the Prince skating on the lake.[1] It turned out afterwards that only Mr. Brown from Windsor was present, Dr. Sieveking arriving five and Dr.

---

[1] The premature birth of the infant Prince, happening as it did just when war between Germany and Denmark had been declared, was the subject of a well-known parody in *Punch*, which happily explained the popular feeling :

"O hush thee, my darling, thy sire is a Prince,
Whom Mamma beheld skating not quite five hours since,
And Grandpapa Christian is off to the fray
With the Germans, who'd steal his nice duchy away.

But slumber, my darling, the English are true,
And will help him, for love of Mamma and of you !
The Channel fleet's coming, with powder and shot,
And the Germans must run, or they'll catch it all hot !"

Farre ten minutes after the event, upon which Sir Charles Phipps declared Dr. Farre ought henceforth to be called Dr. Farther. Fortunately, Lady Macclesfield—herself the mother of a large family—was present, and made a capital nurse. She washed the baby, and wrapped him up in three yards of flannel from Cayley's shop at Windsor, so little were they prepared! Luckily, Lord Granville was staying in the house, and Sir George Grey arrived at 11 p.m. Well, anyhow I shall have cause to remember the birth of the heir to the throne of England. May God preserve both him and his parents!

"*Saturday, January* 9.—The Queen, accompanied by Princesses Helena and Beatrice, and attended by Lady Churchill, Mrs. Bruce and Sir Thomas Biddulph, Sir Charles Phipps, and Dr. Holzmann, departed early. She left a message for me, desiring that I should remain till Thursday—very kind, I am sure, and though it is a bore losing my ball, yet I should have been very sorry to see no more of Princess Helena, and after all this is an event in my life not very likely to happen again. In our walk this morning, Princess Louise revealed that when there was a vacancy among the maids of honour she asked the Queen to appoint me, and Her Majesty would have done this but for the rule that a maid of honour must be a peer's granddaughter. Anyhow, it is flattering to know this, and I am not sure that it would not be rather dull work. Miss Cathcart departed this morning, and in the afternoon Miss Lyttelton [1] arrived for almost her first waiting. She was as shy as possible, so remembering what my own feelings were, I went to try and make friends, and thought her very nice. We all dined together in the Queen's dining-room. Anything half so stiff you never knew! Princess Louise, myself, and Miss Lyttelton enacted the three different degrees of comparison,—shy, shyer, shyest, —and Colonel Ponsonby was just as bad, which is a shame for so old a courtier. I like him so much, and

---

[1] The Honourable Lucy Lyttelton, daughter of Lord Lyttelton, afterwards married (1864) to Lord Frederick Cavendish.

think it very lucky he is married. But we got on better after dinner, when we sat in the ladies' drawing-room, which Princess Hohenlohe thought warmer.

"*Sunday, January* 10.—A letter from Princess Helena, begging me to remain till Saturday. I am glad of this, as it makes it more worth while losing the ball, and I shall see Princess Helena comfortably again. We all went to church at Whippingham, and had a sermon from Mr. Prothero: it was bitterly cold. Afterwards I had Prince Leo to myself for a long while—dear little man, he is quite unchanged. In the afternoon I helped Princess Louise with photos. We dined together again and had much better fun, Princess Hohenlohe bidding me talk German to poor ' Bufflein ' (Prince Leopold's tutor, Herr Buff), and I got on capitally with him, to everyone's surprise, and think he is an ill-used little man. His extreme shyness makes him unpopular here, and they take so little notice of him I think it makes him worse. To-night we were much less stiff—in fact, rather a jolly party. Princess Hohenlohe asked me to play, having kindly ascertained from Princess Louise that I should not mind this very much. Poor little Princess Louise! she loves coming out of her dull schoolroom, and she is such a dear little thing. I am growing very fond of her.

"*Monday, January* 11.—I rode with Princess Louise and Miss Lyttelton on three perfect ladies' horses. ' Bridesmaid,' which I had, has a charming mouth, and we came round by Norris Castle. Mrs. Ponsonby and Lady Biddulph dined. Mrs. Ponsonby sang most delightfully, and I never saw a man more in love with his own wife than *he* is. Miss Lyttelton and I started some squabbles, and shall, I foresee, differ on most subjects. She is deeply religious, and has a strong orthodox bias and some prejudices, combined with lots of good sense and a dash of intolerance. I like her very much; she is so pretty and pleasing, and decidedly clever, although she neither plays nor draws nor speaks German. (Oh, mother, I am eternally grateful to you for having made me a good German scholar!) A budget of letters—not a good account of Edith from herself. Her handwriting is fearfully changed, and I cannot help feeling very anxious about her.

"*Tuesday, January* 12.—I walked to Barton Manor with Princess Louise, and sat with Fräulein Bauer, whom I like very much, for some time. Prince Leo took me to see the French governess, and played to me so nicely on the piano. Mrs. Ponsonby dined, and we had another stiff evening.

"*Wednesday, January* 13.—At breakfast Countess Blücher talked a good deal about Schleswig-Holstein. Princess Louise, Miss Lyttelton, and I walked in spite of the rain to call on Mrs. Ponsonby, and after luncheon I had my precious little Prince with me for some time. The Queen arrived from Frogmore a few minutes earlier than was expected. She had not been in the house half an hour when a letter was brought me, which I read in the Princesses' room, and which conveyed but too surely to my mind what would be the answer to the telegram which I instantly dispatched. Nothing could exceed the affectionate kindness of those dear girls. I kept up pretty well through dinner, and a few minutes before twelve received the following telegram : 'All is over. Come to-morrow.' I felt and still feel stunned.

"*Thursday, January* 14.—I breakfasted in my own room, and remained with the Princesses and Prince Leo the whole morning; their kindness I can never forget. Indeed, *everybody* was kind—Lady Churchill, Lady Caroline, Countess Blücher, Fräulein Bauer, Miss Lyttelton—all. But what an ending to the visit to which I had looked forward so much, and at which she rejoiced for me! I left Osborne by the Messenger's boat at 1.30, and arrived in Arlington Street at 6.30. I am thankful Mamma and Philip are there.

"*Dunwich, Friday, January* 15.—I left town early, and arrived here about two o'clock to find aunt, Mamma, and Philip, all of course in sad distress. My precious Edith passed calmly and peacefully away to her rest a few minutes after twelve on Monday the 11th. Of course they could not let me know before, and it was most considerate to write that preparatory letter, but still it is very painful to think that I should have been riding about and dining with large parties when my sweet child was lying dead. Still, it has all been very merciful. She was unconscious from an early hour on Monday, and literally fell on sleep, without a groan or a struggle. I am so thankful, too, that dear Philip was here. He arrived quite unexpectedly on Saturday, something, he knows not what, having made him change all his plans and start in a hurry. If one had to choose one of the brothers, it would have been him. She received the Sacrament, as she had long looked forward to doing on Sunday, and Philip says, was very cheerful afterwards. I have no doubt the intense cold of last week accelerated her death, but God knows it is mere selfishness to repine at her release from this life of suffering. I can scarcely yet realise that she is gone, still the thought which for years has been constantly in my mind will assert itself : ' I must tell Edith that—Edith would say this.' It is a loss which leaves me very lonely, for the friend of childhood and youth can never be replaced. And yet through all I feel sure

' 'Tis better to have loved and lost
Than never to have loved at all.'

" *Monday, January* 18.—The last sad ceremony is over, and our beloved Edith has been laid in the ruins of the old Saxon chapel, by the side of the sister whom she never knew. Her pure spirit is at rest. I went into her room, where everything remains just as she left it, and almost felt that I was talking to her. It was a mild, springlike day, and I had a budget of kind letters from Court. I cannot resist copying these lines by Lady Emily Ponsonby, which Miss Lyttelton has sent me :

' In suffering and in dreariness,
In sickness and in weariness,
Mortal decay,
Upon her restless bed,
Turning her aching head,
At morn she lay.

In sight of angel throngs,
Filling with their sweet songs
    The vault of heaven,
In peace that knows no care,
No change, or want, or fear,
    She lies at noon.

Seems not the transit strange?
We cannot grasp the change
    To so much bliss.
Grudge not the wasting powers:
The painful, patient hours,
    They lead to this.' "

CHAPTER VI

A Gay Season

1864

THE death of this dear-loved cousin was a great shock to Louisa, but she had many consolations. " We are parted outwardly," she wrote ten days after Edith's funeral at Sotterley, where everything reminded her of her loss, " but for such love as ours there can be no real separation. Her love still holds me fast and watches over me as it were a guardian angel." In due course her youthful vigour and spirits reasserted themselves, and she spent a busy year, throwing herself with all the old eagerness into her accustomed pursuits. As in 1863, most of the season was spent with Mrs. Newdegate and her son in Arlington Street or at Harefield Place, near Uxbridge, while the late summer and autumn were divided between Sotterley and a round of visits, ending as usual with Christmas at Arbury. Mrs. Newdegate treated her as a daughter, and always enjoyed her company, alike in Arlington Street and in her country houses at Arbury and Harefield Place, Middlesex. An old General, who lived near this last-named house, still remembers with pleasure the " beautiful young creature " who sometimes came to the village church with Mrs. Newdegate and her son, and was the object of general attention as she sat in the high family pew, surrounded by the monuments of Newdegate ancestors. Both the society which she met at Mrs. Newdegate's house and her friendship with the Princesses served to deepen her interest in politics, which each year take a more and more prominent place in the Journal. The question of

Schleswig-Holstein excited her greatly, and she followed every step of the war between Germany and Denmark with close attention.

"*Sotterley, February* 3.—The Austrians and Prussians have crossed the Eyder,— their Rubicon,— the first shots have been fired, the first blood shed. Who can estimate the importance of this event, or the extent of its influence upon the future destinies of Europe? Never was there a more complicated question, never one in which right and money were more evenly balanced on either side. You meet no two people whose opinion on the subject is the same. (What a wretched attempt at a leading article I am writing!)

"3 *Arlington Street, Friday, April* 15.—I took advantage of a *tête-à-tête* with Charley at breakfast to hear his opinion of the Danish business, which is simply that the national agitation in Germany is entirely got up by the Jesuits! ! ! . . . In the evening Mrs. Newdegate repeated my speech of the morning: ' If you all think the Danes right, why don't you go and help them?' So it had to come out that I think them wrong, and we had a long discussion; but Charley is always gentle, and they did not murder me. His notion about the Jesuits, which he professes to have derived from a Danish pastor and a Berlin lawyer, might alter the case, but how the world would laugh! However, he made an honest, straightforward speech last night, saying that we could not afford to have a German navy and the Sound under the command of Germany. I call that at least consistent and not humbug! To-night we went to a party at Frances, Lady Waldegrave's, and met all the world plus his wife. I was introduced to Baron Bentinck, the Dutch minister, and to the Duke of Marlborough, who talked too much Toryism even for Charley, about the divine right of kings and the duty of submitting to the powers that be, and abused Garibaldi like fun. I confess I am sick of the sound of his name—dear old fellow. I also saw Mr. Layard of Nineveh.

"*April* 22.—Yesterday morning Charley went to

SOTTERLEY HALL, SUFFOLK.

[To face p. 74.

see Garibaldi — an anti-Catholic move. Oh! it is wonderful to watch the ins and outs of religious and political questions. By the way, Garibaldi himself left town to-day, whereof I am heartily glad. The most absurd *canards* are about on the subject of his visit. Only conceive the House of Commons having wanted to rise to receive Garibaldi yesterday! . . . After dinner, to my great joy, we went down to the House and heard a debate on Colonel Bartelott's motion to repeal a portion of the malt tax with our surplus instead of that upon sugar. We were landed in the Speaker's box, and with the greatest curiosity and interest I looked down upon that assemblage which controls the fate of England and through her that of Europe. It struck me as comfortable, not imposing. However, now when I read the debates, such expressions as ' below the gangway,' ' the bar,' ' the ministerial benches,' etc., will have acquired reality. They were noisy enough when we went in, shouting for ' Bass.' However, Milner Gibson spoke, and was followed by Bass, Bentinck, *Gladstone*,—by far the best, most fluent and eloquent speaker of the night,— Disraeli, whom Mrs. Newdegate said she had never heard speak so ill, and who, they vow, was ashamed of himself. Then came the division, 347 to 99—an overwhelming majority for the Government. I did not understand the question—a very complicated one—enough to know whether to be glad or sorry, but they told me it was a very curious night, and Charley was well pleased.

"*April* 25.—My birthday falls on St. Mark's Day—a thing I never discovered until this my twenty-second eve! —and the beautiful words from St. John's Gospel, ' I am the true vine,' etc., come as a regular birthday greeting. Could one wish for a better one? My presents were Goulburn's *Personal Religion* from dear Mamma, Helps' *Companions of my Solitude* from the Wheatleys, from Princess Louise a little china stand, and—last but not least—from Princess Helena a portrait of my darling father. How much this pleased and touched me I cannot say—it was like a *Gruss* from his dear self.

Dr. Günther called to wish me joy, and walked round the garden with us; and so peacefully, yet joyously, sped the day. And so begins a new year for me. I sat over the fire, reading Helps' book and thinking—thinking of the *juste milieu* in all things, and whether there is not in every quarrel an element of right on both sides, because each of us, poor finite mortals, only seeing one side of Truth, thinks he has the whole. I have long thought this with regard to religion, latitudinarian as it may sound. And I see more and more every day how it applies to politics and to all the affairs of daily life. But perhaps it is well that this is not always clearly seen, because, if it were, little would be done, and there would be few or no men of one idea, like Garibaldi, who will sacrifice all to that one idea. . . . Princess Louise announces Miss Lyttelton's marriage to Lord Frederick Cavendish. He is a lucky man.

"*May* 3.—A few lines before I go to bed, to record the events of the day, comprised in the one great fact of the Drawing-Room. The dear *Madre* looked especially well, and I well enough to satisfy her, which was what I most cared for. It was a very different affair from last year, and admirably managed. People talk of nothing but Denmark, and indeed poor Denmark is being so cruelly punished that I can side no longer with Germany, and indeed hope and wish with the rest of the world that we may take up arms in her defence. Charley put a question to the Ministers as to whether we are going to help Denmark, which was ill enough received.

"*Wednesday, May* 11.—I went down home quite early, to receive our dear little Prince, who came over from Windsor, attended by Herr Buff, and spent a long day with us. Dear little fellow, he looks very well and is quite unchanged. I was surprised to find him a Dane! I hurried back to town, and found Charley very full of a debate which had just taken place on the Borough Franchise, a motion for the extension of which was ousted by moving the previous question and defeating the Government by a majority of 56. Charley told me the gist of his speech, which was that as long as 8,000,000 of borough inhabitants were represented by 338 members to 11,000,000 of county inhabitants represented by only 159 members, he would hear of no other reform. But he did not tell me, what all London was ringing with the next day, that Gladstone had made a speech leading directly to universal suffrage as a right. These are his words : ' Every man who is not presumably incapacitated by some consideration of personal unfitness or political danger, is morally entitled to come within the pale of the institution.' Now that from the Chancellor of the Exchequer is tolerably strong. The question is, Was it a slip ? or is he bidding for power ? Palmerston is ill, and he is eighty. The Whigs, I believe, are aghast ; the Tories are dying to hound him down. C. N. says : ' *No*; don't drive the most powerful speaker in the House of Commons into the arms of the Democrats.' Bright is reported to have said : ' He goes beyond me.' Others say it is the most wonderful thing that has happened since the days of Sir Robert Peel. *Nous verrons.*

" *Thursday, May* 12.—Lord Muskerry came to sit with us in the evening, and sent us into fits with his Irish brogue. He talked over the American question with C. N. One cannot doubt that amongst them slavery will come to an end, but the Union can never be restored, and so one wishes this dreadful war would cease. Therefore, say I, success to the Confederates. In the evening we went to a great party given by Lord Granville at the South Kensington Museum, to meet the Prince and Princess of Wales, and a more thoroughly enjoyable evening I never spent. There was plenty of room, the courts were beautifully lighted, and one roamed at will among the statues and orange trees while the Royal Artillery played delicious music, and we met people we knew in shoals. By and by the Royalties came. We saw them to perfection—the Princess looking bright and well—and followed them through the picture galleries, where between pictures and friends there was *un embarras de richesses!*

After supper the Royalties sat down to whist, the Prince with the Duchess of Manchester, who looked very handsome, and people stared at them and talked with much contentment. All the *beau-monde* were there; in short, it was a wondrous fine party, and not only fine but pleasant, which is not always the same thing.

" *Richmond Park, Tuesday, May* 24.—We drove to Hampton Court, after a long gardening morning, and luncheoned with the Beresfords. In the afternoon we played croquet with the Villiers, and to my great joy won the game out of the very jaws of the evening. Fred Villiers appeared on the scene, having just returned from the seat of the war. He describes the Danes as being in the most frightful state of depression. Sonderburg is *quite* ruined, but the Prussians have not touched the Dybböl fortifications, and their exactions in Jutland have been exaggerated. Most of the people understand English or French, and he got on very well with these two and his broken German. Dear old Phil arrived in the evening, and we were very snug and cosy together. He has been walking up and down Snowdon three times in fifteen hours, forty minutes.

" *Wednesday, May* 25.—Mrs. Newdegate, Charley, and Harry Boucherett (another cousin) all came down to breakfast, which was very merry and successful, the weather being lovely. Then, having started the three gentlemen off for the Derby, we muddled about all day and came up to town, to find ' Blair Atholl ' the successful horse. In the evening we went to a concert at Mrs. Vivian's, where we heard some very fine Italian music which I did not care for, fine as Titiens' and Giuglini's singing was. But we saw a number of friends, among them Sir R., who was so attentive that I foresee it will all have to be done over again. I was perfectly civil, but picked up every stray man I could find to talk to.

" *Thursday, May* 26.— I paraded about all the morning with a footman behind me; called on the Peels, Boileaus, and Thornhills, and saw Emily Smith and her fine boy; had a pleasant practice at Lady Hogg's, where I hooked an invite from Charley Fremantle to his mother's concert. So to Lady Fremantle's Mrs. Newdegate and I did go, and heard some exceedingly charming amateur music, Mendelssohn's *Lobgesang*, which is splendid, and some of his part songs. Oh, I do love that German music!

"*Wednesday, June* 1.—We went with Nora Campbell to a very fine concert at Mrs. Capel Cure's, where, to my delight, I heard Grisi sing for the first time, quite gloriously. Less to my delight were Sir R.'s attentions, from which I in vain endeavoured to escape by flirting with that very safe card, Major Paynter. . . . But oh! I am not happy. When I came in yesterday I found Captain B——'s card, and with it a copy of verses saying that he had staked his all on this one chance. Is not that enough to make one miserable? He will propose, perhaps, at Lady Hoare's ball to-morrow, and my heart aches to think of it, for I love him as a sister does a brother, but not as he would have me. And I can't speak to anybody! If dear Edith were only here! She always wished me to marry, but I won't till I find the right person. 'That's flat,' as Lord Byron says in his letters.

"*June* 4, 11.30 *p.m.*—I cannot go to bed without first recording the events of this strange day. It poured with rain. Mrs. Newdegate went out and left me alone. Miss E——, whose brother proposed to me at Windsor, came and offered to take me to see my cousin, Lou Ridley. I accepted, not without misgivings; but we had not been there long when Mr. E—— was announced. I do not think it was premeditated on the girl's part, but oh! how it grieves me to see that he is still in the same mind. In very deed, I am not worthy of such love. He spoke of dear Edith, and said he had learnt it accidentally, having promised himself to ask no questions about me. Then he said, ' May I stay, or do you wish me to go?' I replied, ' Do precisely as you like.' However, he went after a little while, which was charming of him. Miss

E—— talked of her brother all the way home, and I said much which can be better said through her than to him. But he must not see me, and I must not become her friend. After dinner we posted off to Lady Rowley's and heard more of that everlasting Italian music, for which I don't care a brass button, and then we posted away, finding Sir R—— B—— in the cloakroom. *He* is not to be put off so easily, but I think he sees my game. On to Lady Hoare's splendid ball, two houses connected by a gallery—in short, one of the things of the season. With my usual good fortune, I danced every dance—one was with Captain B——, who, as I feared, came there for the simple purpose of meeting me. What am I to do? I cannot be unkind to him.

"*Monday, June 6.*—We went to the Yorkshire ball, at Willis' Rooms, which is supposed to have been very bad; but I did not care, as I met plenty of people to dance with—Charley, Lord Valentia, Ronald Melville, etc., and Mr. E——, to whom I really do not know how to behave. He started with the assurance that he would not bother me this season at all events! And he is so nice, I am very sorry. Mr. H—— runs in and out of the house like a tame cat. He was here at luncheon, and is coming back to dinner. They are very kind to him, and it is nice of Mrs. Newdegate, for I do not think his own people half look after him, and the consequence is he knows not a soul in London and has rather a *ton de garnison*, which, though it may be better than the *ton de bumpkin*, not all my love of red-coats can persuade me to admire. But I like him very much, and think we shall have a very jolly party for Ascot. I have bought a white bonnet, for which I gave a whole pound. I think it is so plain and undemonstrative that nobody can object to it—all white with a few lilies of the valley. I am naughty enough to be very glad Captain B—— is coming, but I must try and be a good child and not flirt. It is no use worrying oneself about these men, for I can go nowhere without stumbling upon one or other of them. It makes me sad sometimes, but the end of it is I give it up as a bad job and treat them all in the same friendly, sisterly manner.

"*Harefield Place, June* 9.—We were all off for Ascot early, and drove through Windsor Park to the racecourse, where we took up a first-rate position opposite the Stand. We had great fun watching the racing, eating luncheon under difficulties, seeing hosts of friends, and amused with the endless divertisements of a racecourse, portrayed a hundred times by *Punch*, from the ' c'rect card ' to the man who smashes stones with his bare hand. Scottish Chief won the Gold Cup easy. It is such a long race that one has time to observe the intense excitement of the ' ring.' That is the worst of racing, but I am glad to have seen it all once. The Royal Family, including my Princess, were all there. Our return was easily accomplished. But oh! Captain B—— and Mr. H—— were both there.

" 3 *Arlington Street, June* 10.— Dear, kind Mrs. Newdegate came to my room quite early and warned me to be careful about Captain B——, whom she sees clearly means business. I tried, accordingly, to be very careful, and succeeded in pleasing her at all events. She seems so fond of me, it is quite delightful, and I am sure I return it. All the week I have felt afraid of being out of the frying-pan into the fire with Mr. H——, who is staying here and plays croquet with me every morning ; and Mrs. Newdegate told me what I suspected was quite true, and that he had confided his feelings to her. It really is too absurd. We all returned to town after luncheon, and I went with Mamma and Charley to the ball at Buckingham Palace. Somehow I had not thought much about it beforehand, having so many other things to think of, and I was really taken aback by the splendour of the *spectacle*. What pleased me most was that Princess Helena, Princess Mary, and the Prince of Wales all shook hands with us both. Sir R—— B—— asked me to dance, but I had plenty of partners without him. I wore my green gown with the blush roses, and Mrs. Newdegate insisted on sending for a bunch to match for the front of my dress.

"*Saturday, June* 11.—Three of my rejected suitors were in the Park this morning, but, to my relief, I steered clear of them all. After luncheon, at which Mr. H—— appeared, we went down to a party at Pembroke Lodge, where I was surrounded by old friends, and Lord Amberley was as attentive as usual. All this is enough to turn my head, but it **is** no doubt much better for me to have it all out **now** than at eighteen. I shall soon have had my fling, and hope it may please God to grant me a happy meeting with *one* whom I can truly love.

"*June* 20.— I dined *tête-à-tête* with my cousin, Harry Boucherett, who was most agreeable. I am not sure that I don't like him best when he talks sense. We discussed the advantages and disadvantages of living alone, and the reason why the young care so much more for poetry than the old. In short, we grew quite metaphysical. C. N. N. was busy fighting the Gaol Bill. I went to fetch Mrs. Newdegate from her dinner at Mrs. Grey's, and came in for a bit of a very pleasant party. Colonel F—— was there, returned from Paris, where he has left that movable commodity, his heart! I can see, however, 'twill come across the Channel after him ere long, I dare say. At the last party where I met him he never left my side, and yet, fascinating as he is, I do not believe he is worth one half of Captain B——. Lady Mordaunt has actually sent a card for her ball, for Mr. Newdegate and Miss Bowater, and upon Mrs. N. writing to say she thought there must be some mistake, as my mother did not consider her son a sufficient chaperone for her daughter, she sends a card for Mrs. Newdegate without a word of comment or explanation. But not to go would be to punish ourselves! However, last night Charley pitched into Sir Charles, who, of course, vowed it was a mistake. Another amazing event is that Lord Henniker is going to present to-morrow at the levee—how can I write the name?—Madame de Sévigné's expressions on the Grande Mademoiselle's marriage would hardly be too strong! He is going to present—that hater of everything connected with the Court; that persistent fugitive from

Society; above all, that poor invalid whom we ought to be nursing—my Uncle Frederick! And all because it is said that the Prince of Wales is going to give a great entertainment to the Jockey Club. Well! wonders will never cease!

"*June* 21.—This afternoon we heard Trebelli sing Gounod's Serenade and some Spanish songs quite beautifully at a concert at Mrs. Packe's. Afterwards we drove about and found a great crowd in the Park, the Queen having come up and held a reception, after which, to everybody's joy, she actually drove through the Park in an open carriage. She bowed and smiled, and seemed quite overcome by the cheering. No wonder! But oh, I am so glad! We went to Lady Mordaunt's ball, such a good one—lots of room and lots of partners! Colonel Francis was my *vis-à-vis* in one quadrille, and squeezed my hand most affectionately whenever we met, but went away without asking me to dance, whereat I was goose enough to be much disappointed. None the less I enjoyed myself immensely.

"*June* 23.—After dinner this evening, Mrs. Newdegate and I set off on our long drive to the ball at Strawberry Hill. But the ten miles' drive seemed like two, so agreeably did she talk of politics, education, and other matters. She told me, amongst other things, how much Charley has had to suffer from the independent line which he has taken. Lord Derby and Mr. Disraeli, she declares, have done their best to ruin him. Indeed, I never heard a man speak in stronger terms than he did at breakfast to-day of the suffering his enemies have been able to inflict. ' They have bullied my mother; if I had had a wife, they would have crushed her; if I had had a mistress, if they could have hit on a blot in my life, it would have been all up with me!' Once Lord Palmerston offered him a peerage, which he promptly refused. He is a noble character, with all his eccentricities, and sacrifices everything to what he thinks right. I have been reading his articles in the *St. James's Chronicle* aloud to his mother at his request, and cannot help being pleased at the confidence and consideration with which he treats me; but he shan't make a Tory of me, if I can help it!

' In' due course of time we landed at Strawberry Hill — Horace Walpole's Strawberry Hill — and were wandering through its crooks and crannies into the brilliantly lighted ballroom. Of course I danced all night—with Mr. Fane, Sir Malcolm MacGregor, Mr. Dugdale, Mr. Farquhar, Captain C—— (with whom I had a grand squabble, ending in a flirtation—*prenez garde!*), Mr. Campbell, Ronald Melville, Sir Charles Mordaunt. Altogether it was a charming wind-up of my season, and the coloured lamps which illuminated the grounds had faded before the dawn ere we started for Richmond. So now farewell to my gaieties. It has been a very pleasant time, and I think I have learnt something.

"*Richmond Park, June* 28.—After luncheon we went to the Star and Garter, to join the Kenyon and Rowley water-party. We rowed about most of the afternoon, and then sat down to a great dinner. I was between Harry (my guest) and Sir Charles Mordaunt, out of whom I got more political information than he got out of me. It is a wonderfully interesting time. The conference came to an end on Saturday, hostilities recommenced on Sunday, and Alsen was taken on Monday. The papers were laid before the House on Monday evening, accompanied by ministerial statements from Lord Palmerston in one House and Lord Russell in the other, and listened to with breathless attention. On Tuesday, great Conservative meetings were held at Lord Salisbury's and Lord Derby's, but C. N. N. did not attend either, and, in spite of Sir Charles, I do not believe the split in the Conservative party which foiled the attack of a fortnight ago is made up. However, on Wednesday, Mr. Disraeli gave notice that on Monday he will move an address, expressing the regret of the House that England's menaces are not to be carried out, and blaming the foreign policy of the Government. On Thursday, Mr. Kinglake gave notice of an amendment, expressing general satisfaction at the preservation of peace. Whether C. N. N. means to move another amendment, 'I dinna ken.' But on Monday comes the tug-of-war, and it is all intensely interesting. I have wandered far from the Richmond water-party, which ended in a dance and was altogether very good fun.

"*Saturday, July* 2.—C. N. N. moves an amendment to Disraeli's motion, proposing that the integrity of Denmark should be guaranteed on the terms proposed by the neutral powers, *i.e.* the line of the Schlée· and the Dannewerk. But he won't carry that, or I am much mistaken.

"*July* 5.—The great debate began last night. Disraeli and Gladstone fought a regular duel, with all the powers of wit, deadly sarcasm, and withering irony. Mr. D.'s logic is very good, and I do not think Mr. G.'s pulling it to bits very effective. D.'s *péroraison* is magnificent, were it sincere; but his weak point is that he will not commit himself to any line of policy, and here G. has him well. Charley and Kinglake move their amendments in good, sensible, but not brilliant speeches, and General Peel makes a downright, honest, bulldog kind of speech.

"*July* 9.—A majority of eighteen in favour of the Government. Well! I am glad on the whole. But the part Charley took in the recent debate, when his own amendment had been rejected in not supporting the Conservatives, has raised a great storm down in Warwickshire and given him much trouble! From his own point of view, of course, he was quite right, and I must say England has behaved atrociously to the Danes. The German question has assumed a new phase, and Austria and Prussia are playing a bold game."

Early in July, Miss Bowater returned home well satisfied with her lively season and determined to devote her leisure to self-improvement. But she had hardly settled down in her quiet Richmond home than her peace of mind was disturbed by a proposal from Captain B——, the one of all her suitors whom she most liked and respected.

"*Monday, July* 14.—I had settled down quietly to a

working morning in the schoolroom, when post arrived. I scanned my pile of letters, and, strange to say, mistook the writing of one which had been forwarded from Harefield, and did not open it till the last. When I did, it made my heart beat and my limbs tremble, for it contained a proposal from Captain B——, almost stern in its depth and earnestness of affection, such as he may well say I shall not soon find elsewhere. God knows if I did right in declining it as gently but as decidedly as I know how. Even if Mamma approved— and she is strongly averse to the idea of marriage with an officer in a marching regiment—I do not think my decision ought to have been otherwise. I cannot feel for him as he does for me, and he is worthy of something better than I can give him. But it has cost me very much, and at times I feel as if I had flung my happiness away. May God forgive me if I have flirted with him. It is an awful thing to have such influence over a man's life, such a decision to make. Writing this letter occupied the whole morning, and I walked to Norbiton to post it with a heavy heart. How Mamma can treat it so lightly I cannot divine! I almost wish I had not told her. My heart aches sadly for him, and it is of no use for her to tell me not to worry.

"*Wednesday, July* 16.—The early post brought me what I expected, a letter from Captain B——. It is a comfort to me that he says he did not expect any other answer, but I cannot help fearing that he thinks I gave him encouragement. Perhaps this is true. It was *so* difficult, with the whole neighbourhood looking on. However, I feel far happier than I did yesterday, and when we do meet there must be a total change of manner.

"*Monday, July* 18.—We were all of us electrified by the announcement of Lady Florence Paget's marriage, last Saturday, to Lord Hastings. If a shell had exploded in the midst of London society, it could hardly have astonished it more than this! For it is not a month since the town rang with the news of her engagement to Mr. Chaplin. I went to a croquet party at the Old Palace. Nothing talked of but Lady Florence! It appears she was at the Opera on Friday night with Mr. Chaplin, and on Saturday morning walked through Marshall & Snelgrove's shop, stepped into Captain Granville's brougham, and drove off to church to be married. I don't envy the feelings of any of the trio. Even Captain B—— must feel that his fate, trying as it may be, is infinitely preferable to either that of Mr. Chaplin or Mr. Heneage, who three days before his marriage with Lady Adela Hare discovered that it was his money, not himself, she cared for. Poor Lady Florence, hers is indeed a sad story, and not yet all told, I doubt.

"*Saturday, July* 23.—I went with Mary Wheatley to an opera concert in the Crystal Palace, which I thoroughly enjoyed. It was so cool and quiet, the orchestra was perfect, and Mario, whom I heard for the first time, sang in exquisite taste. 'Si la stanchezza,' from the *Trovatore*, was unforgettable, and one was not bothered by a futile attempt to combine music and society; and though I had rather have heard a symphony of Beethoven or a part song by Mendelssohn, taken altogether it was very charming. We were met with a telegram announcing the death of my poor aunt, Laura, Lady Ridley. No one could wish to prolong a life like hers, and it is sad to think that her daughter, Sarah Cookson, who died two days before, had not seen her mother for nearly thirty years. Of her ten children, none but Sir Matthew will mourn her loss. Ah! family quarrels are sad things. But she was a most kind friend to us, and I shall miss her very much. As we drove home, it crossed my mind that my grandmother used to talk of a certain £20,000 which might come to me at Aunt Laura's death. The thought flashed across me, if that money comes, there would be no obstacle to my marriage with Captain B——. But then I felt No! I shall see the place all my life, by the trees on this side of Pembroke Lodge.

"*August* 4.—Sir Matthew came down about 11 a.m., accompanied, to our surprise, by Matt. He brought me my aunt's two legacies, *i.e.* £200, which she sealed up for me on my last birthday, and the gold repeater which she once told me was dear Papa's gift to his mother. I wish she had added the portrait of Mrs. Bowater by Romney, which he left her with the miniature, but otherwise I am quite content. Had she left me more, I should have felt she was wronging her own children. With Matt I was charmed; he is a clever and accomplished youth, and we had a great deal of agreeable conversation during their short visit. . . . Well, I muddle on somehow. Query, Is not life a muddle? Could one organise it? I wonder. I must read Helps on that subject."

CHAPTER VII

A VISIT TO BALMORAL

MAY–JUNE 1865

IN the spring of the following year, Miss Bowater, to her great delight, received an invitation to accompany the Queen to Balmoral for three weeks, and on the 19th of May 1865 she went down to Windsor to join the Royal party.

"*Friday, May* 19.—I left home for Windsor, and did not half like parting from the *Madre*, but got over the *mauvais quart d'heure* of arrival extremely well, and was soon chatting with these dear Princesses. The Drawing-room, it seems, was quite a full one, and Princess Helena played her part admirably, but is terribly knocked up with it. Soon after five we dined in a room commanding the loveliest of views. The Duke of Argyll took me in; the Duchess of Atholl, Mrs. Bruce, Miss Lascelles, Sir Thomas Biddulph, General Grey, Lord De Tabley, Mr. West, Colonel Ponsonby, and Mr. Sahl, made up the party. Immediately afterwards I drove with the Duchess and Mrs. Bruce to the G.W. Station, and punctually at seven the Royal train started. It was lovely all the way to Oxford, of whose spires we caught a passing view; then the shades of night settled slowly down over the rich and *riant* landscape, and it was quite dark before we reached Leamington. At Banbury, some voices sang ' God save the Queen ' and ' God bless the Prince of Wales.' At Stafford came tea, and then the Black Country, with its chimneys sending up flaming tongues to heaven, after which we turned in for the night and made ourselves comfortable on the sofas of our saloon. Before reaching Carlisle, the grey dim dawn had risen, and here and there, through the rolling mists, I caught sight of a purling brook gurgling over the stones. The Borderland suggested Fergus MacIvor and Madge Wildfire and ' The sun shines fair on Carlisle wall.' Then I fell asleep again, and woke with a start to find myself in Scotland, among high, bleak hills, with sheep straying up and down in the cold mists, and here and there a shepherd wrapped in his plaid, surveying us from under his bonnet. Perth was reached about nine, and was more welcome as meaning breakfast than from any historic associations. Then on again, past Scone and Lord Southesk and Lord Strathmore's places to the Bridge of Dun, where Lord Dalhousie met us, and then on to Aberdeen. I only woke in time to see the pretty bit along the coast, where the blue sea comes close in under the rocks. After this we turned sharply to the west, and began to ascend the Dee valley. At Aboyne we left the railroad, and had twenty miles to drive. We passed Abergeldie, and landed here about four o'clock, not sorry to find myself at the end of such a fatiguing journey, and to hear the gurgling of the Dee as it rushes over its grey boulders, instead of the polka which the steam-engine would play.

"*Balmoral, Ballater, N.B., Sunday, May* 21.— It seems like a dream that I should be six hundred miles away from Richmond Park, where I was writing bravely thirty-six hours ago. I did not see the Queen on our journey till we reached Aboyne, where she shook hands as we got out of the carriage. I was glad to see that her widow's cap had given place to a narrow white frill under the bonnet; the Duchess, however, is still in weeds. But last night, Mellish was in the midst of lacing my dress when rat-tat at the door. Mellish went to open it, and in walked—the Queen, come in from a walk with Princess Helena, ' to look after me, as she had promised,' she said. The room was in frightful confusion, and I so scared that I hardly know what I said or did, but I hope I behaved *pretty*, and Her Majesty was most kind and anxious to set me at ease. This morning I went out walking with Princess Helena, and in the afternoon, accompanied Mrs. Gordon to the top of the Cairn above the house. Such a delicious walk, first up among the birch trees, where the ground is covered with anemones and all kinds of wild flowers, and then emerging among heather and grey boulders, to gain a lovely view of the whole valley, with the Castle at our feet, and behind us Lochnagar, towering in majesty with its three snow-clad summits. I should have liked to go to church, but this glorious Nature made it feel like Sunday. This house is very nice, simple, and pretty—not like a palace at all. There are a dining-room, billiard-room, library, and drawing-room *en suite*. The Queen dines in the library, and we go there afterwards. It is a charming room, and any lady may take out any book she likes, by putting her name on a slip of paper in its place. We are a very jolly party, cheery and pleasant. Mrs. Gordon I like extremely. General Grey is a host in himself, full of fun but a man of very decided opinions, not to say prejudices. Still, there is something very lovable about him. He is very wroth because ' little MacCullum More,' as he calls the Duke, won't talk politics with him. The Duke like a wise man, having left all such thoughts behind, is devoted to birds and beetles and sich-like. We had a grand discussion at dinner about whortle-berries and all the different varieties—cran-, crow-, bil-, bla-, dog-, meal-, and bear- berries ! They are almost as bad as the Lochs and Bens and Craigs and all the unpronounceable names of the places about here.

" *Monday, May* 22.—After a great deal of discussion, an expedition, consisting of General and Mrs. Gordon, Mrs. Bruce, Colonel Ponsonby, and myself, was arranged to the Falls of the Gharb-allt. The day was lovely, the air balmy with the fragrance of birch and pine, and just clouds enough to lend softness to the shadows. After driving six miles up the river, we crossed the bridge of Invercauld, and came into the

Forest of Ballochbuie, which was lovely with the sun gleaming through the tall pines upon the bright green carpet of moss and leaves. We crossed the Gharb-allt —a large burn which comes tumbling in sheets of foam over huge masses of granite—and climbed the hill, until, getting clear of the Forest, we had a lovely view over the vale of Invercauld, and saw the long ridge of Ben-na-Biurd, with its snow sparkling in the sun. We returned by this side of the river, through the forest of Balmoral, which to my mind has been ruined by the Prince Consort's objection to thinning trees, and saw a number of roes bounding to and fro. In the afternoon I played duets with Princess Helena, and dined with the Queen, General Grey, and Mrs. Bruce.

"*May* 24.—The Queen's birthday! May God bless and preserve her! Prince Arthur arrived yesterday. He has grown so handsome—and only think! he has brought *me* a beautiful olive-wood book-slide from Jerusalem. I spent the day walking and playing with Princess Helena, who took me to see the Queen's room and her presents, all the children's work, drawings, etc. Portraits of the Prince are *everywhere* ; to me this would be almost painful. In the afternoon General and Mrs. Gordon, the Duke and I set off on an expedition to the Linn of Dee, followed by the rest of the party. We drove through the Forest, by Braemar Castle, to Castletown, where we changed horses, and went on up a wild glen, leading across a desolate tract of country, to Mar Lodge, and at length reached the Linn, a narrow passage between the rocks through which the Dee rushes, like a true mountain stream, changing from clear green to snow-white foam and black pools below. Lord Byron narrowly escaped being drowned here when he was a boy. He fell into the stream, and was only saved by a servant who seized him by the neck and dragged him out. We scrambled about the rocks, and had a beautiful drive home, with the mountains looking like bits of dreamland in the sunset, and the pine woods bathed in golden light. We saw—or rather the Duke saw—the oyster-catcher by the Deeside, and the woodcock and curlews in Ballochbuic Forest, and he pointed out the flat layers of slate which distinguish the Linn from the granite rocks all round.

"*May* 25.—This afternoon there was a grand tea for the school-children, in honour of Her Majesty's birthday—a pretty sight enough, with the Queen surrounded by her children and ladies grouped under the trees. Quite late, I rode with the Gordons and Major Elphinstone to the top of Craig-Lauriben, where is the Prince Consort's cairn. In August 1862, the first visit which the Queen paid to Balmoral after the Prince's death, she and six of her children placed stones on this cairn, carved with their initials. The text inscribed on the tablet was quoted by the Princess Royal in a letter written to her mother shortly after her father's death: ' He being made perfect in a short time, fulfilled a long time. For his soul pleased the Lord ' (Wisdom iv. 13).

"*May* 26.—I was rather alarmed by orders to drive with the Queen after breakfast. Princess Louise came with us, and once we got off it was not so bad. Nothing could be kinder than Her Majesty was, or lovelier than the views in the Forest and glen of Felagie. The Queen did not talk a great deal, but was in capital spirits, and is looking very well. It is such fun to hear her talk to the gillies, John Brown and John Grant, who are certainly most important personages here. In the afternoon I was packed off to ride with General Gordon and Colonel Ponsonby to Alt-na-Guisach. Up Glen Gelder we went to the very foot of Lochnagar, the wildest, most desolate scene I ever beheld, and then up a path cut in the hillside, till we reached the snow-line and saw patches of it all around us, and came down by Glen Muick to the pretty cottage where in happier days the Queen and Prince occasionally spent the night. We returned by the green hills known as the Coyles, after an extremely enjoyable ride of sixteen or seventeen miles.

"*May* 27.—The gentlemen very kindly insisted on taking me with them to the Linn of Muick, through yesterday's glen, to the waterfall down in the woods, and then on to Birk Hall, a pretty little place belonging to the Prince of Wales, with a lovely view over Ballater and the blue hills beyond. We came home by Abergeldie Castle, and I had a long and interesting talk with Major Elphinstone on Goulburn's sermons, science and revelation. Indeed, I often wish I had six pair of ears to listen to all the conversations that take place here. A great discussion has been going on about American affairs. The Duke is a strong Northerner, and said yesterday he did not think they would attack us; but to-day I hear him and General Grey talking of a dispatch from Mr. Adams touching the *Alabama*, which they think looks ugly. General Gordon is an excellent cicerone, having known all this country for more than thirty years, when it belonged to his uncle, and he is so proud of it I think he likes to show it to anybody who admires it as much as I do. General Grey keeps us all in fits, and quarrels amicably with Mrs. Bruce on every possible occasion. I am glad to hear Papa liked him so much, and want to give him one of my photos. Such a bunch of lilies of the valley he gave me this morning! We have taken lately to spending our evenings in the billiard-room, and have grand games at bowls or curling on the billiard-table—a capital game, of which I hear the Prince Consort was very fond. Carl Haag, the painter, has arrived, a clever little man who has plenty to say for himself, so much so that some of our friends mean to put him through a process of *snubbing*, and which I must own he richly deserves.

"*Sunday, May* 28.—We went twice to the little Scotch kirk at Crathie, and heard two fine sermons from the famous Dr. Caird, who arrived last night, and is the most Puritanical-looking party I ever saw. I do not at all dislike the Scotch service, except having to stand when one prays. Dr. Caird's prayers are exceptionally impressive, but one must always be at the mercy of the ' meenister ' ! The ' discoorse ' this morning was from S. Matt. v. 17. He began very politically, by drawing a distinction between Conservatives and obstructers, Reformers and destroyers, and then proceeded to show that Our Lord could not be anything but the fulfiller of the law, because Omnipotence itself could not make a noble action base or a base one noble. The analogy he drew was from that grand principle of submission to Nature's laws, which the Duke of Argyll has so splendidly developed in his papers. Indeed, we were all struck by the similarity between the two, and I was naughty enough to remark that the morning sermon, appealing to the intellect, was intended for His Grace, and the afternoon one, addressed to the feelings, was evidently meant for Her Majesty. The afternoon text was, ' Seek ye first the kingdom of God and His righteousness, and all these things shall be added unto you '—added, either by your being made independent of them, or by their acquiring a depth and meaning that they never possessed before. He drew one or two touching pictures of loneliness— the last of a once gay and happy household, sitting alone in the old home and longing ' for the touch of a vanished hand.' Yet even this loneliness, he said, is nothing to being without God in the world. I thought of Pascal's ' Je mourrai seul ' and Keble's ' Why should we faint and fear to live alone ? ' The language was really very fine, and perhaps on the whole I liked the afternoon sermon best, since it left us all more silent, less inclined to argue, or, as the Duke put it, ' made us feel bad.' Dr. Caird and the Duke talked of Renan and Strauss in the evening, both of whose books, it seems, are much read by the younger Scottish clergy.

" *May* 29.—Princess Helena and I had a glorious ride after breakfast, up Bowment's Moss by a tremendously steep path, with lovely views of the mountains along Deeside. So steep was the path that we were obliged to lead the ponies down, and returned by Glen Gelder, just in time to escape the rain, which set in violently and put an end to my going out this afternoon with Her Majesty. I dined with her and the Gordons, and played bowls as we do every evening.

" *June* 1.—Colonel Ponsonby departed this morning,

leaving me as a legacy some capital doggerel verse about all the Craigs and Bens here and our expeditions. It was cold and gloomy, and I spent most of the day playing duets with Princess Helena and Mrs. Gordon, not forgetting the Guards' Waltz with Prince Arthur. The great news to-day is that Miss Lascelles is to marry Lord Edward Cavendish. It sounds a very nice arrangement, but of course everybody here is very sorry to lose her. The Duke and I are becoming fast friends; he is such a pleasant little man. I have been writing to thank Colonel Ponsonby for the ' Rhyme of Lochnagar,' and General Grey stood godfather to the letter, *i.e.* read and enclosed it in his own, so I think that made it all proper. Lord Charles Fitzroy arrived. It is three years since we parted at Dover. He asked tenderly after Mamma, but looks aged, I think.

"*June* 3.—I started at twelve with Mlle Norèle and the three children for a day at Loch Muick. We rode down to the loch, which, gleaming blue among the green hills, looked like anything but the ' lake of sorrow '; ate our luncheon sitting on the heather, and walked along a path cut in the hillside to the head of the loch. The weather was delicious; the birches hung over the water, the broom was golden on the hillside, and the blue water rippled against the rocks, clear as crystal. After a short rest at a cottage at the head of the loch, just where the Glassalt comes tumbling over the rocks, we rode back the same way, and after tea at the hut, drove home by the Linn of Muick, where we stopped to gather primroses. It was altogether a most delightful day. It was great fun to see Princess Beatrice bullied by her brothers, and a great pleasure to be with my own boy. He is quite unchanged and to me very dear, but I can see that Prince Arthur throws him into the shade, with his good looks and winning ways.

"*Whit-Sunday, June* 4.—The weather, I am glad to say, has improved, and to-day it is quite lovely. If the rain had continued, Her Majesty would have gradually laid up all her children and attendants. Mrs. Gordon is confined to her room, and Princess Helena,

Prince Arthur, and I all have colds ! Mrs. Gordon won the Derby lottery. I am afraid we had a great deal more excitement about that than about the birth of the small Prince,[1] but I am glad to say the accounts of the Princess are excellent. Princess Helena and I walked up Craig Gowan directly after breakfast, and sat there, enjoying the peaceful, lovely landscape, while the words of to-day's Collect rang in my ears : ' Grant us by the same Spirit a right judgment in all things.' In the afternoon I walked to kirk with Lord Charles and Mrs. Bruce. A drowsy sermon sent me to sleep. This to me is the disadvantage of the Scotch Church. The Duke, General Grey, Major Elphinstone, and Prince Arthur went to fish in the Dee. We were a small but jolly party. Lord Charles made himself very pleasant, and we played a spelling game.

"*June* 5.—At 4.30 I started with Her Majesty and Princess Helena for the Sluggan, and rode up a fine wild glen until near the top of the hill we were stopped by a large patch of snow. We had to lead our ponies round it, to gain a view into the next glen, where the sight of Ben-na-Biurd, towering up into the sky, inspired Princess Helena with a plan for another excursion to-morrow. Then we sat down to tea—the snuggest, cosiest little party possible—the Queen so kind and good-natured as to make me feel quite at my ease. Her Majesty having duly ministered to the wants of the gillies, we proceeded to sketch the mountains to the south-west, and then set out on our homeward ride. That ride I can never forget. It would be impossible to describe the colouring of Lochnagar under the setting sun. It was one of those dreams of beauty one sees scarcely twice in a lifetime. My father, Edith, all came to my mind.

> ' Tears, idle tears, I know not what they mean !
> Tears from the depth of some divine despair
> Rise in the heart and gather to the eyes . . .
> In thinking of the days that are no more.'

No less delightful was the drive home. It was half-past eight when we got back to the carriage, and we

[1] His Majesty King George v., born at Marlborough House on June 3, 1865.

bowled home at a tearing pace behind the four greys. Such a sky behind us, and such reflections in the Dee! I dined quite alone with the Queen, the Princesses and Prince Arthur, but it was not a bit formidable!

"*June* 6.—Princess Helena, Prince Arthur, Mrs. Gordon, and I set out for Ben-na-Biurd (3940 feet high) at eleven. We drove to the same point above Invercauld, mounted our ponies and rode up the Sluggan, and then through a narrow glen where we saw a large herd of deer standing or lying in the snow which filled up the opposite crevice of the mountain. Nothing could be more picturesque than the cavalcade, ponies, gillies and all, winding along this steep ascent over the rocks. Soon the path ceased, and the riding got worse and worse, while the views behind us became more and more glorious, range beyond range of blue and purple hills rising one above another with shadows flitting rapidly across them. All too rapidly, alas! for by the time we had reached the huge patch of snow we see from Invercauld, it began to rain. We sat down to luncheon, hoping it might clear, but it did no such thing. However, we were not to be beaten, so off we marched across the snow, Princess Helena, Prince Arthur, and I, in charge of the great John Grant, and precious hard work we found it, both on the snow and over the loose stones at the top. At last we reached the Cairn on the highest point of Ben-na-Biurd, and caught glimpses of lofty ranges of mountains looming grey and mysterious through the mist, which lifted now and then, only to close round us more pitilessly than ever. Anything more absurd than we all looked, tumbling and struggling stick in hand over the loose stones, our skirts limp and clinging (I was fitted out in an old one of the Queen's, which buttoned up in the most comfortable way), and rivulets streaming from our hats, it would be hard to imagine. ' I calkeehlate we were considerabeel wet '! However, by the time we reached the ford over the burn, the rain ceased, and we rode down the glen, and were at home by 7.30, well pleased with our day—ducking and all!

"*June* 7.—We were all glad of a rest after the fatigues of Ben-na-Biurd, but in the afternoon I had a charming expedition with the Duke and Duchess, General Gordon and Mrs. Bruce, to Loch Muick, where the General and I mounted our ponies and scampered up a wild Highland glen to the Dhu Loch, a tiny lake high up in the mountains. To-day the sun shone brightly on its dark water, and the burn which comes straight down from the rocks was like a line of silver. We found the rest of the party scattered about, enjoying the calm beauty of the evening, and had great fun over tea, cooking the fish which the Duke had caught in the loch, broiled on the hot embers of our fire, and watching the evening effects, which are lovelier in the Highlands than anywhere else. All the way home the Duke and Mrs. Bruce quoted poetry, *à l'envi l'un de l'autre*. He is a devoted Tennysonian, General Grey is as vehement against him, and it is such fun to hear them squabble away. I must say, however, that the General recites by far the best. His Grace's manner is, to use the Queen's mild expression, 'unfortunate,' or as Lord Charles puts it, 'it all comes out of his boots.' I was photographed this morning in my brown gown with my lilac hat, which the Queen is kind enough to call very becoming; but I doubt if it will come out well, there was such a wind! Lord Charles and I are rapidly becoming fast friends, and I am glad to find that he does not dislike me, as I fancied at Cannes. When he heard me regret that by staying here a week longer I should miss two balls, he said Mrs. Gordon must take me to Lady Louisa Pennant's ball instead, and would call for me after dining at Camden Hill with the Duke and Duchess of Argyll. Is it not kind of them both? So he is writing to her, and I have arranged to stay in Arlington Street for that night. *Later*.—Matters are simplified by the Duke asking me to dine with the Gordons. He also invites us to Inverary, whenever we come to Scotland.

"*Sunday, June* 11.—An interesting conversation at breakfast between the Duke and Dr. Macleod, who arrived last night, about the Holy Land, Abraham's well, etc. I walked with the children and Mademoiselle, —poor Prince Leo in his little carriage, but very cheery,— and had a scramble to get to church, where Her Majesty came. The sermon was from 1 Thess. v. 10, on the intimate union between the Church militant and the Church triumphant. There was much in it that I liked, but much also which trenched on very uncertain ground.[1] Still, I had rather ' sit under ' him than under Dr. Caird —this great, big, burly, good-humoured, large-hearted ' Norman.' To-night he has been reading Wordsworth aloud to us most beautifully, and I am longing to know his poetry better. How much I shall have to digest when I get home ! The Duke has been making me read his letter in the *Scotsman* on the origin of the American War, ' in hope of curing me of my Southern proclivities ' ! Mr. Theed is here, the sculptor of the beautiful marble statue of the Prince Consort, at the foot of the Queen's staircase. He has come to see about placing a bronze replica of this on the banks of the Dee, but to judge by the cast, which was put up yesterday on the rocks, I hardly think it will look well out of doors.

" *June* 12.—Music and drawing all the morning, then in the afternoon we drove out by Aberarder and Felagie and waited some time in the Forest, listening to the soughing of the wind among the larches and the wild cry of the hawks, and turned into a beautiful green ride above Invercauld, with views of the rushing Dee, through a foreground of birches, juniper, heather, and deer. Then came tea and sketching, and a delightful drive home through the Ballochbuic. Oh ! it was *great* fun, and I

---

[1] In *More Leaves from the Journal of a Life in the Highlands*, p 214, the Queen writes : "*Sunday, June* 11, 1865 —At 12, I went to the Kirk —a great effort—with the girls and the Duchess of Atholl. I had only been once at the end of our stay last year in October 1864, and it made me very nervous. Still, as no one expected me to go, it was better so. Dr. Macleod performed the service very impressively. The sermon was from 1 Thessalonians v 10. No one reads the Bible better than he does, and his prayers were most beautiful. In the one for me, which he always words so expressively and touchingly, he prayed for Alix and her dear babe very beautifully The singing and the whole service brought tears to my eyes. I felt so alone. All reminded me of former blessedness."

am only sorry that this life is coming to an end. I have never laughed so much in my life as since I have been here. The Duchess, for instance, is perfectly killing. Her story of the coaching notice which she saw posted up at Dunkeld sent us all into fits the other evening: 'The Duchess of Atholl (this being the name of the coach) leaves the Duke's Arms (the inn at Dunkeld) every lawful morning at 6 a.m.' She and I have one great subject in common. We drive about these forests marking and thinning in imagination with unsparing hands. Then the scenes that take place in the char-à-bancs, on our homeward drives, are wonderful! To-night there was the Duke reciting Wordsworth, 'out of his boots,' General Grey repeating 'Tam o' Shanter' behind to Dr. Robertson the factor, and Mrs. Bruce shrieking 'Drag!' in front. The Duchess and I laughed till we cried.

"*June* 13.—To-day we all mooned about in a deliciously purposeless way, like babies, enjoying ourselves. I had much discussion with Major Elphinstone, and afterwards with him and the Duke, about Byron, Wordsworth, and Raphael. Also about Goulburn's *Personal Religion.* I don't altogether agree with the Major's theory that we think too little of ourselves, still it is immensely interesting to hear their opinions. I ended the evening by a grand confidential discourse with Lord Charles about the Household—Cowell, Bruce, Phipps, Grey, Biddulph, etc. I am so glad he likes me —for the sake of *auld lang syne* !

"*June* 14.—I sat out with Princess Louise all the morning, which I was glad to do, as I have seen so little of her this time. When I came in, Princess Helena brought me a beautiful shawl and brooch, *de la part de S.M.*, and we sat together writing in my room and talking of the charming little conspiracy which the Duke, Lord Charles, and the Gordons have brewed for me next week. After luncheon I sat quiet, being under orders to go out with Her Majesty, Princess Helena, and the Duchess. At 4.45 we drove to Invercauld, where we mounted our ponies and rode up to the 'Gate,' which I have visited three days running! Here we had tea, and the Queen took me on with her about a mile, to look down another beautiful glen looking eastwards, toward Mount Keen and the Coyles. I had been afraid that this *tête-à-tête* with Her Majesty would be formidable, but it was not, as she rode in front, only addressing an observation to me now and then, and I was quite content to be left to myself and look for the last time on the hills I have learnt to love so well. Returning to the Gate, we sat down and sketched, but rather to my regret were soon joined by the others, and drove swiftly home. Lochnagar was steeped in a lurid crimson glow, and the sun went down in a flood of gold behind Ben-na-Biurd. I dined with the Queen and the Duke and Duchess, and they talked of the Emperor of the French, whom Her Majesty pronounced to be pleasant socially, but dangerous politically. After dinner, I played and won our last game at bowls. I think we all regret the end of our *séjour* here. At night Mrs. Gordon, Princess Helena, and I had a long talk in my room about unbelief, etc. Strange what phases of this we all pass through! But, as Mrs. Gordon justly observed, it is with nations much the same. Still, I feel more and more that few of us enter sufficiently into the spirit of the words, ' Except ye become as little children, ye shall not enter into the kingdom of heaven.' And so ends Balmoral life. It has indeed been a most delightful time.

"*June* 15.—I walked up to the flagstaff on Craig Gowan by myself, for a last sniff of Highland air, a last look at the mountains. It was very quiet and delicious up there. I left Balmoral at twelve with Mrs. Gordon and Mrs. Bruce, getting beautiful views of ' dark Lochnagar ' on the drive down to Aboyne, and admiring the wealth of wild roses and heather along the road. We left Aboyne about two, and troubled our heads little about the scenery after that. At Perth we had a last dinner all together, and the Duchess and Mrs. Bruce left us. I have a pleasant recollection of blue hills in the clear twilight, and after tea at Carlisle I slept till Mrs. Gordon called me to look at the sunrise. Leamington saw me astir, and Oxford up and dressed and enjoying the lovely summer morning. At nine we reached Windsor, and having taken leave of the Princesses and Princes, of Major Elphinstone and the Gordons, who were kind to the last, I drove down to the station in a Royal chariot, postilion and pair, and found myself safe at home by 1 p.m., after an absence of exactly one month. But for my darling mother, I should be very sorry to be back.

"*Sunday, June* 23.—And thus abruptly and hurriedly I took leave of my dear old Journal, the faithful companion of fifteen months, spent amidst an immense variety of scenes and companions, some evanescent and hardly worth recording, others imprinted for ever on my mind. Yet my condition remains unchanged, my heart untouched, calm and fancy free. So be it, if such is the will of God, who links or severs the destinies of mortals here below. To do my duty in that state of life to which He has called me, to live up or at least to try by God's help to live up to the definition of religion which I gave the other day under the green birches, on the grey stones of a Scottish hillside, *i.e.* ' the love of God,'—such, amid many short-comings, is my fixed resolve. For the rest—' Wie Gott will.' "

CHAPTER VIII

BALLS AND WEDDINGS

1865–1866

' 3 *Arlington Street, Tuesday, June* 25.—My last volume began in Passion Week; this commences on the morning of a Drawing-Room day. However, it is likewise the return to ordinary life, after dear, dear Balmoral, where my heart still lingers among the mountains, while my head has not yet recovered from the whirl of the last week. Last night I went with General and Mrs. Gordon to dine with the Duke and Duchess of Argyll, and a very pleasant evening we had, Sir David and Lady Baird, Mr. Howard, and Sir Kenneth Mackenzie being the only additions to our five selves. The Duke, Mrs. Gordon, and I sat together, and were very jolly. I heard from dear Princess Helena. My heart is still on Lochnagar. The Drawing-Room was thin and uninteresting. Princess Helena and I very nearly laughed at each other, but just didn't, and made low curtsies instead.

" *June* 29.—I dined with the Nugents and went on with them to the ball at Lady Louisa Pennant's— the plan brewed so long ago in the Ballochbuic Forest! . . . But rest—rest—rest! that is what I want, after two months of constant society. Rest and time to think. . . .

" *Richmond Park, Sunday, July* 9.—I have lived in such a whirl lately, and feel I do not think enough of the inner life. Dear little Sophy Melville sets me a capital example there, though I cannot quite agree with her that a pink gown is inconsistent with the 'sobriety' of dress recommended in the Bible. . . . I wish for two things—a little more money, and a husband. But I often wonder whether, after all, I shall be called to a single life. It requires courage, but St. Paul tells us that it is the most blessed. I do not *wish* for it, but still I trust I may never be led, from fear of it, to make a marriage without affection. *That* must be lowering to the whole tone of the mind. But sufficient unto the day ! "

The autumn was spent partly in Suffolk, where long rambles along the cliffs at Dunwich and quiet hours in the old home at Sotterley revived Louisa's spirits, and she thoroughly enjoyed her usual tour of visits and gaieties in the winter months. Belvoir Castle, Ely and Lincoln Cathedrals, Boston and Grantham were among the interesting places which she visited, while she greatly enjoyed ten days at Stoke Rochford in the company of her new friend Miss Edith Turnor. " For that dear, almost sacred, name sounds on my lips once more, and another Edith has come to bless my life." Miss Turnor's charm and intelligence had long attracted her, and the two girls now became fast friends.

" *Tuesday, November* 28.—To-day was very wet, but we had much pleasant talk with Mr. Turnor about politics and the study of mathematics, and with Edith about herself, etc. We agreed, for one thing, that nothing would induce either of us to marry a clergyman. These are my reasons. First, I should not like always to be tied down to one spot. Secondly, that as a body I do not like the clergy, and should dislike extremely to be obliged to live among them. I say this not from any disrespect to their office, but I think they are as a rule dogmatical, narrow-minded, and very disagreeable.—L. BOWATER. ' I most completely and entirely endorse the above, and have the greatest objection to the sight of a rook except on his perch—*alias* in the pulpit. Of course there are some exceptions, but I think very few.—EDITH TURNOR.'

" *Wednesday, November* 29.—A last pleasant talk with

Edie. In the afternoon a ride with Mr. Turnor, Edmund, and Edith to Woolsthorpe, to see the house where Sir Isaac Newton was born. It is a quaint little old manor-house, standing in the midst of the village, almost invisible from the main road. We entered through the kitchen, which is low, with heavy beams, as it may have been in his day, and stumbled up a dark little staircase to the room where he was born. There is a quaint carved oak cupboard by the fireplace, and over the mantelpiece the date of his birth and a line from Pope:

'God said, Let Newton be, and there was light.'

The little study is even more interesting. One could fancy the silent, shy boy poring over his books there. Outside the house is covered with ivy, the little old stone mullions peeping out, and at the back there is a sundial carved by his own hand. Altogether, I am glad to have seen the place, though all feelings of pilgrimage to a shrine were dispelled in a breathless gallop against the strong south wind—the pony pulling with all his might. . . . And so ends a very happy, enjoyable visit. I have grown to love Edie very dearly—the Sleeping Beauty, whom life and the world are slowly awakening. May the enchanted Prince soon come and touch the chord that will rouse her from the dreams of childhood and make of her the perfect woman!"

From Stoke Rochford Louisa went on to Arbury, where she spent a happy month with her relatives, talking politics, attending meetings, and going to dances and Christmas entertainments. At Stoke a year before she had enjoyed her first day's hunting—" been introduced," as she puts it, " to the noble sport of fox-hunting," which was afterwards to become one of her regular occupations in Northamptonshire. At Arbury she frequently rode to covert with Mr. Newdegate, mounted on a fiery chestnut mare named Firefly, which she was proud of being able to manage. During this visit to Arbury, Princess Helena's marriage to Prince Christian of Schleswig-Holstein was announced in the papers, and Louisa received " a charming letter from the Princess, telling me of the great happiness which was in store for her." Her excitement was still greater when, on her return home early in March, she heard of the engagement of her intimate friend and constant companion, Miss Bella Mainwaring. Miss Mainwaring lived at the Old Palace, Richmond, a fragment of Henry VII.'s famous Tudor house, and with herself and Lady Sophia Melville formed a circle of friends which Louisa was fond of calling the Trio.

"*March* 28, 1866.—The spell is broken! the Trio is to be dissolved, the triangle will be a triangle no longer. We had scarcely returned from church, when Bella drove up, escorted by a gentleman whom, on my running down to the gate, she introduced as General Milman. Suspecting nothing, I took her into the drawing-room, when she began excusing herself for not having written in so confused a way, that I at once exclaimed, ' You are not going to be married ? ' ' Yes,' she replied, ' to General Milman ' ; and the next instant she informed me that the wedding is to be in May, that I am to be her bridesmaid, and that in July she goes to Mauritius for five years. I did not know whether I stood on my head or heels! However, in five minutes I was dressed and driving back to spend my afternoon with them at the Old Palace. He is twenty-four years older than she is, but very gentleman-like and pleasing, and desperately in love. She is very happy and very much in love. It has just given her the ballast she wanted, and I never saw her appear to greater advantage. Presently Atholl Forbes turned up, and we trotted round the garden, while the General indulged in the most lover-like raptures, and I felt extremely puzzled by the novelty of the situation. And me? I must not think of myself yet! Indeed I cannot bear to think of the blank it will leave in my life. . . . Dear Bella has indeed been one of the stanchest and truest of my girlhood's friends.

"*April* 3.—Sophy and Bella came to luncheon, the latter in a tearing state of excitement, but she soon left, and I had a long, long talk with Sophy, resulting in the melancholy conclusion that although we should be quite willing to marry our respective lovers, if they had £10,000 a year, we are not unhappy to feel that under present circumstances marriage is out of the question for either of us, and that consequently this cannot be the true sort of love. Perhaps that may yet come! Anyhow, it is a blessing that Sophy is not going to be married! If I must lose one, I'd sooner it was Bella.

"*May* 8.—Dear Bella's wedding-day. I can hardly realise that it is all over and that Bella Mainwaring exists no more! The day was cloudless, and by eleven we were all assembled at St. Matthias, the new church at Richmond. The eight bridesmaids—Sophy Melville, Alice Drummond, Annabel O'Grady, Helen Burton, Theo Dallas, two Miss Milmans, and myself—wore white muslin trimmed with blue sashes and Cluny lace, wreaths of white daisies and lovely bouquets of stephanotis, pink geraniums, and fern. Bella looked extremely handsome in her white satin and veil, and behaved so exactly like the ordinary, everyday Bella, walking about showing her presents and introducing people, that you could hardly believe she was the bride. One o'clock brought the breakfast, with shoals of men, and I was soon floated off on a tide of fun and chaff. After going to feed, I was sitting under the portico, engaged in a lively discussion with Mr. Bowles (an ' Owl ') and two or three other men on the respective merits of music and poetry, when suddenly they melted away and left me alone with Captain C——, who, to my utter amazement, took the opportunity of proposing. I was never so much astonished in all my life! For though other men and girls have often chaffed me about him, I never thought for a moment he was in earnest, and even now I can't believe it. The form was much as usual. I answered him quite firmly, but was not the least discomposed, and we were interrupted by the departure of the happy pair, which was an orthodox scene. Then came croquet and dancing, when he renewed the subject, and I flatter myself that I closed it for ever. No! Captain C—— does not care—nobody ever will care—for me half as much as Captain B——!"

Meanwhile, political events were absorbing a large share of Louisa's thoughts. Every day she read the parliamentary debates on the Reform Bill and filled her Journal with comments on the speeches delivered from both sides of the House.

"*April* 17.—The Reform debate continues. Sir Hugh Cairns's speech was very striking, that of Sir Edward Bulwer Lytton one of the best I have yet read. I am, I own, hugely interested in this matter. I don't like the Bill at all, for I object strongly to the indiscriminate lowering of the franchise, without any safeguard against the effect of a more wholesale transfer of power than was effected by the Reform Bill of '32. And it seems to bar the way to the kind of fancy franchise which alone can admit the *un*represented classes without swamping those already represented. As to Mr. Gladstone, nothing can well be more mischievous than his conduct and speeches at Liverpool. But the way out of the mess is not at all clear. What I hope is that the Bill will pass the second reading and be shelved in Committee. Yet I should be very sorry to see Reform shelved altogether. And what is painful to me, no party seems to be acting honestly unless it be the Rads, who say openly that they regard this only as a stepping-stone to more. What will be the end of it?

"*April* 30.—I have not recorded Mr. Lowe's speech, one of the finest in the debate. He describes the franchise most justly as the means to an end and not an end in itself, that end being good government. Mr. Disraeli's speech is a very clever one, but I think his strongest point is where he demonstrates the effect of including the large populations which have grown up without the present borough boundaries in the county constituencies. C. N. N. is never tired of insisting on the present anomalies of county constituencies, which certainly seem to require attention. I am astounded to hear that the clubs described in the two last *Owls*[1] really exist. Lady Burrell (*née* Pechell) is a 'Jolly Dog,' with her attendant cur (Mr. Harvey Pechell), 'Fred Scuffleton' is Freddy Villiers, and 'Augustus Cotillon' Augustus Lumley. I am falling into the Walpole-Berry style, though with small hope of emulating either. That last sentence was evidently written for a posthumous public. After the Duke of Argyll's suggestion last year, who knows what may be the fate of these pages?

"3 *Arlington Street*, *May* 5.—I was wholly stunned by an invitation from dear Princess Helena to Balmoral. It will be charming to see her comfortably before her marriage, and to be at dear Balmoral again, although I am sorry to lose the season. We attended the Queen's Court at Buckingham Palace, for which tickets were issued by the Lord Chamberlain, the number limited to two hundred and fifty. It proved much like an agreeable evening party, with plenty of room to move about. The rooms are handsome. We passed through three saloons and crossed the gallery into the Green Room or Throne Room, the ballroom of my young days. Her Majesty was very gracious. She spoke to Mamma and shook hands with me, as did all Royalties, *i.e.* Princess Helena, the Prince of Wales, Princes Alfred and Arthur, and the Duke of Cambridge. *Pour le reste*, we saw nobody particular, but spoke to Lord and Lady Exeter, General Grey and Sybil, the Ladies Cornwallis, and dear Mrs. Gordon. I am wretched to hear she is not going to Balmoral. People were well dressed; still there was nothing very remarkable about them, excepting the diminution of crinoline, after its eleven years' reign—since the visit of the Empress of the French in 1855.

"*May* 10.—In the evening I went with Mrs. Newdegate and Harry Boucherett to Her Majesty's to see *The Huguenots*. It is certainly a fine opera, and Titiens and Rokitansky both sang gloriously, the latter beating the

[1] A newspaper of the day.

new tenor Mongini into little bits. Charley was to have filled the fourth place in our box, but of course could not get away from the House, and I was glad to have no other man, and could not have flirted in any comfort, as we were exactly opposite the Royal box, in which were the Prince and Princess of Wales, with Mrs. Hardinge and Major Teesdale. In the next box was the Duchess of Manchester and Lady Westmoreland, and beyond that Lady Hastings, Lady Constance Grosvenor, Lady Dunmore, the Duke of Sutherland, Lord and Lady Royston. They all paid each other visits in turn, and it was very amusing to watch them—as good, in fact, as a second opera! The Princess looked far the prettiest of all. Poor Lady Hastings had such a sad, unhappy look on her face, it quite haunts me!

"*May* 11.—There is, we are told, the greatest fear of a commercial panic in the city, and if one house goes there will be a tremendous smash. Last night I heard that one of our biggest tea merchants had crashed. From Vienna jewels are being sent over in shoals. Lord Dunmore was offered a magnificent parure for £4000 by a Bloomsbury diamond merchant, and when he refused, received a telegram from Vienna to say he could have it half-price. To-day we hear that Overend & Gurney have failed for £13,000,000, and there is a rumour that the London Joint Stock Bank has stopped payment. All these things make me very glad that Mamma's fortune is not paid off.

"It was too wet to ride, so I went with Lady Leven and Sophy to the Royal Academy, but the crowd was intolerable and the pictures for the most part abominable. We had scores of visitors all the afternoon, and went to tea with Mrs. Hibbert in Rogers' old house in St. James's Place. His library is still quite untouched, and there is a charming view over the Park. Harry and I dined in Hill Street with his great friends, Mr. and Mrs. Hugo Meynell,[1] whom I have long wished to know, and spent a delightful evening. After that we went

[1] Hugo Meynell-Ingram of Hoar Cross, Temple Newsam, married 1863 Hon. Emily Wood, daughter of Lord Halifax, and died 1871.

to see *The Rivals* at St. James's Theatre. I can't help laughing when I think of my sage reflections on that play when I saw it at Richmond eight years ago. Now I certainly do not see any harm in it, and I fully appreciate the wit and humour wherewith it abounds. I am glad to hear from Princess Helena that she and the Princess of Wales greatly admired my gown at the Court.

"*May* 14.—After a quiet Sunday with Mamma, I came up to town and was astounded and rejoiced to see in the *Times* that the Queen has given up Balmoral and is to go to Cliveden instead. In Arlington Street I found a letter from Princess Helena to say I am to go there. In the evening, after hearing that the Redistribution Bill had passed the second reading, I went to Lady Farquhar's ball, which was a capital one, just the élite of our own set, and I knew every third person in the room, and danced with Ronald Melville, Mr. Fane, Willy Gurdon, Sir Charles Mordaunt, Robert Drummond, Arthur Monck, and Matt Ridley, with whom I have set up a pleasant cousinly flirtation. He is rather handsome and exceedingly clever, but I foresee that on closer acquaintance we should quarrel. Our mutual conceit would clash, and then he has the extremely decided opinions of a very young, clever man, who has lived in an intellectual set at Oxford and has not yet mixed enough with the world to learn to say, ' I don't know— I am not sure.' But I do enjoy discussing books with him — Swinburne's *Atalanta*, Ruskin, etc. Captain C—— was there, but happily only bowed to me in the distance."

CHAPTER IX

WINDSOR AND CLIVEDEN

1866

"*Windsor Castle*, *May* 19.—Princess Helena welcomed me on my arrival, and took me out for a long drive all round Virginia Water and the Rhododendron Walk—too beautiful it is in the first glory of spring. She entered at once upon the subject of her marriage, and talked in the simplest and most natural way of her affection for Prince Christian. Both the Queen and the Crown Princess are devoted to him, and even the Prince of Wales, who from political reasons naturally at first disliked the idea of the marriage, says Prince Christian is so good and excellent he cannot possibly object to his union with his sister. So I can only rejoice in her happiness. Thank God! Our dinner-party consisted of Mrs. Bruce, Miss Macdonald, Lord Charles Fitzroy, Lord Caithness, Colonel Liddell, General Grey, Sir John Cowell, and Dr. Jenner. I sat between the General and Lord Charles, and was very happy. In the evening we were joined by the Duchess of Atholl, the French Ambassador, and M. le Prince de la Tour d'Auvergne, Sir Thomas Biddulph, and Lord Clarendon, who was most entertaining, and delighted me by saying that the Danes were wrong in the first place, to say nothing of their folly at the time of the Conference in London, when they might have obtained much better terms if their demands had been more reasonable. Lady Clarendon is here too, very handsome and attractive. The French Ambassador is very dark and very fat, much younger than I expected, and a thorough gentleman, which is more than can be said of most Ambassadors during the present régime in France. Princess Mary's marriage is to take place on the 11th of June. Everyone says she will be the Queen of English society and means to reform its tone. But people are afraid there may be some difficulty as to her money; it is feared that in the present excited state of politics the Government may be attacked even on that subject.

"*Whit-Sunday, May* 20.—We went to services at ten and twelve, in the private chapel, and I spent the afternoon walking on the Slopes with Princess Louise and talking to dear Princess Helena. I have the most charming little bedroom and sitting-room with a piano in it, up in the Lancaster Tower, looking over the Long Walk, and am very snug there all by myself, reading, writing, and playing! I dined with the Queen, who was most kind; but it is a very stately business, and only the Duchess was there besides. She lunches and dines in the Octagon Room. We breakfast there, and lunch and dine in a room on the other side, but we are a very small party.

"*May* 21.—I sat with Princess Helena, who is very busy and much worried by the warlike reports which Lady Caroline Barrington brings from Berlin, where she has been sent to look after the Crown Princess. At five I drove with her and the Queen by Frogmore and the Mausoleum to Virginia Water, where we mounted our ponies and spent an hour or more, very pleasantly, riding about in the beautiful woods, where it was sheltered from the east wind.

"*May* 22.—Rather a dull day, as Princess Helena went up to town, to have luncheon at Marlborough House and go to the Flower Show with her brothers. But I saw dear little Prince Leo in Mlle Norèle's rooms, where we have planned a daily meeting after luncheon! He looked very well, in spite of his lameness, and played very nicely on his flute. I dined with the Queen; Prince Alfred, who is to be called 'Duke of Edinburgh' after Thursday, was added to our party and made it much more lively. He is certainly very good-looking, and has beautiful large blue eyes, like Princess Mary. I am afraid the Queen is very unhappy about foreign affairs. To-day's news is very warlike, and there seems considerable fear of a revolution in Berlin. The Royalties were much crowded at the Flower Show, the great attraction being the Prince of Teck, who seems to have excited universal admiration among the ladies. Colonel Home Purvis told Mrs. Bruce that the more he saw of him, the better he liked him. But poor Princess Mary appeared at the Flower Show with very red eyes, and had been crying, we hear, because she is told that if war breaks out her bridegroom will have to fight — which does seem too bad !

"*May* 23.—I spent the morning walking round Frogmore with Princess Louise. The sun was warm and everything in blossom, and to me the place seemed quite delicious. Only think of Prince Louis being obliged to join the Austrian Army, while the Crown Prince takes the command in Silesia. Here everyone is much annoyed at the Duke of Saxe-Coburg having asked for a Prussian command, and placed his army at the King's disposal. I think I had rather give up a bit of a kingdom like that than sacrifice the position of head of the Liberal party in Germany ! I sat with Princess Helena while Mr. Thorneycroft worked at her bust, which is getting more like her, although I am not sure that it is altogether good. That done, General Grey came to luncheon. He is a host in himself, and was most amusing, repeating lines from Burns which are very appropriate at the present time :

> ' And a' ye bonny blossoms,
> God mak' ye a' as gude as braw,
> And send ye lads in plenty !
> And oh ! ye British public, know
> That kings are unco' scanty,
> And German princes tho' they're sma'
> They're better just nor wanty ! '

The Drawing-room which most of the party went up

to attend, was a fertile topic of discussion. Everyone was eloquent on the subject of Lady Dudley's beauty and wonderful pearls, and people waited to see her pass after she came out of the throne-room.

"*May* 24.—The Queen's birthday ! The bells rang and a salute was fired in the Long Walk. The Prince and Princess of Wales and Prince Alfred came down to luncheon. There was a grand disturbance, because nobody knew when they were to arrive, and consequently no one was there to receive them but Lord Charles, and that quite accidentally. We had Lady Macclesfield at luncheon, and I have quite lost my heart to her, and remember having always heard Mamma say how charming the Grosvenors were. Miss Macdonald and I walked down into the town, and met Prince Edward and Eliza Alexander, who are here with the regiment for three months. We went on to Frogmore, the only sheltered place, but it must be very hot in summer and damp in winter. There is a pretty drawing-room, beautifully fitted up in white and gold and grey by the Prince and Princess of Wales, but most of the rooms are small and open into a corridor, which makes them dark. Still, it is a very pretty place. After dinner, the Queen sent for the 'three ladies' (the Duchess always dines with her) into the corridor, and was very gracious, shaking hands with Miss Macdonald and myself, and kissing Mrs. Bruce. Prince Edward also dined with her, and joined us in the evening, looking very big. He took a hand at whist, so I sat out and watched the General play—a good lesson for me.

"*May* 25.—Dearest Princess Helena's birthday ! May God indeed send her the choicest blessings, and cause the bright promise of her present life to ripen unblighted by time. It was celebrated by a tea to the servants' children, held in the Conservatory. Never was there such a successful fête ! We all assembled there at five, and the Queen actually walked through, and then dancing began, and for the first time she looked on—an immense step gained. We all joined in it. I thoroughly enjoyed a good country dance, and so I am sure did we all. Princess Helena danced with Löhlein the Prince Consort's valet, Princess Louise with Mr. Stirling, Princess Beatrice with Major Elphinstone, Prince Arthur with one of the dressers, and Miss Macdonald and I each with a page. It was the greatest possible fun, and the Queen remained on a dais at the end, looking on with real amusement, till twenty minutes to eight. ' God save the Queen ' was played, and they all cheered her when she went away, and she looked so much pleased, while I had the advantage of seeing a good deal of my dear little Prince. The Duchess and I dined with her in the evening. All the children were there, as it was a birthday, and dear little Princess Beatrice (who is in great force, in spite of the whooping-cough) proposed ' dear Na's health ' (her name for Princess Helena) ' and many happy returns of the day, as it is her last birthday at home,' a sentiment which was received with shrieks of laughter, resulting in a simultaneous burst of whooping-cough from Princess Louise, Prince Arthur, and Prince Leopold. It was a horrid shame, but it was impossible to help laughing! I never was at such a merry dinner in the Oak Room, and the Queen was most gracious, and came and talked to me for some time after dinner.

" *May 26.*—This morning Princess Helena gave me a dear little thermometer in an ormolu horseshoe, ' in order,' she said, ' that Lady Bowater may not be afraid of your keeping your rooms too hot.' But I don't think that is one of Mamma's bugbears. At 3.30 we started for Cliveden, in three carriages—the Queen, Princess Helena, and the Duchess in the first, attended by Lord Charles on horseback; Princess Beatrice, Prince Leopold, and the two governesses in the second ; and Princess Louise, Miss Macdonald, and myself in the third. The drive was pretty enough, but when we reached Cliveden our exclamations of delight were unbounded, and we rushed about like wild things. Anything more beautiful than this place it would be hard to find ! The house stands on the top of a high ridge, and from my window I look down on a smooth terraced lawn, gay with rose campions and blue forget-me-nots, and on the hanging woods of Cliveden and Taplow, with the river winding below through the meadows like a silver ribbon. Very soon after our arrival, we all—the Duchess, Miss Macdonald, General Grey, Lord Charles, and myself—ran down to the river and, seizing on a boat, had a most delicious row, exploring some of the many little creeks, which with their bulrushes and flags and the shadows and reflections in the water would send an artist into raptures. The place formerly belonged to Sir George Warrender, from whom the Duchess of Sutherland bought it, and soon afterwards the house was burnt down. The present building was only begun in 1851, and is a large Italian villa, beautifully fitted up and full of beautiful things. It is much more cheery than Windsor and much easier to get out of, and in this weather it is too delightful to escape from these great state rooms, without a single book or newspaper to look at. Here every room is full of books, and our dining-room opens into a conservatory, which is a blaze of pink and white azaleas. The grounds are quite beautiful, and remind me very much of Dropmore.

"*Sunday, May 27.*—We had a delightful walk through the Cliveden and Hedsor grounds to a dear little village church, and had a nice service and good sermon on the text, ' He that hath My commandments and keepeth them,' etc. All the Royalties, as General Grey naughtily expresses it, ' were pagans ' to-day, and for some unknown reason did not go to church. In the afternoon I drove with the Queen and Princess Helena, all through the grounds at Dropmore, which are gay with azaleas and rhododendrons in blossom, to Burnham Beeches, which is just a bit of forest with a few picturesque old beeches scattered about. We came back through Beaconsfield, altogether a charming drive, and the Queen was very lively and talked more than usual."

The next week was spent in pleasant drives in the beautiful Thames valley, in the company of her beloved Princesses, in boating expeditions and long walks in the woods, then in the glory of the spring-time. The weather was radiant, and Louisa enjoyed herself thoroughly. The last Sunday was marked by the presence of Charles Kingsley, which is duly recorded in her Journal.

"*Sunday, June* 3.—Mr. Kingsley read the service to-day in the Queen's dining-room. It was very short —only the Litany and Communion Service, with a short sermon on the text, ' Say not thou, What is the cause that the former days were better than these? for thou dost not inquire wisely concerning this.' The burden of the song was that this nineteenth century, with all its imperfections, is better than all that ever went before it, and that we should make a great mistake if we tried to exchange. The language was good, and the sermon very different from those one generally hears, but I don't think it was heart-searching, or likely to do one much practical good. H.R.H. the Duke of Edinburgh rode over to luncheon, so we had Mr. Eliot Yorke to amuse us, and I frittered away the afternoon between him and the Princesses. We had *meant* to walk to Hedsor Church—V.V., as General Grey puts it : G.V. we call it sometimes, for he never will do anything but just what he pleases. The other day he went to Windsor, and instead of coming back to dinner, stayed to dine with his own people and did not return till past eleven, and there were the Queen and Princess Helena sitting up for him with a pile of dispatch-boxes, which arrived by messenger from the Foreign Office just after dinner. I fear the news is very bad again, and it is really too much for my small mind to have the war and Reform Bill to look after at once. It shows, however, that reading the *Times* is as good as being at headquarters, for the first leading article in yesterday's paper contained precisely the same news as reached the Queen at 9.30 on the previous evening. Mr. Kingsley dined with the Queen and joined us later, and made himself very pleasant during the short time that he remained. He told us all to read *Madame Thérèse*,[1] which he calls ' a perfect idyll.'

"*June* 4.—The last day at Cliveden ! I went out

---
[1] A French story by Erckmann-Chatrian.

directly after breakfast with Princess Louise—dear little thing, I have seen a great deal of her this time and we are capital friends. But the Queen overtook us, and picked us up to go and perform a grand ceremony of planting an oak in one of the more retired avenues. Never, I should think, were those quiet glades so gay, for Princess Beatrice and Miss Bauer followed in an open phaeton-and-pair, and Prince Leopold and Mr. Stirling in the pony-carriage. To me the Queen was most gracious, as she has been all through this visit; but all the same I was not sorry when it was over, and we all dispersed. Princess Louise and I took a charming drive through Hedsor Park, and after luncheon I sat first with Princess Helena and then with Princess Louise till 4 p.m., when we had agreed to have another game of croquet with dear Prince Leo. Our pleasure, however, was sadly spoilt by the dear boy having an attack of faintness which alarmed us all. Happily he recovered quickly, and the Queen, who was going out driving, did not know of it till her return. I dined with her, and was afraid that she might blame us for playing croquet on so hot a day; but she was kind and gracious as ever, and took leave of me in the kindest way. At night I had a long talk with the dear Duchess, of whom I have seen a great deal this time, and who is always most kind to me.

"*June* 5.—I took leave of the Princesses before breakfast, and started directly afterwards for Windsor, and was home with the dear mother by luncheon-time. I talked and slept all day, and in the evening drove up for the Palace ball, which was about as amusing as usual. I saw shoals of people, danced every dance, and met Edith Turnor, Mrs. Gordon, etc. Princess Mary asked us to come and see her presents at St. James's Palace, which we did the next day. There was a large, pleasant assembly, and lovely *cadeaux*, especially a necklace of crystal flies given by the Duke of Edinburgh. Her Royal Highness was exceedingly kind and civil, but I was dead tired, and refused to do anything else but go home to Arlington Street."

CHAPTER X

POLITICS AND SOCIETY

1866-1867

DURING the next two years Louisa Bowater's life was, as, looking back on this period in her Journal, she pronounces, comparatively uneventful. She rode and danced, read and wrote, and enjoyed dinners and balls as much as ever. Her friends were more numerous than ever, fresh suitors presented themselves constantly and were freely discussed in the pages of her Journal. But none of these made any lasting impression on her heart. On the whole, the man who exercised the greatest influence on her at this time was her cousin, Charles Newdegate. Much of her time, as before, was spent in Arlington Street or at Harefield or Arbury, and her growing interest in politics was largely due to his society, while her regard for him and her affection for his mother deepened each day that she spent in their company. A few extracts must suffice as specimens of the many interesting events recorded by her busy pen.

" *3 Arlington Street, June 7.*—Mrs. Newdegate and I went to the House and heard some rather dull speeches on the County Franchise, from Mr. Liddell, Mr. Adderley, Mr. Stanhope, and Sir George Grey. Mr. Walpole's amendment, proposing £20 as the franchise qualification instead of £14, was lost by 13, the Opposition having weakened themselves by a motion brought on earlier in the evening by Lord Stanley without any notice, to take the Redistribution Bill before the Franchise Bill. The Whigs, meanwhile, affect a virtuous indignation;

and so they fight and squabble, and the true interests of the country are neglected. Ugh! I am sick of the whole thing!

"*Harefield Place, Sunday, June* 10, 2 *a.m.*—I don't feel the least inclined to go to bed, and shall amuse myself by writing an account of our evening at Lady Emily Peel's. Lady Waldegrave had a rival party, so the members of the present and of the *ci-devant* Government were not very civil to each other. We went very early to Whitehall Gardens, followed Lady Ely upstairs, and found a large dinner-party. The Duke of Cambridge was standing near the door talking to Lord Dudley, whose pretty bride sat on the sofa behind in white satin and lovely diamonds. In the middle of the room the Bishop of Oxford and Lord Derby were deep in conversation, and were shortly joined by Lord Chelmsford and Sir Robert himself, who went about bowing and smirking; he may be excellent, but he has very bad manners. Smaller fry followed — though 'Jacob Omnium'[1] scarcely comes under that denomination. Then, in quick succession, came the Clarendons, Lady De Grey, Lady Churchill, Lady Burrell, Lord and Lady Queensberry, Sir Francis and Miss Grant, Adderleys, Henniker, and Boscawens—in short, it was a very fine, very Tory party. In the cloakroom we met Mr. Norton, at whom I stared with great interest, and Lord Houghton, to whom I was introduced. Meantime Charley had been dining with the Newspaper Press Fund. Lord Granville was in the chair, and annoyed Charley by describing him as a great Conservative, in opposition to himself as a Liberal. It is very amusing to live even on the outskirts of 'the circles of power.' Oh! how ambitious I should be if I was one of them! I was very sorry to leave town, but it is delicious here. Now to bed and to put by such thoughts for Sunday. The nightingales will sing me to sleep.

"3 *Arlington Street, June* 12.—We went to Lady Dartmouth's ball, a great crush at first, but afterwards there never was such fun. Almost every man I knew in

[1] Matthew James Higgins.

London was there, and I did not think it was left in me to enjoy a ball so much. I talked politics as usual with Sir Charles Mordaunt. His tone is very different to what it was at Lady Farquhar's a month ago, when, according to him, the Tories did not choose to take office. *Now* he thinks the party is going to smash, and he says that neither he nor C. N. N. have a chance of winning their elections with the £14 franchise.

"*June* 19.—We were astounded by the news of the Government's defeat by 11, in consequence of which they have decided to resign. The question was such a comparatively trifling one, whether the borough qualification should be stated according to the rental or the rates. The Queen is at Balmoral, and the whole affair is very inconvenient. She ought not to have gone. I had a long letter from Princess Helena, who is much worried about the war and the illness of the Crown Princess's youngest boy.

"*June* 20.—The Prussians have overrun almost all Northern Germany without opposition. We live in wonderfully exciting times.

"*June* 26.—We drove into the city to leave cards at the Mansion House, and found the Lady Mayoress 'receiving,' a rare chance for me, and admired the fine but rather dark rooms, fitted up with old-fashioned magnificence. Charley came up and reported that the ministers were out. Gladstone made a very temperate speech, while Lord Russell and Lord Derby pitched into each other upstairs. To-night at Mrs. Packe's ball I danced with Mr. Gladstone's secretary, Willy Gurdon, who seems glad his chief has resigned, and says they will come in all the stronger in six months. But, on the whole, nobody seems to care much.

"*June* 27.—We dined with Mr. and Lady Harriet Ramsden in Portman Square, where a Mr. Pennington took me in, but I got into talk with my other neighbour, who said almost directly, 'Is that Mr. Newdegate?' 'Yes.' 'Oh, I'm so glad! I have long wanted to know him. I must have a discussion with him after dinner.' 'What about?' I asked, premising that Charley was my cousin and guardian. ' I want to know why he so persistently attacks the Roman Catholics.' ' Are you one ? ' ' Yes ; I belong to one of the oldest Roman Catholic families in England.' ' Ah ! ' I said, ' he likes them a great deal better than he does the recent perverts.' ' Well, he has a strong *collaborateur* in Mr. Whalley.' ' Mr. Whalley,' I retorted, ' is no friend of his.' Then on to a thousand other subjects, scampering over the ground, *effleurant* everything— French society, German novels and metaphysics, Schiller and Goethe—and I was not surprised to find that he had been brought up in Paris and taken his degree there. Ere long we exchanged names : mine conveyed nothing to him, but *his*—Jerningham—took us at once into Norfolk. Then I bade him attend to his other neighbour, and we agreed to meet at Mrs. Paynter's ball. After dinner he got his talk with Charley, and later in the evening I sat out with him at the ball for twenty minutes, fighting the Roman Catholic subject. He tried in vain to persuade me that ' the end justifies the means ' was an exploded doctrine, but had me more in a corner touching convents, of which I know too little to speak. He said he did not like them himself, but complained that Charley was hard and bitter, although every one allows him to be honest. I told him that there must be war between us, as the Roman Catholics were so aggressive, and that the British public was asleep and wanted rousing, and that the Jesuits' view of implicit obedience rendered them not responsible and therefore doubly dangerous. Of course the end of the talk left us just where we were, but it was intensely interesting, and altogether a curious adventure.[1]

" *July* 4.—I sat at home all the morning reading

[1] Sir Hubert Jerningham, born 1842 ; entered the Diplomatic Service, 1866 ; served in Paris, Vienna, and as agent at Belgrade, 1878 ; Governor of Mauritius and Trinidad, 1887-1889 ; died in London, April 3, 1914. Sir Hubert was the author of *Life in a French Château*, and of several other books, and was considered, with Lord Chief Justice Cockburn and Lord Granville, to be one of the three finest French scholars of the day in this country.

George Eliot's (Miss Evans) new novel *Felix Holt, the Radical*. Wonderfully clever it is, reminding me of the best Dutch pictures. Her studies of middle and upper-lower class life are admirable. Charley knew her well, and says that all her life she has been mortified by her want of beauty. This, I suppose, explains why many characters in her books—Hetty, Esther, etc.—are lovely but not always wise. I had a long argument with him to-day on the Schleswig-Holstein question. All turns upon this: Did the Duke of Augustenburg sell his rights to the Duchy to Prussia, or not? The best informed people say that he did not. Meantime, Charley wishes success to the Prussians, and his wish is gratified, as we have just heard of their great victory. After tea we had a long chat about his political position. It fills me with profound admiration when I realise how his whole life has been one long sacrifice to duty. His life all work, mine all play—what a contrast! And yet I can't help it. But I wish I could find a principle to guide one in judging of the doctrine of nationalities. One is very anxious that Venice should belong to Italy, Schleswig-Holstein to Germany, and then why should not Ireland be free? I mean logically. It is hard to draw the line between a just resistance to oppression, and rebellion.

"*Thursday, July* 5. *Marriage of Princess Helena*.— I was up betimes and got into my wedding clothes at once, and was off by 10.30 to Paddington Station, where Lord Alfred Paget handed me out of the carriage, and I found myself in Lady Augusta Stanley's charge. The station was gay with uniforms and ladies in full evening dress, but we soon found seats in a compartment of the special train, with Mr. Disraeli and Lord Eversley in the next. They were busy discussing the Austrian reverse, but we could not hear much of what they said. The streets of Windsor were gaily decorated as we drove up to the Grand Entrance and marched through St. George's Hall to the top of the equerries' staircase, where Miss Maude and I were separated from our chaperons and shown into the White Drawing-room.

Here we found a number of invited guests, including the mothers of the bridesmaids and others, who were not to take part in the processions. The Duke of Argyll and I had a great greeting. He was full of the war news. The Austrian army, it seems, was completely routed at Königgrätz, and there is now nothing between the Prussians and Vienna. 'Tis but a few weeks since people were saying there was nothing between the Austrians and Berlin. And all this Benedek has thrown away. Ere long we were summoned to the Chapel, where I found myself in a line with Miss Seymour, Miss Maude, Miss Wood, and Sybil Grey. Opposite us were seated the whole of the ex-Ministry, who do not give up their seats till to-morrow. Lord Derby, General Peel, and Mr. Disraeli were the only representatives of the new Cabinet, the latter sitting next but one to Mr. Gladstone. It was a curious study of faces, and very suggestive was the fact that Baron Brunnow and Count Bernstorff never ceased talking. Poor Count Apponyi, the Austrian Ambassador, sent an excuse. And now a flourish of trumpets and a grand march announced the approach of the first procession, that of the Royal Family, headed by the Maharajah, in gorgeous Indian array. He was followed by the Princess of Leiningen, the Duchess of Cambridge, Princess Louise, and Prince Leopold, able to walk, I was glad to see ; Prince Arthur and Princess Beatrice, the Duke of Edinburgh and the Princess of Wales, and the King and Queen of the Belgians — an Austrian archduchess, who must have felt very heavy-hearted. Another pause and a burst of martial strains heralded the bridegroom's approach. I looked anxiously at the Prince to whom my darling's destinies are to be committed, and when he rose from his knees he stood exactly facing us. It is a fine manly presence and an open face, younger and better-looking than his photos lead one to expect. He turned many eager glances towards the door, and soon the bride advanced slowly, with flushed cheeks and eyes bent on the ground, looking very handsome. The Queen and Prince of Wales supported her, and her train was borne by eight bridesmaids: Lady Caroline Gordon Lennox, Lady Margaret Scott, Lady Albertha Hamilton, Lady Laura Phipps, Lady Alexandrina Murray, Lady Ernestine Edgcumbe, Lady Muriel Campbell, and Lady Mary FitzWilliam. I listened with beating heart to the solemn words of the service. Both 'I wills' rang out clear and distinct, the Queen gave her daughter away, and all was completed. It gave me pleasure to see the Prince kneeling with one arm on his mother's chair, and to see the hearty embraces between the bride and her mother and brother. Then the procession wheeled and passed out, and we found ourselves back in the drawing-room, where Major Elphinstone came and talked freely to me in the crowd. Presently we were told to go in to see the Queen, who was in the next room. I wanted to wait for Lady Mary Hood, but General Grey pushed us on, so I took heart of grace and followed Miss Maude to the door. People were shy, and ranged themselves on each side, instead of going up to the Queen, who stood in the middle of the floor evidently in a state of despair. Suddenly she caught my eye and beckoned me forward, so I went, made two curtsies, shook hands with her, and got a cordial grasp from Princess Helena, with a 'Thanks very much,' in reply to my whispered greeting, and found myself alongside of Lady Augusta, nearly tumbling over Prince Christian *en route*. But I never was more frightened in my life. The Royalties soon retired, and I had a bow from Prince Alfred and Prince Arthur, and took a good look at the King of the Belgians, who is much changed from the fair stooping youth I remember as Duc de Brabant. The Queen is plain and not graceful. Now came a move for luncheon, and to my great surprise and delight General Peel took me in. Didn't I feel cock-a-hoop! I am not sure that the scene in the Waterloo Chamber was not the prettiest of all—plenty of space, a buffet round three sides of the room, and the sun streaming down on gay uniforms and dresses. I saw no end of friends, including Mr. Stirling, who came and talked to me of Prince Leo, and then went back to town with Lady Augusta and the Dean."

The autumn was once more spent in a round of visits, ending with a month at Sotterley and Christmas at Arbury, where Louisa enjoyed meeting her old friend Miss Tina Montgomerie, the companion of many happy days spent under the same roof.

"*Arbury, December* 14.—Once more the anniversary of that sad day comes round, and even in the midst of gaiety one's thoughts turn to the Sunny South and that slowly darkening room. None the less I am happy, happier than I ever thought I could have been. Dear Papa would have been glad of this. We went a huge party to Gopsall ball, which was very lively, although not so smart as last year. It is curious the revolution that is taking place in dress and how we are going back to Empire fashions. Lady Mary Hervey was the handsomest girl in the room.

"*December* 15.—The hounds met at Arbury, but it was a pouring wet day, and we saw nothing. The party all dispersed, except four pleasant men—Colonel Wynne-Finch, Sir Theodore Biddulph, Captain Rowley, and Mr. Boughton Leigh, a snug combination, which Tina and I appreciate. Are we rivals? I sometimes think it. I can never visit the Gallery without a pang, when I remember that first visit to Arbury which brought me a friend, in Tina—and a lover! To-day my dreams are changed. *He* no longer occupies the prominent place which he did in my thoughts. Will the other dream come to anything? Is it for his happiness or for mine?—and more than all, do I care? does he think of me? The gentlemen hunted, and we walked to Astley and had a long, long talk, ending by touching on the subject which so deeply interests us both. I could not help admiring her unselfishness when she said, 'The question is, would marriage be for his happiness?' Is she fond of him, I wonder?

"*December* 28.—Yesterday we rode to Coventry, which looked very picturesque with its quaint old towers and market-place lined with stalls of ivy, holly, and mistletoe, Peeping Tom at the corner, and the tall spires rising through the fog. To-day Tina and I drove to the meet at Fillongley, a very pretty village with a fine old church and yew tree. Dear Tina departed in the afternoon, to my great regret.

"*December* 29.—I rode about with Charley, and had a long, long talk with him about the Roman Catholics and his lifelong struggle against them. ' It is hard,' he said, ' to be obliged to fight so constantly, but that is God's will, not mine. I have never suffered a personal interest to stand in my way.' That explains much. I can hardly trust myself to write what I think of him. Wild dreams again! He is persuaded that the Roman Catholic Emancipation Bill led to the passing of the last Reform Bill. ' The Jesuits,' he declares, ' wish to have absolute power, and when the people find that, they will take the power more and more into their own hands, and the consequence will be revolution and democracy.' Apropos of John Bright's firm having thrice been prosecuted for disregard of the Factory Acts, Charley lamented the inconsistency of so-called patriots, and gave it as his opinion ' that no one who read history could be sanguine. It gives one such an idea of the finality of things.' But is it really so? Surely the human race, take it for all in all, *has* advanced, *is* advancing, and *will* advance. It makes me feel how little I go to the root of things or judge them on fixed principles. Read—think—read—that is the only way to improve.

"*Willingham, January* 5, 1867.—A long talk with my cousins, Jessie and Louisa Boucherett, about the enfranchisement of women, for which they are most anxious. They told me some curious facts—the right of women to vote in Yorkshire under the House of Lancaster, their present right to vote in Sweden and Austria (much good it has done them there!), their right to vote in parts of France before the Revolution —a right of which they have since been deprived. Apparently aristocracies are more favourable to women's rights than democracies. I am not quite sure about it, and fear that in Roman Catholic countries female franchise would only give more votes to the party of the priests. Women are such fools, I believe even here half of them would vote as their parson or apothecary bade them. Jessie says, ' Enfranchise them, and they will obtain a better education.' I should be tempted to get the education first. I finished *Madame Thérèse*, which Mr. Kingsley so strongly recommended. I quite see its perfection from the artistic point of view—the perfection of extreme simplicity. I also see another thing. It points out the good and noble side of those ideas about *les droits de l'homme* which were afterwards so much trailed in the mud of the Revolution that their original beauty was altogether lost, and we fail to comprehend the enthusiasm which they at first inspired in many good men and true.

" *Stoke Rochford, January* 16.—We all went out to look for the shooters, and had enormous fun, tramping about in the snow and going off into shrieks of laughter, as also over a noisy round game in the evening. It is good to be young and foolish sometimes. In the afternoon I put on skates for the first time since 1859, and got on pretty well, considering. All the shooters came down, and the scene was gay and picturesque in the snow. Still more enjoyable was the late walk home through the still, calm air by the light of a brilliant moon. I sat by Mr. Heathcote and talked German to him, he being half a German by birth, and got on to Prussian politics. Lady Mary Turnor (Edmund's wife) is quite charming—so bright, clever, and sensible. He is indeed a lucky man.

" *January* 21.—We were kept in all day by the snow —playing battledore, writing, talking, playing whist, and roaming about the beautiful library, seeking honey from many a flower—a rare dissipation for me! In the evening had a long chat with Edith—she is a dear little thing, and I am sorry, very sorry, this visit has come to an end.

" 38 *Beaufort Gardens, March* 12.—A letter from

Lady Susan Melville, written at Princess Christian's desire, with a very alarming account of the poor Princess of Wales. Meanwhile, the political world looks dark and gloomy. Ministers shilly-shally with Reform, there is a Fenian rising in Ireland,—martial law to be proclaimed after two years' peace,—the Eastern question lowering ! Only Germany prospers.

"*April* 15.—Last night's post brought the welcome news of dear Bella's having a son, born on February 26.[1] This morning I hear that dearest Princess Christian is safe with a son, born at 5 p.m. yesterday. It was curious my getting news of these events two days running. God bless both the young mothers and their bairns.

"*April* 22. *Midnight.*—I positively cannot go to bed without writing a few lines to record my impressions of Mrs. Scott Siddons, whom we have just seen at the Haymarket as Rosalind in *As You Like It*, and in two scenes from *Romeo and Juliet*. I scarcely know which I admired the most. Her exquisitely lovely face lends itself equally to Rosalind's archness and to Juliet's despair. I only quarrel with the *scenes*—it should be the whole play. But she *must* take the town by storm. It is unworthy of the *Times* not to recognise it.

"*Richmond Park*, *May* 2.—I am sorry to leave London, but it is charming to be at home again, and I cannot describe what a delight this weather is to me —the delicate tints of the green, the hazy blue of the distance, the lark by day and the nightingale by night. I saw the poor imbecile wandering about, and even he seemed happy. Then I had a curious encounter with an old man who looked like a watchman and came and sat down by me. A troop of children gathered round us, and a casual remark on the beauty of the weather led insensibly to a long conversation on Scott and Irving, in whose works he seemed extremely well read. At night we went to Lady Harberton's ball, which has created great excitement, and proved a *grand succès*. All the pleasantest people in the neighbourhood were

[1] Miss Mainwaring, married to General Milman in 1866.

there, enough for spirit and not too many for dancing, lots of men, and everything well done. I danced all night without stopping. . . . A charming, happy letter from my dear Princess and an invitation to Arlington Street from Mrs. Newdegate. I finished *Le Conscrit*. It gives a most vivid idea of the miseries which these poor people endured in 1813, but is not as pretty as *Madame Thérèse* "

CHAPTER XI

London, Suffolk, and Frogmore

1867–1868

"3 *Arlington Street, May* 18.—Mrs. Newdegate, Harry, and I tried hard to understand last night's work in the House. It has resulted in the abolition of that wretched Compound Householder, whom we have been at such pains to realise, and a return to direct personal payment of rates—*i.e.* household suffrage pure and simple! What would have been said to this two years ago? I am very angry with Mr. Gladstone for condescending to threats of agitation. George Ridley says household suffrage is a return to the ancient basis of the Constitution. But in what altered conditions!

"*May* 22.—We went down home for our usual Derby Day party, and found it very pleasant but bitterly cold. We heard the result on our return to town,—'Hermit,' 'Marksman,' 'Vauban,'—whereby Mr. Chaplin, Sir F. Johnstone, and Captain Nicholl land £250,000—downright wicked, I call it. Lord Hastings says he shall win again in 1869.

"*May* 29.—I went to the Academy with Mrs. Newdegate, and was pleased to find that my taste coincides in a great measure with hers. Goodall's 'Rachel' and Frith's 'King Charles the Second's Last Birthday' divide the popular favour; Landseer's picture of the Queen on horseback, with John Brown holding the bridle and the Princesses in the background, creates a good deal of comment, but does not please me in the least. Mr. Weigall has painted a speaking likeness of Lady Rose, and there is a portrait of 'Herr Joachim—

a lamplight study,' by Mr. Watts, which in richness of tone recalls the Old Masters. We went to the Feildings' party, which was almost too small, but very pleasant, Lady Sherborne and Ida singing charmingly, and Sir Hope Grant accompanying on the 'cello. St. John joined us here, and went on with us to Mrs. Weguelin's ball—the cheeriest, jolliest, merriest concern I have been at for long. St. John went on swimmingly. I danced with him and C. Heathcote, Edward Ridley, etc., and Alpin took me to supper. Altogether I enjoyed it to an absurd extent.

"*June* 5.—A pouring wet day, which gave one time to write letters. In the evening to three parties, Lady Boyne, Mrs. Adderley, and the Ridleys, where all the cousinhood were collected, and very charming it was to see that splendid house open once more and the whole family assembled under its roof. The papers full of alarming accounts of robberies committed in broad daylight in the most public thoroughfares.

"*June* 6.—We rode with Robert Gurdon, J. Angerstein, etc. In the afternoon paid twenty-one visits without finding anyone at home. Dined with the Melvilles, and sat by Mr. Cumming Bruce, a most agreeable old gentleman. No subject amiss to him—society, politics, art, he talked about all agreeably and well. He said of C. N. N. that someone had lately remarked that he had more of the Demosthenes element than anyone in the House, the only fault of his speaking being that it was often too grandiose, ' always Cæsar saving Rome.' He told me a capital story of the Duchess of Gordon, when valsing was first introduced. When Mr. Whitbread remonstrated with her on allowing so indelicate a dance, she replied, ' Why, Mr. Whitbread, I thought you were the last person to object to the liberty of the press.'

"*June* 25.—I went to Ella's with Mrs. Hoare. Rubinstein played grandly, but the only piece I cared very much for was the Adagio from Beethoven's Quartett in G. At night to the Palace ball, which was quite unusually pleasant, less crowded, more dancing, and everyone looking uncommonly well. Royalties were few and far between, but Princess Louise looked very pretty and shook hands cordially, so did Princess Louis of Hesse. I danced with Mr. Abbot and Mr. Stirling, and had a long talk with the latter,—poor little man, he is so sorry to have left Court, —also with Charley, a quadrille half a mile long, and went to supper with him. Lady Adelaide Talbot looked lovely, and Lady Alice Hill very handsome, flirting with Lord Kenlies ; and Miss Wilbraham, Miss Napier, Miss Grant, Edith Turnor, and a number of pretty women were there.

"*July* 5.—Yesterday at the Levens' breakfast everyone was talking of the alarming accounts from Mexico and the probable postponement of the Review. This morning we found the sad news was but too true. Poor Kaiser Max![1] true, he was a usurper, but a usurper seeking to restore the blessings of peace and settled government to a country which for twenty-five years has been a prey to the most fearful anarchy. Of course it would have been wiser for him to have retired with the French troops, but one cannot help admiring the gallant, chivalrous spirit which fought so bravely to the last. And that poor Empress—bereft of her reason ! It is *too* sad. In the evening, we dined with Sir George Chetwynd, and I sat next to Mr. Clements, who is private secretary to Colonel Taylor. It amuses me to see how these people, Mr. Clements and Charley Fremantle,[2] worship Dizzy. It makes me fancy there must be something more about him than one gives him credit for. Perhaps, however, it is only that, as Mr. Clements observed, he knows how to govern men, and Gladstone does not. Mrs. Newdegate does not think Gladstone honest. I do, though it seems odd

[1] Maximilian, Archduke of Austria, brother of the Emperor Francis Joseph, elected Emperor of Mexico, 1864, deposed and executed by rebels, June 19, 1867.

[2] Hon. Sir Charles Fremantle, K.C.B., third son of 1st Lord Cottesloe, private secretary to Mr. Disraeli, 1866–1868 ; Deputy-Master of the Mint, 1868–1894 ; born 1834, died 1914.

that his own father and brother should have thought so ill of him. But of Dizzy's principles I have no opinion. See the dirt he has eaten this session! Only a fortnight ago he declared that if the House of Commons decided to give an additional member to six large towns, the Government must reconsider the whole Bill and their position. Of course some people were fools enough to believe him, and give him a majority of 8! And the following week he himself gives the additional member to four out of the six towns. I should like to know what mighty difference there is between four or six towns having an additional member to authorise such a line of conduct! C. N. N. is much disappointed at the rejection of the Cumulative Vote, brought forward by Mr. Lowe—a rejection due to unworthy party motives. . . . Colonel G——'s presents, letters, visits, and constant attentions worry me greatly. We do not know what to make of them, and it becomes every day more difficult to choke him off. Our friend James Hewett was married on Thursday to that nice, pretty Miss Hodgson. God grant it may turn out happily, but it was an ill omen, the news of his brother's death coming in the midst of the breakfast. Ah me! 'tis a strange world we live in.

"*July* 12.—I went to Mrs. Hardy's in Carlton House Terrace to see the entrance of the Sultan—an exceedingly fine sight it was. From Buckingham Palace to the Horse Guards the line was kept by the Guards, whose scarlet uniforms looked well against the bright green of the trees, while the grey towers of Westminster were immediately opposite. I could not help thinking how astonished some of those who sleep in the Cathedral would have been to see the Commander of the Faithful passing, not as a captive, but as an honoured guest through the heart of London. The procession was imposing, state coaches and Royal liveries, and an escort of Blues escorting the carriage containing His Imperial Majesty and the Prince of Wales. Big Ben boomed out as he passed, and he acknowledged the salutes of the crowd, which was neither very dense nor very enthusiastic, by raising two fingers to his forehead.

"*July* 15.—At 4 p.m. I was suddenly summoned back to town by a telegram from Harry, to go to the Opera for the Sultan's state visit. I rushed up, but it was already late. I got into the string at St. James's, Piccadilly, and never arrived till after the Royal party. However, it was a brilliant sight, the Royal box being placed in the centre of the house, immediately facing the stage and reaching up to the top, under a canopy surmounted by a crown. The Sultan sat in the middle, with the Prince on his right and the Duke of Cambridge on his left. His little son was in the next box, and a brilliant suite of both nations. The house was crammed, the most conspicuous figures being Madame Musurus,[1] the wife of the Turkish Ambassador, and Lady Dudley, who wore the most magnificent diamonds and emeralds which I have ever seen. The opera was *Masaniello*, a very pretty spectacle, with plenty of gay choruses and a good deal of dancing. We had only three acts, and then 'God save the Queen' was played, and they clapped the Sultan, who advanced to the front of the box, smiling and bowing and laying his hand on his mouth. He is an uninteresting-looking man, with a fat, roundish face, and a dark beard and moustache.

"Meanwhile, a scene of another kind and of far weightier import was going on at St. Stephen's. The Reform Bill has passed the third reading. This volatile world is thinking too much of Turks and Belgians[2] to attend to such grave matters, but it is a night to be remembered. This country is entering on a new era, and though we may hope and earnestly pray that all may yet be well with us, and that Mr. Lowe's and Lord Cranborne's lugubrious predictions may not be realised, it is beyond all human foresight to tell what will be the results of this session's work. One thing is certain, that all confidence in the heads of the Conservative

---

[1] Madame Musurus died on the following Friday, at the India Office ball.

[2] A corps of two thousand Belgian Volunteers came over on a visit to London in July, and were present at the Wimbledon Review.

party must be at an end. As far as they are concerned the results of the session may be summed up in General Peel's bitter words : ' There is nothing so insecure as a security, nothing with less vitality than a vital point, and nothing so elastic as the conscience of a Cabinet Minister.'

"*Richmond Park, Saturday, July* 20.—Harry Boucherett came to luncheon, and escorted us to the Camp at Wimbledon, where Princess Mary of Teck gave away the prizes very gracefully, assisted by Lord Spencer, who this year succeeds Lord Elcho as Chairman of the National Rifle Association. At the conclusion of this ceremony the Sultan arrived, and his whole procession drove in front of the Grand Stand— where we sat—to the Cottage. Then he mounted a milk-white Arab charger, superbly caparisoned, and rode down the lines, accompanied by our Princes and the Duke of Aosta, and attended by a brilliant staff. They took up their position by the flagstaff, where the Duchess of Cambridge and her daughters, Princess Mary and the Grand Duchess of Mecklenburg, and Duchess of Aosta were seated, and the march past began. First came our Belgian guests, with their priest, their *vivandière*, and their gigantic drum-major—a smart-looking body of men enough ; then the Artillery and Household Cavalry, the Third Hussars, and four battalions of our beloved Guards, Grenadiers, Coldstreams, and Fusiliers. It was a glorious sight ; they marched past like a solid wall, with their fine bands playing, and it sent a thrill through one to look at them. Then came the long, long stream of Volunteers, grand also, not only in outward strength and appearance, but with a moral grandeur of their own—making us all feel proud of a country which can send forth such an army of unpaid soldiers. It was indeed a memorable sight, and as one looked at the Sultan and his Circassians and Albanians in their white burnouses and turbans, one felt as if the whole thing had walked out of the *Arabian Nights* and might incontinently vanish.

"*July* 22.—Dear Mrs. Newdegate left us, after a

two days' visit, which has been a great treat. Among other interesting things, she told us a curious story of Lady Byron, which throws some light on the strange history of her separation from her husband. Mrs. Henry Tower (from whom Mrs. Newdegate heard it), a cousin of Lady Byron, was staying with her at her mother's place, Kirkby Mallory, in January 1816, six weeks after the birth of her child, Ada Byron, when a woman asked to see Lady Byron, and handed her a packet of papers. The contents of these papers Lady Byron never communicated to her cousin, but when Mrs. Tower came to her room afterwards she found her in a state of the greatest distress. When, at a later period, Lord Byron wished to induce his wife to live with him again, Lady Byron took these papers to the Lord Chancellor, whose comment after reading them was, ' Lady Byron is quite right, there can be no suit.' "

After another visit to Arbury, where Louisa made friends with Mr. Cecil Parker and Mr. Thurlow Astley, and enjoyed a lively dance at Mr. Dugdale's at Merivale, she went to spend the winter with her uncle and aunt at Sotterley. Here she took up parish work vigorously, held evening classes, trained the choir and played the harmonium in church, and arranged school-treats with renewed enthusiasm. A few shooting-parties and the company of her favourite cousin, St. John Barne, helped to enliven an otherwise quiet time, and her leisure hours were devoted to French literature, of which she never tired.

"*Sotterley, Friday, November* 22.—Parliament met on Tuesday, but what they have done as yet I hardly know. I have so many irons in the fire—a working-party for East London, teaching in the school, canvassing, playing chess every evening with my uncle—I have no time, and am getting into a chronic state of overwork. Colonel Charteris and Colonel Baring, who came to shoot the Big Wood, departed, both very pleasant men, and the latter a great flirt. Colonel G——, too, left, but not till he had taken a walk with me and frightened me nearly to death with his affectionate manner, poor dear old gentleman !

"*December* 12.—A most horrible Fenian outrage, in the shape of an attempt to blow up Clerkenwell Prison and rescue the Fenian prisoners. It failed as far as they were concerned, but spread death and destruction around. Six or seven people were killed, and thirty seriously injured. In truth, I do not know what we are coming to—the state of the country grows more serious every day. The alarm is universal in London, and more than thirty thousand special constables have been sworn in.

"*Sotterley, January* 1, 1868.—St. John arrived from Osborne, where he was ordered, at ten minutes' notice, with a hundred men, to guard Her Majesty from an apprehended Fenian plot. It appears these men had really formed a conspiracy to carry her off, and being on guard at such a time, as St. John observes, is anxious work.

"*January* 24.—On entering the dining-room this morning, I was shocked to find Mamma bathed in tears. My uncle was my first thought, but it was even worse —dearest Mrs. Newdegate is gone from among us. We were so utterly unprepared for the blow that it seems to stun one, and I can hardly realise it. She was quite well last week, but had a shivering fit and took to her bed on Friday. On Tuesday a change for the worse took place, and she died at seven. Oh, what a loss! To me she was a second mother, and next to my own darling mother there is no one in the wide world whose loss I could more deeply deplore. And I am but one among so many who will mourn for her. She filled a great position nobly, and was as fearless in her pursuit of duty as she was kind, generous, and large-hearted. As to Charley—to him it is an incalculable loss, and his grief is almost too sacred to be dwelt upon. Never was there such a beautiful relation between mother and son. Well may Mrs. Clerk write to me, ' We are all, rich and poor, panic-stricken.' One comfort I have in looking back: I do not think I ever grieved her. I think she was really fond of me, and once she went so far as to tell Mamma that she wished I would ' set my cap at Charley,' as she would like to have me for her daughter. It is gratifying to know this, for I never thought she wished it. That, however, will never be. Dear, dear Mrs. Newdegate! Well, hers has been a long, useful, and happy life, and now she is gone to that rest for which no one was ever better prepared. But oh—poor Charley!

"*February* 28.—I was totally flabbergasted by an invitation to Frogmore for this day week. Much as I like going to stay with my Princess, I am really sorry to leave the work here, which has been very satisfactory. Thank God for a pleasant and I hope useful winter, in spite of the one dark cloud which has overshadowed these last weeks. Now for a very different phase of life!

"*Frogmore House, March* 6.—This afternoon I drove to the equerries' door of Buckingham Palace, and was conducted the whole length of the building, to my dearest Princess, who received me in her own kind and cordial manner. Prince Christian soon joined us, and we three drove together through the Park to Paddington, where I was deposited in a saloon carriage with my dear Duchess of Atholl, Lady Clifden, Miss Stopford, and Lady Caroline Barrington. At Windsor, Prince and Princess Christian, Colonel Gordon and I drove straight here, and Princess Christian herself installed me in my pretty little room looking out on the water in front of the house, with Mellish next door and Baby on the other side. Our dinner-party consisted of Mr. Duckworth, Mr. Sahl, and Mr. Woodward, and was very agreeable. Both the Prince and Princess are so goodnatured, and set everyone at ease. Mr. Duckworth is young and good-looking, and very fond of Prince Leo—who sent me many affectionate messages. Only think what he told me about old Lady Smith of Lowestoft. She wrote a critique of the Queen's book to a friend of his, who thought it so wonderful for an old lady of ninety-six that he sent it to Mr. Duckworth, to show to the Queen, who was charmed. But poor old Lady Smith was much disconcerted when she discovered what had been done with her letter. We spent the evening over photos and autographs, of which both the Princess and

Prince Leo are making collections. It might have been an ordinary country house-party!

"*March* 7.—I breakfasted *en famille* with the Prince and Princess, and spent the whole morning hard at work gardening with her—planting violets and pinks, hoeing, raking, and watering! After luncheon, drove up to the Castle with the baby, a splendid boy, and went to see Princess Louise and Prince Leo, who has grown tall and *élancé*, but looks fearfully thin and transparent. There is an almost unearthly look about him, as if he would not abide long here; but this may only be my fancy. In the evening I drove up to the Castle with Colonel and Mrs. Gordon, who are kindness itself to me, and make me feel I shall always be grateful to anyone of the name of Gordon. Prince Christian told me to ask the Duchess of Atholl to look after me, but I was all right. We dined with the Household—a very large party. I sat between Major Elphinstone and Mr. Sahl, and after dinner we were joined by Prince Christian and Prince Arthur, who is exactly the height of Major Elphinstone now, Lord Bagot, Lord and Lady Tankerville, and Lady Clifden, who looked lovely, also came in, and we played a round game, a modification of Muggins, called 'Keep your Temper.'

"*Sunday, March* 8.—We drove up to service in the private chapel. A Mr. Rowsell preached extempore on 'charity.' Afterwards I was very graciously received by Her Majesty, who gave me a kiss and asked after Mamma. I spent the time till luncheon with Princess Louise and the Princes, looking over autographs, and we were as jolly as sandboys. After luncheon in the Octagon Room, I came back with the Princess, who presented me with the Queen's book, in which Her Majesty had written this inscription : ' To Louisa Bowater, in remembrance of Balmoral, from VICTORIA R. March 8, 1868.' I am very much pleased. At four we rushed up to St. George's, and had an unusually fine service, with the Hallelujah Chorus by way of anthem, the solo parts sung by the most exquisite boy voices. The recollections stirred up by the sight of the historic banners and the love of chivalry imparted by the prayer, ' God save our Most Gracious Sovereign the Queen and all the Companions of the Most Noble Order of the Garter,' combined to render the service very impressive, and the beautiful words of the Lesson rang in my ear : ' Set your affections on things above, not on things on the earth.' I dined alone with the Prince and Princess, played chess with His Royal Highness, and had a long, long talk with my beloved Princess, who is just as dear as ever. The more I see of Prince Christian, the better I like him. He is so pre-eminently sensible,—the very thing for her generous, impetuous nature,—and he is extremely kind-hearted, and most universally liked. Major Elphinstone spoke most highly of him last night. It is so pretty to see her little matronly ways, ordering the dinner and attending to her household, and so wisely careful, which makes me respect her all the more.

"*March* 9.—This morning Princess Christian went out with the Queen, and I rushed up to St. George's, left Mellish with the Duchess's maid, and walked home alone, as it is *selon les règles* for me to go backwards and forwards to the Castle alone. Colonel and Mrs. Gordon came to luncheon—she is so nice and kind to me—and the Duchess of Marlborough with Lady Cornelia Churchill, who is very pretty and pleasing. Princess Christian drove them back to the station, while I went up to the Castle and took a charming drive with Princess Louise, and had tea with her and Prince Leo. I dined alone with the Prince and Princess, and talked chiefly of politics—even of that delicate subject, German politics. I like all he says, he is so wise and just ; and he is so devoted to her, and she to him. There cannot be the shadow of a doubt as to their perfect and entire happiness.

"*March* 10.—Princess Helena was strumming valses on the piano to me after breakfast when the door opened and in walked the Queen, followed by Princess Louise. Her Majesty was very kind, as indeed she has been each time I have seen her. The Prince and

Princess went off at twelve to luncheon at Marlborough House, and I went up to the Castle, where we had a large and amusing luncheon-party—the Duchess of Wellington, Lord Bagot who goes out of waiting to-day, and Lord Skelmersdale who comes in, a very handsome and agreeable person, Lord Bradford, and Mr. Gathorne-Hardy, who came down for a grand ' function,' to use the Court word, *i.e.* the presentation of an address to the Queen on the subject of the Fenian outrage. We waited in the corridor to see the City magnates arrive, 125 strong, which they did in three fine coaches and a long procession of Windsor flies. Poor people! they had exactly fifteen minutes for luncheon and three for the presentation of their address, as it was not read, so their loyalty was scarcely appreciated as much as it might have been, but some of them were allowed to see the rooms; so we skedaddled, and I waited in Miss Stopford's room till the rain was over. We dined with the Queen, rather a large party—Sir Thomas and Lady Biddulph, the Duchess, Lady Clifden, and Dr. Robertson of Balmoral. It was decidedly lively for Court, and I was amused talking to Lord Skelmersdale and Lady Clifden, who are both charming, and so pleasant to look at. The Queen was most gracious to me, as usual, and expressed her regret to hear I was leaving to-morrow.

" *March* 11.—And so ends another Court visit. The Princess told me when I arrived that the 11th was the first anniversary of the death of Prince Christian's mother, so he might prefer to be alone, and they both took the kindest and most cordial leave of me. It has been a most charming visit, without a contretemps of any kind; and it is the greatest pleasure to see my beloved Princess so thoroughly happy, with a devoted husband and one who is so pre-eminently sensible and kind-hearted. I feel thoroughly satisfied and very grateful."

CHAPTER XII

A VISIT TO SILESIA

1868

"*Richmond Park, Saturday, July* 4.—Strange that on the fourth anniversary of the reception of a letter which, to say the least of it, has tinged my thoughts for the last four years, another important communication should reach me. Princess Christian asks me to go with her to Germany for seven weeks at the end of this month. So flattering and delightful an offer was of course instantly accepted, and I look forward with unmingled satisfaction to the trip.

"*Osborne, Cowes, Isle of Wight, July* 25.—I came down here *via* Surbiton and Southampton, met Colonel Finch on board the steamer. He made himself very agreeable—got me a fly when we landed, and told me that Mr. Disraeli was coming here to-night. I was shown to my room by a pampered menial in red, who brought me some tea, and Princess Christian and Lady Augusta Stanley came to see me before dinner. I dined with the Household. Our party was neither large nor lively, and included two of Prince Louis's gentlemen and the Princess's lady, Fräulein von Graney, who is very nice and kind. Lady Clifden, Lady Augusta, and Mr. Disraeli joined us afterwards. The latter is evidently an original, to judge from the scraps of conversation which reached my ears : ' Passion and fashion are the two things which divide human nature,' ' When you do away with the indefinite, you destroy the romance of life,' and some remarks on travelling in the days of

Roderick Random, in a waggon, being much more amusing and improving than it is now.

"*Sunday, July* 26.—We have just been listening to a very good sermon preached by Mr. Prothero, at service in the house, before a very small party. Neither the Queen nor Princess Louis was there, but I saw Prince Leopold, much grown and looking very well. It is a beautiful day, and the Queen breakfasted out of doors. Princess Louise came to see me, and I gave her the autographs, which pleased her very much. At tea I saw Princess Alice's three dear little girls, such pretty children—Victoria, Elisabeth, and Irene, a two-year-old child.[1] Dizzy did not show all day, but at dinner I had the luck to sit by him. He was very sententious and pedantic, I thought, affecting to be superior to hunger, which he called a savage passion; but I liked what he said of Prince Christian, that he combined tact with a deep, slow-moving mind, and agreed that he was both sensible and good-natured.

" At ten o'clock the whole Household assembled at the Queen's Entrance, and Her Majesty and all the Royalties came down to see us off—our party consisting of Prince and Princess Christian, Mr. Sahl and myself. Prince Louis of Hesse and Prince Arthur accompanied us on the barge to the Admiralty yacht *Enchantress*, which was anchored in Cowes road. It was like a Venetian scene, rowing in the still starlight night, and the splash of the oars and the lantern-light falling on the bronzed faces of the sailors reminded me of the lovely spring twilight when we landed at Osborne six years ago.

"*On board the 'Enchantress,' July* 27.—When I woke we were off Eastbourne. It was a most lovely day, and the white cliffs of Dover looked beautiful as we steamed past them and made for Ostend. We sat on the bridge all day reading and working, and I wrote a letter to

---

[1] Victoria, born 1863; married Prince Louis of Battenberg, 1884. Elisabeth, born 1864; married Grand Duke Sergius of Russia, 1884. Irene, born 1866; married 1888, Prince Henry of Prussia, brother of the Kaiser.

mother under difficulties, using the paddle as a desk, while Princess Christian held my paper. We landed at 5.30 p.m., travelled by Bruges and Ghent to Brussels, where we had an hour to wait, and trotted out over a fine ' Place ' to supper at a restaurant, where the Prince and Mr. Sahl were busy mixing the salad. At 10 p.m. we went on by Aachen and Düren, reaching Cologne on a glorious summer morning.

"*Central Bahnhof, Cologne, Tuesday, July* 28.—We had some difficulty in getting rooms, but I ended in getting two hours' delicious sleep on a pile of feather-beds on the floor, and felt as fresh as a four-year-old when I woke. Prince Christian and Mr. Sahl took me out at twelve to see the Cathedral, which is certainly wonderfully fine, especially the west front, where you see the new and old part of the building side by side, the grey weather-beaten stones with tufts of grass here and there contrasting with the whiteness of the new work. I was struck with the deep devotion of the people attending Mass, and saw the Schatzkammer with the richly worked shrine of the Three Kings, and the great painting known as the ' Dombild,' representing the Adoration of the Magi, with the patron saints of Cologne, Ursula and Gereon. A Prussian General, who was Colonel of the Prince's old regiment, came to dinner, a pleasant old gentleman, covered with decorations—which, however, do not count for much here—and buttoned up to his throat in uniform. We left the hotel at three, driving round the Dom, and suddenly through a quaint old archway I saw a swift-flowing green stream—it was the Rhine. Our journey lay along its banks at first, but we changed at Giessen, and the railway made a great bend round a valley studded with picturesque villages. This was the former territory of the Duke of Nassau, and a good deal of bitter chaff passed between the *Herrschaften* and Mr. Sahl touching the treatment he has received from the King of Prussia. The transition must be very painful to many, but the gain to Germany as a whole is undeniable. After Giessen came Marburg, with the beautiful church and castle which was the home of St. Elizabeth of

Hungary; then Luther's Eisenach. But by this time it was quite dark, and as nothing was to be seen we sang and made ourselves very merry by the way. Soon after one, we reached Gotha, where we were met by Prince Christian's elder brother, the Duke of Augustenburg, whose name is familiar as the claimant of the Schleswig-Holstein duchies, of which Prussia deprived him. He brought us to his house, where his wife, the daughter of Princess Hohenlohe and niece of our Queen, received us in the most friendly manner, and after a comfortable high tea we were glad to go to bed.

"*Augustenburgisches Palais, Gotha, July 29.*—I spent the morning in my rooms, going down to luncheon at one and to dinner at five, after which we took a drive by Goldbach, all through this fertile valley, bounded by the blue hills of the Thüringerwald. The villages are dirty; the men wear blue blouses, and the women carry baskets on their backs, like the Boulogne fishwives, and seem to work very hard. Princess Hohenlohe, the Duchess's mother, whom I once met at Osborne, is staying here and is particularly pleasant; and there are four charming children—Princesses Victoria, Carlina (short for Caroline Matilde), Louise, and Prince Ernst Günther.[1] I have made great friends with their little Swiss governess, Mlle Bost, and see a good deal of her.

"*July* 30.—At 12.30 we all drove to Rheinhardtsbrunnen, a *Jagdschloss* belonging to the Duke of Coburg, about nine miles from Gotha, at the foot of the Thüringerwald, which has been lent to the Crown Prince and Princess of Prussia, who are staying here for six weeks. It is an exceedingly pretty little place buried in trees,

[1] Augusta Victoria, born 1858; married William II., Emperor of Germany, 1881.

Caroline, born 1860; married 1885, Frederic, Duke of Schleswig-Holstein-Glücksburg. Her daughters—Victoria, married 1905, Charles Edward, Duke of Saxe-Coburg, son of Prince Leopold, Duke of Albany; Alexandra, married Prince Augustus of Prussia, 1908; Helena, married Harald, Prince of Denmark, 1909.

Feodora-Louise, born 1866; married 1889, Frederic Leopold, Prince of Prussia.

Ernst Günther, present Duke of Schleswig-Holstein Augustenburg, born 1863; married 1898, Dorothea, Princess of Saxe-Coburg.

something like Balmoral, and as we drove into the courtyard we saw a dead stag lying on the pavement, shot by the Duke, who is here for a day or two as his niece's guest. It was shy work being launched into such a large party of strangers, but all the Crown Princess's ladies and gentlemen were most kind to me and made me cordially welcome. They were already at luncheon when we arrived, and made me sit down by Herr von Seckendorf, a Prussian officer who had been attached to our Abyssinian expedition and told me much that was interesting. Count Kalckreuth, a distinguished painter, and his daughter, Countess Anne, a nice little thing of sixteen, Count Eulenburg, Countess Reventlow, who is the Lady Caroline Barrington of the Household, and Mlle d'Harcourt were among the party. After luncheon, Countess Brühl took me a beautiful drive up into the hills, which are clad to the very summit with magnificent woods—such Scotch firs as I have never seen in England mixed with maples and sycamores, and here and there great rocks like those in the Happy Valley at Cannes, with clear streams running between the red stones—as one of the ladies put it, ' *ein echt classischer Wald.*' We returned to the Castle about seven, had a fussy sort of high tea, after which I was presented to the Crown Prince and Princess, who were both extremely kind and spoke quite affectionately of dear Papa. The Princess remembered how he used to carry her about in his arms, and the Prince says he knew him as early as 1851. I hope to see them again at Potsdam, where they return next week, when we go to Berlin. The Crown Princess wants us to go and stay there, but as the palace they occupy there belongs to the King of Prussia, his leave must be asked, which my Prince and Princess will not hear of, and considering the present state of things one can hardly wonder. We left about 8.30 and drove back to Gotha, after a very enjoyable day. I forgot to mention that we also saw the Duke of Coburg; he is not particularly good-looking, and not at all like the Prince Consort.

"*July* 31.—Directly after breakfast I marched off

with Mellish to the Schloss, a large ugly building, finely situated on the top of the hill round which Gotha is built, and commanding beautiful views of the surrounding mountains. It contains a fine collection of paintings, including a curious screen of 1526, with most realistic renderings of New Testament subjects, one of which, the Parable of the Mote and the Beam, struck me especially. In the Kunstkammer upstairs are many interesting relics—an ivory prayer-book exquisitely bound by Cellini which once belonged to James I., a ring of Mary Stuart's, the Duke of Alva's dagger, the hat, gloves, and boots worn by Napoleon at Tilsit, and a wonderful cabinet of Chinese and Japanese antiquities. This Castle is not inhabited by the Duke of Coburg, who during the six months which he spends here lives in another palace, near our house. In fact, the place swarms with palaces and shady *Alleen*, which with the pretty green boulevards make Gotha a very pleasant town. In the afternoon I took a walk with the little girls and Mlle Bost, through the Orange Garden, to Friederichsthal, a pretty little palace occupied in 1862 by our Queen. The Crown Prince came to dinner, and was full of fun. One curious scrap of conversation I overheard. They had been talking of coronations, and Prince Christian remarked that King Christian IX. of Denmark had never been crowned. ' It is true,' replied the Crown Prince, ' I wonder why ? ' ' He had no time,' put in the Duke of Augustenburg quickly; ' your father spoilt his appetite for that ! ' In the evening some Gotha people came to tea—a Herr von Holzendorff, whose daughters were full of enthusiasm for England, and one of whom sang very prettily with her mother, a pupil of Mendelssohn. We were rather jolly at our side table, and I was glad to see another little specimen of German life.

" *Sunday, August* 2.—I have had two rather dull days, as Prince and Princess Christian go to Rheinhardtsbrunnen every day, and the evenings are not particularly amusing. To-day I went to the Lutheran Church in the Castle with Mlle Bost, and heard a very good sermon on ' Judge not, that ye be not judged.' After luncheon, we had a delicious drive with the young Princesses, and some people out of the Duchies came to dinner. It is touching to see the devotion of these Holsteiners to the Duke. It puts me in mind of the Jacobites and Charles Edward.

"*August* 3.—Countess Brühl came over early from Rheinhardtsbrunnen and took me by train to Weimar. We passed the strong fortress of Erfurt, where Luther lived in the Augustinenkloster, and the picturesque castles of the three Gleichen, from which Count Gleichen takes his name, and reached Weimar, which is just such another pretty little town as Gotha, only that it lies in a hollow, instead of being on a hill. Count Kalckreuth and his nice little daughter met us at the station, and lionised us in the most friendly way. We visited Schiller's tiny little house, passed Goethe's, which unfortunately is not shown, and the Theatre where so many immortal works saw the light—a wretched little building. The town is rich in statues—we saw those of Schiller and Goethe, standing hand in hand, as well as those of Herder and Wieland, who both lived here. We visited the Stadtskirche, which has several portraits of Luther, and the Palace, which contains priceless treasures of art, including ten of the original drawings of the Apostles' heads in Leonardo's ' Last Supper,' and a fine collection of drawings by Raphael, Michelangelo, and Leonardo. Last of all we drove to the Friedhof, or cemetery with the Grand Ducal vault, where Goethe and Schiller are buried. Our hospitable friends took us back to dinner in their own abode,—a flat in a big old house once occupied by Marlborough, with a lime avenue before it,—and after a good rest we returned to Gotha, greatly pleased with our day.

"*August* 5.—We all drove out into the mountains and walked through the Thüringerwald to Rheinhardtsbrunnen, getting lovely views of the Inselberg, the highest peak of the range, and sat out under the trees at the inn, like ordinary mortals, drinking our coffee. We got back to Gotha about eight, and found the evening a little long, for at 1 a.m. we left the Augustenburg Palace and travelled by night to Berlin.

"*British Embassy, Berlin, August* 6.—I slept all the way, and saw nothing of the country but one or two old castles in the moonlight. Lord Augustus Loftus, the British Minister, met us at the station, and took us to the Embassy. One of the Crown Princess's ladies came to drive about with the Princess on a shopping expedition, so I was free, and after a scrub and an hour's sleep, Adèle Arnold, my old Sotterley friend, took me for a drive through the Thiergarten, a sort of combined Hyde Park and Bois de Boulogne, and then all along Unter den Linden, which is certainly a very fine street. At the east end are a number of stately buildings : on the right the King's Palace, Opera House, and Crown Prince's Palace ; and on the left, the University, Arsenal, and Guard House, with Rauch's imposing monument to Frederick the Great in the centre. Adèle dropped me at the Crown Prince's Palace, where I lunched with the Household, while my *Herrschaften* were lunching with the Crown Prince, who since he dined with us at Gotha on Friday had *only* been to Ems to dine with the King, to Coblenz to breakfast with the Queen, to Bonn to receive a D.C.L. degree and take part in the festivities on the Jubilee of the University, to Hanover for a public banquet, and to Stettin on military business. A pretty good round ! However, there he was, as fresh as a lark and as merry as a cricket, when after luncheon we set out with him as our cicerone to see the sights. We drove in two Court carriages (the first decent turn-outs I have seen in Germany) first to the Gewerbe Museum, a sort of South Kensington Museum, in which the Crown Princess takes great interest, and then past the Schloss, a huge pile of buildings in the Lust Garten, to the Fine Arts Museum. This is a handsome building outside, but still handsomer inside, with a grand double staircase adorned with frescoes by Kaulbach. We walked through the Sculpture Gallery and Egyptian Museum, but did not attempt to look at the pictures. What struck me most was the size and space of the Galleries and the beauty and appropriateness of the decorations. Our collections may be as fine or finer, but we do not half do justice to them. After this we drove by the unfinished Rath-haus, a handsome red-brick building in Italian style. Everything at Berlin, I notice, is either Italian or Greek—there is nothing Gothic.

"I was not sorry when at last we returned to the Embassy, for I was almost giddy with all I had seen. We dined at eight, and were a snug little party—only the attachés, Mr. Plunkett and Mr. Lascelles with his nice little wife, a daughter of Sir Joseph Olliffe, the physician to the Embassy at Paris. Lady Augustus is at Baden, and Berlin is as empty as London in August. Only Lord Augustus annoyed me by insisting on dragging forward the Schleswig-Holstein question and saying he wanted justice done to the Danes, by giving them back North Schleswig—a great want of tact and good taste when the Prince and Princess were his guests!

"*August 7.*—We left Berlin for Potsdam at ten, and were met at the station by the Crown Prince and Princess, two or three gentlemen, and kind Countess Brühl, who started with me and Mr. Sahl at once on a lionising expedition. First we visited the Orangery, a handsome Italian building in the style of the Medici Villa in Rome, with pretty views over the terraced gardens which have been so marvellously created out of the barren sandy soil. Then we drove to Sans Souci, passing the famous Windmill, and saw the rooms once occupied by Frederick the Great, and left untouched, with the clock still pointing to the hour of his death. A portrait of him on the wall struck me immensely by the air of strong determination and the keen blue eyes which seem to look one through and through. We crossed the Havel and drove along its banks to Babelsberg, the present King's favourite plaything—and a charming toy it is! Every tree has been planted by his own direction; the grass is kept like an English lawn, and the views over the river and lakes are delightful. Within, it is furnished in the simplest way. The King has just a camp-bed, and the walls of his rooms are hung with military prints. I was amused to see a large map of the campaign of 1866! The Crown Prince told me that our Queen was delighted with the place when she stayed here in 1858, and made several very pretty sketches in the gardens. We drove back to Potsdam through the Park, past Glienike, the home of Prince Frederick Charles, the Red Prince, who played so distinguished a part in the late war, and were thankful to reach the New Palace and sit down to luncheon. They were all so kind and pleasant, and after luncheon took me all over the Palace, which was built by Frederick the Great at immense cost, after the Seven Years War, to prove to the world that his resources were not exhausted. In one of the state apartments we fell in with the Crown Prince and Princess, who were most kind and good-natured, and told Countess Brühl to show me their own rooms. She has grown stout, but has the same round bright face, and her voice is exactly like the Queen's. He is a charming man, so frank and genial, and he looks so well in the dark blue uniform faced with red, and white duck trousers, which he and all his gentlemen wear. Everybody goes about in uniform here, and every second building you see is a barrack. The Crown Prince and Princess's rooms are very pretty and comfortable. Her audience-room is lovely, all fitted up with blue and silver; and his big writing-table amused me, with a high stool in front, like that of a clerk in a counting-house. After that, we visited the Friedenskirche, which was built, on the pattern of a basilica surrounded with cloisters, by the late King, who is buried here. A little chapel close by contains the grave of the Crown Princess's little son Waldemar, who died just before the war. There was a sleeping head of the child, quite buried in flowers. As we drove to the station I had an animated discussion with a Lieutenant von Magdeburg, who escorted us, on Macaulay's sketch of Frederick the Great, with which to my surprise he was well acquainted. He fired up indignantly when I expressed my entire agreement with our historian's condemnation of that King's father,

Frederick William I., and defended his cruel treatment of his wife and children with a heat which I could not have shown if the character of any of the Georges had been attacked; but, as Countess Brühl remarked to me, these are sacred traditions for the Prussians. I must say I think few young English officers that I know are as well read in German as the Lieutenant is in English literature.

"*Schloss Primkenau, Waltersdorf Schlossen, Saturday, August* 8.—Last night Her Majesty's Mission saw us off from Berlin station at 11 p.m. We had a very hot journey, passed Frankfort in the moonlight, changed at Haasdorf, and reached Waltersdorf this morning at 5 a.m. Here an open carriage met us, and we had a pleasant drive over flat country, half marsh and half forest, until we came suddenly upon an extremely pretty Castle, surrounded by other houses, in the midst of a fine wood. Here the old Duke's daughters and Prince Christian's sisters, the Princesses Augusta and Henriette, received us, and I was thankful to go to bed in my pretty little room. This property, I learn, was bought by the Duke, when he was compelled to leave the Duchies in 1853, as a shooting-box, and has only gradually become his home. The marshy land has been reclaimed by a judicious system of drainage and irrigation, neat farmhouses have been erected, and the condition of the peasants greatly improved. The Castle lies between the village and the wood, and consists of several different houses. I live in one of these with my Prince and Princess, and we trot over to the Duke's house, the Castle proper, for luncheon at one and dinner at five. A public road runs between our house and the courtyard of the Schloss, and flocks of sheep, carts, and droves of pigs are constantly passing by, and in the evening the village children often come close up to the windows and stare at us. In fact, it is the most primitive and patriarchal kind of life I ever saw. At 1 p.m. we crossed the courtyard to luncheon in the Schloss, and I was presented to the Duke, a very courteous and gentlemanlike old man—rather an invalid.

His three daughters, Princesses Augusta, Amelia, and Henriette, are each kinder and more amiable the one than the other, and I especially like the youngest one, Henriette, who reads a good deal and is very intelligent and sensible.[1] After dinner, we went out for a long drive in open carriages—the only thing to be done in this intense heat—and had a thorough farming expedition. The Duke is a great farmer, and breeds horses and cattle on a large scale, and is proud of his fine race of horses, half Arab and half Percheron—a French breed. All the women work in the fields and go about barefoot, with large straw hats and very short skirts. The carts are mostly drawn by bullocks. There are no gates or hedges, only now and then a ditch divides the fields. The wages, as a rule, are two Thalers or six shillings a week, but this includes the rent of their very miserable-looking cottages."

The next four weeks were spent at Primkenau, where Louisa was treated with the utmost kindness by the Princesses of Holstein and their ladies, and saw an interesting side of German life. But it was, as she often repeats in her letters and Journal, in many respects a dull life, and the extreme heat made it almost impossible to take any exercise or even sit out before evening. Occasionally she took early rides with one of the Princesses in the beautiful Oberwald surrounding the Schloss, and enjoyed driving a pair of pretty little piebald ponies bred on the Duke's farm, while Princess Christian drove in a carriage drawn by a pair of greys. Sometimes a few neighbours came to dinner, and once or twice heated political discussions took place, to which Louisa listened with keen interest. On Sunday, August 23, an address of welcome to Prince and Princess Christian, which was to have been presented on their arrival had it taken place at a less unearthly hour, was finally delivered, and by the Princess's desire Louisa wrote the following account of the ceremony to the Queen:

"About half-past six, the procession approached,

[1] Princess Henriette, born 1833; married 1872, Dr. Jean d'Esmarch of Kiel.

headed by the town band, followed by the Schützengilde, the Bürgermeister, and thirty young girls dressed in white with red and blue scarves, to represent the English colours. Seventy had wished to take part in the procession, but, alas! enough white muslin was not to be had in the neighbouring town. Fortunately the sun shone, and the scene was a very pretty one. When all had taken their places, the schoolmaster's daughter presented the Princess with an immense bouquet of white roses, scarlet geranium, and heliotrope, and recited a marriage ode, composed by the pastor's son for the occasion. The Bürgermeister then made a speech, expressing the pleasure which the news of Prince Christian's marriage had given the inhabitants of Primkenau, and their regret at being unable to express their satisfaction at the time of the Princess's visit last year, on account of the Duchess's death a few weeks before. A loud ' Hoch ' was then given by all present, and the Prince expressed his thanks and those of the Princess in a few short, well-chosen words, after which a hymn was sung. Then the old Captain of the Schützengilde came forward, and apologising for a *third* expression of welcome by the old German saying, ' Alle guten Dinge sind drei,' congratulated the Prince as a member of their fraternity, and added that he hoped His Royal Highness would prove as successful in life as in sport, and would not fail to attain perfect happiness. A ' Hoch ' was then given for the Duke as head of their ' Gilde,' and for the ducal house, to which the Duke responded very briefly; and the Prince and Princess walked round and spoke to several of the people, whose evident attachment to the ducal family it is very pleasant to see.

" *Friday, August* 28.—Princess Augusta's birthday, so there was much giving of presents, health-drinking, etc., and I had a lovely bracelet from my Prince and Princess. They do seem such a happy, united family party, it is quite a pleasure to see them. We all went in spite of rain and cold to watch the shooters and have luncheon with them—and a very merry one it was—at one of the farms, called the Adelaiden Au, where a small room has been built for this purpose. A Kiel Professor, Herr Mikkelsen, was my neighbour, and amused me very much, although I think he is a little inclined to evolve camels from his inner consciousness. Perhaps we all of us are. He is writing a life of George I.'s unfortunate Queen, Caroline Matilda. Princess Augusta gave a most interesting account of the interview which she and Princess Amelia had with the King of Prussia at Baden last summer, and how they pitched into him. Certainly the whole family has been most extremely ill-used by him, especially as he always professed such affection for them, and began by acknowledging their claims. Doubtless the annexation of Schleswig-Holstein will be better for Germany in the long run, but there has been a deal of dirty work to achieve it. The other evening I had a long talk with Princess Augusta, in which she endeavoured to convince me that it was not for Germany's advantage that the little Courts should be swept away and the privileges of the nobility diminished; she even declares that in the Duchies, for instance, people look for the coming of the French as a deliverance. But all this is hard to believe. Heavy taxation and other hardships there must be, no doubt, but better Germany as she now is than as she was in the beginning of this century.

"*August* 31.—A lovely morning after the rain, and I took a walk by myself in the Oberwald, examining the beautiful trees which grow with such wonderful luxuriance in this sandy soil, and wondering if our system of forestry is the right one. In the evening we drove to a long-talked-of party at Count Lohgau's at Reuthe. We started before 6 p.m., and did not return till 1 a.m. I never was more amused. There were about fifty people—some marvellous figures—and a few Prussian officers. We began with some music, which was wonderfully good for this out-of-the-way part of the world. Then came dancing, two polkas, far better danced than we in England can dance it, and three quadrilles with a most complicated last figure, directed by a Prussian officer with spectacles and stentorian lungs. Excepting the Duke of Augustenburg, who came with us, I knew none of my partners; but here it is the fashion to dance what are called 'extra-tours.' Anybody may come up and making a bow to your partner, twirl you off for a turn and bring you back to him. I enjoyed it, as the men were all alike to me, and I love dancing, but it would be a great bore if one had a really pleasant partner. After the dancing came supper, which was very funny. We sat down to little tables without cloths, and helped ourselves to plates and knives and forks from trays which were handed round. An interminable number of dishes followed, and the whole thing lasted an immense time. But that did not matter, as we were so jolly at our table and made a furious row. Count Ranzow, my partner, is most amusing, and made noise enough for two; and I never would have believed that Fräulein von Krogh, the Princesses' companion, had it in her to 'chaff' so well. Princess Christian looked so nice, and it is a pleasure to watch her constantly-changing expression.

"*September 2.*—I spent the morning copying a letter from the Queen to Princess Helena, to be sent on to the Crown Princess, giving an account of her ascent of the Righi, which she enjoyed thoroughly. The heat has been intense at Lucerne, but it is cooler now, and Her Majesty is very well and in great spirits. Five wretched Prussian officers came to dinner, looking very miserable, and Fräulein von Krogh being ill in bed, a young Fräulein von Buchwald and I had to manage the tea, which was rather fun, but not altogether easy in a country where the men never dream of helping you, and only make endless bows.

"*September 6.*—And now the last day has come, and to-night we start for home. Although quiet, it has been a pleasant *séjour*, and I can never forget all the kindness that I have received in Germany. Much, too, I have seen and learnt during the past weeks, and I shall always look back with pleasure to my Silesian visit."

CHAPTER XIII

Sir Rainald Knightley

1869

THE year 1869, which was destined to be so momentous a one in Louisa Bowater's life, opened under somewhat gloomy auspices. The death of her kind relative, Mrs. Newdegate, and the consequent cessation of her pleasant visits to Arbury and Harefield, and of her gay seasons in Arlington Street, made a considerable change in her circumstances. At the same time, the end of the year 1868 saw the last of her yearly visits to the old home at Sotterley.

"*Monday, December 7.*—Prince Christian says he thinks a Journal is a bad thing, because in the heat of the moment you record things which had better be forgotten. Maybe! nevertheless, to-day's record must be written. Family troubles have compelled my mother to come to the irrevocable decision—which had I been a free agent should have been made long ago—that this place must see us no more. I don't deny that I feel it deeply, more deeply than I could have believed possible, but so it must be: the comfort is that Mamma sees it quite as I do. And so the happy life here is over for ever! The bitter thoughts with which I started on my morning walk faded before the serene beauty of the day, which succeeded a night of fearful storms, and it was with a calmer feeling that I looked round on the beloved landscape. Ah! well-a-day! Doubtless it is best so—God will find other work for me to do. . . . I do try to do the little things that come in my way, but oh! it seems so sad to think of

SIR RAINALD KNIGHTLEY, BART.
1869.

[*To face p* 160.

the mass of want and misery there is in the world and to be able to do nothing.

"*Christmas Eve*, 1868. — Another Christmas at Sotterley and the last! I little thought, when eight years ago we spent our Christmas alone together—Mamma and I—that thus it would be. I don't feel very Christmassy, and yet as long as my sweet mother is spared to me the world can never be very desolate. The wind moans and whistles sadly, and I do not feel attuned to the angels' song. God comfort all who are in trouble, sorrow, need, sickness, or any other adversity.

"*January* 2, 1869.—I took leave of poor old Hannah, and said good-bye to several of the old friends whom I have known from early childhood. It seems very hard to leave these poor people with no one to look after them; but God's ways are not our ways, and He will doubtless provide for them, and give me other work to do. We leave early to-morrow for Norfolk. And so ends life at Sotterley.

"*Weeting, Brandon, January 7.*—Certainly this is a very amusing party—quite out of the usual Norfolk groove—Mr. and Mrs. Gurdon, Colonel and Mrs. Gardiner, Count Maffei and Lord Henley, whom we met last year at Haddon. I walked with Colonel Gardiner, Mr. Gurdon, and the children to join the shooters, and watched a very exciting 'hot corner,' and had a pleasant chat and much chaff with Lord Henley on the way home.

"*January* 8.—I had a most charming walk with Colonel and Mrs. Gardiner all across country to join the shooters on the other side of the Ouse; and the sky reflected in the water, with the river winding away into the distance, and groups of tall Scotch firs scattered about, while the afternoon sun lighted up the red houses of Brandon, formed a picture worthy of one of George Eliot's novels. It was quite dark when we returned, and I sat by Lord Henley again at dinner, and listened with amusement to a conversation between him and Count Maffei on proposing and being refused!!!—a matter of which I have had some experience, although I naturally kept my own counsel. Count Maffei was also very interesting about the impending appointment of a new Italian Minister, saying that it was of the utmost importance to a new country like Italy to be socially as well as politically represented in this country.

"*Richmond Park, March* 13.—I was much shocked by the news of the Duke of Schleswig-Holstein's death. I feel so sorry for those poor Princesses, hurrying the one from England and the others from Pau, to arrive only in time to see their father die. It takes my thoughts back to Primkenau—to the last drive on the last evening, and to the pleasure that it was to him to see all his children around him. How well I remember the way in which he paced up and down the gallery one evening, cursing Bismarck, and lamenting the folly of his son in ever putting trust in his promises. Certainly he was a fine old gentleman. We drove in the Hammersleys' beautiful open carriage, which they have kindly placed at our disposal while they are at Brighton, and called on Lady Alice Peel at Marble Hill, the abode of George II.'s mistress, Lady Suffolk, and one of the few remaining villas which the last century made famous or infamous. Lady Alice was most interesting, and amused us with a story of 'Lady Beaconsfield,' as Mrs. Disraeli is now styled, taking her home in her carriage from the Drawing-room, after Lady Alice and Lady Salisbury had been discussing if they would speak to her! I had no idea the split in the Cabinet of 1867 was carried as far as that."

Louisa's interest in politics remained as keen as ever, although she seldom now had the opportunity of discussing these questions with Mr. Newdegate. Her remarks on the admission of John Bright into the Cabinet are characteristic of the period, liberal as she considered her own opinions to be.

"*December* 4, 1868.—Ministers have resigned! The decided Liberal majority, 112, — chiefly, however, furnished by the borough,—made it evident that there must be a change before Christmas, so Mr. Disraeli has adopted the wise and dignified plan of resigning at once, and Mr. Gladstone was with the Queen for two hours yesterday. And that artful dodger, Dizzy, has got his wife made Viscountess Beaconsfield, so he keeps power and she gains rank. I really give him great credit!

"*December* 12.—The new Cabinet is formed, and the Right Hon. John Bright has been *not* sworn of Her Majesty's Privy Council, but has made the affirmation required by law. Alas, poor Queen! However, maybe he will be more moderate when shackled with the responsibilities of office. The other members of the Cabinet are not very Radical. Mr. Lowe is Chancellor of the Exchequer; Lord Clarendon goes to the Foreign Office; the Duke of Argyll is Secretary for India; Lord Granville, Colonial Secretary; Mr. Cardwell, Secretary for War; Mr. Bruce, Home Secretary; Sir W. Page Wood, Lord Chancellor; Mr. Goschen, Poor Law; Lord Hartington, Post Office; Mr. Childers, Admiralty. Well, pray God it may go well! We live in anxious, troublous times."

Her affection for the members of the Royal Family was undiminished. She records the birth of Princess Christian's eldest son with joy, and thanks God for the safety of her beloved friend. A month later she heard of Prince Leopold's Confirmation with deep interest, and read Archbishop Tait's beautiful charge on this occasion, which the Prince had sent her, with a heartfelt prayer that its "noble aspirations for his future career may be realised."

On the 29th of March she officiated as bridesmaid at the marriage of her friend Lady Julia Melville to General Robertson, and made the now habitual reflection that she herself seemed destined for a single life. She frankly admitted that she would have preferred to be married had the right man presented himself, but at twenty-seven she hardly thought this to be likely. She had, as we have seen, refused many offers and never regretted her decision, and although in one case she owned that her feelings had been at the moment touched, she remained heart-whole. She little dreamt when, on the day after the Roehampton wedding, she accompanied her mother to pay a visit to Mr. and Mrs. Gage at Firle, that she was about to meet her future husband.

" *Firle Place, Lewes, Tuesday, March* 30, 1869.—We left home early and went up to London Bridge, whence we had a charming *trajet*, through very pretty country, to this delightfully quaint old place at the foot of the Downs—a great rambling house with a central courtyard, a splendid hall and fine picture gallery. A most agreeable small party—our kind host and hostess, Mr. and Mrs. Gage, her brother, Sir Rainald Knightley,[1] and Sir Thomas Munro, two exceedingly pleasant men, with whom I thoroughly enjoy mental trotting out.

" *Friday, April* 2.—The morning was devoted to croquet, which we played insanely all yesterday in the teeth of a cold east wind. In the afternoon we had a charming walk to the top of the Downs behind the house. We could not see the view, but it was great fun scrambling down, and I had much talk with Sir Rainald. I wonder if I begin to understand him? He strikes me as a very good average sort of man: clever, without being a genius; good, without having a very high standard—in short, not unlike myself. I wonder what his faults are? Mr. Thomas arrived, and nearly killed us with his Sussex stories of stool ball—a curious game, not unlike cricket, which the women in this part of the world play. Oh dear ! how I wish I could remember what I read ! I stumbled so fearfully over Madame des Ursins, in our conversation at dinner, and I *did* think I knew her !

" *Saturday, April* 3.—We travelled up as far as Croydon with Sir Rainald and Mr. Thomas—a most amusing journey. I seldom remember so agreeable a party, and am quite sorry the visit is over. We got home by 3 p.m., and I devoted myself to copying some interesting notes which I read at Firle on Browning's ' Childe Roland to the dark tower came.' It is

[1] A day to be kept for all time.—L. K.

wonderful how they clear up its meaning, though I doubt if the best sort of poetry ought to be a sealed book to all but the very choicest spirits. George Eliot's ' Spanish Gypsy ' is, I confess, far more to my mind."

That first meeting at Firle made a deep impression on the girl's mind, and she returns to it in her Journal at intervals all through the next few weeks.

" My head very full of last week," she writes on April 15, " but I must not dwell on it too much. . . . Nora Campbell told me of Sir Rainald's long devotion to Lady ——. It is a touching story, and I like all I hear of him."

One day at the end of April Louisa caught sight of Sir Rainald in the Park, and was much provoked because, seeing a crowd of men round the carriage in which she was sitting, he only bowed and passed on. A month later, she and her mother came up to spend a month with a cousin, Miss Wheatley, in Beaufort Gardens, and met Sir Rainald several times. He called on Lady Bowater, joined Louisa out riding in the Park most mornings, and danced with her at the Palace ball. Political interests drew them together, and the Irish Church Bill, which had lately been brought forward by Mr. Gladstone, was the subject of many of their conversations.

" *June* 19.—A charming ride in the morning, and a long talk with Sir Rainald about last night's division in the House of Lords. There was a majority of 33 in favour of the second reading. The Bishop of Peterborough's peroration was certainly magnificent. Lord Derby says it has never been surpassed during his long parliamentary career ; Lord Ellenborough, that there has been no such speech since the days of Plunkett. Certainly there never has been a question in my time which has agitated the upper classes so much, but still I hold to my opinion that it is a simple act of justice and earnestly trust that the Bill may pass. Sir Rainald has done his best to induce Lord Salisbury to vote in its favour, and, humanly speaking, this has decided the fate of the Bill and avoided a fearful collision. But many good men and true look on this as an act of sacrilege, involving the country in a downward course of irreligion. And yet! do not justice and truth go before everything? and may we not on our side say, ' Fais ce que dois, advienne que pourra'? God alone can know what were Mr. Gladstone's motives for bringing it forward. I wonder if he has misgivings? Expediency would have been best consulted by leaving it alone.

"*June* 27.—My thoughts were busy with the important event apparently impending in my life. I am anxious and nervous about this week, yet why be so? All is in God's hands : He will guide all as is best.

> 'I see my way as birds their trackless way. . . .
> In some time, His good time, I shall arrive;
> He guides me and the bird. In His good time!'

"*June* 28.—We went to a breakfast in Buckingham Palace Gardens, at which the Queen herself was present and the Viceroy. It was a pretty sight and a fine party, but—tell it not in Gath!—very cold and very dull. The Queen did not speak to us, and Sir Rainald was, to say the least of it, very odd, very different from what he has been. I can't make him out.

"*July* 2.—I rode with Miss Mordaunt, and Sir Rainald joined us. We had the pleasantest talk that we have yet had—all the uncertainties of the last two days have quite vanished. Dear mother is so good. That is the worst part, but I think, with God's blessing, we shall be very happy."

Several pleasant rides and political discussions followed. Then came a large dinner-party, after which Louisa had a long talk with Sir Rainald, and a ball at Mrs. Angerstein's, which she enjoyed more than any other of the season, and ended by going down to supper with him. On Lady Bowater's return to Richmond Park, Sir Rainald came down with his sister, Mrs. Gage, to a large croquet party, and invited Louisa and her mother to pay a visit to Fawsley, his country place in Northamptonshire, during the second week in August. This time there could be no doubt as to his intentions. "To think," adds Louisa, in recording the fact on July 17, "that probably the greatest event in my life will be decided in less than a month."

On the 10th of August she accompanied her mother to Fawsley, and describes the beautiful drive from Weedon and through the park to the fine old house, which Sir Rainald had recently enlarged and restored.

"*Fawsley, Daventry, Wednesday, August* 11.—We took a long and charming ride in the morning round this beautiful park, with its woods and glades, deer, water and distant views, and had much pleasant talk, though upon everyday subjects. In the afternoon we played croquet. Sir George Osborn and his daughter arrived to luncheon, Lord and Lady Listowel came to tea, and Charley Newdegate arrived to dinner. I sat between him and Sir Rainald—a curious combination. All seems to me to be passing in a dream. I am not excited, only quieter than usual, but very happy.

"*Friday, August* 13.—No, I can't write any description of to-day, but I have plighted my troth to Rainald Knightley, and from the very bottom of my heart I pray God that He will help me to be a good wife to him. He is so good and nice, I am sure we shall be happy together. There is but the *one* wrench —of leaving Mamma. It was all settled coming out of the dear little church here, which Rainald took me to see this morning.

"*August* 14.—The Osborns departed, to our great joy, and we had a long, long talk, and a delightful ride in the afternoon. What have I done to deserve such love, such happiness? I can only pray God to help me to be a little worthy of it. There is not a word he says that does not realise my highest ideal. And the Gages are so kind.

"*Sunday, August* 15.—A very, very bright and sunny bit of life. The agitation of the last few days has a little bit subsided, and every hour makes me know him better and love him more dearly. We had such a nice walk together all round the lovely Dingle, where the sun was shining through the trees, as it will, I hope, shine into our lives. Church was not till late in the afternoon, but it was very nice to tread that little path again and in God's own house to pray for a blessing on our new life.

"*August* 16.—Papers and carriages!—sublunary, practical considerations, but very pleasant ones withal. He is *so* kind, only too much inclined to spoil me and waste money upon me. We had some nice walks besides, and long, happy talks.

"*August* 17.—Another happy walk and talk before we left. He is so nice and good—well, I can't write about it, so it is no use trying. We came home. What a change since we left here!

"*Richmond Park, August* 18.—I was hard at work all the morning, writing letters to announce the happy event. I really do not know how to be happy and thankful enough—there never was anything so perfect as it all is—as *he* is. I only hope my head will not be turned! I am not worthy of such happiness, but it comes from God. I only hope it will not make me selfish. Dear Mrs. Gage has been so good to me—she *must* feel it, but she is so unselfish; and Mr. Gage and Mr. Knightley are so kind too. Never was anyone more affectionately welcomed.

"*August* 19.—I had my first letter from him— such a nice one—and answered it. I hope he will like mine. I am getting a little more used to my happiness now—but oh! it does seem so wonderful. I destroyed all memorials of my foolish old penchant for Captain B——, and have told Rainald all about it, except the name.

"*August* 21.—Letters! letters! letters!—and another charming one from him. Lady Leven came in the afternoon, and brought me my first wedding present. I sometimes still feel as if I must pinch myself, to be sure it is really me!"

The next week Sir Rainald Knightley spent a few days at Thatched House Lodge, and Louisa enjoyed showing him her favourite haunts. Together they rowed on the river and drove or walked to Hampton Court, Coombe Wood, and White Lodge. When he left for Scotland she was surprised to find how much she missed him, and how she hungered for his letters, and began to wish for October 20—the date on which her wedding day had been fixed. A busy month followed, during which crowds of visitors found their way to Richmond Park. Princess Mary and Prince Teck, Lord and Lady Russell, and many other old friends came to wish Louisa joy, and presents from Princess Louise, Prince Leopold, the Duke of Grafton, and many of the Royal Household arrived. Early in October her " absent Knight " returned to town, and she spent her days shopping with him in town and walking about Kensington Gardens, or riding in their former " happy hunting-grounds "—Rotten Row.

" Such lovely things he gives me ! " she writes,—" a dressing-case, sets of pearls and diamonds,—all quite too beautiful. I hardly feel as if they ought to belong to me. To-day he brought with him a beautiful pair of carriage-horses, which he has bought for me, and we went together to Heal's after furniture. I felt so odd, choosing and ordering things, for he doesn't help one bit ; and then we walked home to Beaufort Gardens through the closing twilight, arm in arm. Oh dear ! this is such a happy time—happier than my brightest dreams could ever have pictured it ! "

" *Richmond Park, Sunday, October* 17.—The last Sunday of my maiden life. All day yesterday I was very busy tearing up and arranging old letters, finishing all my preparations. It is rather sad closing the old, happy life. But next Sunday, please God, I shall kneel beside my husband at His altar and consecrate our new life to Him. Now I look back, I see how God has been training me all along for the work He intended me to do in life. I have been waiting, how often impatiently and faithlessly, with little of that concentration of purpose of which Stopford Brooke speaks so well in a sermon which I read this morning. Standing on the eve of a new life, I dedicate my future to Him to-day. May He teach me to be a loving, obedient wife, a kind, wise mistress! May He—I know He will—give me strength to do my duty in the state of life to which He has called me!

" . . . It is the last day—dressmaker, shopping, signing settlements, arranging presents which poured in all day, and finally exhibiting them to any number of people. Such was its outward history. Within, I am perfectly calm, peaceful, happy, thankful ; and my darling mother bears up bravely. I cannot write more —*Mit Gott.*"

CHAPTER XIV

Marriage

1869

On the 20th of October 1869 Louisa Bowater was married to Sir Rainald Knightley in the church of St. Peter, Eaton Square, from the house of her cousin, Martin Smith, in 13 Upper Belgrave Street. The wedding is best described in her own words.

"*Fawsley, Wednesday, October* 20.— Our wedding day! The new life has begun, our solemn vows have been plighted before God's holy altar, and my darling Rainald and I are man and wife. Now—odd as it seems—my Journal must be true and faithful still, and give an account of our wedding day. A glorious day it was, sunny and bright as heart could wish—a glad omen, I verily believe. I did not feel in the least nervous— at least I felt there was too much to be done and thought of, to allow myself to give way. My exquisite wedding bouquet was a present from dear Princess Christian, as well as the lace veil which I wore. When I was dressed and waiting, the band of the Scots Fusiliers marched past. It was a most curious coincidence, like a greeting from my dearest father, and it brought tears to my eyes. Martin Smith was most kind, and came to fetch me when all was ready. Of course Uncle Frederick Barne, who gave me away, behaved in an eccentric manner; but my bridesmaids were all there to time, and looked very pretty and nice in their pink frocks. They were Fanny Corbet, Tina Montgomery, Susan Rowley, Julia Angerstein, Evelyn Bathurst, Helen Ellice, Frances Vanneck, Caroline Duncombe, and

Mina Nugent. I had a long time to wait first for Rainald and then for Mr. Knightley and Mr. Story,[1] who married us ; but I did not regret this, as it gave me plenty of time to collect my thoughts. Dear Rainald was very nervous, Mr. Knightley still more so. I felt so perfectly happy in my choice that I could repeat the solemn words quite steadily, although Mr. Knightley went so fast, it was very difficult. It was very soon over, and Mamma, Uncle Frederick, Charley Newdegate, Mr. Gage, and Sir Thomas Munro witnessed the marriage. The next half-hour was rather trying, going about talking to people. I seem to have seen most of my old Sotterley friends—Adèle Arnold, Lucy Wormald, and St. John. At one they all went in to breakfast, and we retired to a snug little luncheon upstairs. At 2 p.m. we went down, took leave of a few, very few, people, my darling mother bearing up beautifully and dear Tina being most helpful—and were off, the group of pink bridesmaids looking so pretty on the steps. The N.W.R. were most polite, giving us a saloon carriage all to ourselves. Lord Denbigh came and congratulated as we started, which also recalled dear Papa, and then away we sped to Blisworth, where a special engine brought us to Weedon. Here our new carriage was awaiting us, and at Dodford the Daventry volunteer corps was drawn up and gave us a hearty cheer. Our progress through Newnham was a small triumph, bands playing, bells ringing, arches of evergreens and flags and loud cheers all the way. The tenants, about thirty in number, very well mounted, were drawn up at the park gates, and escorted us to the house, the foot-people racing alongside, tumbling over each other in the fern in all directions. The bells of the dear little church that we love so well rang merrily, and all the school-children were drawn up in front of the house. As the carriage stopped, the tenants formed up outside the portico, and a very pretty and touching address

[1] The Rev. Valentine Knightley, Rector of Preston Capes and Charwelton (1836–1878), and Rev. W. Story, Rector of Fawsley, both cousins of Sir Rainald.

was read. My darling husband spoke well and clearly in reply, and did not break down as I feared he would, for he felt it deeply, and his golden heart was indeed touched. The children strewed flowers at my feet as I stepped out of the carriage and we passed in, and so ended the long, trying, but happy day, and Rainald and I entered on our new life in our own home. May God bless it to us!

"*Fawsley, October* 25.—The days go by so quickly it is hard to keep account of them. But it is very nice being quietly at home after all the excitement of the last few weeks. Of course one feels rather shy and strange, but dear Rainald is so thoughtful and considerate that I shall soon feel quite at home. We take walks round the Dingle and all about this beautiful park, and have paid visits to the gardeners' and woodmen's cottages, and went all through the hothouses with the very loquacious head-gardener, and saw the nursery, which would fill mother with envy and is in beautiful order. So indeed is everything about the place, although I plague Rainald's life out with chaff for his ignorance of the cottages and farms, and most of his own concerns. Yesterday we drove in Rainald's American spider to Canon's Ashby, a most deliciously quaint old place with a very fine church, and met the owner, Sir Henry Dryden, a still quainter person, with blunt, rough manners, and such queer old-fashioned clothes, looking exactly as if he had stepped out of Dickens's novels. To-day I have entered on my housewifely duties and been all over the house with the housekeeper, Mrs. Eaton, and an upholsterer from Daventry, arranging, contriving, and glorying in my new domain. I felt myself to be my mother's own daughter! I hope the workmen who are still busy decorating the new rooms will be gone in a day or two, and then we can arrange the furniture and chintzes, etc. Rainald went to Daventry on justice business this morning—absolutely the first time we have been separated for half an hour. I was much gratified by a most kind and gracious letter from the Queen with a very pretty turquoise and diamond locket, containing a photo of dear Prince Leo, with a lock of his hair and underneath ' From V. R., October 1869.'[1] I have been strolling about alone, and enjoy feeling myself the mistress of this beautiful place. There are lovely walks and rides in all directions, and I have been riding one of Rainald's hunters, which carries me very well, in the afternoons, or driving my new pony-carriage, which is charmingly light and easy. Last night we talked politics, and Rainald showed me the correspondence about last year's election, in which he was very badly treated, also Lord Derby's letter of 1866, offering him the Under-Secretaryship of Foreign Affairs, ' the best thing out of the Cabinet,' which he refused because he would not serve under Disraeli. He told me of his attack on the Whig Government that year and of a lucky hit which he made in comparing the Premier to a tipsy man, clinging to a lamp-post, unable to advance, fearing to retreat, unable to stand, yet afraid to fall. He said it set both sides of the House in a roar, while Mr. Gladstone sat scowling with rage, quite unable to see the joke. He also showed me a curious letter from Lord George Bentinck, giving the whole history of his resigning the leadership of the Conservative party, on the Jew Bill in 1848, and another from Lord Cranborne, the

[1] The following is the text of the autograph letter addressed to Lady Knightley on this occasion by Her Gracious Majesty, Queen Victoria:

"BALMORAL, *October* 22, 1869.

"MY DEAR LOUISA,—I was unfortunately not aware that your marriage was to take place *before* the end of this month, and therefore delayed sending you my offering. This morning I see that your marriage took place on Wednesday, and I hasten to write these lines to wish you every possible happiness in your married life for *many, many* years to come! I need not say that I shall ever take the warmest interest in your welfare. The accompanying locket contains the likeness and hair of Leopold, the poor little boy whom you were so kind to, when God took your dear fathers both away on the same day. I hope you will often wear it, in recollection of him and me. You will be glad to hear that he is particularly strong and well—*unberufen*, as the Germans say. Your dear mother will, I fear, miss you dreadfully. Hoping ere long to have the pleasure of seeing you and your husband,—Believe me always, dear Louisa, yours very affectionately, VICTORIA R.

" Pray send me your photograph, as well as Sir Rainald Knightley's."

present Lord Salisbury, anent the Reform Bill of 1867, in which he says that 'John Bright has been haranguing Beaumont on the dangers of household suffrage and this democratic Bill!' It is curious to see how they all seem to treat Delane, the Editor of the *Times*, as a power in the State."

The hunting season opened early in November, and meets of the Pytchley, Bicester, and Duke of Grafton's hounds were the leading events of the winter at Fawsley. Lady Knightley began by driving her husband to the meets, and before long took to riding to hounds herself, and became Sir Rainald's regular companion in the hunting field. Another occupation which proved of absorbing interest was the state of the cottages on the estate, to which she early turned her attention.

"*November* 18.—Rainald and I walked to Down Farm directly after breakfast to look at a cottage where some people called Ames live, which has only two bedrooms and where a third is wanted. Imagine how much I felt in my element! I hope we shall be able to make a tidy job of it. But I am not quite happy in my mind about these poor people, since, as they live in a 'shod,' *i.e.* a cottage attached to an outlying farm, the farmer, not unnaturally, objects to their keeping a pig. I was glad to find out, however, that they have two sons living at home, one earning fifteen shillings a week as blacksmith here, the other working as a shoemaker at Badby. . . . I must say the people here are much better off than with us in Suffolk, and you see big flitches of bacon hanging up in every kitchen. But I fear it will be some time before much can be done here in the way of cottage-building, the farms absorb so much money, and even now all the cottage rents are spent in repairs."

Lady Bowater, to whom her daughter confided her new anxieties, offered to bring a little book of Lord Cawdor's on *Housing* with her to Fawsley, a proposal which Louisa welcomed eagerly, being, as she says, "always on the look-out for hints." But Sir Rainald added a postscript—half in jest, half in earnest—to his wife's letter, begging Lady Bowater on no account to bring Lord Cawdor's book, adding : " Louisa's bother about Ames's cottage has cost me thirty pounds already. She and her cottage improvements are the plague of my life ! "

" *November* 19.—This afternoon we drove out in what Rainald calls ' prelatic pomp,' to return visits in the neighbourhood, and found every single mortal at home. Rainald's face of utter despair was very amusing. I am afraid our near neighbours, as I have seen them so far, are indeed ' nigh-bores.' I never saw a less promising set. But I dare say I shall find some people worth knowing. When we return from the round of visits over which Rainald is already groaning, I must go and see some of the poor people and begin to know them, which I have not yet had any opportunity of doing."

Two days afterwards Sir Rainald and Lady Knightley left home to pay visits to old friends in Suffolk, and she had the great pleasure of taking her husband to see Sotterley on the way to Lord Stradbroke's house at Henham. After a day or two at Claridge's Hotel, they went on to Longleat, where Lady Knightley found plenty to interest her in Lord Bath's noble house with its pictures and splendid library. A visit to the Duke of Beaufort at Badminton was followed by a few days at her " dear old Arbury," where she had the joy of meeting her mother, and only longed that Mrs. Newdegate could have been present to share in their happiness.

" *Saturday, December* 18.—We left dear Arbury with regret, but oh ! with what exquisite happiness did we find ourselves once more in this beautiful home— all the new rooms we have furnished ourselves waiting for us, and presents and letters without end. This first return home was indeed a happy one.

" *December* 22.—I was hard at work all day, arranging books and furniture, up to the last moment, when I had the pleasure of welcoming the dear mother to my own home ! Dear Mary Wheatley arrived soon afterwards. It does seem so natural and pleasant to have them here. The ground is covered with snow, and there is a sharp frost. A real Christmas scene!

"*December* 23.—The whole evening was spent in the servants' hall, assisting in the distribution of dear Rainald's charities to the inhabitants of these six villages — Charwelton, Hinton, Woodford, Badby, Newnham, Everdon, and Preston. The system is admirable, and has gone on for generations, and it was pleasant to see the poor women trotting off with bundles of calico, flannel, and blankets. In the afternoon arrived Sophy and Henry Gage, their boy Harry, Sir Thomas Munro, and Val—a charming family party. My dear old Philip also came.

"*Christmas Day.* — Our first Christmas together! It seems so strange to think that this time last year we did not even know each other by sight. Certainly this is far the happiest Christmas I have ever spent. How shall I ever be thankful enough? Was ever mortal so blest as I am! Everything this world can give is bestowed upon me, and it all flows from my husband's love, and that is the gift of God. Work too He has given me—the work I have wished for so long. Oh, may He also give me grace to do it faithfully! My heart is full. I cannot write all I would."

These passages from Lady Knightley's Journal show how complete her happiness was in these early days of her wedded life. Marriage not only satisfied the cravings of her heart; it placed her in a position for which she was admirably fitted, and above all it supplied the opportunities for work which she had long desired.

The family into which she had married was one of the oldest and proudest in Northamptonshire. The Knightleys traced their descent lineally from Sir Rainald de Knightley, who came over with the Conqueror and is mentioned in Domesday as "lord of the manor of Knightley in Staffordshire." They settled at Fawsley in the reign of Henry v., and in the course of a few years became the owners of no less than thirty-three manors in Northamptonshire. The oldest part of the house goes back to the first half of the fifteenth century, and the kitchens and noble hall with its fine oriel date from about 1500. Early in the sixteenth century, a Sir Richard Knightley married the daughter of the Duke of Somerset, who was Lord Protector during the minority of Edward VI., and became notorious for his championship of the Puritan cause. The " Martin Marprelate " tracts, the first of which appeared in 1588, the year of the Armada, are said to have been issued by a secret press set up at Fawsley in a small chamber above the oriel window of the great hall. His descendant, another Richard, inherited the Puritan traditions of the family and was a strong supporter of the Parliamentarian party. An interesting record of proceedings in Parliament from 1623 to 1640, in his handwriting, is still preserved at Fawsley, and has been partly printed by the Camden Society. Many conferences between the chief Parliamentarian leaders took place at Fawsley, and during the Civil Wars a printing press is said to have been set up once more in the secret chamber. Sir Richard's eldest son married a daughter of Hampden, but opposed the King's execution and took an active part in the restoration of Charles II., who knighted him at his coronation. These historic memories were of the deepest interest to Lady Knightley, who devoted herself eagerly to the study of the Knightley pedigree and portraits, and made many fresh discoveries in the family history. The leading part which the Knightleys had played in more recent county politics was to her a still greater source of pleasure. From 1852, when his father, the venerable Sir Charles Knightley, retired from Parliament, Sir Rainald had been one of the representatives for South Northamptonshire, a post which he filled during the next forty years. Lady Knightley, we have seen, had been keenly interested in politics from her childhood. Now she threw herself with ardour into all her husband's pursuits, and afforded him invaluable help in his public career.

On the other hand, the situation was in many respects a difficult one, and all her courage and wisdom were needed to overcome the obstacles in her way.

Life at Fawsley was fashioned on the most antiquated pattern. As Disraeli wrote of his Buckinghamshire home: "It was sylvan and feudal." Sir Charles Knightley had been a typical country gentleman of the good old days. He farmed his own land, brewed his own ale, and reared a famous breed of cattle known by the name of the Knightley shorthorns. After he gave up his seat in Parliament to his son in 1852, he lived altogether at Fawsley, surrounded by the members of his family. His wife, Selina Hervey, granddaughter of the first Earl of Bristol, had died in 1856, but his only daughter, Sophy, who married Lord Gage's son in 1840, made her home at Fawsley during most of the year, together with her husband Mr. Gage and their only son, Harry. Two nephews who had taken orders and held family livings—Valentine Knightley, rector of the neighbouring parishes of Preston Capes and Charwelton, and William Story, who was at the same time rector of Fawsley and curate to his Cousin Val—made up the party, while Mr. Gage's old friend, Sir Thomas Munro of Lindertis, also spent the winter at Fawsley and brought his horses with him for the hunting season. Fawsley, situated as it is in the heart of South Northamptonshire, was an admirable hunting centre, and, after the fashion of their neighbours, all the men of the party rode to the neighbouring meets of the Pytchley, Bicester, Warwickshire, and Duke of Grafton's hounds. Sir Rainald himself always said that he began to hunt at the age of six, and never left off till he was seventy-six. As in many other of our remote country districts, the feudal system still prevailed to a remarkable extent on the vast estates which had so long been Knightley property. Women and girls dropped low curtsies, men and boys touched their caps and pulled their forelocks at the sight of any of the quality. Doles of warm clothing, boots and shoes, flannel and calico, sheets and blankets were distributed in the great hall every Christmas. A fat ox was killed, and joints of beef were given to labourers and cottage tenants. But of the real existence of their poorer neighbours and dependants, of their habits and thoughts and ways of living, the inmates of the big house knew nothing. It was much the same with their more well-to-do neighbours, the smaller gentry and clergy of the neighbourhood. Once a year a haunch of venison from Fawsley Park was sent to each of these as a graceful recognition of their existence, and before an election Sir Charles himself drove round in his high phaeton and called at all the principal houses to ask the owner to do him the honour of recording his vote in favour of Cartwright and Knightley, the Conservative Members who had represented the county for many years. Sir Charles kept this practice up to the time of his death, when he was over eighty, and drove round in his American spider, attended by a single groom, to canvass his old constituents on behalf of his son Rainald, who was about to take his place. There are many Northamptonshire folk who still retain a lively recollection of the fine old man as he was in these last days of his life. I remember myself how my brother and I used to be taken as children to have luncheon and play with his little grandson, Harry Gage, and a very awe-inspiring function it was. We were solemnly ushered into Sir Charles's presence, and followed the little procession, led by the bent, silver-haired old man, who walked leaning on a gold-headed cane and supported by his daughter, a gentle, sad-faced lady, into the dining-room. Tall liveried footmen stood round the table, the old butler behind Sir Charles's chair, and a haunch of venison on a massive silver dish was always set before him. We were naturally very shy on these occasions, and our elders were very silent. The Gages said little; Mr. Knightley, in our eyes a very formidable personage, never opened his lips; and Sir Charles generally contented himself with patting my brother's head and giving me a kindly smile. But what made up for all was the sight of the glorious riband border, for which in those days the gardens of Fawsley were famous, and which attracted visitors from all the countryside. I can still remember the glowing colours of the long rows of hollyhocks, gladioli, brilliant Mrs. Pollock geraniums, blue lobelias, and yellow calceolarias, between the grass walks and ponds, surrounded by the red-brick walls of the old kitchen garden.

When in 1864 Sir Charles died, full of years and honour, the famous riband border was broken up. A troop of gardeners were dismissed, and thousands of geraniums and lobelias were given away. The house was shut up. Mr. and Mrs. Gage settled with old Lord Gage at Firle, and Sir Rainald went to live in town. Up to this time he had always said that it was impossible to marry, since, as he explained to his old kinsman, Lord Cottesloe, if he left Fawsley it would break his father's heart, and if he took his wife to live there it would certainly break her heart. But now he felt that it was incumbent on him to marry for the good of the family. So he determined, first of all, to improve the house at Fawsley and adapt it as far as possible to modern requirements. With this object, a whole suite of new living-rooms facing south and an entrance porch were added, which certainly increased the comfort of the house if they could scarcely be said to add to the beauty of the old Tudor buildings. Then, with his sister's help, he deliberately looked about him in search of a suitable wife. In a fortunate hour he met Louisa Bowater, and wooed and won her for his bride. Many of her friends wondered how this brilliant, handsome, and much-admired girl could be content to marry a man who was more than twenty years her senior and who had little that was likely to attract her fancy. Sir Rainald was a singularly silent and reserved man, with none of the geniality which had made his father so popular with his neighbours and constituents. Tall and dignified, with fine features, iron-grey hair, and a slight stoop, he was an aristocrat to the tips of his fingers. But his courtly manner and distinguished bearing attracted Louisa from the first. He talked well when he chose to exert himself, had a considerable knowledge of French literature, and was a great authority on whist. His abilities commanded the attention of his colleagues in the House of Commons, and his utterances, although rare, were always thoughtful and to the point. As an old county member and a foremost representative of the large landowners in the Midlands, he was treated with respect by successive ministers and was distinguished for his personal devotion to Lord Salisbury and his aversion to Mr. Disraeli, whom to the end of his life he regarded with deep-rooted distrust. Mr. Gladstone always said that he considered Sir Rainald to be one of the cleverest members of the old Tory party and beyond doubt the most dexterous debater in the House. His fastidious taste and pride in his ancient lineage often excited the mirth of his opponents, and on one occasion, when he was sitting in the smoking-room of the House of Commons descanting on his favourite topic, Sir William Harcourt exclaimed, in the words of Bishop Ken's evening hymn :

" And Knightley (nightly) to the listening earth
Repeats the story of his birth ! "

Such were the husband and home with which Lady Knightley's destinies were henceforth associated. Happy as she was in her new surroundings, dearly as she loved her husband, her keen perception quickly realised the defects of the system to which she now belonged. Its narrowness and exclusiveness repelled her from the first. " We live in a groove here," she exclaims repeatedly in these early years of her married life, " and this is a bad thing for us all." With her love of reading and travel, and her eagerness to acquire fresh knowledge, she could not long remain content with this narrow circle. She used to declare laughingly that when she first came to Fawsley no one read any newspaper but the *Morning Post*, and that the only magazine ever seen on the drawing-room table was the *Quarterly Review*. But she quickly changed all this, and was soon able to introduce at least a measure of sweetness and light into her new home. The neighbours might, as she remarked, be an unpromising set at first sight, but closer acquaintance revealed the existence of more than one whom she felt to be worthy of respect and whose friendship she became eager to cultivate. " I like to go to Edgcote," she writes a year after her marriage, " and see the Cartwrights. These girls read and think, and it does me good to see them and discuss books and music with them and hear them play, which they do quite admirably, I must say." She never forgot hearing Schumann's " Warum ? " played at a rainy garden-party at this particular house, and declared that it gave her a new idea of the power and meaning of music. But whether her neighbours were dull or interesting, clever or stupid, Lady Knightley was determined to have a share in their joys and sorrows, and if possible make Fawsley a centre for rich and poor alike. This was no easy task, and many years of resolute and persevering effort were needed before it could be accomplished. But from the moment of her marriage Lady Knightley's charm and goodness made themselves felt by all those with whom she came into contact. This radiant young bride, beaming with happiness and goodwill, brought a new element into life at Fawsley, and her coming was welcomed by all ranks and classes. From the first, as we have already seen, she threw herself into the lives of farmers and labourers on her husband's estate, and used her influence to improve their condition. " Louisa loves all this ! " Sir Rainald remarked one day to a guest who was tramping over a ploughed field to visit a farm : " I hate it ! " Church life, again, was at a very low ebb in these villages " Sundays here," she wrote soon after her marriage, " are very unsatisfactory." As long as Sir Charles lived, both his nephews, the rectors of Charwelton and Fawsley, had made their home at the big house, but when Dr. Magee became Bishop of Peterborough he insisted on these clerical gentlemen residing in their respective parsonages and attending to their parochial duties. But how lax this observance still remained may be realised from the fact that on Sundays only one service was held in Fawsley church, and that this was alternately Matins at 12 and Evensong at

12.15, while Holy Communion was celebrated four times in the year.[1] Lady Knightley's deeply religious nature was sorely distressed at this state of things, and she did her best to improve the services as far as this was possible. She started classes on Sundays, read with her own young servants, and set to work to train a choir. She made a point of never missing the weekly practices when she was at Fawsley, and took the keenest interest in the task. "Our first performance in church!" she writes on March 26, 1870. "It went off much better than I had expected. I really think we have the making of a very nice choir, and I only hope the singing, which makes them all come to church, will not have the effect of diverting their attention from the service." But she found little sympathy with these aspirations in her husband's family. Both Sir Rainald and his sister, Mrs. Gage, a genuinely pious and devout woman, had been brought up on strictly evangelical lines, and disliked all innovations in the services to which they were accustomed, and it was many years before the church services at Fawsley were conducted in a manner congenial to Lady Knightley's feelings.

[1] A friend of Lady Knightley's who was a frequent guest at Fawsley gives a graphic account of the Sunday services. After taking morning service at Charwelton, where he was curate to Mr. Valentine Knightley, Mr. Story would appear at the house about noon, to collect a congregation. Anyone who felt inclined to attend service, then accompanied him to church, where he proceeded to read Matins and deliver a sermon in a monotonous voice, without any attempt at punctuation. On one occasion he complained of a sore throat, and Sir Charles, who was then living, desired him not to preach a sermon. However, his voice improved, and he was on his way to the pulpit, when the old clerk rushed forward with outstretched arm and, seizing him by the gown, cried out, "Sir Charles says ye mayn't!" The Rector withdrew obediently, and no sermon was preached that day.

SIR CHARLES KNIGHTLEY, BART.
1813.
(From a miniature at Fawsley.)

CHAPTER XV

Hatfield and Brook Street

1870

POLITICS, as we have seen, had occupied much of Lady Knightley's time and thoughts in her girlhood, and her marriage brought her into intimate contact with the leading statesmen of the day. One of the first visits which she paid with her husband, in the winter of 1870, was to Hatfield.

"*Friday, February* 4.—How little I imagined, when gazing at this fine old house from the railroad, that I should ever find myself a guest beneath its roof! However—to proceed soberly—dear Sophy Gage and Henry left us directly after breakfast, and we travelled by the old familiar way of Leighton and Luton, catching a glimpse of the dear mother at Wheathampstead. We walked up from the station with Lord Carnarvon, and by degrees made out all this immense party—beside the Carnarvons, Mr. and Mrs. Gathorne-Hardy, Count Streleczki, Mr. and Mrs. Froude, Lord Percy, Mr. John Murray, Mr. Fergusson (author of the *Handbook of Architecture*), Lord Verulam, Sir Henry Drummond Wolff, Lady Alderson and two daughters, a Mr. and Mrs. Drew, and Dr. Frankland, an eminent chemist. I sat between Lord Percy and Lord Salisbury, and after dinner talked to Mr. Froude, who is certainly very agreeable. He gave a most extraordinary account of dinners in old days at Lord Houghton's, and of Swinburne standing on a sofa, reciting some of his most passionate verses, 'making himself as wicked as he knew how,' and of Ruskin sailing up to the poet with outstretched arms, exclaiming, ' Exquisite ! divine ! '

" *Saturday, February* 5.—After breakfast, I went all over this very fine house—one of the finest, in some respects, which I have ever seen. The gallery is a dream, and the armoury below also very fine, and the pictures—chiefly family portraits—most interesting. Afterwards I pottered about with Mr. Fergusson, looking at the Old Palace in which Queen Elizabeth lived, which is now turned into stables, but has a quite magnificent hall. It really requires all one's eyes and ears, for meantime Rainald and Mr. Hardy were sparring very amusingly over politics—Mr. Hardy reproaching him and Lord Salisbury with preferring to keep up personal enmities, instead of sacrificing them for the good of the party, to which Rainald retorted, ' Oh ! if you had gone when he did, that Reform Bill would never have been passed.' In the afternoon we drove to the Vineyard, a quaint old garden near the river, with yew hedges, putting me a little in mind of Sans Souci. At dinner I sat between Lord Carnarvon and Mr. Murray, both of whom I found very agreeable, as also Sir Henry Wolff, to whom I talked afterwards. Lord Cairns came.

" *Sunday, February* 6.—We all went to the parish church, where we heard a very young sermon from a very young clergyman—not a wise sermon, perhaps, in view of his congregation, but honest, modest, and, as Lord Salisbury added, ' original,' besides having the merit of keeping us all awake. The rain drove us back from our walk this afternoon, but at tea we had some pleasant discourse from Mr. Cyril Graham about the religion and language of the native Indians who inhabit the Hudson's Bay territory. They speak no less than forty distinct languages, and singularly enough among their traditions is that of Cain, whom they believe still to exist as a being ten feet high, of most malignant temper. I again sat between Lord Percy and Lord Salisbury, and talked a good deal to the latter about the condition of religious thought in this country. He thinks we are rapidly approaching a state of religious chaos, what will come after it is hard to say, and with his far-reaching, statesmanlike eye, he seemed to pause and look on into the future. He was rather consoling about Education; and also spoke of Dean Stanley, whom he does not think very profound, and the Archbishop of Canterbury (Dr. Tait), whom he defines as being very just, capable of seeing both sides of a question, but also very imperious. The Bishop of Peterborough (Dr. Magee) he described very contemptuously as 'an excellent speaking-machine,' adding that his speech on the Irish Church possessed every element of a fine speech save one—it was not in the least the speech of a Bishop. That quality, he added, was possessed by the Archbishop's speech on this occasion. In the evening we had conjuring tricks, etc. It is pleasant to see how utterly unaffected Lord Salisbury is, ready to laugh at anything, how fond he is of his children, too, and how much he cares for what is right. We had evening service at 6 p.m. in the private chapel, and very impressive it was. In short, I think—in fact I am sure—I never enjoyed a visit so much. It is indeed rare to meet so many clever, remarkable men at one time, yet they none of them seemed to clash, but all enjoyed themselves equally."

From Hatfield Lady Knightley accompanied her husband to town for the meeting of Parliament, and paid a flying visit to her old home and to Frogmore, where she lunched with Princess Christian, who entered most cordially into her friend's new-found happiness, and then returned to Claridge's Hotel for a couple of nights.

" *Wednesday, February* 9.—In the evening we went to a very amusing party at Lady Cork's, my first *début en femme mariée*. Everyone was particularly civil and pleasant, and I think I shall get on. There were a great many celebrities—Lowe, Goschen, Childers, Sir Roundell Palmer, Sir Roderick Murchison, Lord Houghton, etc. Mr. Lowe was particularly amusing, saying that Dizzy's speech last night, on the state of Ireland, was a very feeble affair—' Bite deeply, or bite not at all!' At least he was reassuring as to the future of Ireland; and altogether I enjoyed myself immensely."

The next two months were spent at Fawsley, where the building of a new farmhouse, the instalment of a schoolmistress at Badby, and the training of the village choir made Lady Knightley busy. Sometimes she drove to hounds, sometimes took long walks with her husband in rain and snow to inspect farms or visit outlying cottages. " But whatever we do, all our life is sunshiny, thank God for it ! " she writes. Occasionally some county function demanded the Member's presence, and then his young wife always accompanied him.

"*Fawsley, March* 1.—Rainald and I made a very early start in the high dogcart, and had a pleasant drive of fifteen miles, through Preston, Canon's Ashby, Moreton Pinkney, Weston, and Helmdon to Brackley, a townlet reminding me of Beaconsfield. We went at once to the newly restored Chapel, founded by the Knights of St. John of Jerusalem, now the property of Magdalen College, which was formally reopened to-day. The full Church service was refreshing, and I liked Mr. Thicknesse's sermon on 'The poor have the Gospel preached to them.' As he spoke of close parishes and village schools, of bad cottages and the alarming aspect of affairs, warning us, the prosperous ones of earth, to fight against these evils lest our national greatness and virtue should crumble to decay, one felt nerved and encouraged to do one's very best. At luncheon I sat between him and the Duke of Grafton, and had a good deal of interesting talk about the Education Bill. Lord Ellesmere, the Bishop of Peterborough, Mr. Thicknesse, and the President of Magdalen all spoke, and then we adjourned to the parish church, where the Bishop consecrated the new burial-ground and gave an address which, although very eloquent, disappointed me by its lack of serious thought, reminding me of Lord Salisbury's ' excellent speaking-machine.' The drive home over rolling stones, in pouring rain, was hardly pleasant."

A second visit to Claridge's, although chiefly spent in house-hunting, was made memorable by another party at Lady Cork's, where Lady Knightley was introduced to Mr. Gladstone.

"*Claridge's Hotel, March* 9.—I went to Buckingham Palace and spent an hour with dear Princess Christian. We dined with the old Duchess of Cleveland, which was not lively, though I was pleased to meet Lord Hotham, such an old friend of my dear father, with whom he went out to Spain in 1812. On to Lady Cork's, which was very amusing. I was especially interested in a conversation between Rainald and Mr. Gladstone, who was most particularly courteous and pleasant. He began by remarking on the change in social intercourse since he first entered Parliament in 1832, when, he said, it was limited by politics, whereas now all parties mix freely. Then they talked about the Irish Land Bill, which he said, he and his colleagues had endeavoured to make as distinctly Irish as possible, so as to preclude all notion of it being applied to England. Rainald remarked that the scale of compensation was too high, upon which Mr. Gladstone replied, as he has since said in his speech on the conclusion of the debate, that if the Bill passed, it would add seven years' purchase to the value of land, and that the hardship of being turned out bore far more severely upon a man who paid £10 a year than upon one who paid £100. Of course I listened with all my ears, and eyes too. He is a plain man, but has a wonderful brow and piercing eyes. The beauty of the evening was Lady Wentworth—a clergyman's daughter married last August to 'Ada's' son. A sweet, innocent face—may it long remain so! I looked at Lord Wentworth with great interest, remembering my father's school-friendship with his grandfather, Lord Byron, and the letter which Lady Milbanke wrote to my grandfather, Admiral Bowater, from Seaham, announcing her daughter's marriage to the poet. . . .

"*March* 17.—We have taken 18 Upper Brook Street from Easter till Michaelmas. May God's blessing be upon the event which we hope will take place there!

"*March* 23.—I had rather an unhappy, worrying

day. An interview with Dr. Farre damped instead of confirming the hopes in which we have been so sanguinely indulging. The suspense and anxiety are very trying, and even worse to me than my own is my darling's disappointment. May God give us strength to resign ourselves to His holy will, and to be thankful for the many blessings we enjoy, even if it should please Him to withhold this—the crown of all! I went to the Palace to see dear Princess Christian, who was kind as ever, and in the evening to Lady Margaret Beaumont's ball. Shall I, or shall I not, record with what results? I think I will, for I do not wish to forget that, if Rainald was cross, for the first time in five months, it was entirely my selfishness and thoughtlessness which made him so. For these there was no excuse, while his vexation was more than palliated by a long day of worry and disappointment. But it is all right now.

"*March* 24.—My darling's morning greeting was more than enough to compensate for last night, and all is sunshine again. We dined with Lord and Lady Donegall in Grosvenor Square, and had an agreeable party. My neighbour, Lord William Osborne, amused me much with his stories of Lord Lytton, the old Duchess of Cleveland, etc.; and Mr. Montague Corry was also very pleasant.

"*Fawsley, March* 29.—We all went to Daventry steeplechases. Dear Sophy Melville and I in my pony-carriage, the rest of the party—Lady Francis Gordon and her daughter, Mr. Cheney, the Tomlines, Sir Thomas, Mr. Edgell, and Philip—in the omnibus with four horses. It was an amusing day altogether, and I enjoyed walking about with Rainald and making acquaintance with his farmer-friends. The last race was tremendously exciting, ending in a dead heat at the end of four miles. Lord Donoughmore, Val, and William Story dined, and we had great fun at a round game.

"*March* 31.—A lovely morning! I drove Lady Alwyne Compton to the meet at Shuckburgh, and seldom enjoyed anything more. She goes at once into the category of the very choice spirits of this earth, who act on one mentally and morally as a tonic, and are as good as they are clever. We talked much of art, which has, I feel, this winter occupied a smaller place in my life than it ought to. I must give myself up to it more in the summer. It is quite curious how well we agree about everything. Rainald, Sir Thomas, Sophy, and I played croquet,—a delicious little party,—and the evening was pleasant with three such agreeable men."

In the following week, a large party arrived for Northampton Races—a proceeding with which Lady Knightley owns she was frankly bored. "I hate races!" she writes. But the second day was enlivened by the arrival of the Bishop of Peterborough, who, much to the general consternation, came to hold a Confirmation at Badby in the race-week, and paid his first visit to Fawsley. To the surprise of the whole party, he proved a most agreeable guest, and laid the foundations of a lasting friendship with Lady Knightley.

"*April* 6.—The Bishop followed us up here after the Confirmation, which Sophy Gage and I attended, and we found him an immense acquisition to our party, so very agreeable and easy to get on with, full of good stories—in short, exceedingly pleasant. He talked a good deal about Education, and thinks the Irish plan works very well. This would save an infinity of trouble, as the system must be more or less alike in both countries, and denominational education in Ireland means Ultramontane education.

"*April* 7.—Before breakfast I took the Bishop to the church, with which he was much pleased, and I am quite sorry his visit should have been so short. All our guests departed, save Henry and Sophy—which was an immense relief. The exertion and strain of so big a party is very great, and none of the lot suited me particularly. But we did an immense amount of civility in the way of asking people, and it was quite the right thing, this first year, to take a good party to the Races. We shan't do it again in a hurry!"

Easter was spent at Firle, where, to her daughter's joy, Lady Bowater was also asked, and Sir Thomas Munro made up just the same party as that of the year before, when she met Sir Rainald for the first time.

"*Firle, Easter Day, April* 16.—This day seemed to breathe the spirit of those beautiful lines from the *Christian Year*:

> ' And there are souls that seem to dwell
> Above this earth—so rich a spell
> Floats round their steps, where'er they move,
> From hopes fulfilled and mutual love.'

All together—dear little Harry for the first time—we knelt together in the primrose-decked church to receive Holy Communion, dearest Rainald remembering how last Easter Day he had prayed that he might find the right wife; so that we may humbly hope our happiness is even more than in the common sense God-given.

" . . . All these days have been most enjoyable, the brightest sun, the bluest sky, tempting one to be out the whole day, doing nothing but read and play croquet. A very bright and sunny bit of life. . . .

"*Richmond Park, Monday, April* 25.—My twenty-eighth birthday, and I may truly say the happiest I have ever spent since the famous fourteenth one—fourteen years ago. We left Firle with much regret after a very happy week, went to London and inspected our Brook Street mansion, with which we are much pleased, and paid a visit to Hatchard's, where Rainald gave me no end of charming books, the *Idylls of the King*, all Miss Austen and Sheridan, besides a new parasol—the very same present dear Papa gave me fourteen years ago. Then we came here by the old familiar route, down to this dear old home. It is such a pleasure to be here again with the dear mother and to revisit all the familiar holes and corners.

" 18 *Upper Brook Street, April* 28.—We took leave of dear Mamma after our happy little visit, and came up here, where I was busy the rest of the day, settling

FIRLE PLACE, SUSSEX.

[*To face p.* 192.

into our new abode—which will, I hope, be a happy and eventful home to us."

The season which followed was a gay and pleasant one for the young wife. She thoroughly enjoyed the pleasures of London society, and dined out with her husband and went to balls without, " strange to say," she remarks, " feeling the least wish to dance." But she saw a great deal of her old friends, and was never so happy as when she could drive her mother out in her " beautiful new carriage," or better still, spend the day with her at Richmond. Sir Rainald knowing her love of riding, gave her a " delicious little horse," which rejoiced in the name of " Meggie," and on which she rode most days in the Park, with or without him. They gave a few dinners at home, which no one enjoyed more than Lady Knightley herself, who delighted to collect congenial persons, and made an admirable hostess. Sir Rainald was fond of plays, and took his wife to all the best theatres, especially the Robertson plays, *Caste*, *School*, etc., which were then the great fashion. On Sunday mornings, Lady Knightley generally took Sir Rainald to hear her favourite preacher, Mr. Stopford Brooke, whose thoughtful sermons she had always appreciated, while in the afternoon they often went to hear Mr. Brookfield. A few passages from the Journal are given below :

" *May* 27.—Rainald and I went to luncheon with the Speaker, and saw all over the House of Lords, which I thoroughly enjoyed. The Speaker's dining-room is one of the most fascinating rooms in London. You see the traffic over Westminster Bridge, yet never hear a sound. You gaze down upon the river, and see St. Paul's in the distance, while opposite, St. Thomas's Hospital is rapidly approaching completion. We admired the mosaics in the Central Hall of the House of Lords and the small frescoes in the Corridor, and peered into the actual House, where the Lord Chancellor was hearing appeals, saw the Queen's Robing-room, which has some fine oak-carving, and descended into the Crypt, where the Abbots of St. Stephen's are buried, which has lately been restored, and is used as a chapel. After looking at the statues of statesmen in St. Stephen's Hall, we took our departure, well pleased with our day and our guide, Mr. Edward Denison, the Speaker's brother.

"*Fawsley, Saturday, June* 4.—We left London about twelve, travelled down with Major Whyte-Melville—a most amusing companion—and arrived at this dear old place on a lovely summer evening, the thorns still in full bloom, the air sweet with their perfume—everything in the greatest beauty. Together we strolled about—oh! so happily. The sky is so blue, the sun gleams so brightly through the full fresh foliage of leafy June, the air is so pure—I never saw the place look so beautiful. And I am so happy with my darling. I do not feel our one trial so deeply as he does. His deep love for me, I believe, helps him over what he must, to a certain extent, feel as a want of sympathy in my sunny but shallow nature, which ever turns away from all that is painful. I often feel that I am not worthy of him, but I do love him with all the power I have, and I think he knows it now, although the other day I dragged out of him that he had long thought my feeling for him was only liking, fondness, not love. But it *is* love—the deepest, truest, best I have to give.

"*Castle Ashby, Northampton, Tuesday, June* 7.— Another bright and sunny bit of life! We left Fawsley early, and were here soon after twelve. Dear Lady Alwyne received us; and Lord and Lady William, Lady Marian Alford, Miss Mary Boyle, and the poor invalid, Lord Northampton, make up the party. We wandered about the gardens, feasting our eyes on the wealth of roses, and resting by the fountain in the conservatory garden, which, in its deep rest and shade, is unlike anything else I know. After luncheon, we drove up the avenue and through the woods, which a little bit reminds me of the Thiergarten at Primkenau —oh! how long ago that seems now. We visited the two giant oaks, Gog and Magog, which stand in a field near a farmhouse, with a few other equally ancient trees and a great ring of wood all round. Lady Alwyne then took me over the house. There is—as at Longleat—a quaint old library at the top of the house, and a fine room called ' King William's dining-room,' otherwise the interior is chiefly remarkable for its rich, luxurious, and artistic atmosphere—bright touches of colour and a wealth of flowers and books everywhere bearing witness to the refined and cultivated tastes of the whole family. Sad it is, in the midst of these delights, to see the shrunken, attenuated form of the man who owns them all, doomed to a life of pain and privation. Yet as I sat by his chair to-night and listened to his explanation of the exquisite designs which he has made for a dressing-case for Lady Brownlow and his other beautiful drawings, I could not help seeing how art brightens and cheers his existence. The day ended with service in the lovely little church, which seemed to give reality to the unseen communion which links heaven and earth together.

"*Fawsley, June* 8.—Only too early we had to tear ourselves away from this ' Earthly Paradise,' and drive to Northampton, where I had to appear at my first public meeting. However, as it was merely to give away prizes for patching and darning to small girls, I did not much mind, and should not have minded at all if it had not been for the vote of thanks. It is not pleasant to have civil speeches made about one to one's face, before two hundred people! After it was over, we went to see the famous Round Church, built like the Temple Church, in imitation of the Church of the Holy Sepulchre at Jerusalem, and came back to play croquet in the warm summer evening.

" 18 *Upper Brook Street, June* 10.—I did not stir out all day, being entirely occupied in doing the flowers for our dinner. However, I had Sophy Melville to help me, so didn't mind, and later Mary Wheatley and Nora Campbell came in. Our dinner consisted of Lord and Lady Cork, Lord and Lady Ellesmere,

Mr. and Lady Margaret Beaumont, Lady Francis Gordon, Lord Sligo, and a few others. It was very cheery, and went off well; and Rainald was very well satisfied, which was a great thing. I went on to Lady Margaret Charteris's ball, which was very pretty, very smart, and very enjoyable. I am getting to know people well enough not to feel forlorn. I feel the world before me 'like an oyster,' and am determined to open it—though not with my sword, and the slight difficulty one experiences only makes me more determined not to be beat.

"*June* 16.—I went with Sophy to hear the debate on Education in the House of Commons, and most amusing it was. Mr. Gladstone made a long, confused, diffuse speech. I thought it was my stupidity which prevented me from understanding it, but I soon found other people were in the same case. Afterwards we discovered that its purport was to accept Mr. Cowper-Temple's amendment that no Catechism or distinctively denominational formularies should be taught in the rate-founded schools, and that the voluntary schools should be independent of the new School Boards. As soon as he sat down, up sprang Dizzy, and in the cleverest, most aggravatingly-amusing speech, avowed his utter inability to comprehend the proposed changes. An animated discussion followed, which ended in the debate being adjourned till Monday. We trotted back to Whitehall, where I dined; and the evening was enlivened by a magnificent thunderstorm, which lighted up the Towers of Westminster quite beautifully.

"*Sunday, June* 19.—I spent the morning quietly, sitting out in the garden—which does not sound like London, although the blacks destroyed the illusion—and reading *Récit d'une Sœur*, which grows more and more touching and heartrending. Ah me! I feel now, as the Queen says she used in happier days, so sorry for a widow. I know that was the thought that passed through Rainald's mind yesterday, when we were looking at Millais' picture of 'The Widow's Mite,' in the Academy. In the afternoon we went to Grosvenor

Chapel to hear Dean Goulburn, towards whom I feel almost as if he were a friend—from knowing his books so well. He preached what Rainald called 'a sensational,' but what I thought a very excellent sermon on 'Inasmuch as ye did it *not*,' bringing out very forcibly the actual guilt of sins of omission, as shown by the three parables of the foolish virgins who took no oil, the unfaithful servant who hid his talent, and the sheep and the goats. Indolence towards self, towards God, and towards our neighbour, how little do we contemplate it in this awful light ! Oh ! may God deepen the impression these solemn words made on my mind, that I be not carried away by this pleasant, luxurious, idle life !

"*June* 22.—The heat was tremendous, and I only drove about with my dear old companion and governess, Agnes Lentz—a thing we have talked about doing for fourteen years ! We went to see Mr. Murray about the Maintenon letters, which I copied from the MSS. in my father's possession and sent to him. He says they have not been printed, but that Lord Stanhope thinks too much of this lady's correspondence has been already given to the world for their publication to answer. Mr. Murray, however, intends to submit them to the Duc d'Aumale, with a view to their being printed by the Philobiblion Society, of which he is the head, and also recommends me to communicate with the Frenchman who is now editing Madame de Maintenon's letters in Paris.

"*June* 24.—We had a very enjoyable expedition down to Windsor for the Queen's breakfast. It poured with rain all the morning and all the way down, but by the time we had wandered round the state apartments it cleared, and by degrees a bright stream began to trickle slowly down the staircase outside the White Drawing-room—the gay colours which are so much the fashion contrasting well with the grey stone of the Castle. The weather afterwards became lovely, and it really was very pleasant. The British public chose to grumble, but I think they enjoyed it, all except the wretched peers and commons, who had to return almost as soon as they got there, for divisions on Irish Land and Education. Dear Prince Leo was too ill to do more than look on from a terrace.

"*Sunday, June 26.*—I was off betimes to breakfast with Nora Campbell and hear Mr. Liddon preach at St. Paul's, Knightsbridge. His text was: 'He that seeth his brother have need and shutteth up his bowels of compassion from him . . . how dwelleth the love of God in him?' The first part, on the necessary interdependence of the love of God and man and the impossibility of loving an abstraction labelled God, was very fine. The second part was a lecture on Political Economy and Pauperism, especially applied to demolishing what I have always felt but could not prove to be the false doctrine of maintaining that increased luxury and expenditure on the part of the upper classes is good for the lower. Certainly, morally, it is bad for both. Still, altogether I don't like him as well as Stopford Brooke.

"*July* 1.—I started early with Mr. Heathcote, Mary Wheatley, and Nina Packe for a sketching expedition to Windsor, which, alas! was ruined by a heavy storm. We dined with Lord William Osborne, and went on to Sir Dudley Marjoribanks' fine new house in this street, where was all the world. It is very handsome certainly, especially the staircase, and I think the public ought to be much obliged to him for adding a really fine house to the few there are in this monotonous city of ours. Now I want to see Dorchester House.

" I am a good deal annoyed, I must confess, by Lady Holland having only asked us to her last two breakfasts. It is a trifle in itself, but shows very plainly the way the current flows, and that instead of having, as I hoped, succeeded in society, I have failed, at all events for this season. It is foolish to care so much, but I do. Perhaps the mortification is good for me, and I certainly should not mind so much if it did not mortify Rainald too! Yet when one reads *Le*

Récit d'une Sœur, and breathes that purer atmosphere, one can only despise oneself for clinging so desperately to this foolish world.

"*July* 3.—Nora came to breakfast, and as in old times we set forth early to hear Mr. Stopford Brooke, and were amply rewarded. It was on the woman with the alabaster box of ointment and Judas's protest against the waste. The lesson deduced was that it is downright wrong for artists and poets and men to whom the power of discovering and expressing beauty, and of raising, refining, and beautifying men's lives, has been given, to leave this their own work and waste their energies on the war with material evil, which is quite a right work for others. Incidentally, he said a great deal about the degree of expenditure which is right for food and dress, and the motives which should govern all expenditure. Like Liddon, he inveighed against the false political economy which upholds luxury because it is good for trade. Somehow, curious as some of the sermon was, it made one feel stronger and better for one's work, anxious to regulate one's expenditure aright, to spend wisely, feeling that even in things which are not immediate charity one may be doing work for God. I am sure he would appreciate the tone of the Northampton family.

"*July* 6.—We went late in the afternoon to Holland House, which has long been the object of my ambition. Imagine, so to speak, in the heart of London, a delicious old Elizabethan house, with a fine avenue of elms, and a park which entirely shuts out the world, a garden— oh ! but a garden one sees in a dream, so exquisite in colour, so deliciously framed in by quaint hedges with tall white lilies gleaming against them, and the rich red of the house as a background—a garden in which to sit and dream away the happy hours, and where one would not be the least surprised to see a fairy spring from the white bells. Even the people, bright as were the dresses and pleasant the society, seemed almost *de trop*. Rainald introduced me to Mr. Delane, the Editor of the *Times*—a mighty power in the State.

We went to the Palace concert, which is always enjoyable, and I liked hearing Mlle Nilsson sing, ' Kennst du das Land ? ' out of Thomas's opera, *Mignon*. Lady Marjoribanks' ball in that beautiful house was also extremely pleasant. I do like going out ! I hope not *too* much.

" *Saturday, July* 9.—We went to Lord's for the last day of the Eton and Harrow match, which was tremendously exciting—the closest match known for years, Eton winning by only 21 runs. The scene afterwards would have amazed a foreigner ! Everyone shrieked and yelled violently, while the victorious Eleven were hoisted—a remarkably honourable, but I should think very unpleasant process. All along of eleven little boys having beaten eleven other little boys at a game probably quite incomprehensible to two-thirds of the spectators !

" *July* 13.—I went off very early with Mamma to see the opening of the Thames Embankment. It was a gay and pretty spectacle, and the Embankment will be an immense gain to London. We went to Holland House, which was charming as ever, so fascinating indeed that we did not get home till late, and found the Cavendish-Bentincks had already sat down to dinner, much to Rainald's disgust. I sat between Mr. Leopold Rothschild, who was pleasant and Lord K—— who was dull, but we talked across to Mrs. Cavendish-Bentinck and Mr. Cheney, and altogether I enjoyed my dinner and a party afterwards. Evidently Apollonia, as Dizzy calls her in *Lothair*, understands Society. I went on to Lady Otho Fitzgerald's for five minutes—a dull party, but worth going to for the sake of the picture framed in by the open window of the Towers of Westminster with the full moon hanging immediately over them. It carried one's thoughts—oh ! so far away !

" *Knole Park, July* 14.—This is a day which must be chronicled before I sleep—it has been so bright and beautiful. I left London at twelve for Sevenoaks, and a drive of little more than a mile brought me to this really magnificent old country house, with its courtyards, arcades, and quaint low rooms. The party consisted of the Duchess of Montrose, Sir Frederick and Lady Elizabeth Arthur, Mr. Primrose, Mr. Cornwallis West, and Prince Lichtenstein—'un gentil petit prince,' an attaché of the Austrian Embassy. The three young men were nice enough, especially Mr. West, but the rest not *simpatici*. We strolled about the garden, admiring its dazzling flowers, tall overarching trees and deep shady glades, and I sat out under the limes, heavy with bees and blossom, to sketch a bit of the oldest part of the house, with its black and yellow gables and lattice windows. Later, we set forth in a cavalcade of pony-carriages, which reminded me of Silesia, to drive down some of the long grassy glades and then through shady lanes and hop-gardens to the most delightful old place that was ever heard or read or dreamt of—Ightham Mote. Deep down in the valley the old house stands, built round a courtyard gay with creepers and surrounded by a clear deep moat. Beyond is a smooth bowling-green, bounded by grassy terraces, with tall white lilies and a yew hedge shutting out the world. We spread our tea on the banks of a little stream under a fine cedar, and I longed for a more sympathetic party to share my delight. Mr. Cornwallis West, my charioteer, was the only one at all in harmony with the place! Afterwards, Lord Buckhurst drove me back to Knole by an even prettier way, through woods and glades innumerable. We dined in the long gallery of James the First's days, lighted by old silver sconces; and Rainald and I gazed long on the moonlight in the courtyard from our latticed window before ending this ever-memorable day.

"*July* 15.—After breakfast, Lord Buckhurst took us all over this most interesting old house. We saw the state bed-chamber of James I., with its beautiful repoussé silver mirrors, sconces, dressing-plate and silver table. Another room had been fitted up with Venetian chairs and tapestry for the reception of some Venetian ambassador. One gallery was hung with portraits by Mytens, another with paintings by Sir

Joshua, another with portraits of wits and poets of the two last centuries—Ben Jonson, Dryden, Pope, Garrick, Locke, Newton, etc. I particularly admired a portrait of the Earl of Surrey, and one of Sir Thomas More, ascribed to Holbein, with a wonderful look in the eyes, as if he were gazing into another world. There are no less than fifty staircases, springing up in every corner; and there is a chapel, hung with curious tapestry of Tudor times, and with a group of small figures given by Mary Queen of Scots. But what I can never forget when I think of Knole is the startling news which reached us there. We were standing in the great hall—Rainald and I, Lord Buckhurst and Prince Louis—when a servant ran in with the *Morning Post* in his hand, and we read the words: 'War inevitable.' Comment is useless, save to say that I think a more unjust and unprovoked war never stained this earth. Reluctantly we tore ourselves from this beautiful old-world place and returned to town. Rainald went down to the House, and found Mr. Gladstone replying to Mr. Disraeli's question as to the foreign news in a very despairing tone. Later in the afternoon, Nora came in with the actual Declaration. Public opinion in this country is strangely divided. 'I hope those rascally Prussians will be beaten,' is the cry of the common herd. The more thoughtful ones see the wickedness of the way in which it has been rushed into.

"*July* 17.—Mr. Stopford Brooke gave us a sermon entirely upon the war—too much so, I thought—and violently anti-French. As I came home I met Mr. Gladstone in Berkeley Square, walking along with his head thrown back and his lips compressed, evidently far from pleased.

"*July* 20.—We went quite late to Holland House, which is always a pleasant gathering. I trotted about independently, having got to know the greater part of *le beau monde* one meets there. It would be curious to count up the number of new acquaintances that I have made this summer. There were a great many Royalties at to-day's party, and I noticed His Royal Highness the Prince of Wales conversing with Mr. Gladstone for nearly half an hour. Somebody suggested that Lord Houghton, 'the cool of the evening,' be requested to step up and ask what they were talking about! Later, I went with Lady Alwyne Compton to a small party at Mrs. Cavendish-Bentinck's, to meet Mlle Nilsson, the Swedish *prima donna*, whose pretty manners charmed us. The Dukes of Manchester and Wellington and Lord Longford carried her off to play whist, so we saw but little of her; but Mrs. C.-B.'s *salon* is always pleasant.

"*July* 25.—There is great excitement to-day at the publication in the *Times* of an alleged *Projet de Traité* between France and Prussia, proposing to add Belgium to France to compensate for Prussia's recent annexations, and compel the King of Holland to sell Luxembourg to the Emperor. Bismarck swears he had this in Benedetti's handwriting, but great stress is laid on the bad French and the fact that the King of Prussia is named first, as it is diplomatic etiquette to name one's own Sovereign first. At all events, it seems a pity such a document should have been published just now. The dispatches relating to the declaration of war are sad reading. Bismarck and Napoleon seem equally to blame.

"*Richmond Park, July* 28.—We left Brook Street with mixed feelings. It has been a very happy time, but I could not help thinking of the hopes with which we took possession, and which were so soon dashed to the ground. Otherwise I have had enough of London, and am glad to escape to the rest and quiet of this dear old home."

On the 2nd of August Lady Knightley left her "dear old home" for her "dear new home." The return to Fawsley, she owns, was a little painful. "We had so fully hoped to come home three! But with so many blessings we ought not to murmur if one is withheld, and I really think every day we are more and nearer to each other."

CHAPTER XVI

Harrogate, Scotland, Osborne, and Burghley

1870–1871

The year 1870 was rendered memorable in European history by the Franco-German War, and Lady Knightley's Journal reflects the anxiety with which the startling events of that summer were followed in this country. The usual family party, consisting of Mr. and Mrs. Gage, their son Harry, and Sir Thomas Munro, spent August at Fawsley, and were joined by Lady Bowater. After her gay season, Lady Knightley thoroughly enjoyed what she calls the happy-go-lucky idle country life—croquet or driving every afternoon, whist every evening, the newspapers being the only excitement.

"*August* 8.—News of a great victory gained by the Crown Prince over Marshal MacMahon at Weissenburg, while on the same day (August 6) the Prussian centre under Steinmetz repulsed the French before Saarbrück. Paris is in the greatest consternation, while the Emperor telegraphs, 'Tout peut se réparer.' We live in stirring times. Anyhow, I had rather see the French beaten than the Prussians.

"*August* 10.—Our first big garden-party. We asked everybody we could think of for miles round to croquet from four to seven, and they came to the number of about a hundred. We had a band and refreshments in the old hall, and it all went off very well.

"*August* 20.—Croquet the whole morning, which I won't do again. It is so idle. Drove Mamma to Canon's Ashby, which was a perfect picture of olden time, with

FAWSLEY.

[*To face p.* 204.

its quaint gateways and terraces and bright flower-beds. The war news is most exciting. The accounts of the fighting near Metz have been most conflicting, each side claiming the victory; but there can be no doubt Marshal Bazaine was routed in a tremendous battle near Gravelotte, and is now besieged in Metz and cut off from the rest of the army. Meantime preparations are being made for the defence of Paris under General Trochu, the Ollivier ministry having fallen after the defeat of Worth, since which we have heard little or nothing of the Emperor. Private accounts represent the spirit of the common people as very bad, and France is evidently on the brink of a revolution. How will it all end? Meanwhile the sum of human misery is fearful to contemplate, and one can think and talk of little but the war. Henry and Sophy are so strongly Napoleonic, it is often difficult to keep the peace. I am very sorry for the French, Emperor and all, but should have been more sorry for Germany.

"*Arbury, August 29.*—We managed to have a parting game at croquet, Rainald, Val, Harry, and I, and came on here after luncheon with the Gages. The place is looking so pretty, I hardly recognised it in its summer attire. But one does miss dear Mrs. Newdegate dreadfully!

"*August 30.*—We all went to Birmingham for the *Elijah*, which I enjoyed immensely. Nowhere is it given in greater perfection than here, where it was first performed in 1846, conducted by Mendelssohn himself. It always strikes me afresh as singularly dramatic. Perhaps the finest of the choruses are 'Thanks be to God' and 'Behold God the Lord passeth by,' while I enjoyed every note of 'Lift thine eyes!' and 'O Rest in the Lord.'

"*August 31.*—We played croquet all the morning—the weather being most enjoyable, and the place looked lovely. We drove in the afternoon to a harvest-home at Astley, at which I danced vigorously and listened to a capital speech from Charley. He began seriously by saying how thankful we ought to be, even if the pastures are burnt and the hay crop is short, that our fields are not trampled down and our homes destroyed by hostile armies, and ending jocularly with a reference to my marriage and his own bachelorhood.

"*September* 1.—We were all off early and heard the *Messiah* to absolute perfection. Alas! how painful is the contrast between the words, ' Peace on earth, goodwill toward men,' and the news which reached us just as the oratorio was beginning : ' Total defeat of MacMahon.' A battle seems to have been raging for four days between Sedan and Montmédy, along the banks of the Meuse, in which MacMahon was totally defeated, while at the same time Bazaine's sortie from Metz appears to have been utterly frustrated. In our eagerness for news, we six ladies—Lady Manners and her daughter, Mrs. Gregory, Julia Boucherett, Sophy, and I—actually stormed the Stock Exchange, where none but members are by right admitted. But these events are far the most remarkable that have occurred since 1815."

It was at Harrogate, where Sir Rainald and Lady Knightley spent the next month, drinking the waters, that the news of Sedan reached them.

"*Queen's Hotel, Harrogate, September* 3.—We were busy settling down in our rooms and seeing a doctor, when Horne (the butler) rushed in with a telegram : ' Emperor Napoleon surrendered to King William—the whole army of Sedan capitulated.' Such astounding news absolutely takes one's breath away, and one can form no opinion of the course events are likely to take. How little we anticipated such a catastrophe on that memorable 14th of July, only six weeks ago, when in the old hall at Knole we learnt that war was inevitable.

"*September* 5.—Events succeed each other with such startling rapidity that it is almost impossible to keep pace with them. The *Observer* begins a striking article with the words : ' On Friday, July 15, the Emperor declared war against Prussia ; on Friday, September 2, he surrendered to King William.' Although we knew it by twelve on Saturday, it was not till 1 a.m. on Sunday that at a special sitting of the Corps Législatif, the ministers, Count Palikao and General Trochu, announced to Paris the greatest disaster that has ever befallen her arms. The net result is that they have accomplished a revolution, happily so far bloodless, and proclaimed a Republic—whereupon the brutes, fools, idiots, fell into a state of exuberant joy! This with masses of their countrymen slain, and an enemy's army marching on Paris. The Emperor is gone to Wilhelmshöhe, near Cassel, where I hope the Empress has by this time joined him. Good heavens! what a fate! A most interesting letter from Russell gives particulars of the surrender. Late on the afternoon of the 1st the Emperor wrote to the King: ' Mon frère : N'ayant pu mourir à la tête de mon armée, je dépose mon epée aux pieds de votre Majesté.' Firing immediately ceased, but, the French army being entirely surrounded, the King of course insisted on an unconditional surrender. And so the night passed—what a night it must have been! At early morning, the Emperor came in his carriage to seek an interview with Bismarck, at a cottage door. Later he saw the King, and finally departed for his German prison. Oh, if it would only bring peace! I began my water-drinking and walking before breakfast, and don't on the whole dislike it. We took a walk to a height from which we had a most lovely view of the country round with the grey houses and spires of Harrogate in the foreground—very Scotch in colouring and quite distinct from the yellow-brown of Northamptonshire and the ruddy hues of the southern counties. I really think we shan't be so much bored here after all."

In pursuance of this resolve, during the next three weeks Lady Knightley explored the charming neighbourhood of Harrogate with her accustomed energy. In company with Lord and Lady Lyveden, and one or two other friends, she visited York Minster, Fountains Abbey, Ripon, Bolton Abbey and Wharfedale, Temple Newsam and Harewood House. The beauty of these Yorkshire dales, with their leafy woods and running streams and purple hills, delighted her, and the wonderful collection of Turners at Farnley Hall were a revelation. Leaving Harrogate at the end of September, Sir Rainald and Lady Knightley went on to Sir Thomas Munro's place, Lindertis, near Kirriemuir, visiting Edinburgh and Holyrood on the way. Here Lady Knightley was thoroughly happy. The freedom of life in the Highlands, the long rambles in the deep glens and along the wooded mountainside, golden and russet with autumn tints, recalled old days at Balmoral. She took excursions to Glamis Castle and Airlie, and played battledore and shuttlecock on rainy days with the young Munros. At Tullyallan, near Stirling, where the travellers paid another visit on their way south, she found a very amusing party, including M. de la Vallette and Mrs. Norton.

"*October* 16.—This party is certainly an odd one. M. de la Vallette and Mrs. Norton have not met for years. On their first acquaintance, she stared so hard at him that he asked for an explanation, and she answered : ' I see in your eyes that you will die a violent death.' Upon which he replied, much annoyed : ' Madame, j'ai toujours su que vous étiez enchanteresse, mais je ne savais pas que vous étiez aussi sorcière.' ' Si vous saviez,' he added, in relating the story, ' les émotions que cette femme m'a causées.' I had a charming letter from Prince Leopold, announcing Princess Louise's marriage to Lord Lorne. I am sure I trust it will be for her happiness. M. de la Vallette told us the story of General Bourbaki, whom a Polish gentleman got out of Metz, pretending that he came from the Empress, and bearing as his credentials a photo given him by the Prince Imperial of the inn at Hastings where he was staying. When Bourbaki reached Chiselhurst, and found that the whole thing was a trick, he was ready to blow out his brains ! M. de la Vallette thinks it was a ruse to implicate the Empress in a plot with Bazaine. He added that the General had done all in his power to prevent the declaration of war, but was not allowed to go to Paris to take part in the deliberations."

A week later, Lady Knightley met Mr. Motley, the historian, at Bretton Park, Mr. Beaumont's place, near Wakefield, and had a very interesting conversation with him.

"*October 22.*—We began by talking of English places, and ended in the one all-engrossing subject—the war. We discussed the Bourbaki mystery, and then he told me all the story of the Empress's flight from Paris on the celebrated 4th of September. She left the Tuileries on foot, immediately after luncheon, attended only by Madame le Breton, without any preparation for her departure, merely snatching up a hat and grey shawl which lay on a sofa in her boudoir. They got into a fiacre, followed for some way by a man who recognised them but did not betray them, and having only four francs between them, drove to the house of Dr. Evans, an American dentist, where they passed the night. Early the next morning, they drove about forty miles out of Paris, in his private carriage, and after sleeping at some small village inn finally reached Trouville, where Mrs. Evans was staying. Dr. Evans took them on board Sir John Burgoyne's yacht, in which they crossed the Channel, and after a very rough passage arrived at Ryde early on Thursday morning."

The autumn and winter were spent at Fawsley, where Lady Knightley had the pleasure of welcoming her Boucherett and Corbet cousins at Christmas, and Lady Bowater came to join the usual family party. She took organ lessons, attended choir practices, paid frequent visits to Badby tenants and cottagers, and accompanied Sir Rainald regularly to the hunting field, mounted on her new mare Meggy. Public events occupied much of her attention. She waxed indignant at Prince Gortschakoff's circular announcing that Russia held herself free from any obligation to keep the Treaty of 1856—a most violent proceeding, which, to her mind, Lord Granville hardly answered with sufficient spirit. The siege of Paris and the subsequent disorder of the Commune filled her with deep compassion, horror, and dismay.

"*November* 23.—The investment of Paris continues. We hear occasionally by balloon from the besieged city, which has been tranquil since October. But they have already arrived at eating dogs and cats. The accounts of successful sorties are so conflicting, it is difficult to arrive at any satisfactory conclusion. I have been reading Sir Henry Bulwer's *Life of Lord Palmerston* and the eighteen years during which he held the seals of the Foreign Office. I wish we had him now, with his bold, plucky bearing. Certainly I must do the Emperor the justice to say that he has been a far better friend to England than any previous Government of France. I think and hope the Russian affair has blown over, but we shall see what comes of the conferences. But oh dear ! I have had a dreadful blow. Bismarck has written a circular in which he announces that, owing to some alleged infringement of neutrality on the part of Luxembourg, he no longer considers himself bound by the Treaty of 1867, which, when Prussia's susceptibilities were aroused by France's attempt to buy that Duchy from the King of Holland, was entered into by all the Powers to secure its neutrality. This most unprovoked breach of good faith puts an end to my sympathies with him."

A visit to Ickworth in December was interesting on account of the Knightley connection with the Herveys, and the opportunity which it afforded of seeing Bury St. Edmunds with its ancient Priory and memories of Abbot Sampson. The party itself was a pleasant one. "Certainly," she remarks, "four prettier women than Lady Bristol, Lady Buckhurst, Lady Mary Hervey, and Mrs. Forbes are seldom got together. To-day Mrs. Forbes received a telegram announcing the death of her father, Mr. Dudley Ward, which was of course a shock, although hardly a sorrow, as she had only seen him once since she was ten years old. We were struck by the singular coincidence that after luncheon we had all been gathering rosemary and talking of its meaning. I had been thinking of Cannes and the rosemary arbour there."

With Lord Stanhope, thé historian, who was one of the guests, Lady Knightley struck up a fast friendship, which lasted until this nobleman's death and proved a source of great pleasure to her in after years.

"*New Year's Eve*, 1870.—There is always something solemn about the end of another year, especially one so laden with sorrow and suffering as this has been to many thousands, nay millions, of our fellow-creatures. Certainly, as far as Europe is concerned, this has been the most eventful year since 1815. For us it has been a very happy one, though marked by the downfall of the hopes which made that fortnight at Firle the happiest of my life. But in this, as in all else, may we say from our hearts, God's will be done."

In the midst of these happy Christmas festivities great consternation was caused by the arrival of a Royal invitation to Osborne for Thursday the 29th, a most inopportune event. Sir Rainald absolutely refused to take so long a journey for only two nights, in such bitter weather. Lady Knightley was sorely perturbed, and divided between loyalty to Her Majesty and duty to her husband, but in the end an excuse was sent. Fortunately the invitation was repeated a week later, and she had the pleasure of revisiting her old haunts in her husband's company.

"*Osborne House, January* 5, 1871.—We left town at eleven and had a prosperous journey and quite a pleasant crossing, falling in with Mr. Baillie Cochrane and his daughter, and the weather having suddenly become quite mild, after this long and severe frost. We were shown up to our rooms, where the two Princesses presently found me. I had a long talk with my own dear Princess. We dined with the Queen, the party including the Duke of Cambridge, Prince and Princess Christian, Princess Louise, Prince Arthur, Prince Leopold, and the Duchess of Atholl. It was a very favourable specimen of a Royal dinner, the Duke of Cambridge talking loudly and continuously and so making cover for the others, and I sat between the young Princes, who were both very pleasant. After dinner the Princes and ourselves retired as usual to the council room, where we found Miss MacGregor, Lord Alfred Paget, Colonel Elphinstone, Colonel Ponsonby, Colonel Clifton, Dr. Poore, and Mr. Collins. Dear me! it all seemed so natural, only being married makes it much pleasanter.

"*Friday, January 6.*—After breakfast Rainald and I went out walking with Prince Leo and Mr. Collins, and spent a good two hours roaming about the grounds and inspecting curiosities in the Swiss museum, including a mummy brought from Egypt by the Prince of Wales. It was an immense treat to see my own dear little Prince so comfortable, more comfortable than I have ever seen him since we left Cannes. He has come out wonderfully, grown quite into a man, with the precocious development of Royalty, aided by his own bad health. Certainly he is a singularly pleasant companion, and is, I am glad to find, devoted to Princess Louise. It seemed quite odd to be trotting about together again —like old times. Princess Christian sat with me most of the afternoon, and took me over to tea with Prince Arthur and Prince Leopold, finishing with snap-dragon as in old Christmas-times here. We again dined with the Queen, and Lord Alfred Paget gave us some interesting details of his visit to the Empress at Chiselhurst, when he took her the news of the fall of Strasburg. The Queen was most gracious, and altogether the visit has been a remarkable success, to my great joy, for Rainald was quite ready to take huff, if there had been anything to take huff at."

At the end of January, Sir Rainald and Lady Knightley paid another pleasant visit to Lord and Lady Exeter at Burghley House, in the north of the county.

"*Burghley House, Wednesday, January* 25. — We came here by Rugby in bitter cold, the frost having set in with renewed severity, and walked about the quaint old town of Stamford, before coming up to this magnificent place, which certainly ranks with Hatfield and Longleat among the finest houses in England. It was built by John Thorpe about the same time for Queen Elizabeth's Lord Treasurer Burghley. An enormous party, thirty-four in number, and dinner in the great hall was a very stately ceremony. About a hundred of the neighbours came to a dance afterwards, which I enjoyed thoroughly. The house-party consists of Sir Stafford, Lady and Miss Northcote, Lady C. Wellesley and two daughters, Sir Lawrence, Lady and Miss Palk, Lady Penrhyn and Miss Pennant, Lord Strathallan, Miss Drummond, Mr. and Mrs. and Miss Pakenham Mahon, Lord and Lady Hatherton, Lord Raglan, Lord Ranfurly, Lord and Lady Powerscourt, Mr. Walrond, Colonel Lee Seymour, Mr. Montagu Corry, Lord and Lady Brownlow Cecil, Lord Burleigh, etc. I sat by Sir Stafford Northcote, and liked him very much.

"*Thursday, January* 26.—I drove with Lady Powerscourt, whom I like, and Lady Exeter, whom I don't like, and stayed at home in the evening, while most of the party went to a dance at Uffington, and played whist with Lord Hatherton and Mr. Corry, which was much better fun. In fact, the party was improved by being halved. I hate such a mob—it is not society, but is more like a big inn.

"*January* 27.—I went all over the house with Lady Powerscourt. It is a fine place certainly, though I prefer the outside of Longleat and the inside of Hatfield. There are quantities of good pictures and china, many portraits of Angelica Kauffmann, who spent some months here and painted a fine head of Garrick; but what interested me most was Lawrence's full-length of the Lord Exeter who married the village maiden of Tennyson's poem, and of his wife, the lovely 'Cottage Countess,' with their little daughter. My room, the 'Purple Satin Chamber,' is entirely hung with fine tapestry, of which the house is full. In the afternoon I walked with Lord Brownlow Cecil and Mr. Tryon to the kitchen-garden, which covers fourteen acres and is managed by a very clever head-gardener. Afterwards we took a fast, pleasant walk to Stamford. The Bishop of Peterborough and Mrs. Magee arrived, and by good luck I sat next him at dinner, and found him as agreeable as ever.

"*January* 28.—I sat between the Bishop and Sir Stafford at breakfast and discussed the new Education Act. The Bishop dreads its ultimate effect in secularising, and fears there will be squabbles between the sects on the Boards, and that for peace's sake the schoolmaster will leave off teaching any religion at all. But he agrees that at present the Act is doing an infinity of good, and both he and Sir Stafford spoke very highly of Mr. Forster, a most high-principled and conscientious man.

"*Fawsley, January* 30.—The capitulation of Paris was signed on Saturday, together with a twenty-one days' armistice for the whole of France. One cannot but rejoice at the termination of a resistance which, heroic as it has been, has been long known to be hopeless, and involved such a fearful amount of misery. Sophy is in a dreadful state of mind, quite curiously indignant, and anticipating much danger to England from the Prussian success.

"*February* 26.—Thank God! peace was signed at Versailles yesterday by Thiers and Bismarck, but upon what terms! Alsace and part of Lorraine, including Metz, to be given up, a war indemnity of two hundred millions to be paid by France, and the Germans to occupy part of Paris. They are brutally hard."

CHAPTER XVII

A London Season and a Foreign Tour

1871–1872

"*Claridge's Hotel, March* 7.—I spent the whole day on the trot, shopping and looking at houses—a dreary occupation. After much hesitation, we ate humble pie and took Sir Edward Colebrooke's house, 37 South Street, for the season. It is an excellent house, in a charming situation, but the rent is very high. There is much talk of Mr. Gladstone's strange appointment of Mr. Goschen to succeed Mr. Childers at the Admiralty, thus adding another to the many shuffles which have taken place in the Ministry since July, without adding any strength to the Cabinet. It is curious to see perhaps the most popular Ministry there has been in my time floating slowly to destruction. Gladstone gets more and more irritable every day. But who or what is to succeed him ? Had there been any cohesion in the Conservative party, he would certainly have been beaten on this foolish and mischievous secret Westmeath Committee—a cowardly attempt to shuffle the responsibility which attaches to the Government on to the House of Commons."

The season which followed was a very pleasant one. Lady Knightley enjoyed society to the full, and she remarks, " Now that I know all the smart people, it is very jolly." A visit to the National Portrait Gallery with Lord Stanhope as cicerone was one of its more notable events.

" It is perhaps more historically than artistically interesting, but it is very pleasant to see what manner of men they were with whom one becomes so intimately acquainted in books. There is the Chandos portrait of Shakespeare, with a forehead which reminds me of Lord Salisbury; a finely painted picture of Sir Joshua by himself, with his hand across his forehead; Walter Scott in his study; Hogarth at his easel; Nelson's Lady Hamilton—oh, such a lovely face!—Waller looking prim and starched, by no means as if he were writing verses to Sacharissa; Thurlow looking wiser than ever man was—in short, to enumerate all would exhaust the list of remarkable Englishmen. It was very interesting going with Lord Stanhope, who is so full of anecdote and information, and we were accompanied by Mr. Scharf, the keeper of the gallery, a great authority, Mr. and Mrs. Edward Stanhope, and Mr. Banks Stanhope.

"*May* 9.—I was all day at the Drawing-room—the most crowded one I have ever seen since the Princess of Wales's first. We had to go half-way down the Birdcage Walk to get into the string and slowly past the Horse Guards and down the Mall. The Queen stayed to the very end, having no one to depute, for dear Princess Christian is laid up with congestion of the lungs. There was a wonderful display of lace and jewels, but the pushing and squeezing were frightful. There was a debate on Mr. Miall's proposal to disestablish the Church of England, for which I am sorry to say eighty-nine M.P.'s were found to vote. Mr. Bruce made a very shuffling speech; Mr. Gladstone an admirable one. If only he could be trusted!

"*May* 13.—Rainald went to the levée, and afterwards we went together to Miller's about lamps. The shopman gave a strange account of things in Paris, the utter standstill to which everything has come, and told us that out of twenty-five of their men who had been with them some twenty years, no less than eight went on strike the other day, simply because they objected to working with a German who had been taken on during the last few months—a perfectly quiet and inoffensive man. The shopman himself remarked, ' Frenchmen were not foreigners '—a strange turn for

British sentiment to take! We had a very successful dinner—Lord and Lady Bristol, Lady Cork, Lord Barrington, Lord and Lady Cawdor—and I went on by myself to a very pleasant party at Lord Stanhope's. He was very civil and made much of me, which is always agreeable, and introduced me to the French ambassador, the Duc de Broglie, and to Mr. Lecky. I like meeting remarkable people.

"*May* 17.—We dined with Mr. and Lady Elizabeth Villiers in Lady Jersey's old house in Berkeley Square. It was a dinner of reconciliation, so I think it right to go there, but it was painful to Rainald for more reasons than one, and he shrank from revisiting the home of his old love, Lady Clementina, where he had spent so many happy days. It was a very dull, bad dinner, too. I sat between Lord Bagot and Sir William Ross, and was a good deal bored, but enjoyed meeting Lord Charles Fitzroy and his nice daughter. The Communists, who are now masters of Paris, have pulled down the Column on the Place Vendôme, because, forsooth, it recorded victories, and so hurt the feelings of other nations—as the *Spectator* says, a ' nobly childish ' sentiment. I fear there are awful scenes going on in that doomed city. The accounts of the horrors are too sickening. Rome, Jerusalem, Babylon, fearful as was their destruction, at least fell before an enemy, not before their own inhabitants.

"*May* 21.—Mr. Thomas came to luncheon, also Lord Stanhope (for the third time), and, much to my surprise, Mrs. Norton. However, they made themselves very agreeable, talking, among other things, of dreams, which recalled to my mind one that I had, a few nights ago, so vivid and singular that I must record it. I dreamt that I had been elected to the House of Commons, though I tried in vain to recollect for what constituency I was about to take my seat. The floor of the House was covered with members, through whom I threaded my way very shyly, following someone to a seat on a bench below the front Opposition bench, but above the gangway, which I did not like, as it made me a supporter of Mr. Disraeli, and I looked about for Rainald, that I might secure a seat behind him, thinking of him quite in his right place. There were other ladies in the House, but as I was the only M.P. they had to leave when the debate began. I waited impatiently for this, and wondered why I was not asked to take the oath. After this my dream became more confused, the Queen came down and hindered business, and I kept looking out of the window at her guard crossing Westminster Bridge, and up at the new Speaker's Gallery, thinking, with the inconsistency of dreams, how nice it would be to go and listen to the debates there, while at the same time I was deeply impressed with the responsibility of my new position. Suddenly I awoke and realised where I was, and began to ask myself if this were an omen of the future.

"*Whitsunday, May* 28.—I went with Rainald to Mass at the Roman Catholic church in Farm Street. The music was splendid, and I liked the quiet time for meditation. It made me feel that, however they may differ from us on certain points, we are entirely one in the great central doctrines of Christianity—far more, indeed, than with many who profess to belong to our Church. In the afternoon, Sophy took me to the Chapel Royal, a sleepy service, which was a great contrast to the devotion of the Mass at Farm Street. But it is a fine hall, with a ceiling painted by Rubens, and I can never forget that from its window Charles I. stepped out upon the scaffold. As we walked home, through the Green Park, we met Lord Enfield, who told us the horrible news of the murder of Archbishop Darboy of Paris—the third who had died a violent death. For the last seven days, Paris has been the veriest hell upon earth—an awful punishment for her denial of God. The Communists both in Versailles and Paris are shooting men and women down by hundreds. It is as bad as in the Revolution, and with far less cause. Meantime, I am reading Carlyle's *French Revolution* with deep interest.

"*June* 24.—I went off quite early to Buckingham

Palace to see Princess Christian, and had a great lark, as she insisted on coming home with me, startling Rainald and taking a drive through the streets alone with me. It was great fun, and I had Mamma in the afternoon, and after dining with the Dartreys, I went on to a smart little party at the Duchess of Marlborough's, to meet Prince Arthur, which I much enjoyed. In fact, the public have at last been pleased to come round, and I feel I have safely turned the corner in society. I am glad for Rainald's sake and my own. I like society, and to fail would be mortifying.

"*June* 26.—We had a most agreeable dinner at Lady Molesworth's, quite the pleasantest I have had this year—Carnarvons, Carysforts, Shaftesburys, Peels, Stratford de Redclyffes, the Duke of Rutland, Marquis d'Azeglio, Lord Lytton, Lord Stanhope, etc. I sat between Lord Stratford and Lord Carnarvon, to whom I am devoted. It is seldom one sees anyone so honest and earnest, and I am sure it must do good. To a party at Lady Charlotte Denison's. The beautiful rooms were not too full, and I stood for a long time talking to Mr. Lowe and gazing upon the lovely river view with the lights of Westminster Bridge reflected in the water.

"*June* 29.—I went with Rainald to hear a bit of the celebrated Tichborne trial, which has been going on for weeks, and seems likely to occupy many more. I had never been in a Court of Justice before, and was interested in realising the whole thing. I have not the slightest doubt that the claimant is a gross impostor, but Sir John Coleridge, who was cross-examining him, seemed to do it in a slow, tiresome way, while the man himself (although totally uneducated) is evidently sharp and very self-possessed. It will certainly rank among the *causes célèbres* of the century.

"*July* 5.—A charming dinner at Lord Stanhope's—Ashburtons, Listowels, Avelands, and Lady Leconfield, a wonderful *réunion* of beauty. I sat between Mr. Cheney and Lord Ashburton.

"*July* 6.—Yesterday Prince Arthur, whom I ran against in the street, came to tea, and was very pleasant, full of the Waverley ball, to which all the world is going—he as Charles Edward, which I think a mistake ! To-day I had my dear Princess with her Prince and Lady Susan to luncheon—a real pleasure.

"*July* 12.—I went with Rainald, Lady Francis Gordon, and Lily to Holland House, which was most delicious. All the rooms were thrown open, and we wandered all over the charming house described by Macaulay thirty years ago. We especially admired the library, which he says combines the antique gravity of a college library with the grace and wit of a drawing-room, where the shelves are loaded with the varied learning of many ages and many lands, and the walls adorned with portraits of the best and wisest Englishmen of two generations. The gathering to-day was not unworthy of former times. The foremost lion was the Crown Prince of Germany. Just a year has elapsed since war was declared. What events have taken place in the interval ! I had a warm greeting from my old friend of Berlin and Gotha, Count Eulenburg, and shook hands with His Royal Highness. This is my last party. I hate doing things for the last time, I hate giving up this charming house, yet I never was so glad to escape from London."

After drinking the waters at Schwalbach, by her doctor's orders, Lady Knightley and her husband travelled by Heidelberg and Bâle to Lucerne and Interlaken, a trip which she enjoyed immensely, never having been in Switzerland before. The beauty of the Lake of the Four Cantons, the first sight of the Jungfrau, an expedition to Andermatt and the Grimsel Hospice, alone with her husband, all filled her with delight. " I don't think," she writes, " anybody ever had so much enjoyment crowded into one week as I have had in this last ! " And again, on the last Sunday at Geneva, she writes :

" *Hôtel de la Paix, Geneva, September* 11.—Rainald called me at 5 a.m. to look at the Mont Blanc range, which, veiled in cloud last night, stood out clear and sharp against the sky, while the yellow light of the rising sun streamed up from behind, and a few rosy clouds were reflected in the lake. It was a very lovely scene to carry away as one's latest recollection of this beautiful country, and I shall always look back on this fortnight as one of the brightest and happiest bits of my life. It is impossible to have seen Switzerland under more favourable circumstances."

The homeward journey through Paris was full of melancholy interest.

"*Hôtel Bristol, Paris, September* 12.—Alas ! we had not far to go before we saw heart-rending proofs of the destruction which has fallen upon this fair city. In our short drive from the station to this hotel, we passed the ruins of the Hôtel de Ville, of the Ministère des Finances, and, last not least, of the Tuileries themselves, besides many ruins of private houses at the corner of the Rue Rivoli, to say nothing of the Colonne Vendôme, of which only the pedestal is left. And in cruel mockery of all this desolation, on every public building the words ' Liberté, Egalité, Fraternité ' are scrawled, while on the smokened and blackened ruins we read : ' La République une et indivisible.' In every photographer's window are endless pictures of the ruins. A few caricatures of the Emperor and portraits of his marshals are exhibited side by side with those of Orleanists and Republicans. There is even a play announced, which is called *Le double Siège de Paris*, and *objets* made from fragments of Prussian shells are sold in several of the shops. It is a strange people. No photographs seem to be more popular than those of the shooting of Monseigneur Darboy and his companions. Next to those in popularity are symbolical groups of ' Alsace et Lorraine ' and of ' France en 1870 ' as a pale, bleeding, dishevelled woman, surrounded by Prussian generals, while others represent the awful visions which are supposed to haunt King William's slumbers, clamouring for vengeance. I was rather pleased with a sacristan in Notre-Dame, who, after showing us a gorgeous cope given by Napoleon III., remarked, 'He did more for Notre-Dame than all the other kings of France put together.' We took a drive in the Bois de Boulogne, which is a melancholy scene! More than half of the trees are cut down, and those which remain are more or less marked by cannon-balls, as our *cocher* pointed out with apparent satisfaction. He told us with much glee how 'au temps des Prussiens' he managed to draw double rations for his children, how horses were requisitioned for sale at f. 1.50 the kilo, how a donkey sold for a thousand francs, etc. We went out by train to Versailles, passing Neuilly with its broken bridge and ruined St. Cloud, and stood at the foot of Louis XIV.'s statue, with the inscription, 'A toutes les gloires de la France.' It was there that, exactly a year ago, the German Crown Prince distributed medals to his victorious troops. We wandered through the stately gardens to Trianon, passing through a part of the camp, where 80,000 troops are still quartered. Very dirty and dreary looked the tents, depressed and downcast the men, slouching about, without a vestige of smartness, with all the life and heart taken out of them, apparently without occupation or interest of any kind. 'Le Petit Trianon' seems to have passed unscathed through all the storms which have swept over France, and remains precisely as it was in the days when Marie Antoinette used to take refuge here from the wearisome grandeurs of Versailles. Here are her spinet, the very pieces of music which she played, her dressing-table and jewel case, a bust of her son, the silk curtains, but little faded, presented by the city of Lyons on her marriage; the satinwood chairs, tables, and bureaux bearing her cipher—in fact, the whole atmosphere breathes of the ill-fated Queen whose creation it was, and whose memory still lives in this charming little spot.

"*September* 15.—We left Paris without any other incident to remind us of the recent invasion than the sight of a few Prussian soldiers on guard at some of the northern stations, and arrived safely in London soon after five. Gladly did we shake off the dust of foreign shores, joyfully did we hail our own, and, much as we have enjoyed our tour, I don't think anything will tempt us abroad again for many a long year! Oh dear! the delight of being at home again, after five months' absence—words cannot express what I feel."

The chief event of the following winter was the dangerous illness of the Prince of Wales, which stirred the nation to its depths. Lady Knightley's intimate connection with the Royal Family naturally made her follow the course of the fever with profound anxiety.

"*Fawsley, December* 8.—I walked to Charwelton after luncheon to look at some very unsatisfactory pigsties. This illness of the Prince makes one feel very anxious about sanitary reforms in every direction. It is clearly to be traced, both in his case and in that of Lord Chesterfield, whose death broke up our party at Ickworth this week, to poison from the drains at Londesborough Lodge, Scarborough, where they successively occupied the same bedroom.

"*December* 9.—A most alarming change for the worse in the Prince's condition. The Queen, Princess Louise, Prince Arthur, and the Duke of Edinburgh have all gone down to Sandringham, and the case is said to be almost hopeless. A telegram received at Daventry at 3.30 p.m. said he was still alive. What an awful visitation! God comfort that poor Princess! I do feel for her and the Queen and for them all. It is just ten years since his father died. I could think of nothing else.

"*Sunday, December* 10.—The Prince was still alive at 7.30 p.m. last night. I have an almost superstitious feeling that if he can survive this week, he will live. Ten years ago, his father died on Saturday the 14th, at 11 p.m. What a strange thing loyalty is! Here is a man whom I scarcely know, yet, because he is the Prince of Wales, I and thousands of others, who have not my associations with his family and affection for them, are watching as if it were at the sick-bed of a dear friend. Oh! how vividly it recalls that awful time at Cannes ten years ago.

"*December* 11.—The Prince is still alive—yesterday there was a slight rally, but this morning the telegram is as bad as bad can be. The account of the poor Princess slipping away for half an hour to church yesterday is most touching. May God comfort her!

"*December* 12.—Thank God the Prince is still alive! —at least, he was still alive this morning. The intense feeling all over the country is perfectly beautiful, and the united prayers offered up by the whole nation are touching beyond words. Sophy and Henry arrived about 3 p.m., and said that all along the line the excitement was intense—heads hung out of the windows at every station asking, ' Is he still alive? Is there another telegram? What is the latest news?' If God spares his life, he can never forget it.

"*December* 13.—But little change—but what there is, is not for the worse. If he outlives to-morrow, I shall believe that God has granted his life to the prayers of the nation.

"*December* 14.—This day ten years ago the Prince Consort died, and now his son lies at the point of death. But thank God to-day's telegram is better. If he outlives the day, I shall believe in his recovery. It recalls that awful time so vividly. And dear Princess Christian is there.

"*December* 15.—We drove into Daventry, and were rejoiced by a decidedly improved report of the Prince. I do think he has turned the corner and will be spared to say, like Louis XV., ' Qu' ai-je donc fait pour être tant aimé?' "

Two months later, Lady Knightley was present in St. Paul's at the solemn thanksgiving service for the Prince of Wales's recovery.

"*Claridge's Hotel, Tuesday, February* 27, 1872.—A day long to be remembered in our annals—the nation's thanks to God for hearing the nation's prayers. All ordinary traffic was suspended and all the shops were shut as we drove to the House of Commons. Here the two Estates of the Realm embarked on board steamers and sped down the silent highway, where the Embankment, St. Thomas's Hospital, and the Houses of Parliament hold their own even against Somerset House, Lambeth, and the Temple. The day was perfectly fine, and the sun shone while we were in St. Paul's. It was a grand sight, tier upon tier of faces rising on all sides in that vast dome, which forms a better centre than could be found in any Gothic church. Our wait was a long one but full of interest, as we were surrounded by all that is most distinguished and fairest in the land. Lady Bath, Lady Cowper, and Lady Brownlow—to my mind three of the loveliest of women—sat opposite, and 'Mr. Speaker' was escorted to his chair of state in front of us with great ceremony. It is indeed a proud position to belong to the Commons of England, the most distinguished body in Europe. They are not all gentlemen—why should they be, as they represent the whole nation?—and I have no patience with people who are too grand and too exclusive, forsooth, to sit among them. Soon the Lord Chancellor came in, and then the organ pealed out 'God save the Queen,' and we all rose to our feet as Her Majesty came in. She looked ill and worn, as if the intense anxiety had told upon her, and may well have been overcome by the extraordinary enthusiasm of the welcome which she received, I learn, all along her route. The Prince looked pale and hollow-eyed, as one might expect. He looked about a little at first, but seemed suddenly to recollect himself, and bent his head in deep devotion. The Princess looked pale, but very charming in a bright blue velvet gown, and Prince Leo had an expression of awe upon his face, as if he felt the solemnity of the occasion deeply. The service was short, and the most impressive moment seemed to me that when the whole assembly sat hushed to hear the Archbishop's sermon. Oh! I think and trust God's blessing is upon us, as a nation—little as we deserve it!"

CHAPTER XVIII

POLITICAL PARTIES AND CABINET MINISTERS

1872–1873

"*Burghley House, January* 31, 1872.—We arrived here to-day, to find a tremendous political gathering, literally almost the whole of the ex-Ministry, with the important exceptions of Lord Salisbury and Lord Derby. But the Duke and Duchess of Marlborough, Lord and Lady Cairns, Sir John Pakington, Mr. and Mrs. Gathorne-Hardy, Lord and Lady John Manners, Sir John Hay, Mr. Chaplin, Mr. Graves (M.P. for Liverpool), Colonel Annesley, Lord and Lady Eustace Cecil, Mr. Ward Hunt, Mr. Corry, and six of the family, make up a goodly collection. They are all in great excitement, expecting a stormy session, while the Alabama question is the unknown quantity which may upset all calculations. I sat between the Duke of Marlborough and Lord Cairns, whom I found very agreeable. He told me a capital story of Mr. Morris, Solicitor-General for Ireland. He was pleading before 'Alphabetical Smith' when the latter interrupted him testily with—'Mr. Morris, I don't understand your argument.' 'So I presume, my lord,' replied the lawyer, 'but I'll repate it till yer doe l' Lord Cairns declares that he told Lord Derby this story when he recommended Mr. Morris's appointment and that it tickled him greatly. I actually sat down solemnly to whist with three ex-Cabinet ministers: Mr. Gathorne-Hardy, Lord John Manners, and Mr. Ward Hunt, and although in a great fright, got on very well.

"*February* 1.—The usual kind of country-house

day—stitch all the morning, after luncheon a visit to the kitchen, a most lordly apartment with a splendid groined roof and a picture of a huge ox, said to be by Rubens. Then Lady Exeter, Lady John Manners, and I drove into Stamford and ransacked an old curiosity shop, where much to my delight I discovered a whole set of china with the Bowater arms, which came from a Mr. Sawyer, who was connected with our family. I invested in it on the spot ! The Northcotes and Finches arrived—Mrs. Finch, *née* Edith Montgomery, looking exceedingly lovely. I sat between Lord John and Mr. Hardy and discussed politics, and afterwards played whist with Mr. Hunt, Mr. Chaplin, and Mr. Hardy.

"*February* 2.—I sat at work steadily all the morning, with much pleasant talk circulating round me, especially on Women's Franchise, of which I was rejoiced to find Sir Stafford and Lady Northcote staunch supporters, while Mr. Graves confessed that his colleague, Lord Sandon, had been converted by his contact with Mrs. Anderson and Miss Davies on the London School Board. We paid a visit to the plate closet—and a most gorgeous collection it contains, from Queen Elizabeth's exquisitely fine silver filigree drying-plate to the gold breakfast service in relief, bought in Rome before the present Queen's visit. There were some beautiful old chased silver decanter-stands, silver wall-sconces, etc. We left after luncheon, travelling as far as Rugby with Mr. Graves, a shrewd, clever, sensible Liverpool merchant, who is strongly in favour of the State-control of railways, which would, he declares, enable us to pay off the National Debt. The Alabama question seems to be uppermost in men's minds just now. The Americans have certainly perpetrated a gigantic fraud, and our Commissioners were idiots to be so easily imposed upon.

"*Claridge's Hotel, March* 5.—After a morning spent in house-hunting, I went to the House of Commons and heard the debate on my beloved Education. Mr. Dixon, the head of the Birmingham League, moved a long string of resolutions condemnatory of the Act of 1870. He spoke fluently, but not to the point, without daring to bring forward the real object of all his efforts and agitation—the exclusion from the schools of all religious teaching. He was followed by Mr. Richards, the member for Merthyr Tydvil, with whom I was much better pleased, for he spoke as if he honestly believed that what he advocated was for the good of the country. Then came Mr. Forster, who spoke as he always does, in a straightforward, manly way, but said that a general compulsory measure might be necessary next year. I came back after dinner, and heard Dr. Lyon Playfair and Professor Fawcett, who both made good speeches, and saw the division taken about twelve o'clock—95 to 355. This was on the whole satisfactory, although several voted in the minority of whom I should not have expected it.

"*Fawsley, March 20.*—The House behaved very idiotically last night, hooting and shouting like a set of schoolboys and turning out the reporters. Sir Charles Dilke had only three supporters; but the business will leave a bad impression on the country, I fear. All about here, we are much worried by the agricultural labourers' strike, instigated by Arch and a few others. It is quite a new phenomenon in these parts, but *cela donne à penser.* I read Burke's fine speech on Economic Reforms, and thought how much times had changed since his day, and what a contrast there was between the spirit in which he brought forward his motion and Sir Charles Dilke's attack.

"6 *Great Stanhope Street, April 24.*—We went to luncheon with Lady Anna Stirling-Maxwell. Sir William was most agreeable, and the house is full of lovely things. I wonder how far it is right to spend so much in that most fascinating form of refined self-indulgence—Art! In the afternoon we went to one of the most agreeable parties I ever remember at the Palace—entirely indoors, and everybody in high good-humour—in short, a real success. I had great fun; for the Archbishop of York took me to have tea, and, *chemin faisant,* I fell in with Prince Leo, so that between the two I was fairly puzzled, and was obliged at last to say to Prince Leo, ' You know, sir, I can't keep an Archbishop waiting with my cup of tea in his hand!' So I went to fetch it, and then had a good long talk with my dear Prince. After that, I had quite an interesting conversation with Mr. Gladstone— chiefly on the merits of tea, which he praises as the best possible restorative, and says that he always drinks it when he comes in from the House, as well as after his favourite physical exertion of cutting down trees. He has certainly most agreeable manners, but I still think a very sinister expression.

"*St. Mark's Day, April* 25, 1872.—My thirtieth birthday! I can hardly believe it. I feel still so young, so joyous and happy—younger in some respects than I did five years ago. Yet it is an era in life—the close of a decade. Youth, one may say, is over; middle age beginning. It was a very happy birthday. Rainald gave me such a lovely emerald and diamond ring, and we went together to see a charming collection of pictures at Christie's. Mr. Gladstone told us of it yesterday, and Sir Joshua, Turner, Crome, Linnell, etc., were all well represented. At five I went to St. Peter's, Eaton Square, and heard an admirable sermon from Mr. Wilkinson, drawing both warning and encouragement from St. Mark's character—bidding us rejoice in every little cross in our self-indulgent, luxurious lives, and at the same time speaking in words soul-stirring as the trump of battle, of the certainty of victory that awaits us if we fight on to the end, not in our own strength, looking for our exceeding great reward. It was a sermon to do one good in all the turmoil of this busy world. Mr. Wilkinson certainly does appeal to me with quite peculiar force. He has a wonderful power of fitting into one's daily life, and I go to hear him whenever it is possible to get a seat in that crowded church. I feel every day more strongly that it is not right to spend one's whole life for three months simply for one's own amusement. God help me with this workhouse visiting which I am so anxious to undertake!

"*May* 1.—Rainald voted for the Women's Franchise Bill, much to my joy. The more I think about it, the more convinced I feel that it is only just women should have the vote, and that many injustices under which they labour will never be removed until they do have it. Rainald met Lord Salisbury, who is full of the idea of moving the rejection of the Ballot Bill in the House of Lords, and strongly urged him not to do so foolish a thing. Strange that so clever a man should not know the feeling of the country better! Such an act would only give a factitious popularity to a measure which now needs but very little to become very unpopular.

"*May* 3.—A very amusing day! Lord Stanhope and Mr. Lowe joined us out riding, and I had a good deal of talk with the former about the excavation of the Temple of Diana at Ephesus, and then about Goethe, whom he quoted freely. Then the King of the Belgians rode up to Mr. Lowe, who, taking His Majesty for Mr. Mundella, gave him about the most discourteous reception ever experienced by a crowned head. It was a funny scene, and how Mr. Lowe did chuckle over it when, after riding some time with the King, whose identity he had by this time discovered, he returned to us. Meanwhile King Leopold's attendant, Baron Lunden, gave us a very amusing account of the late carousal at Berlin on the Emperor's birthday, just as I remember hearing Countess Savernia describe it, one hot afternoon at Primkenau. Mr. Lowe and Rainald then fell to talking politics, recalling the time when they worked so hard together in 1866, and had so nearly created a strong Constitutional party to see it all destroyed the following year, and *selon eux* the country ruined by Mr. Disraeli. I can fully enter into their feelings, although how far the country is ruined remains yet to be proved! 'But after that,' continued Mr. Lowe, 'having done what I could for my country, I resolved to do a little for myself. I remember Lady Lansdowne telling me that I could never again join either party, but must remain "in a solitary cave," and so I might if I had been Marquis of Lansdowne, but being only a lawyer with a small practice, the case was different.' There was a delightful honesty about the confession, I must say, but one could not help feeling glad there should be some politicians, such as Lord Lansdowne, who are both socially and pecuniarily independent. Mr. Lowe and Lord Stanhope afterwards had a discussion on literary monarchs, apropos of the King of the Belgians presiding on Wednesday at the dinner of the Literary Fund. It is curious how few they were able to mention. Frederick II., whose fighting, however, was certainly better than his writing, Nero, Claudius, Louis XVIII., seemed to exhaust the list. They might have added James I. of Scotland and Charles I. In the evening we had the most successful dinner, I think, that we have ever had. Lord and Lady Salisbury, Lord and Lady Stanhope, Lord and Lady Aveland, Mr. and Lady Margaret Beaumont, Colonel Tomline, Lord and Lady William Osborne, Lady Donoughmore, and Matt Ridley. How they did talk! I got on a great deal better with Lord Salisbury than I did at Hatfield, and found him most agreeable and interesting. We talked of the Athanasian Creed, which he thinks the Reformers ought not to have put into the Prayer Book, although he doubts whether their mistake can be remedied now. Of the Conservative reaction, which he thinks is in some measure due to the alarm caused by the Commons. Of Mr. Gladstone, whom he does not appear to dislike as much as many people do. Of Mr. Forster, whom he does not seem altogether to trust, saying that we shall have rate-schools all over the country in ten years, and then no schools at all, owing to the opposition to Local Taxation. Of the Women's Franchise, for which he would certainly have voted had he been in the House of Commons: he can see no reason against it, although he does not consider it to be a pressingly needed reform at the present time.

"*May* 6.—I went to the Drawing-room—truly a dream of fair women! Lady Brownlow, Lady Dudley, and Lady Ilchester form a trio not easily to be surpassed in any country or generation—whatever one's elders may say! Violent contrasts of colour seem to be much the fashion, and unless managed with consummate taste and skill, are to my mind very ugly. The prevailing rage for two shades of the same colour also strikes me as very inartistic. It is curious how very few people make any attempt to dress artistically. I don't pretend to do it myself, but I flatter myself that my gown, pink with a black and pink train, softened with white lace and long trails of horse-chestnut blossoms, was effective and in good taste. It was a long business, and the Queen had left when we passed, which I did not much mind, as Princess Christian came to take her place. I met her last week at tea at Emmy Hamilton's, looking uncommonly well after spending two months abroad.

"*May* 10.—Rainald dined with the Speaker, I with the Petres—sat between Lord Calthorpe and Mr. Leopold Rothschild, and was not particularly amused, except by Lady Margaret Beaumont; went on to a small party at Bridgewater House, which is always pleasant. The hall is, to my fancy, the finest thing I know in London, to say nothing of the pictures. Lord Granville and Mr. Gladstone in deep confab upset a lamp between them. Is it an omen of coming events? To a charming ball at Lady Bristol's, with — oh! such flowers. The centre court was roofed in and turned into a perfect bower, and there were very many pretty faces; but I don't much care for balls. Rainald moved an amendment in the Report on the Ballot Bill last night, —' That the declaration of a voter that he cannot read or write shall be enough for the returning officer to mark his paper for him, without going to a magistrate,' —and nearly beat the Government, 168–183. It is pleasant to see him taking a real interest in politics.

"*May* 15.—Last night we dined with the Donegalls, and I went to some charming music at Mrs. Loyd Lindsay's, with lovely pictures and a few really pleasant people scattered about—not placed formally and not too many of them! Hallé and Madame Norman

Neruda played beautifully, and I had a little talk with Mr. Gladstone and the Bishop of Peterborough. This evening I went to a small but very new and amusing party at Princess Louise's. I liked seeing her receive for the first time. It seems only the other day we were all girls together. At dinner at Colonel Tomline's I sat between Gerald Lascelles and Mr. Hayward—a clever enough man, if what he says is to be trusted. He told me a curious story about Lady Waldegrave's influence with the Duc d'Aumale, which is so great that the Comte de Paris wrote to her only last week to beg her to induce him to speak in the Assembly—which he did two days ago.

"*June 27.*—Off at cockshout to the Pro-Cathedral at Kensington—a fine building of which one little suspects the existence—to attend the wedding of Prince Louis Lichtenstein and Miss Marie Fox, Lady Holland's adopted daughter. We were invited by the express wish of the bridegroom, with whom I made friends two years ago at Knole. All the Royalties and diplomats were present, and quite a crowd of smart people. The lively little bride, with her black hair and sparkling eyes, was a marked contrast to the Prince, tall and brown-haired, with his pale, thoughtful face and earnest expression. Lord Granville gave away the bride, and Archbishop Manning, in white and gold cope and jewelled mitre, performed the ceremony. I was deeply interested in seeing him again, remembering his visit years ago to that quiet little Sotterley Rectory. He looked exactly like the Doge of Venice in the National Gallery—hard, stern, and impassive; but when I saw him nearer I was struck by his worn and weary expression. Has he found the Church of Rome a gigantic mistake? In his address, he spoke very strongly of the indissoluble union of marriage, describing it as a state full of duties and obligations, of joys and sorrows. This young couple had launched their barque on a bright summer sea, but they would soon be overtaken by storms and tempests, and unless the Redeemer of the world was in the barque that bore them, these storms and tempests would be too much for the frailty of human happiness. Had the scandal of the day—the escapade of that pretty Lady Wentworth, whose fair, innocent face charmed me, I remember, little more than two years ago—given emphasis to his words? I could not help wondering.

"We all went on to Holland House, and well may the *Times* say that all that is most distinguished in the society of England was there. We wandered about for some hours in that most interesting house and garden, every inch of which is full of historic memories, and met many friends. I noticed Mr. Gladstone in earnest conversation with Lord Russell, looking radiant owing to the decision volunteered by the Arbitrators in the *Alabama* case, that they cannot entertain the Indirect Claims.

"*June* 29.—Last night Rainald made a short speech on the Ballot Bill, which seems to have told; for one member after another came up this morning in the Park to chaff and congratulate him about it. It was on making use of the schools as polling-places. He told them that in cutting out this clause, the House of Lords had with perverse ingenuity contrived to take out almost the only good clause of an extremely bad Bill. This change would increase the expense of elections, and enhance the difficulty of getting candidates recommended by other qualifications than wealth. 'The Reform Bill of 1867,' he continued, 'has produced one result we none of us anticipated: we have now the richest House of Commons we have ever seen, but although it is certainly the wealthiest, I am very far from saying it is the most eloquent or the most intelligent.'

"*July* 4.—I drove with Mamma to Lady Leven's breakfast at Roehampton, which was peculiarly pretty and successful on this lovely day. It seemed like a bit of old times, roaming about that lawn, meeting old friends at every turn, most of them with little ones clustering around them. Ah well! I must not repine. One piece of news I heard which touched me more nearly than I had thought possible—my old lover, Captain B——, is said to be dying. Rainald was very dear and kind when I told him about it, and full of concern. In the evening, I went to a ball at Northumberland House, a very stately mansion of olden time, with a beautiful gallery and many other rooms looking on the gardens, which were gay with coloured lamps. I shall have been in nearly all the big houses in London this year.

"*Holmbury, Dorking, Sunday, July* 7.—We came down late yesterday to this most delicious little place, and had a charming drive from Gomshall, the station, through deep ferny lanes, over hills covered with furze and heather, by picturesque red-roofed cottages, and then such a view from the house, perched as it is on the side of a hill and looking over a wide stretch of richly wooded country. The party consists of our pleasant host, Mr. Leveson-Gower, Mr. and Mrs. West, Lady Alwyne Compton, Lord Arthur Russell, Mlle de la Peyronnet, and Mr. Cheney, and very well chosen it is. To-day we drove to a quaint old church with Norman arches and a pretty rectory hard by, sat out in this delicious garden all the afternoon, and walked up the breezy hill behind the house, covered with gorse and heather.

"*July* 8.—We had a delightful ramble through the woods, passing close to Wotton, John Evelyn's beautifully wooded home. Never was there such perfect country so near to London. It seems like a bit that has been forgotten by the world. I could linger for ever among these Surrey commons, with their waving foxgloves, long trails of wild roses, climbing honeysuckles, quaint farmhouses, rustic inns, cottages smothered in roses, and water-meadows rich in meadowsweet! Most reluctantly we tore ourselves away from this paradise, and returned to smoky London with our host.

"*July* 17.—I was very nervous and uneasy about our first party. We went out riding, and kept quiet later. Prince Arthur dined with us, and was very nice and friendly. We had the Spencers, Baths, Bradfords, Listowels, Lord Sefton, Lord Burghley, Lady Manners, etc., to meet him, and a small party afterwards. They all knew each other, and it did very well. I went on to Lady Penrhyn's ball, which was very empty, and actually danced several times: I am an old goose, but I do enjoy dancing for dancing's sake!

"*Dunwich, July* 24.— Dear Edith's birthday! I thought of her so much coming down here. Rainald went off early to Lord Southampton's funeral, and Mellish and I came down here, and found my uncle and aunt, St. John and Constance,[1] all kinder and more cordial one than another.

"*July* 27.—St. John drove me over to Sotterley quite early, that I might have a long day there, and I *did* enjoy it. It all seemed so natural that I could not believe four years had elapsed since I was there even for a day. The only thing that seemed strange was the heat and the luxuriant summer foliage, having never been there in July before. I went to see several old friends,—one I found had died last week,—played on the harmonium in church, and visited my dear father's grave, where the growth of the trees more than anything else reminds me of the lapse of time. As to St. John, he is completely his old self, only more courteous, more anxious to be kind and friendly than of yore. It is a great pleasure to be here again. Each morning I take an early walk by the sea, as I used to do in old days, and sketching and chess fill up most of the day; and after tea I dawdle with my uncle over the purple heaths I love so well. I have enjoyed my visit thoroughly, and they have all been most kind to me."

A month at Buxton that August afforded the opportunity for visits to Hardwick, Chatsworth, Haddon Hall, and Bakewell, where the Vicar, Dr. Balston, formerly

---

[1] Lady Constance Seymour, daughter of the Marquis of Hertford; married in 1871 to Lieut.-Colonel F. St. John Barne, late Scots Guards. He died in 1898.

Head Master of Eton, took Sir Rainald and Lady Knightley over the ancient church, " doing the honours in the most friendly manner," and showing them the famous runic cross and the Vernon Chapel with the tomb of Dorothy Vernon, who ran away with John Manners and took Haddon into the Duke of Rutland's family. Lord Redesdale was their companion on several of these excursions in the Peak Country, and proved an admirable cicerone.

A visit to Colonel Tomline's, at Orwell Park, Ipswich, was the chief incident of the following autumn. Lady Knightley thoroughly appreciated her host's fine collection of paintings, and was taken a drive to Felixstowe, then " a tiny watering-place in embryo, which may be developed in the future."

" *October* 16.—This party is too amusing. I long for a really clever pen to describe it. Lady Cork alone, with her unfailing wit, her continual flow of talk and chaff, her endless stories, keeps one in fits of laughter. She is never tired of recounting her battles with Lady Waldegrave for precedence. On one occasion, at Strawberry Hill, Lady Cowley was told off to go before her with Count Apponyi, upon which she hooked up ' Dot and go one,' as she called Lord Grey, and bustled in first, to her hostess's great discomfiture. Then there is the Duke of Somerset, quiet, gentlemanly, full of information, but not very ready with conversation. Mr. Milner Gibson is lighter in hand than the Duke, and very easy to get on with. One sees at a glance that he does not know what principle means, but he is shrewd and clear-headed to a degree. He disapproves highly of the retrospective clauses of the Washington Treaty, and seems to doubt whether the *Alabama's* escape was an infringement of international law, as it then existed. He talked a good deal about Disraeli, as did the Duke, and told me an anecdote which shows how intensely he cares for the Jews. When there was a question of Rothschild being debarred from sitting in the House, on account of some contract, he moved heaven and earth to influence the decision of the Committee appointed to decide the question—and succeeded.

"*October* 18.—In spite of a threatening morning, the Duke of Somerset and I started soon after twelve for Helmingham, of which I have heard so much all my life. It is certainly a very perfect specimen of an early Tudor house, entirely unspoilt, built round a courtyard, with moat and drawbridge still in perfect preservation. The rooms are small, but have a good deal of character. In the library, Mr. Tollemache showed us a very choice collection of Caxtons, including the first, the *Treatise on Chess*, and some exquisite illuminated MSS: one of the thirteenth century was a copy of King Alfred's translation of Orosius. We saw Queen Elizabeth's room, and her virginal, as well as her portrait, which she afterwards presented to Lord Dysart. Mr. Tollemache also showed us a letter which he had just received from Mr. Gladstone, enclosing a newspaper extract recommending that each labourer should be given ten acres of land, with which sage proposal Mr. Gladstone expressed himself as much struck! The Duke, who is by no means devoted to his former colleague, marvelled with me over the total ignorance of all knowledge of rural life which this betrayed. Oh dear! I am so sleepy, I had better go to bed, for I can't even write English, but one does not go driving about every day with ex-Cabinet ministers!

"*Claridge's Hotel, March* 7, 1873.—We went to see the Old Masters at Burlington House, and Rainald recognised an exquisite portrait of Miss Linley, afterwards Mrs. Sheridan, by Gainsborough, which used to be at Delapré Abbey. It is a sweet face, with dark eyes, regular delicate features, and a mouth just ready to break into smiles. Rainald used to say he would never marry till he had found a woman like it! Luckily for me he did not keep his word. Another Gainsborough which interested me was the portrait of a 'Lady in a blue dress,' which I find is the Mrs. Bowater whose china I picked up so curiously last year at Stamford.

"Meanwhile the debate on the Irish University Bill drags its slow length, and Rainald is sorely troubled what to do. If, as seems probable, the independent Liberals vote against the Government, the issue lies mainly in the hands of the small section of independent Conservatives, among whom he is a ruling spirit. Mr. Hardy made a speech last night which certainly admitted of the interpretation that in the event of the Ministry being defeated, he should refuse to take office under Disraeli, and Rainald went to him this evening and asked if that was his meaning. He pledged himself distinctly to that effect, so now Rainald can vote with a clear conscience, without any risk of bringing in Disraeli to carry more revolutionary measures than ever! It has made his course plain, anyhow. He dined with Baron Ferdinand Rothschild, and sat next Lord Hartington, who seemed in a piteous state of mind about the Government's prospects, and hinted that if they were beaten it was not unlikely that Mr. Gladstone himself would retire. A Conservative has been returned by an immense majority (1354) for Mid-Cheshire—the first county election under the Ballot.

"*March* 11.—At 3 a.m. this morning, after Mr. Gladstone had summed up the debate in what Rainald says was one of the finest speeches he has ever heard him make, full of humour, pathos, tact, and good temper, so that Rainald said ' it quite went to my heart to vote against him,' Ministers were defeated by a majority of three! If Rainald had not been in town, this result would not have occurred. It was he who read between the lines of Mr. Hardy's speech the assurance which the independent members needed, and by his interview with him made assurance doubly sure. Lord Salisbury, who is in a certain sense their leader, sent them word to stay away; and Lord Eustace Cecil, Mr. Beresford Hope, and a few others did so. The rest minded Rainald, and so turned the scale.

"*March* 12.—Of course we could think and talk of little but politics. The House is adjourned till Thursday, and Mr. Gladstone has had two interviews with the Queen, who by great good luck is in town. Beyond that, nothing is known. There is an admirable leader in the *Times*, which might have been written by Rainald himself, alluding pointedly to the ' understanding ' between the leaders of the Opposition and the independent members.

"*March* 14.—Ministers have resigned, and Mr. Disraeli has been sent for.

"*March* 15.—Mr. Disraeli has refused to form a Government. It was, of course, impossible, after Mr. Hardy's distinct pledge. Gladstone and Disraeli's explanations are the chief topic of conversation. Disraeli's speech, giving his reasons for not taking office, is extremely clever and dexterous. For once he has behaved in a statesman-like manner. I asked Rainald to-day when he first began to distrust him. He said, ' Very soon after I first came into Parliament, I was desired by the whip to do all I could to get our men to vote against the Government on some question—not a very important one—on which they seemed to me to be in the right. However, I trusted our leader, and thought he probably knew more about it than I did, so I did as I was bid. When we got into the Lobby, we found ourselves in a minority, upon which Disraeli said, " There! we've sacrificed our characters, and voted wrong, and haven't beat the Government after all!"' Comment, I think, is superfluous.

"*Fawsley, March* 18.—Rainald was very much annoyed by a printed notice, purporting to emanate from the Badby branch of the National Agricultural Labourers' Union, desiring him to raise all his labourers' wages to 15s. a week with beer, or 16s. without, for a day of ten hours, excepting on Saturdays, when they are to leave at four o'clock. Similar notices have been sent to every employer of labour, and he is the more angry because he says the farmers have behaved with great forbearance, paying good wages all through the winter, so he thinks it most ungrateful of the men. I regret it more than I can say, the more so as it will prevent me from carrying out a scheme for a coal club which I have been very full of. I can't do it without the farmers, and I could not appeal to them for help just now.

"*April* 15.—And so ends another winter at dear Fawsley, in some respects the most satisfactory we have yet had. May God bless and prosper all the various works we have started, especially the systematic district visiting, which has brought me into touch with all classes of people in Badby and Charwelton, and gives me some real insight into the lives of Rainald's cottagers."

CHAPTER XIX

ROYALTIES—ENGLISH AND FOREIGN

1873

"*Firle, Lewes, Sussex, April* 17.—The usual happy holiday life here, which I always thoroughly enjoy, especially after the hard work of the last few weeks. The weather deliciously spring-like, and flowers everywhere. I played croquet most of the day, and went to evensong at six, which was very restful and pleasant, and I felt I might well say a thanksgiving for the weather and my holiday.

"*Saturday, April* 19.—Before I go to bed, I must write an account of our charming day at Hurstmonceaux, a place which *Memorials of a Quiet Life* has made classic ground. We went by train to Hailsham, and had a pretty drive through the Sussex lanes, just bursting into leaf under the cloudless sky. We went first to the church of which Augustus Hare tells us that Julius would ' look across the Level to the sea against the shining line of which the grey stunted spire of the hill-set church stood as if embossed.' The interior is very simple, its only feature a fine tomb, of 1534, to Lord Dacre. Just on the edge of the hill stands the beautiful old yew tree with the three graves, that of Julius Hare, Marcus Hare, and Mrs. Frederick Maurice, and a little farther off the white cross with its simple inscription : ' MARIA HARE, Nov. 22, 1798— Nov. 13, 1870. Until the Day break.' We walked down from here to the magnificent ruin of the old Castle, built in 1440, and of which Horace Walpole gives so amusing an account, when he visited it in 1752. Then it was perfect and inhabited, and many were the reproaches showered upon the memory of Mrs. Henrietta Hare, who reduced it to its present lamentable condition. The outline of the great hall and of the chapel and most of the rooms can still be traced, and the beautiful oriel window of the 'Ladies' Bower' is still standing. We had a charming luncheon in the ruins, and drove round by Lime and the Rectory, to see the position of houses where we have lately been dwelling so much in thought.

"1 *Park Lane, Piccadilly, April* 28. — There is always a certain degree of solemnity in taking possession of a new house: one never knows what may befall one in it. We were very sorry to leave Firle, where we have had such a happy time; but we had a prosperous journey, and I was busy all the afternoon, settling into this most fascinating abode.

"*May* 1.—A most extraordinary thing took place in the House of Commons. The adjourned debate on Mr. W. H. Smith's resolution on Local Taxation was resumed. A tremendous whip had been sent out on both sides, the House was crowded with more than 500 members, Mr. Disraeli wound up the debate in most pugnacious terms, daring Gladstone to a division, when lo and behold! it all collapsed, because when the question was put and the Liberals said 'No,' not a soul on the Conservative side challenged a division. Such a thing has hardly ever, if ever, been known in Parliamentary history, and it shows how unanimous was the opinion of the party against the course their leader tried to impose upon them. Rainald has gone about for several days saying it was madness to divide, and the greater part of the world has come round to his opinion. We should have been beaten by 90, instead of winning by 100, as we did last year, so ill-timed and ill-placed was the resolution, to the principle of which—*i.e.* the necessity for some relief to local taxation—we all agree.

"*Sunday, May* 4.—We walked to Whitehall, to hear Bishop Wilberforce. It was a very interesting sermon on St. Paul's word to the Thessalonians, ' Remembering without ceasing your work of faith and labour of love and patience of hope,' three things which ought to characterise all Christian life. I was struck with one remark he made—' that the present age is so impatient for results.' I must not expect Badby to mend its ways in a year, or in many years. And then, oh! who—at least not I—can say that they work faithfully?

" *May* 24.—I walked into the Park with Rainald and Harry Gage, to see the meet of the Four-in-hand Club. It was quite like a scene in some foreign town—the crowds of people wandering up and down on the grass under the green trees in the bright sunshine, and strings upon strings of carriages blocking the road in every direction—the Princess of Wales driving by with her own pretty, gracious smile, and then these beautifully-turned-out teams bowling along.

" *May* 26.—I had a delicious ride with Rainald, and Mr. Hardy joined us, which is always pleasant. It really is worth almost any exertion to get that charming hour of air, exercise, and society. We dined at Lady Stanhope's, a most agreeable party—Motley, Froude, Hamilton Aïde, etc. I sat between Edward Stanhope and Mr. Froude, whom I found very amusing, although we hardly agreed at all. I told him he was very hard upon the landlords, which he did not like. He maintains that people ought to be governed, not to govern themselves, and says you don't take a vessel out to sea and let the sailors vote every day how she is to be managed, and that in the same way the vessel of State ought not to be at the mercy of the multitude. He hates political economy from beginning to end, and would like all the trades organised in Guilds, as in old days, which at least ensured good work, and says Trades Unions are only inarticulate endeavours after the old organisation. He does not approve of the modern idea that every man is as good as any other, and thinks nothing will be mended till the present enormous increase of expenditure on personal luxury is checked."

The visit of the Shah to London in the summer was

the occasion for great festivities ; most of the big houses were thrown open, and Lady Knightley thoroughly enjoyed the succession of brilliant entertainments in the Persian monarch's honour.

"*June* 18.—We drove down to Carlton House Terrace to see the Shah's arrival, which has sent the whole of London clean out of whatever little mind it possessed. Certainly it is a remarkable thing the way these Eastern potentates are attracted by Western civilisation. First the Khedive, then the Sultan, then the Shah of Persia ! We only want the Emperor of China and the Mikado of Japan to complete it. Unfortunately, the pageant was marred by a terrific thunderstorm, and the rain came down in buckets as he emerged from the Horse Guards. He was delayed first by a fog in the Channel, then by the heating of a wheel in his train, so was more than an hour late, and arrived without a scrap of luggage. We dined with the Poltimores to meet Princess Mary and the Duke of Teck.

"*June* 20.—A long and busy day. We walked into the Park to see the Shah, which we did with much success—an ugly, sulky-looking individual he is ! In the afternoon to the Heathcotes' very pretty amateur exhibition of drawings, after which I had a long visit from dear little Lady Constance Lawley and an interesting talk over home duties. Then came our dinner, which we flatter ourselves was a great success, in spite of the kitchen chimney taking fire in the middle —which, however, we did not know at the time. We had Princess Louise and Lord Lorne, the Baths, Seftons, Corks, Bradfords, Mahons, Lord Hartington, and Lady Sophia Macnamara. Then off to the Guildhall, where we arrived in a scrimmage of Royalties, just as the Shah left ; but we had a good stare at him in the carriage. The ball was a fine sight in that grand old Hall, and I had a valse with Charley Newdegate.

"*June* 23.—This Shah excitement makes one feel horribly idle and *désœuvré*. While I think of it, I must record Lord Odo Russell's *mot*. Seeing His Persian Majesty slightly overcome at one banquet, he remarked to the French Ambassador, ' Oh! la nuit tout chat est gris.' In Paris the Shah was saluted by the mob with nothing but ' Miau-miau '! This evening, Mamma, Val, and I went to the Albert Hall, which the hard-worked Shah visited in state. The whole of that enormous building was densely crowded, tier upon tier rising up to the top of the vast dome, while every face was turned to the central dais. Certainly it was a sight to remember !—the Shah of Persia seated between the Princess of Wales and her sister, the Czarevna. The Shah has an intelligent face, and uses much gesticulation. He talked a great deal to Princess Dagmar, whose animated expression was pleasant to watch. The Shah wore the famous diamond aigrette in his cap, his coat was studded with pearls and diamonds, and a great rope of pearls and emeralds hung round his neck. When, at last, the whole assembly rose for ' God save the Queen,' a strong magnesium light was flashed down on the Royalties, making the whole house as light as day—a very striking scene, which I shall not easily forget.

" *June* 24.—We went to the Court Theatre to see the *Happy Land*, a clever satire on the Government in general and Messrs. Gladstone, Lowe, and Ayrton in particular, which has acquired a wonderful popularity by reason of the Lord Chamberlain having freely used his scissors on the more personal portions and forbidden the actors to make up their faces in imitation of Messrs. Gladstone, Lowe, and Ayrton. On to Lady Manvers to hear the Hungarian Band, which the Prince of Wales heard at Pesth and induced to come over. They played with wonderful *verve* and *entrain*, and keep marvellous time.

" *July* 9.—We drove down to Lady Leven's at Roehampton, a very pretty, pleasant party ; dined with Lady Margaret Beaumont, and sat between Lord Eliot and Lord Bute—a curious combination. I may not agree with them in their High Church and Roman views, but it is pleasant to feel one is with people who are deeply religious and really do *care* for God. It does one good in this whirl of worldliness! On to a smart little party at Lady Bradford's, where I met Princess Mary; and then to Lady Listowel's, which was all garden, moonlight, and music. It is such a pretty house—a long vista of brilliantly lighted rooms ending in a conservatory full of palms and flowering shrubs. Princess Louise and Prince Arthur were there, and Princess Christian was at Roehampton—really there is no end to Royalty this year.

"*July* 14.—I went to a very pretty ball at Lansdowne House, where the Princess and Czarevna were again dressed alike, as they were at the Albert Hall and the Palace concert. It is very pretty and nice of them, and they seem such affectionate sisters. It amused me to watch the Royalties dancing—the Prince of Wales with Lady Cuckoo Bingham, the Princess with Lord Dupplin, and the Czarevna with Teck. I also had a long talk with the Duke of Argyll, whom I have hardly seen since Balmoral days.

"*July* 17.—I spent a very pleasant morning with Lady Frederick Cavendish, visiting the new 'Girls' Public Day School' at Chelsea and listening to an extremely able lecture on Political Economy, given by the clever little mistress, Miss Portal. It may seem nonsense to teach girls such a subject, but I am persuaded that no one could watch their eager faces, or listen to their intelligent questions, without seeing that they were receiving a mental training of the most valuable kind; nor could one help feeling that some knowledge of the principles on which the taxation of their own country is managed must be far more useful than an acquaintance with the exact functions discharged by Roman ædiles. I only wished that I had received such training in my youth! This whole movement for the education of girls is no doubt an experiment, especially when one considers the mixture of classes which it involves, but I sincerely hope it will prove successful. I was very glad of a quiet afternoon; and Rainald, who went down to Northampton for the opening of a new cattle-market, returned barely in time for our dinner, at which were present Lord and

Lady William Osborne, Lady Francis Gordon and Lily, the Lowthers, Sir Thomas, Harry Gage, Major Whyte Melville, Sir John and Lady Sebright, and Mr. Motley, whom I found very pleasant, although rather too much of the writer, too much inclined to lecture instead of conversing, not remembering La Bruyère's maxim, ' L'esprit de la conversation consiste bien moins à montrer beaucoup d'esprit soi-même que d'en faire trouver aux autres.' He expressed himself in the most friendly terms as regards this country, saying that a war between England and America was impossible. I did not dare reply, as I should have liked, ' Of course it is, as long as we concede everything you choose to ask ! ' We talked a great deal of Education, which he says is necessarily the basis of the whole State fabric in America, since direct self-government by an ignorant democracy would mean simple mob rule, and it is difficult enough to keep pace with the ignorance imported by the ceaseless stream of immigration. It is entirely free, and the State of Massachusetts alone spends as large a sum annually on Education as that which is voted by the House of Commons here. After dinner, I went to a ball at Apsley House, which I was glad to see, although it will not bear comparison with Bridgewater, Grosvenor, or Dorchester Houses. Some of the pictures are very good, and I was struck with the numerous portraits of Napoleon, including a colossal statue at the foot of the stairs.

" *July* 18.—To-night I went to a ball at Bridgewater House—quite the prettiest of the many pretty fêtes I have seen this season. The flowers were so lovely, and it was so delightful sitting in the arcades and looking down upon the grand hall. The Prince and Princess of Wales and the Czarevna, dressed alike as usual, were there ; but I never even went near the ballroom, and was quite sorry to tear myself away at 1.30 a.m. I suppose there never was a year when so many of the big houses in London were thrown open.

" *July* 19.—We took the most delightful excursion to Ham House with Mr. Tollemache, his four chestnuts bowling along in a way that made driving almost as exciting as a good gallop! The day was perfect for the drive and the row up from Richmond, and the quaint old place looked its best, with the sunshine streaming under the great lime trees, and the old-fashioned flower-borders with their delicious scent. A large party from Sion came over to meet us, among them the late Lord Chancellor, Lord Hatherley, whom I looked at with great respect as the man who amidst all his business avocations taught regularly in the Sunday school and attends daily service in Westminster Abbey. Ham House itself I know by heart, but I was delighted Rainald should see it, and we did not return till past nine—altogether a most enjoyable day.

"*July* 21.—We were terribly shocked to hear of the sudden death of the Bishop of Winchester, who in riding with Lord Granville from Leatherhead to Holmbury, to stay with Mr. Leveson-Gower, was thrown from his horse and killed on the spot. No man was ever better prepared to meet his end, and no one will be more missed both in the Church and in Society. It is very curious that he should die on those lovely Surrey downs where we spent such a happy Sunday just a year ago. I never heard him preach till this summer, when, oddly enough, I have heard him three times; and only a fortnight ago, at Lady Margaret Beaumont's, he shook hands with me at the top of the stairs, whether mistaking me for someone else or because I was with Rainald I cannot tell, but I was pleased, and told Rainald at the time that I hoped to keep up the acquaintance. And now he is gone—behind the veil.

"*Richmond Park, July* 25.—I am staying with the dear mother, enjoying the country quiet and this dear little home, and seeing any number of old friends. To-day, Dr. Günther and his wife (!) came to luncheon, which seemed like a bit of very ancient history dug up again, with a very modern bit patched into it. I always like talking to him, he is so clever and intelligent. But what *old, old* days it recalls!

"*Dalzell, Motherwell, N.B., September* 25.—Yesterday

we left Lamington, a most attractive little place in the hills, and came on by train to this charming old Castle, perched on the side of a wild glen and beautifully restored. It is a pity that the smoke and chimneys all round spoil it so much! To-day, Mr. Hamilton took us for a most fascinating expedition to Bothwell and Cadzow. It was a hideous drive, through the almost contiguous towns of Motherwell, Hamilton, and Bothwell, amidst a teeming mining population, ill-housed and ill-clad, though earning as much as ten shillings a day. We crossed the Clyde at Bothwell Bridge, the scene of the battle in *Old Mortality*, and saw the fine old ruined Castle, hanging over the richly wooded banks of the Clyde. Opposite are the ruins of Blantyre Priory and Cadzow Castle, the earliest seat of the Hamiltons. We visited Barncleuth, a quaint old tiny house with a charming old-fashioned garden, terraced along the glen, with clipped yews and sweet-scented flowers wandering at their own will—a garden out of a story-book. Then, amidst the gnarled, stunted trees of the old Caledonian forest, we saw a herd of fifty wild cattle, splendid white beasts with black ears and muzzles.

> ' Mightiest of all the beasts of chase
>   That roam in woody Caledon,
>   Crashing the forest in his race,
>   The Mountain Bull comes thundering on.
>   Fierce on the hunter's quiver'd band,
>   He rolls his eyes of swarthy glow,
>   Spurns with black hoof and horn the sand,
>   And tosses high his mane of snow.'
>   (*Cadzow Castle*, by Walter Scott.)

" *September* 26.—We ' did ' Hamilton Palace with the Lambtons, who arrived last night. A dreary, hideous, depressing pile it is, though crowded with priceless art-treasures, beautiful cabinets which belonged to Marie Antoinette and to Napoleon, and many fine pictures. A Vandyck portrait of Gustavus Adolphus struck me particularly, and there are good Titians and works by Florentine masters. But the truth is, there is far too much of *everything* for real enjoyment;

and then the pomp and vanity of it all, the living for self and dying for self, seemed stamped upon the whole place, most of all upon the huge Mausoleum, where the last Duke but one rests, embalmed in the sarcophagus of an Egyptian queen, on a splendid marble floor. It gave me a cold shudder, and I escaped joyfully to the pure air and sunshine, which thank God are common to all men.

"*Highclere Castle, Newbury, November* 18.—Tired as I am, I must write a brief record of this interesting day. Rainald and I left home early, and drove in the dogcart to Banbury, where a brief half-hour took us to Oxford, where Charlie and Harry Knightley met us and showed us a good deal of the ancient University, Christ Church itself with its three quads, curious old Cathedral and magnificent dining-hall, and several other Colleges, Magdalen, etc. Then away, with tired brain, to spend an hour at Reading, owing to the breakdown of a goods train in front of us, and arrive here just in time for dinner. It is an interesting and suggestive party—Count Beust, Mr. Browning, Mr. Townsend, editor of the *Spectator*, who in five minutes got into a spar with Rainald over his pet idol, Gambetta ; Mr., Mrs., and Miss Holford, Mr. Cockerell, General Scott, etc. etc.

"*November* 19.—Talking to remarkable people is certainly very hard work! Here I have been divided between Count Beust and Mr. Browning nearly all day. The occupation, amusement, or whatever you like to call it, has been a walk and luncheon at a little house by a lovely lake. Mr. Browning is as different from his poems as anything one can imagine—a loud-voiced, sturdy little man, who says nothing in the least obscure or difficult to understand! Count Beust is a typical *homme du monde*—pleasant enough, as Rainald remarks, when you can stir him up, which is not always an easy task. General Scott is a clever, sensible man, a great authority on sewage. To-day Lady Dorothy Nevill and Meresia have arrived, also Mr. Morier and Mr. Henry Cowper, whom I found very pleasant at dinner.

"*November* 21.—Lady Portsmouth came to luncheon,

and very charming I found her. Miss Holford, too, is a nice, natural, and very pretty girl, whom I like particularly. We all walked up to the top of the Beacon, to see the fine views from the British Camp. Mr. Browning talked a great deal of Carlyle, telling us how he will walk and talk for two hours at a stretch, without letting anyone else get in a word. I wish I had the pen of a Boswell, to put down one-half of the things which I have heard here—instead of which I must go to bed.

" *Ickworth, Bury St. Edmunds, November* 24.—And here I am at Ickworth, giddy and bewildered with all I have done in this last week. After a few days in town, chiefly spent in house-hunting, we came on here, to find a very large party—Lady Howard de Walden and her daughter, Lord and Lady Augustus and Lord John Hervey, Lord and Lady Penzance, Lord and Lady Ruthven, Mr. Manners, Colonel Annesley, Sir Charles Ellice and his wife. I sat between Sir Charles Ellice and Lord John, both of whom were very pleasant. We discussed Mr. Disraeli's fine speech and the striking sentence with which he concludes, saying that England will soon have to take her stand on the principles of the Reformation, in the fight with Ultramontanism, which is about to invade Europe, and ' save civilisation from the withering blasts of atheism and from the simoom of sacerdotal usurpation.'

" *November* 25.—A most lovely day, and we went out to luncheon with the shooters—the wives all trotting after their husbands in truly conjugal fashion. Lord Penzance, who by the way is very agreeable, would not find much work here! Lady Howard de Walden is one of the very few women who visited the old Holland House. She gave us an amusing account of the society over which Lady Holland ruled with a stern and despotic hand. Once she quarrelled violently with Lord George Bentinck because he would not, at her command, break off a conversation in which he was interested. I sat by Lord Charles Bruce at dinner, and was delighted to find him devoted to Mr. Wilkinson, and full of interest in all good works.

"*Chevening, Sevenoaks, November 29.*—We arrived here yesterday, to find another pleasant party—Colonel and Mrs. John Stanley, Mr. and Mrs. Graham, Mr. Delane, Dr. William Smith, editor of the *Quarterly* and of all the Dictionaries, Lord and Lady Mahon, and Mr. Weguelin. The political fighting that goes on is very good fun, Mr. Weguelin being such a terrific Rad, and Colonel Stanley an equally hot Conservative! But the pleasantest thing is seeing all the curiosities in this house. Lord Stanhope showed us his gallery of prints and famous autographs, including a beautiful little poem by Macaulay, the original MS. of the ' Maid of Athens ' (' *Girl* of Athens,' Byron first called it), notes for a speech by Mr. Pitt, a letter from Charles Edward in '45, another from the Duke of Marlborough, etc. Then he took us all over the libraries, which occupy a number of rooms in the wing of the house. That of the first Lord Stanhope remains exactly as he left it. After tea, we had a long *séance* over autographs and epigrams—altogether it was very amusing.

"*Advent Sunday, November 30.*—Not a very Sunday-like Sunday, but a very agreeable one. After morning service, we admired Chantrey's beautiful monument to Lady Frederica Stanhope, the daughter of Lord Mansfield and mother of James Banks Stanhope. She died at the birth of her second son, and is represented with the babe clasped to her bosom. It is the most lovely thing in the world, and I do not wonder to hear that the sculptor himself preferred it to all his other works. It is, to my mind, infinitely more beautiful than the Children in Lichfield Cathedral.

"After church, I listened with keen interest to a long conversation between Rainald and Dr. Smith on the state of the Conservative party, the missed opportunity of forming a strong Coalition in 1866, and the personal antagonism between Lowe and Disraeli, which was one cause of its failure. They further discussed the probability of Lord Salisbury ever joining the Cabinet with Disraeli in it. Incidentally it came out, in the course of conversation, that Lord Carnarvon wrote the article in July on the Lessons of the French Revolution, Dr. Smith himself the one on Grote, and Lord Salisbury, as one had guessed, the political article last October. Then we paid another visit to the library, where we saw a number of Lord Peterborough's letters to the first Lord Stanhope, and ended by taking a walk through the park by an exceedingly pretty drive laid out by the great Lord Chatham, who spent a summer here and took great pleasure in many of the improvements. In the evening, Mr. Philip Stanhope arrived from Moldavia, where he has been acting partly as a civil engineer, partly as a diplomatic agent. He says that Russia is making stealthy strides in the East by means of Panslavism, and thinks that in the event of a war all the Christian subjects of the Porte, of whom there are twelve millions in Turkey alone, would rise against her. Altogether, this has been a most interesting visit, and I can hardly believe that it is not a fortnight since the day we left home.

"*Fawsley, December 8.*—We hunted with the Duke from Hinton—one of those still, grey days, and a capital scent. This evening I finished the Autobiography of J. S. Mill, one of the saddest and most remarkable books that I have ever read. Brought up from infancy to look on Christianity as a superstition and too clear-headed to console himself with *le grand peut-être*, anxious to make the good of others his object yet dimly conscious of the lack of a supreme motive-power, the whole history is a gigantic example of what a broken, distorted thing can be made of life by the finest intellect without the great key which alone can unlock the puzzle."

CHAPTER XX

A Conservative Ministry

1874

The great excitement of the coming winter was the Dissolution of Parliament, followed by a General Election, a surprise sprung on the nation by Mr. Gladstone, and to Lady Knightley's delight her husband was again returned, together with Major Fairfax Cartwright, for South Northamptonshire.

"*Fawsley, Saturday, January* 24.—I had just taken up Grote's *History of Greece* for half an hour to read before luncheon, when Rainald startled us all by announcing, ' Parliament is dissolved ! ' This sudden and, I believe, unprecedented *coup de theâtre* has occupied all our thoughts ever since. Mr. Gladstone publishes a very long, very elaborate address to his constituents, in which he certainly endeavours to be, like St. Paul, ' all things to all men ! ' I think he tries to catch too many kinds of fish, and will probably not succeed, although his bait of repealed income-tax, reformed local taxation, and other remission of taxes, is no doubt very glittering. In other respects the address is a mischievous one, full of impossible schemes mixed up with desirable and needful reforms, while he pledges himself to nothing. What a state of excitement the whole country will be in for the next six weeks ! And oh ! what part in the great drama shall we enact ? May we be guided to do our duty, whatever it is l

" After writing this, Rainald and I had a long, grave talk. Sunday morning brought a letter from Major Cartwright, saying that he meant to stand again, and hoped his colleague would not fail him. In the end, my darling husband decided that it would scarcely be fair on the constituency for him to retire on such short notice, seeing that the elections must all be over in the next fortnight. How thankful I am for this decision I cannot say; with brains like his, and with the insight and influence which he possesses, whenever he chooses to exert himself, it would be a thousand pities to let constitutional indolence induce him to desert his post. The country needs all her good men and true, I am sure, of whatever party they may be. I think we should both go mad over a real contest. Even this mild excitement tires and worries us both a good deal.

"*January* 27.—Sophy and Henry and Sir Thomas Munro all left at an early hour, and Nora Campbell followed later to London. Rainald wrote his address, and I copied it for the printers. It is very short and simple, but manly and dignified. The nomination is fixed for Monday, and on that day, if all goes well,— and every day diminishes the danger of a contest,—it will be all over.

"*February* 1.—Rainald went off early to Northampton, and returned soon after 3 p.m. once more duly elected M.P. for South Northamptonshire. Hurrah ! hurrah ! hurrah !

"*February* 7.—Last night I went with Val to a pretty dance given by the Weedon officers, and we were all greatly excited to hear of the Conservative gains in London. W. H. Smith and Sir Charles Russell are returned with enormous majorities for Westminster, and Mr. Goschen only creeps in at the bottom of the poll for the City, where Cotton, Twells, and Hubbard are triumphantly returned. The Conservatives win ten seats in London alone, and a good many all over the country. Indeed, the long-talked-of reaction has proved itself infinitely more real than could have been anticipated, and for the first time since 1841 the Conservatives will find themselves with a real working majority in the House of Commons. The causes of this extraordinary change are hard to decide, but I think it is in a great measure due to the disgust felt by moderate Liberals at Mr. Gladstone's imperious proceedings.

"*Thursday, February* 19.—On Tuesday Mr. Gladstone went down to tender his resignation, and yesterday morning the Queen sent for Mr. Disraeli. The great news to-day is that Lord Salisbury has joined the Ministry. I *cannot* help thinking that it is far grander and more patriotic on his part to do so than to sacrifice to personal dislike and distrust of Disraeli the services which he must feel he can render to his country. Rainald thinks otherwise, and is of opinion that for the country it would have been better he should stand by and criticise. That may be useful, but can hardly be the highest function of the statesman. He puts Lord Salisbury's action down to love of office and fear of being left out in the cold. I, on the contrary, believe it is inspired by the longing to try and save India from this fearful famine, which he if any man can do.

"*March* 28.—We hunted with the Pytchley from Stowe and came home at 6 p.m., having done nothing, but I much enjoyed a long talk with Lord Granville about education and books. He remarked that the present intellectual position of Christ Church bodes ill for the future of our upper classes. It is melancholy that at our crack college it should be the thing to do nothing. I bemoaned my inability to remember much of what I read, to which he replied that he too had a bad memory, but is satisfied that what one reads, although mainly forgotten, still manures the mind. I was struck by his diplomatic way of asking questions and finding out who people were, etc. Altogether I found him extremely pleasant and light in hand. So ends my hunting season. I have been out nineteen times.

"*4 Grosvenor Crescent, April* 22.—We took possession of our new house two days ago, but still have the house full of workmen. Dined in Carlton House Terrace and sat between Sir Matthew and Mr. Sclater Booth, the new Local Government Board Secretary. He has an idea that Dizzy does not tell the *Times* things, which if true is very imprudent. On to Lady Derby's party at the Foreign Office, a most horrid squash, much worse than in Lady Granville's days. Mr. Lowe, who had been dining at the Speaker's with the late Cabinet, was very good fun about their fall. Rainald was very naughty, chaffing Lord Salisbury for having taken office. He introduced me to Mr. W. H. Smith and Sir Samuel Baker, both of them remarkable men in their way. Mr. Smollett, the member for Cambridge, made a savage attack on Mr. Gladstone in the House on the late Dissolution. Certainly 'Trickster,' the term employed by Mr. Smollett, is scarcely Parliamentary language; still I had rather be called that than to be told, as Mr. Gladstone was by the Duke of Somerset, that he had ' licked the dust off the feet of democracy.'

" *May* 4.—To-night I went to the French play with Prince and Princess Christian, the Princess of Wales, Colonel Teesdale, and Lord Dunmore. We saw *Gavant Minard*, a regular Palais-Royal piece, which I did not like much. Meanwhile Rainald was distinguishing himself in the House. Mr. Hanbury had proposed a resolution pledging us to extend and consolidate our power on the Gold Coast. Sir Wilfrid Lawson had moved an amendment saying it was desirable we should withdraw at once, which he refused to drop. It was most undesirable that we should be committed to either course, but no one saw any way out of the difficulty until Rainald jumped up and, in six sentences, listened to with profound attention, after the previous speaker had been drowned with cries of ' Divide, divide,' moved the adjournment of the debate until July 31. All parties were charmed, and he carried the motion by three to one. To-day men of all shades of opinion are congratulating him, and it is very pleasant to see what weight he carries with him on the rare occasions when he chooses to speak or act.

" *May* 6.—To-day Rainald received an invitation to dine with Mr. Disraeli, which sorely perplexed him. He came, however, I think, to the right decision to decline very courteously in a friendly note, such as he has not written to him for many years. To accept the invitation would be to hamper his power in the House of Commons as an independent member, in which position he can be of great use, while to decline in a formal manner would mean closing the door upon all communication for ever. But how much importance was evidently attached to the matter is shown by the way in which we were attacked on the subject by both of his private secretaries, Monty Corry and Algy Turnor.

"*May* 16.—Rainald and I went to see a collection of paintings and *objets de luxe* made by a Mr. Barker who has died lately, at his house, 103 Piccadilly. From the top to the bottom, the house was crowded with pictures, chiefly pre-Raphaelite, rare china, and fine old furniture—but so crowded together that the only way to make it comfortable would have been to turn out half the contents! We dined with Sir Stafford Northcote, and I had the good luck to sit by Sir Garnet Wolseley, the hero of the Ashanti expedition! I found him most easy and pleasant, bright, simple, and unaffected. He says the Fantees were not as ugly as they have been represented, and that they had generally beautiful figures and sometimes small and well-made feet, very different from the flat foot of the negro. The great height of the trees and the entire absence of animal life were the two things that seemed to strike him most in the Bush. He spoke most highly of Lord Cardwell, and seemed to think his scheme for reorganising the army will answer. He also talked a good deal of China, and is satisfied that the Chinese are the people of the future. Already, he says, they are breaking out of their boundaries towards Kashgar and have compelled Mr. Forsyth to abandon his mission there. On to two great squashes at the Duchess of Marlborough's and Lady Salisbury's, where we found most of the ministers, and Rainald chaffed them about Dizzy's clever speech on the county franchise, which, while opposing the lowering of it now, quite leaves a door open for himself to bring it forward some day. I seem to myself to have been talking to distinguished people without end— Lord Salisbury, Lord Strathnairn, the Bishop of Peterborough, Mr. Lowe, Lord Cairns, etc. I do enjoy it so! Lord Salisbury spoke of Sir Garnet as our general of the future.

"*Sunday, May* 17.—In the evening we did what I am not fond of doing on Sunday, dined out with the Bradfords, a very small party, but a remarkable one, as it included Mr. Disraeli! It is very flattering to see the anxiety which is displayed to bring about a *rapprochement* between him and Rainald. It was evidently an arranged thing, but in spite of the smallness of the party not much came of it, and I do not think they exchanged more than two or three sentences. He came and talked to me after dinner. I thought him affected and sententious, as I did when I met him at Osborne in 1868, but could have got on better if we had been left to ourselves.

"*June* 10.—In the evening we went to the palace concert, and I had a good look at the Duchess of Edinburgh. She is very like her brother, but so gay and animated. As Princess Christian told me the other day, the precedence about which there has been so much talk has not been altered, nor could it have been without an Act of Parliament. The Princess of Wales and Princess Christian walked first, then the Duchess and Princess Louise. While noting all this, I had a long talk with Lord Cairns about the Public Worship Bill. He is evidently out of patience with the bishops, who are most difficult to deal with, and never, he says, know their own minds for two minutes together. I see the Bill is very unpopular, and much doubt it passing. Lord Selborne, who put me into the carriage to-night, is evidently unhappy about it. All the world is talking of the great marriage just announced between Lord Grosvenor and Lady Sybil Lumley. I hope it will turn out well. She is a lovely girl, and said to be perfectly charming.

"*June* 12.—Our first dinner in this our own house went off wonderfully well, although Lady Manners failed at the last minute! We had the Cawdors, Adderleys, Buxtons, Gages, Hanbury Tracys, Lord Manners, Lord Cottenham, General Airey, and Mr.

Browning, with whom I do not get on as well as I should like. Then off to Dorchester House, where were he and she of Edinburgh. I valsed with Lord Hertford and several others, and enjoyed myself hugely, as I always do at that beautiful house.

"*Osterley Park, June* 16.—We drove down here yesterday to stay with the dear old Duchess of Cleveland, whom Rainald and I both like so much. The house, which I remember seeing years ago, when I rode over here with my father, is very quaint and finely decorated in the best style of the last century. Lord Jersey has 3000 acres here, which must be very valuable, and the kitchen-gardens are let to a market gardener at £12 an acre. Lady Jersey and Mr. Brandling, Lord Alington, Matt and Polly Ridley, Reggie Villiers, and Lord Zouche are here. To-day we drove in Lord Alington's drag to Ascot, all through Windsor Park, but the intense cold quite spoilt the races, and made one long for sealskins! There were very few people, and no smart gowns in consequence. Here is Horace Walpole's description of Osterley, as he saw it a hundred years ago:

" ' On Friday we went to see oh! the palace of palaces—a palace sans crown or coronet, but such expense! such taste! such profusion! and yet half an acre produces all the rents that furnish such magnificence. In short, a shop is the estate, and Osterley Park is the spot. The old house I have often seen, which was built by Sir Thomas Gresham, but it is so improved and enriched that all the Percies and Seymours of Sion must die of envy. There is a double portico that fills the space between the towers of the front, and is as noble as the Propylæum of Athens. There is a hall, a library, a breakfast-room, an eating-room, all *chefs d'œuvres* of Adam, a gallery 130 feet long, and a drawing-room worthy of Eve before the Fall. Mrs. Child's dressing-room is full of pictures, old filagree, china, and japan. So is all the house. The chairs are taken from antique lyres, and make charming harmony. There are Salvators, Gaspar Poussins, a beautiful staircase and ceiling by Rubens, not to mention a kitchen-garden that costs £1400 a year, and a menagerie full of birds that come from a thousand lands, which Mr. Bankes has not yet discovered. Then in the drawing-room which I mentioned, there are door-cases and a crimson and gold frieze that were, I believe, borrowed from the Palace of the Sun. The Park is the ugliest spot of ground in the universe, and so I return comforted to Strawberry.'

"Glowing as this description is, it is not in the least exaggerated, and I seldom enjoyed anything more than going over the house with the stately old lady who inhabits it, and suits it so well. There is a boudoir hung with the most exquisite tapestry, put up two years after Horace Walpole wrote; a state bed which the Duchess occupies, embroidered in a way to drive the School of Art mad with envy; a dressing-room elaborately decorated in the Pompeian style; while every bit of door, shutter, frieze, and cornice is finished in the same exquisite taste.

"*July* 12.—We went down by train to Hatfield, to a grand fête given for the Prince and Princess of Wales and their guests, the Crown Prince and Princess of Prussia. Alas! just as we arrived, the rain came down in torrents, and entirely spoiled what would have been a most charming entertainment. It cleared later fortunately, but the grass was soaked, and one could not wander about in the gardens as one would have liked. I was in luck when dinner came, as Lord Strathnairn took me in, and I sat between him and Lord Carnarvon, and for the first time assisted at a real state banquet, a very fine sight in the grand old hall. I talked to Lord Carnarvon about Mr. Plimsoll's Bill, and to Lord Strathnairn about the Public Worship, or, as Sir Thomas Munro calls it, 'the Clerical Meeting's Bill.' The line Mr. Gladstone is taking seems calculated to break up the Liberal party still further, and Dizzy, it is supposed, supports the Bill, to please the Queen, annoy Lord Salisbury and Mr. Hardy, and complete the disruption of the Opposition.

"*July* 13.—I went to Prince's to see the skating on rollers which has become the fashionable amusement.

It is a pretty sight, but not very good for the bodies or minds of the youthful generation. The former are over-exerted, while the latter remain totally uncultivated. I wonder how long it will last! On the way home I began to wonder if I had done anything to be of use to anybody these last few months. It has been a gay, pleasant season, I have never enjoyed one more, but I am afraid I have become very worldly and pleasure-loving. Rainald and I talked a good deal about expenses to-day. It is difficult to know how to apportion one's expenditure, how much is inevitable, and how much may be fairly counted selfish. I am afraid I feel responsible for much of our expenditure this year, *i.e.* on the house which we have bought and furnished. Oh, how often I wish I had never set my heart upon it! We had some nice grave talk about the future world to which we are wending, and about which we know so little.

"*Sunday, July* 19.—I went with Rainald to Lady Charlotte Schreiber's, to look at her almost unequalled collection of Bow, Chelsea, Worcester, Plymouth, Derby, and Bristol china, all beautifully arranged in chronological order. She and her husband thoroughly understand it, and I was much interested in all they told us. Flowers, birds, figures are the ascending scale as regards painting on china, and coloured ground is preferable to white. Plymouth is the first English china made with hard paste, raised flowers on white are characteristic of Bow, and the raised conches on Chelsea are especially valuable.

"*Monday, July* 20.—I finished up the season with a pleasant little party at Lady Henniker's, where, besides talking to Lord Aberdeen and Lady Edith Ashley about Plimsoll, I had a very interesting conversation with Lord Selborne about the Public Worship Bill and the prospects of the Church. He agrees it is necessary that something should be done, but dreads whither the ball now set rolling may go, saying he should not wonder if blood were one day to be shed in a religious war in this country. Really Charley Newdegate is not so far wrong after all! He told a curious story of the present Bishop of London, Dr. Jackson. The living of St. James's, Piccadilly, being vacant, Dr. Blomfield offered it to a Mr. Harvey of Hornsey, who declined it, but wrote: ' If you want a good man, take Jackson, the under-master of the grammar school at Islington.' The Bishop sent for him, heard him preach, and appointed him then and there. Lord Selborne also told me that Mr. Gladstone, after his fine speech on the second reading of the Public Worship Bill, exclaimed, ' I have killed that Bill!' Never was any man more mistaken!

"*Althorp, September* 18.—We drove over here on Wednesday, and went to Northampton yesterday for the Agricultural Show. It was my first experience of a public dinner, and a very long process it is, but I confess to having been rather amused than otherwise, although of course the exclusion of politics made the speeches rather dull. This morning Lady Sarah showed me some of the most valuable books of the famous Althorp library. I believe it is the finest private library in the kingdom— a *Biblia Pauperum* printed by Fust and Gutenberg, in 1455; several early Caxtons; a book of Types from the Apocalypse printed from coarse blocks before movable types were invented; a Decameron, which was bought in 1807 for £2260; a Book of Hours, which belonged to a Spanish queen, with all manner of good resolutions written on the fly-leaves; and Aldines without end! I had to hurry over it, for we came home to luncheon and played croquet, alas! for the last time. And so ends another happy summer at home. Thank God for it!"

Sir Rainald and Lady Knightley spent the next few weeks on a round of visits in Scotland. They began with Lamington and went on by Dunkeld to Guisachan, Sir Dudley Marjoribanks' beautiful place in the Highlands, where they were the guests of her cousin, Matthew Ridley, whose name often figures in these pages, and his wife, Sir Dudley's elder daughter.

"*Guisachan, Beauly, N.B., September* 23.—Tired as I am, I must try to write a few lines about this most enjoyable day, every hour of which has given me the keenest pleasure. After leaving Dunkeld, we dashed through the beautiful Pass of Killiecrankie, where the Garry rushes along its deep gorge, and by Blair Atholl to the wild Pass of Drumouchter, and then descended into Strathspey and came down on the sea at Forres and by Culloden to Inverness and Beauly. There we left the train and drove for twenty-three miles along beautiful wooded glens with glorious views of purple hills till it was too dark to see anything, and very glad we were to get here at eight. The party consists of Matt and Mary Ridley, Colonel and Lady Emily Gore, Mr. and Miss Hughes, Lord Vernon and his daughter, Mr. Newton and Mr. Delane, who amused us with a queer story which he had picked up in the train that Rainald was going to be made a peer.

"*September* 26.—We came here on Wednesday, and this is Saturday night, and I have not written a line of my Journal. I feel as if I could not describe the ever-changing beauty of these mountains and glens, rocks and waterfalls, these bleak moors and soft mossy woods with gnarled firs and slender birches. We ride and ride. I long to be alone and listen to what Nature has to say in these wonderful solitudes. Yesterday we took a most delightful expedition over the hill to Affric, which sits on its fir-clad isle between two still, clear lochs, shut in by high mountains. Lady Fanny Marjoribanks and Lady Blandford were there, and gave us luncheon. Mr. Newton, Mr. Delane, and the Vernons are gone, and Lord and Lady Frederick Cavendish have arrived. *She* is an immense addition to the party. I must rescind my former statement about Mr. Delane, who certainly knows everything that happens to Dizzy, and informed us that he had heard some days ago that the Prime Minister was not going to Ireland, nominally because of a bronchial attack.

"*September* 29.—Every day we take rides in new directions through these beautiful hills and get exquisite views of blue peaks and sunny lochs and far-away mountains standing out against the clear green of the evening sky. Altogether I am very sorry to turn my back on beautiful Guisachan, which I am never likely to see again, and both Ishbel Marjoribanks and Lady Frederick are very congenial companions and delight in this Highland scenery as much as I do.

"*Glen Ferness, Dumphail, September* 30.—We had a charming drive to Beauly, and a long and rather dreary one from Nairn to this place. Dear old Lord Leven welcomed us most cordially. He is in his eighty-ninth year, and I am glad to have managed a visit to him and Sophy. The Findhorn flows close to the house, between rocky banks, richly wooded, with views of wild moorland and here and there glimpses of the Moray Firth and distant hills.

"*October 2.*—In spite of a terrific gale—the barometer down at 28—Sophy and I had a very pleasant drive to Cawdor Castle, looking across to the Moray Firth and Sutherland and Cromarty on the opposite shore. We found Lady Cawdor, who took us all over this very perfect specimen of an old Scottish castle. It has the usual central keep with four turrets and a moat and drawbridge, and in the very centre of the house is the hawthorn tree and the coffer in which the founder of the castle was carrying his gold when he was told to build his house at the third hawthorn which he reached. King Duncan is said to have been murdered in one of the rooms here. I was greatly fascinated with the whole place, it is so unspoilt, and I liked the old spiral staircases and the arras hanging on the bare stone walls.

"*Fawsley, October* 21.—Rainald went to Quarter Sessions, and I trotted down to Badby, where as usual I found plenty to do till luncheon, soon after which the Bishop and Mrs. Magee arrived. In the evening I listened with great interest to a conversation between Rainald and the Bishop about the steps to be taken by Convocation and Parliament as to the proposed alterations in the Rubric, as to legalising the eastward position, etc. The Bishop feels strongly the importance of the two bodies acting together, and deprecates Parliament taking any action on its own account, as more likely than anything to lead to Disestablishment. We had a few neighbours to dinner, and the Bishop, after his wont, made himself most agreeable, telling story after story. Carlyle's definition of Dizzy and Gladstone amused me especially: 'Dizzy prays morning and evening that people may not find out what a humbug he is; Gladstone, that he himself may not find out what a humbug he is.' He lately heard a lady remark, after reading J. S. Mill's *Autobiography*, ' What an extraordinary man! He appears to have had no mother and no God.' Speaking of the sad fact that seventeen hundred men in Northampton voted for Bradlaugh, he said that this was to be chiefly accounted for by the bad hands into which two of the chief parishes of the town had fallen—men who had been there twenty years and had done *nothing*—and ' the worst part is,' he added, ' that I as Bishop can do *nothing*!' His remarks about speakers in the House of Lords were particularly interesting. He spoke of the sharp thrusts which Lord Granville can give from under his velvet paws, and expressed the warmest affection and admiration for Lord Salisbury, and, to my joy, approved entirely of his taking office. He also said that the attendance at the House of Lords had improved immensely since the new peers had been made. Formerly, when important questions were discussed, often not half a dozen peers were present. In talking of the clergy, he amused me by saying how difficult it was to keep them straight on any point. ' The fact is, when they get together, they are like wet hay and begin to heat.' He also gave an interesting account of the Metaphysical Society, to which he belongs. The members meet and dine together once a month and hold a discussion on some given subject, premising that no one is to be offended at what anyone else says. A necessary provision, when you get together Archbishop Manning, Mr. Froude, Mr. Greg, Mr. Roden Noel, the Duke of Argyll, and two or three English bishops and deans, and then proceed to discuss Miracles. On that occasion he was very much struck with the feeble nature of the anti-Christian arguments. But I could write pages about the interesting and curious things which he told us. He certainly is one of the most agreeable people whom I have ever met, besides being a man to whom I look up with the greatest respect, because of his earnestness and sincerity of purpose.

"*October* 26.—We are both of us absorbed in the Greville Memoirs, and seeing how interesting they are makes me resolve to be more careful to put down the various curious and amusing things that I hear. His stories about William IV.'s undignified proceedings remind me of one I have often heard Sophy tell, of his coming to call on Sir William Fremantle, at Englefield Green, perched on the box of his own carriage, that he might see how a new pair of horses went! Rainald told me a curious story of Mr. Disraeli, how that after he had written his Memoir of his intimate friend, Lord George Bentinck, he went to Mr. Charles Greville, who had always been on the worst possible terms with Lord George, and asked him to review the book in the *Quarterly*. Mr. Greville declined, alleging as his reason the known enmity which had always subsisted between them. A few days later he was surprised to receive a visit from Mr. Delane with a similar request for the *Times*. He again declined, giving the same reason, adding, ' Mr. Disraeli cannot wish it, after what I told him the other day.' ' Why,' said Delane, ' Disraeli himself desired me to come to you! '

" Between his interminable relations of party politics, Mr. Greville gives one occasional glimpses of the horrible state in which the people were at that time. Although there is, no doubt, still ample room for amendment, I am sure that things are much improved since those days.

"*Euston, Thetford, November* 1.—We arrived here with the Sydneys and Lord Charles, the rest of the party being the Duke of Cambridge and Colonel Macdonald, the Ashburtons, Lady Marian Alford, and Sir R. Errington's elder brother, Mr. Stanley. All the world are talking of the Greville Memoirs, and I was amused to hear Lady Sydney say that Mr. Greville had resolved never to record any gossip about the

Royal Family, upon which the Duke exclaimed, ' Bless my soul ! I think he has given us a pretty good dose of it.' The Duchess of Grafton came to tea, and I thought her very pleasing. It is a pity she does not make more effort to appear, but she is no doubt very delicate. The Duke of Cambridge was my partner at whist, very good-humoured and jolly as usual. Lady Marian Alford and Lady Sydney talk away together, and relate much that is amusing, and I gaze my fill at pretty Lady Ashburton. We discussed the article in the *Edinburgh* on the Session. It is a regular party attack on the Government, grouping all their blunders dexterously together. But certainly the most extraordinary thing was Mr. Disraeli's violent language about Lord Salisbury, in the last days of the debate on the Public Worship Act. Such language, I suppose, was never used before by one cabinet minister about another. Rainald says he has thought a great deal about it, and I cannot imagine what his object can have been. Rainald's position, I am sorry to say, becomes daily more isolated, since on the religious questions, which unhappily are becoming the burning questions of the day, he cannot act with his former friends, Lord Salisbury and Mr. Hardy, feeling as he does entirely with Disraeli on these matters. I doubt if either he or I shall long continue to care for our present position, such as it is, in the world of politics and fashion.[1] I have never really been ' of it,' and home duties and country life become daily more attractive. But I shall not vanish without a pang from London—the centre of everything.

"*November* 5.—The anniversary of Inkermann ! so we drank to the health of the three who were present on that great day, the Duke of Cambridge, Colonel Macdonald, and Lord Charles. How long ago it all seems ! and must be, since Lord Sydney has been telling us all about his visit to St. Petersburg last year, to attend the Duke of Edinburgh's marriage. The Czar there drives about everywhere without an escort, and goes to the theatre on gala nights with no escort but the man

[1] A true enough prevision.—L. M. K., 1882.

who drives him, and walks about the streets entirely unattended. A great contrast to the fright he was in here, when every Pole was watched by a detective, and he drove in a close carriage and made one bound in and out of it.[1] Lady Ashburton and I had a pleasant day, lunching with the shooters and walking about with them—the weather marvellously still and bright. Two curious little announcements were read out of to-day's paper. At a meeting of the Corporation of London, it was proposed to give Mr. Disraeli the freedom of the City, but after a warm debate the matter dropped. Mr. Gladstone announces the publication of a pamphlet on *The Vatican Decrees in their Bearing on Civil Allegiance*, upon which Lord Sydney groaned out, ' Why can't he keep quiet ? '

"*Fawsley, Saturday, November* 7. — We had a prosperous journey home, travelling with the Sydneys, who were good company to the end. Lord Sydney said he dined one evening at Gloucester House, and the Duke of Cambridge and Lord Clarendon kept him there till 2 a.m., harping on all the Prince is doing to pull down the monarchy. They slyly suggested that he should remonstrate, but it was a case of ' people who live in glass houses ! ' Lady Sydney told us that the *Inconnue* of Prosper Mérimée's *Letters* was a Mrs. Dagineau, whose mother was English, and that no one suspected the existence of the friendship. The Empress herself told Lady Sydney that, well as they knew Mérimée, they never dreamt of it. When his house was sacked in the Commune, the packet of letters fell into the hands of a stranger, who brought them to England, and Lord Henry Percy has actually seen them. I am extremely interested in Mr. Gladstone's pamphlet. It is impossible not to agree with every word of it, and equally impossible not to wonder what is his object in writing it. Does he mean to join the Old Catholics ? He has been staying with Dr. Döllinger this autumn, and went to Lord Acton's the very day his letter to him appeared in the *Times*. Or is it to spite

[1] Six years after this, he was murdered in his own capital.—L. K., 1880.

the Romans for having rejected the Irish University Bill, and thus paved the way for his great fall last year? Or is it an attempt to outbid Dizzy for Protestant support? Probably it is none of these things, but simply the outcome of a mind which, great as it is, becomes entirely absorbed in the one subject which occupies it at the moment.

"*4 Grosvenor Crescent, November 22.*—There is a great stir about Mr. Disraeli's speech at the Guildhall, in which he said that the British workman was in a better position than many a foreign nobleman who was liable at any moment to arbitrary arrest. Of course he was supposed to refer to Count Arnim, who has been again arrested for political reasons, and all the foreign papers commented upon his remark, whereupon he inserts an official disclaimer of any such reference in the *Times,* and of course makes matters ten times worse, as it is immediately assumed on the Continent that he did this at Bismarck's bidding, which is certainly not true.

"*Crichel, Wimborne, December 7.*—We came here from home to-day, and find the Ashburtons, whom I am delighted to meet again, Lady Alington, Lord Winchelsea, Big Ben,[1] Lord Henry Lennox, and Lord Bingham. After dinner Lord Winchelsea and Lord Henry Lennox both broke out into violent abuse of Mr. Greville's book, which is to be accounted for by the fact that Mr. Greville had been the main instrument in turning Lord Winchelsea out of the Jockey Club, and that he speaks in a most impertinent way of the Duke of Richmond.

"*December* 10.—We drove to St. Giles's, Lord Shaftesbury's place, and admired the fine old yews round the house, and on to Cranborne Manor, a most delightful old place belonging to Lord Salisbury. One room is called King John's, and there is a charming panelled hall with a minstrels' gallery, very like Haddon in miniature.

"*Somerley, Ringwood, December* 14.—We came on here on Saturday with Lady Normanton and the

[1] George Cavendish Bentinck, born 1803, died 1886; M.P. for West Norfolk.

Dowager Lady Barrington and her daughter Augusta. The Crichel party amused me, but this one is far more to my taste, always excepting dear Lady Ashburton. I have been admiring the beautiful Sir Joshuas and Gainsboroughs in the fine picture gallery here, and enjoying Miss Barrington's really delightful music, and taking long walks through the fir woods with which this house is surrounded. Mr. and Lady Rose Lovell, Colonel and Mrs. Henry Byng, Lord Calthorpe, and Mr. Montague Guest arrived—a very pleasant party. Miss Barrington told me that *A Week in a French Country House* is taken almost exactly from life at Frankfort, the Marquis de l'Aigle's place near Compiègne, with which she is intimately acquainted through her elder sister's marriage to Mr. Alfred Sartoris, a brother of the Marquise. The story was written by another sister-in-law of the Marquise, Adelaide Sartoris, Fanny Kemble's sister, and the painter described in its pages is Leighton.

" Meanwhile Count Arnim's trial proceeds, and is most bewildering. Bismarck's language to him seems to have been most insulting, while the Count himself seems to have been careless and not always accurate in his dispatches. How Bismarck can allow his personal views on French politics to be published in this manner is beyond comprehension.

"*Fawsley, December* 24.—We came home to find snow on the ground, and the trees bending under the weight. I went to the Workhouse at Daventry, and had my first Christmas good wishes from the poor old women there. Mamma, Sophy, Henry, and Harry arrived in the evening, only Sir Thomas is unfortunately detained in town by illness. I went to Badby to help at a Christmas tree and tea for the children, and distribute Rainald's gifts, and had the Preston singers as usual at night. It is really like Christmas in a story-book, with our happy family party, and the snow on the ground, and the dear old hall hung with garlands, and carol-singing all round, and underlying it all the deep, real joy of our Blessed Lord's birth. How thankful I ought to be!"

CHAPTER XXI

LONDON AND HOMBURG

1875

"*Fawsley, January* 22, 1875.—The Liberal party are in despair at Mr. Gladstone's resignation, and are sorely exercised as to the choice of a leader. It appears to lie between Mr. Forster and Lord Hartington, and the latter will no doubt have it, although far the least able man of the two, just because he is a Duke's son. As the *Daily News* neatly puts it : ' They think a party leader should be also a party giver, and cherish a humble hope of a share in the festivities of Devonshire House.'

"*January* 30.—An immense meet at Charwelton, where the Pytchley had not met for forty years, when Mr. Osbaldistone was Master of the Hounds. It was an extremely pretty sight and a lovely morning. Lord Hartington was out, and told Rainald that he thought he should be chosen leader of the Opposition without a division. I suppose he knew what we know now—*i.e.*, that Mr. Forster intends to retire from public life. We had a nice gallop up here through Badby Wood and by Badby House and Staverton, ending at Shuckburgh.

"*February* 10.—The session really promises to be the long-dreamt-of one devoted to social reforms. Last night Sir Stafford Northcote brought in a Bill about Friendly Societies, Mr. Cross another for improving London dwellings, and Sir Charles Adderley a very bad Bill (I fear) about Unseaworthy Shipping. Still, it is a cheering and promising sign that so much prominence should be given to measures of this class. I wonder what will be the result ?

"*Richmond Park, April* 12.—I left dear Fawsley for the first time without regret, the weather is so cold and ungenial, and we have been very quiet for a long time. Travelled up with Charley Newdegate, who still defends Bismarck in spite of his outrageous conduct. He is actually stirring up a row, and a most unprovoked one, with Belgium in particular, and all Europe in general. What it all means I have not a conception! It almost seems as if ' Whom the Gods doom to destruction they first make mad.'

"*April* 13.—Mamma and I drove to Richmond and called on Lord and Lady Russell. The old Lord was as bright and cheery as possible, asking a Colonel Fletcher who had just returned from Canada many questions about the Colonies, and expressing his great satisfaction that there was now less inclination to snub them than there was. Mr. Lowe, he said, was always for abandoning our Colonies, and ' breaking up the sun of our vast Empire into spangles.' Even Lord Granville gave a man leave to wear a United States decoration, to whom it had been given solely because he expressed an opinion that we ought to give up Canada to the States! I said at least Lord Carnarvon had plenty of backbone, whereupon he replied that a statesman who did not belong to the vertebrate order of animals was of no use. He really was most agreeable, talked of Lady Mary Wortley Montagu's letters, and although deaf and infirm is a wonderful specimen of eighty-five!

"*April* 14.—To-day we drove to Roehampton, and thought Lord Leven, who is eighty-nine, even more wonderful than Lord Russell.

"*4 Grosvenor Crescent, April* 21.—We came to London in time for luncheon. The house looks very comfortable, and it certainly is nice settling down in one's own town house. In the evening I went to a huge squash at the Foreign Office, where I met my old friend Sir Howard Elphinstone, who has just returned from the East with Prince Arthur. He says ' Chinese Gordon ' is doing wonderfully well, and the Khedive asks, ' What manner of man is this you have sent me, who won't take money?' His predecessor, Sir Samuel Baker, seems to have been a great failure, as one reads between the lines of his very self-glorifying book. And he accepted £20,000 as a compensation for his alleged grievance in leaving before his time had expired!

"*April* 27.—To-day Rainald witnessed a strange scene in the House of Commons. It was crowded in every part, especially in the Strangers' Gallery, and among other strangers were the German Ambassador, Prince Christian, and the Prince of Wales, who was on the Royal Commission about horses, and had come to hear Mr. Chaplin's motion, when suddenly up got Mr. Biggar, the deformed Irish pork-butcher who spoke for four hours last week on the Peace Preservation Bill, and cried, 'Sir, I spy strangers!' and out they all had to go! However, Dizzy moved to suspend the standing orders, Lord Hartington seconded the motion, and in half an hour they were all let in again. But it was a curious episode, and not exactly creditable to the House. Rainald says that many years ago,—in 1863, I think,—when the Radicals proposed to give Garibaldi an ovation when he came to the House, he and Big Ben went to the Speaker and threatened to spy strangers, and so put a stop to what would have been a very improper proceeding. I remember the incident perfectly, but did not know how it had been stopped.

"*May* 4.—Nora Campbell dined with us, and by a most happy inspiration we went down to the House together, and were in great luck. Lord Hartington moved his resolutions respecting the rules of the House by which reporting the debates is nominally a breach of privilege, and any one member may espy strangers. He is a dull speaker, but what he said was very sensible. Mr. Mitchell Henry, who followed him, spoke well, but at inordinate length. Then came Charley Newdegate, who spoke to the point as an old member and was altogether worthy of himself; then Dizzy, who disappointed me. He spoke with effort and by no means fluently, although he raised a laugh when he said the two last speakers wanted an Act for the preservation of speeches. Then Mr. Lowe, clear, fluent, and commonsensical, brushing away musty cobwebs. He sat down, and Mr. Hardy had just got up, when Mr. Sullivan jumped up, saying, ' Mr. Speaker, I spy strangers!' whereupon of course there was a great row, and all the occupants of the Strangers' Gallery had to be bundled out, including Lord Spencer; but we remained safe, behind our grating. The members in their turn yelled, howled, and hooted, even I was sorry to hear, hissed Mr. Sullivan, who raved and stormed in his turn, saying that as a journalist he was determined to speak for his brother-journalists, and that they would no longer continue on sufferance in the House, but would resist to the last the tyranny which kept the Press in slavery, with more bombast of the same kind, amid frequent interruption. Lord Hartington then got up and said that he could not approve of what Mr. Sullivan had done, but that he was only following a very respectable precedent in showing the absurdity of the rule excluding strangers. Lord Eslington said that there was one thing that the House never tolerated, and that was being threatened, as Mr. Sullivan had done, and proposed to refer the question to a Select Committee—a proposal which Rainald supported. Mr. Disraeli then said that Mr. Hardy had been about to make some very valuable suggestions, which would probably have settled the question, if he had not been so improperly interrupted, and finally proposed the adjournment of the debate.

"*May* 5.—We had a pleasant ride with various House of Commons men, Mr. Noel, Mr. Sandford, Mr. Neville-Grenville, etc., all full of last night, and all agreeing that something must be done. But Mr. Lowe, to my surprise, was eloquent on the folly of the line Dizzy took. ' Wisdom of our ancestors, indeed! is it likely that when rules have been carefully framed for the express purpose of keeping people out they are likely to prove the best means of letting them in?' Lord Redesdale, who came to see me later, takes the ultra-Tory view, and asks ' why a rule which has been in force for so many centuries should not continue?' I am rather inclined to think the power should be vested in the House, not in one member. Rainald insists that by simply threatening to enforce the rule in 1863, he and Big Ben saved the House from the undignified proceeding of rising to receive Garibaldi, and that if for instance Prince Bismarck came and the Protestants tried to cheer and the Romans to hoot him, such a scandal might be averted by a single man of sense and courage.

"*May* 31.—I went to the House to hear the end of the debate adjourned from May 5. Mr ⁓⁓ 'y was just finishing his speech when I got there, and Colonel Mure made a long, fumbling, rambling speech, during which there was much buzz, which ceased entirely when Rainald rose. He spoke low at first, and somebody cried, 'Speak up!' and then he did speak up, slowly, distinctly, shortly, with much point and purpose, frequent 'hear, hears,' and one genuine burst of laughter. Above all, his whole manner and bearing were essentially those of a gentleman, and I felt very proud of him, while the compliments we have since received have been innumerable. Mr. Roebuck followed, and was received with respect; but his proposal, which *I* thought a very good one, was not approved. Then Mr. Beresford Hope and Sir William Harcourt, who certainly speaks uncommonly well; and then Mr. Ward Hunt and Mr. Horsman rose together, and there were such loud cries of 'Horsman, Horsman!' that the former was obliged to give way, and we had a most clever and amusing speech—far the best of the evening—from Mr. Horsman. Both the front Opposition Bench and Mr. Sullivan got it hot and strong, and they didn't like it; while 'our fellows' kept cheering and laughing, in no low tones. The House was densely crowded, and the debate ended by Lord Hartington's resolution being rejected by 107— poor dear Charley, with an excellent amendment, only getting 30 men of the very worst type in the House to vote with him. Mr. Disraeli's motion to expel strangers by a vote of the House was then agreed to, without a division. Altogether, it was exceedingly amusing, and I enjoyed it very much. Rainald's speech was very well reported, as well as flatteringly spoken of, in the *Times*; and what pleased him most of all was General Peel telling him, 'You are my leader now,' which he values more than all the compliments that have been paid him.

"*The Deanery, Christ Church, Oxford, Whit-Sunday,* 1875.—I hardly know where to begin, I have seen so much in these two days! Oxford in the most ideal weather is indeed charming, and is a romantic place in what he\ begin a new volume of my Journal—the faithful companion of over nineteen years. Yesterday Paddington Station was simply a pandemonium, exactly like Frith's picture, and the contrast was all the more charming with this quiet Deanery garden, between the fine Cathedral and Christ Church library. We had tea in Harry Gage's rooms, and at dinner I sat between Lord Brooke and dear Prince Leo. It is quite charming to see him so well, able to walk about easily, and so much come out in every way. There was a large party, including Mr. Montague Bernard, late Chichele Professor of International Law, and Sir Henry Maine, Professor of Jurisprudence. After service, the Dean took us all over the Cathedral, and I admired the beautiful new windows designed by Burne-Jones. We lunched in All Souls with Edward Ridley, and saw the fine library, which contains some of Sir Christopher Wren's designs for St. Paul's. One of these, which was approved by Charles II., but happily not carried out, had an immense steeple at the top of the Dome. Rainald and I and Alice Liddell—a most fascinating girl, the original of *Alice in Wonderland*—dined with Prince Leopold in his own rooms, where Harry and Lord Ramsay came to meet us. It was amusing to go in to dinner with him in his own house, and he was so nice. Altogether, these two days have been full of enjoyment, and I could spend hours poking about old Oxford.

"*Frampton Court, Dorchester, May* 18.—We drove into Dorchester, a pretty old town with avenues all round it, like a foreign place, and visited a quaint old house called Wolverton, now inhabited by Mr. and Mrs. Albert Bankes. I was thrilled to hear that *Far from the Madding Crowd* was written by a stone-mason at Poole, Thomas Hardy, who is familiar with all this country. We also saw the clergyman of a parish close to Dorchester, a Mr. Barnes, who has written some very pretty poems in Dorsetshire dialect. He has a fine head and long grey beard, but wears the most eccentric attire—a long flowing robe of grey waterproof lined with scarlet, and black stocikngs with buckled shoes.

" In the evening Mr. Sheridan, who is staying here, showed us a very interesting letter from Mr. Motley, written in 1872, when he was staying with Prince Bismarck at Varzin for his silver wedding. Bismarck gave him a very curious account of his interview with Thiers and Jules Favre, when the peace preliminaries at Versailles were discussed. Favre with much effort compassed the shedding of a few tears, and then begged Bismarck not to reveal his weakness. Not long afterwards, a pathetic account of his emotion, given by Favre himself, appeared in the French newspapers. Thiers made Bismarck a long oration, upon which the latter begged him not to address him as if he were the Assembly, saying that their business could be arranged in a few words. Thiers then began a second oration, to which Bismarck replied in a German speech, of which neither Thiers nor Favre understood a word. They remonstrated and wished to send for an interpreter, whereupon Bismarck said that this was quite unnecessary if only Thiers would come to the point, but that he understood eloquence as little as Thiers understood German! Nevertheless, Bismarck liked Thiers, saying that he had quite the manner of the old school.

" *June* 29.—We dined with the Duke of Grafton, and went to an amusing party at Lady Salisbury's, where was the Seyyid of Zanzibar, who greeted us most politely with a sort of kiss of the hand, like the Shah, as he went out, and I am told blessed the house as he took his leave. He retires everywhere for prayer after dinner, and sets an example which Christians might well follow. Afterwards I listened with amusement to a discussion between Rainald and Lord Salisbury over the Agricultural Holdings Bill and the recent meeting at the Carlton. The landlords are evidently much exercised over it. I own to being puzzled, and am not sure whether I agree with the Government or the forty-five county members who met at the Carlton and objected to the provision that improvements for which the farmer is to be compensated should be such as add to the rateable value of the land. I also had a little talk with Mr. Forster, who knows me at last! He has just been in Northamptonshire, and is struck with our old-world look. I can understand his feeling the contrast with his busy, modern North! Last night we met Captain and Mrs. Richard Burton, the travellers, at dinner at the Sheridans'. She was an Arundel of Wardour and would marry this most cut-throat-looking individual. I wonder if she is happy? Anyhow, she told us many wonderful stories, ending with an account of poor Janie Teleki, who died in her arms at Damascus, having been received into the Church of Rome on her death-bed.

"*July* 1.—I went with Nora and Harry to hear *Lohengrin*, the much-talked-of. Decidedly I prefer the music of the past to that of the future, Mozart to Wagner. But when I have said that, I must add that as a music-drama it is glorious! The instrumentation is so rich, the recitation far finer than any other, the libretto charming, and the whole thing rolls along in one grand full stream of harmony. Albani was ' Elsa,' and Niccolini ' Lohengrin,' but somehow the singers seemed subordinate to the orchestra. There are no pauses for applause, and the densely crowded house hardly got a chance of once clapping. Altogether, I was deeply interested, and to me the three hours passed with incredible rapidity.

"*July* 22.—Rainald came in late from the House, and told me of a most painful scene which took place when Mr. Disraeli announced the abandonment of the Merchant Shipping Bill. Poor Mr. Plimsoll, between mortification and excitement, went almost off his head, denounced the shipowners as scoundrels, and would not withdraw a word, even when threatened with the censure of the House. Poor man! he has been badly treated, and I cannot say how sorry I feel about it."

At the end of the London season, Sir Rainald, who suffered from frequent attacks of gout and rheumatism, was ordered by his doctor to drink the waters and take the baths at Homburg and Wildbad. Lady Knightley, although somewhat reluctant to leave home, thoroughly enjoyed the trip abroad, and as usual managed to do and see much that was interesting during the seven weeks.

"*Brussels, Hôtel Mengelle, July* 25.—I left London *without*, England *with*, regret, and had an excellent journey and passage to Ostend. Belgium looks like one vast field of allotments, and it is wonderful how every scrap of ground is turned to account. We admired the great church of Ste. Gudule with its fine windows and old glass, and went all over the beautiful Hôtel de Ville. After table d'hôte, we walked about in the charming Park, and thought Brussels a very attractive town.

"*Homburg, Kisseliff Strasse, July* 31.—*Les journées se succèdent et se ressemblent, beaucoup même!* Homburg is much the prettiest and nicest of the German watering-places that I have seen, but I do not care for German bath-life, I confess! Up at six; off at seven to the Elizabeth Brunnen, drink three glasses, walk twenty minutes between each and an hour after the last, in a crowd of every nationality, German predominating. Home tired as a dog to breakfast without butter! Then a quiet morning, which I enjoy, having gone in for a solemn study of Fawcett's *Political Economy*; a light luncheon, consisting of what the Germans call *verlorene Eier*—poached eggs; at three down to the springs again, to drink two more glasses; then to the Kursaal to listen to the music, till it is time to go home and dress for table d'hôte at 5 p.m.; back to the Kursaal at seven for coffee and music, and home to bed at ten; lights out at eleven. Such is our daily programme, with occasional variations. To-day we went over the Schloss, where King George III.'s daughter, Princess Elizabeth, Landgravine of Hesse-Homburg, resided, and which would have been our Princess Alice's country house if the war of 1866 had not cost Hesse-Darmstadt this principality. The Schloss stands well, and has a fine view of the Taunus range, which explains what I never understood before, why Homburg is called *vor-der-Höhe*. The gardens are very pretty, and the house itself well furnished and quite habitable. I do not wonder Princess Alice grudges the loss of it, and the Crown Princess refuses to live in what should have been her sister's home. This evening a grand military band from Mainz played beautifully in the Kursaal, and the gardens were lighted up. The place is chock-full of English and Americans, and there are a certain number of people we know—Her Grace of Montrose, the Duke of Montrose, Lord Chelmsford, etc. Altogether, it is a queer, odd sort of life—a thing one is glad to have seen once.

"*August 7.*—I started with Batten directly after breakfast, and in spite of feeling rather nervous, achieved a successful journey to Darmstadt—a dull town with fine wide streets, and the grass growing in them. Princess Alice's new palace looks like a bad copy of Buckingham Palace. We drove out through woods for about three miles to Kranichstein, a ramshackle old *Jagdschloss* of the Grand Duke's, which had been empty for a hundred years before Prince and Princess Louis took it, and is now only half furnished. Here I spent a few hours very pleasantly with Princess Christian, which I really enjoyed. Our party at the very simple two-o'clock dinner consisted only of Prince and Princess Louis, Princess Christian, a Countess Ixelheim, and the six children—five charming little girls and a delicate-looking boy, with their English governess. The youngest but one of the Princesses, Alice, a fascinating child, came running up in high glee to show us her birthday present, a locket ' from Grandmamma Queen ! ' [1] Princess Alice made herself very agreeable, and is, as I have always heard, a most accomplished and superior person—more attractive, perhaps, than any other member of our Royal Family.

" *August* 8.—We dined at the ' Victoria '—a parting dinner to Lord Chelmsford, who made himself most agreeable. He told us how Lord Lyndhurst made his last speech in the House of Lords on the eve of his ninetieth birthday, and said that both the late Lord Derby and Sir Robert Peel were exceedingly nervous when they spoke. But the best thing was his own joke to Lord Derby on his retiring in favour of Mr. Disraeli. ' Do you know the difference between your Administration and his ? Yours was the Derby, this is the *Hoaks* ! '— Mr. Disraeli's only change having been to substitute Lord Cairns for Lord Chelmsford as Chancellor. Lady Emily Dyke also told me an amusing story of the Whitebait Dinner at Greenwich,'where it seems it is the custom to give a wooden spoon to the Minister who has attended fewest divisions. This year it fell to Dizzy himself !

" *August* 20.—Our last day at dear little Homburg. I have really become quite fond of the place. Yesterday I had a long talk with our friendly little host, Herr Deininger, and gleaned a variety of information. Labourers' wages are about one and eightpence a day ; at harvest-time they sometimes get as much as three shillings for fifteen hours a day. The best land lets for about a pound for half an acre. Most of the large properties are strictly entailed in perpetuity, but it is the custom of the peasant-proprietors who own the rest to divide it among all their children, till the waste of land in division becomes

---

[1] (1) Victoria, born 1863 ; married 1884, Prince Louis of Battenberg, (2) Elizabeth, born 1864 ; married 1884, Grand Duke Sergius of Russia, uncle of the present Czar, who was murdered at Moscow, 1905 ; (3) Irene, born 1866 ; married 1888, Prince Henry of Prussia, brother of the Kaiser ; (4) Alix, born 1872 ; married 1894, Nicholas II., Emperor of All the Russias ; (5) Marie Victoria, born 1874, died 1878 ; (6) Ernst Louis, born 1868 ; succeeded his father as Grand Duke of Hesse-Darmstadt, 1892 ; married Victoria, second daughter of Duke of Saxe-Coburg, 1894.

enormous. All the meat comes from a great distance, Munich, Stuttgart, Coburg, and is consequently very dear. The best beasts come from Hungary, and coals from Dürren. At dinner to-night I sat next to a very pleasant individual, who turned out to be Prince d'Aremberg. We began talking French, but after a time got into German, which did much better. He spoke in no measured terms of his dissatisfaction with the present state of affairs in Germany, saying that Bismarck had snubbed and set aside all the old families, of whom but very few would go to Berlin, and that he was surrounded by Jews, who managed everything. He himself is a Catholic, but Catholics and Protestants alike are in despair at seeing all religion banished from the schools. In short, I was quite surprised at the open way in which he spoke, frankly anticipating the break-up of the German Empire, and saying that had they known how things would turn out, he and many others would never have fought as they did in the late war. I only wish I had made him out before."

From Homburg, the travellers went on to Wildbad, where the beautiful wooded valley and charming walks and drives laid out by the sovereigns of Würtemberg, and the primitive habits of the peasants, delighted Lady Knightley, and she took advantage of the opportunity to inspect the schools and study the German system of elementary education.

"*September* 5.—One morning I went with Sir John and Lady Kennaway and the German pastor, Herr Bartholomeï, who by the way has translated Dean Goulburn's *Personal Religion*, to see the schools. There are 500 children under six masters and two mistresses who teach the infants, working thirty-six hours a week. The head master gets about £60 a year. The religious instruction is given by the pastor, leave to withdraw children being granted if desired, which is very seldom. The school is a building of three storeys, divided into a number of classrooms. The system of teaching is very minutely prescribed by the Stuttgart Educational Board, even to the number of chorales to be learnt, amounting to eighty in the course of the year. The girls sing very nicely, and the arithmetic is of an advanced order, children of seven doing addition up to 100. The attendance is compulsory, a fine of one mark being inflicted for nonattendance, and the fees vary according to the parents' means, some being as low as two marks per year. All classes sit side by side, the sons of the doctor and pastor with those of the poorest wood-cutter, but those who choose can go on to a so-called *Real-schule*, or Secondary School, held in the same building. The pastor is himself the inspector. There seems to be very little poverty in Wildbad, the revenues of the town amounting to £10,000 a year, and every male receiving £5 a year and enough wood to keep a stove burning. The land is divided into small plots, carefully irrigated, and as is generally the case with peasant-proprietors, they seem a thrifty, hard-working set."

After visiting Baden, which in spite of its charming situation struck the writer as "a deserted place since play and the French have alike forsaken it," Sir Rainald and Lady Knightley returned home by Strasburg and Paris. They crossed the frontier at Avricourt, and looked with keen interest at the scenes of the Franco-German War, that were still fresh in everyone's mind, "Toul, Saverne, Lunéville, and Châlons-sur-Marne, where one thought of Attila and his Huns," and realised for the first time "what an immense tract of country the Germans have taken from France." At Paris, Lady Knightley paid a visit to some relatives living at St. Cyr, near Versailles, and saw the École Militaire, which occupies the same building as Madame de Maintenon's Pension des Demoiselles.

"*Paris, Hôtel Bristol, September 9.*—I do love a day in Paris ! To-day I spent much of my time in the streets with my maid Batten. Paris looks much gayer than it did four years ago, though of course this is the dead season. They have built up the Colonne Vendôme, and have cleared away some of the ruins and opened a new street, which they are pleased to call ' du 4 Septembre.' I was also struck by seeing scrawled on a wall at Versailles, ' Le suffrage universel c'est la ruine.' At least there is one sensible mortal in France. But oh! what a queer people the French are! We went to see the 'Panorame de la Guerre,' an exceedingly clever representation of the siege of Paris, taken from the Fort d'Issy, and giving an excellent idea of it all. But how strange that they should care to make such a thing, and still stranger that they should like to go and see it, as they do, in crowds! This time I had the great pleasure of seeing the pictures of the Louvre, which were not put back when we were here in 1871, and looking at Raphael's 'Belle Jardinière,' and many others which I remember twenty years ago. Altogether, I have enjoyed these two days immensely."

The return home was saddened by the death of Mr. Henry Gage, who had been seriously ill some time, but whose actual death Lady Knightley first learnt in Paris from a newspaper paragraph. Besides feeling deep grief and sympathy for her widowed sister-in-law, Lady Knightley had an affectionate regard for Mr. Gage, who had been her first friend in the family, and to whom, humanly speaking, she owed the chief happiness of her life.

CHAPTER XXII

THE GIRLS' FRIENDLY SOCIETY

1876–1880

THE year 1876 was noteworthy in Lady Knightley's life as that in which she first became a member of the Girls' Friendly Society, in which she afterwards took so great and prominent a part. From her girlhood, as we have seen in these pages, she had been eager to devote herself to the service of others, and after her marriage she took a leading part in all movements connected with the training and improvement of women. Her intercourse with her own servants and with her poorer neighbours in Badby and the other parishes round Fawsley convinced her of the need of some organisation for girls in domestic service, and when Mrs. Townsend founded the Girls' Friendly Society in her Warwickshire house of Honington, Lady Knightley welcomed the scheme warmly and set about forming a branch of the Society in Northamptonshire. The following entries refer to her earliest attempts in this direction. Like everything of the kind with which she was connected, they met with complete success, largely owing to the charm of Lady Knightley's own personality, and to the earnest religious convictions which lay at the root of all her endeavours.

"*February* 26.—I am much delighted with a scheme for a Girls' Friendly Society which Lady Dryden has sent me. It seems to have been started in a Warwickshire village by a friend of hers, Mrs. Townsend, and is approved by the Archbishop. I do really think it is the thing which I have so long wanted.

"*March* 9.—I rode to Hellidon to see our Rural Dean, Mr. Holthouse, about the Girls' Friendly Society, which he quite agrees may be very useful in our villages.

"*March* 25.—I went to see Lady Massey and Miss Collyns at Daventry, to talk about G.F.S., and was charmed with their kind reception of the idea.

"*April* 5.—To-day fourteen ladies came to talk over the G.F.S. We had a very satisfactory meeting, and I trust the ' Daventry Rural Deanery Branch ' is fairly organised, and pray most earnestly that by God's blessing it may prove a living, working power for good among our girls.

"*Easter Eve, April* 15.—A beautiful day and a very long and busy one, first decorating the church, then going down to Badby and round to the mistresses and mothers of the girls whom I hope to enlist for G.F.S. My mind is quite full of it, but I was glad to go to the quiet five o'clock service and prepare for to-morrow's festival.

"*Easter Day.*—This afternoon I had the pleasure of enlisting four of my own maids as members of the G.F.S. I must not expect too much ; if it does but ever so little good, I shall be thankful.

"*April* 17.—Another long, busy, and very happy day, ending with a tea at Badby, where I enlisted seventeen girls as members of the G.F.S. There are sure to be many disappointments, but I do trust it may be a means of helping them to keep steady, and can't help being pleased at having succeeded so far."

From this time the Girls' Friendly Society occupied an important place in Lady Knightley's time and thoughts, and frequent mentions of it appear in her Journal, both in London and at Fawsley. She took an active part in its development and contributed largely to its immediate success in her neighbourhood.

"*January* 24, 1877.—I drove over to luncheon at Edgcote, and was present at the first meeting of the Brackley Deanery G.F.S. It is delightful to see it spread ; if only it will work well !

"*4 Grosvenor Crescent, May* 10.—Miss Augusta Barrington (afterwards Mrs. Maclagan) came to talk G.F.S.

"*June* 1.—Harriet Cartwright and I went to a meeting of G.F.S. Branch Secretaries, at which Mrs. Townsend (Lady Dryden's friend and the foundress of the Society) presided. I am very glad to have seen her; the spiritual depth of her writings and her powers of organisation make her certainly a remarkable woman. Afterwards we went on together to Mr. Wilkinson's Bible Class. It is 'wonderful how he takes for granted that no one who really is striving to lead the higher life will *wish* to go out, while fully acknowledging that it may very often be people's *duty* to go. Then it is all right, he says, and one may serve God in society just as well as anywhere else. I wonder how far it is *my* duty to go out. To a certain extent it undoubtedly is, but then, I like it. Does it ' weaken my spiritual life ' ?

"*Fawsley, October* 17.—I had my first G.F.S. meeting of the Associates belonging to our Branch. We had a grand discussion about paying premiums. I wish we could get out of that fog.

"*Fawsley, June* 11, 1878.—A very happy day for me, and I hope for about sixty members of the G.F.S., who by kind Rainald's permission held their picnic festival here. We met at the church at 2 p.m. Mr. Collyns read the service—the special one appointed for the occasion, with the lesson about Naaman's little maid, and Mr. Holthouse gave a short address on Purity. Then we walked round the Dingle and gardens and had tea in the coach-house, and afterwards there was tea in the dear old hall for the eighteen ladies and gentlemen. It doesn't sound much, and the weather was most unfavourable, but still I think it seemed to give a certain reality to our Association, and Rainald and I both felt real pleasure in sharing the delights of this beautiful place with those who have so few pleasures."

It was indeed greatly to Lady Knightley's credit that she succeeded in interesting her reserved and fastidious husband in this branch of her work and obtained his consent to opening Fawsley to her G.F.S. Associates and Members. Although Sir Rainald always affected to laugh at his wife's labours in this direction, and was fond of calling the G.F.S. the " Great Fuss Society," he was undoubtedly proud of her success as a speaker and organiser, and seldom hindered her from carrying out her plans.

"4 *Grosvenor Crescent, June* 27.—I went with Harriet Cartwright to the Third Annual Meeting of Branch Secretaries of G.F.S., this year so numerous that we were obliged to assemble at Willis's Rooms. It was a curious experience, having a purely feminine meeting. I was struck with Miss Hubbard's remark, that they all looked very much in earnest, while I am afraid I was only thinking what dowdies they looked! One disadvantage we labour under is the difficulty of making ourselves heard in a large room, with the noise of the traffic outside. A very clear and comprehensive scheme of organisation was proposed, and a very good speech made by a young woman—not a lady—on the need of help for the ' business girls ' of London.

"*Fawsley, December* 10.—Thermometer at 18 degrees, trees covered with snow; a picture of a winter's day, but not a nice one to turn out in. However, I went warm and snug in the brougham (thanks to kind Rainald) to Northampton, where we had a most successful meeting of about thirty ladies, and did a great deal of business in about two hours, fairly launching our Diocesan organisation. I am to be President, at all events for the first year. The one contretemps was that Miss Oxenham missed her train, so that we had no representative of the Central Council, and I had to take the chair and do all the work, and could not answer half the questions.

"4 *Grosvenor Crescent, April* 22, 1879.—All the last week my whole mind has been occupied with the public meeting for the G.F.S., which is to take place at Northampton. I do so earnestly wish it to be a success! Great was my despair yesterday at receiving

PLAN OF FAWSLEY.

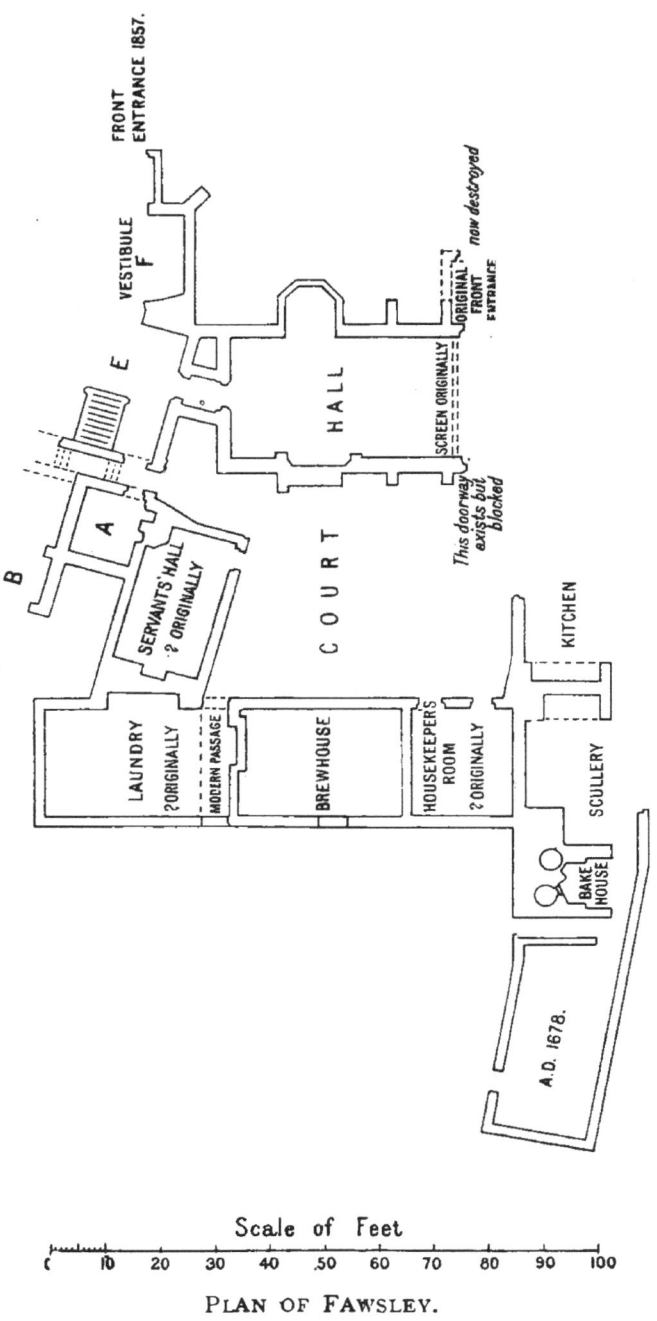

[*To face p.* 290.

a letter from Mrs. Townsend to say she feared she would not be able to come. I felt very low in mind, but dear kind Rainald came to the rescue and went down with me to Northampton, which was a most untold comfort. We had a council meeting first, which was very satisfactory, and got through a good deal of business, then after luncheon at the 'Angel' came the important part—the big meeting in the Town Hall. The Bishop, who presided,—not merely as chairman, but as the warm advocate of the Society,—spoke long and eloquently, dwelling on the womanhood of England as its most precious possession, and saying that a pure and virtuous maidenhood, and pious, well-ordered families, are the very strength and life of any nation. Then came the awful moment. Rainald said that my voice shook very much at first, but when I got reading I did not so much mind. I had put some notes together, and read extracts from the report, and went on for about twenty minutes. The hall was about half full, chiefly of parsons and parsonesses; but they seemed interested, and I do hope it will give the Society a push, and I shall be rewarded for the mental terrors that I suffered. I am quite sure that I did not like doing it at all, but it was inevitable. The Bishop and others were very civil, and as long as Rainald approves, it does not matter what anybody else says!"

As a matter of fact, Lady Knightley's speech on this occasion produced an immense impression, and is still remembered by many who were present and heard her speak. It was no doubt largely due to her exertions and influence that during the next year as many as fourteen branches were started in the diocese of Peterborough. Still more important for the general work of the G.F.S. was the energetic part which she took in framing the constitution in 1880, after the rupture threatened by Mrs. Papillon's attempt to alter the central rules, which in Lady Knightley's eyes was equivalent to starting an entirely new Society.

"All through these troubled years of our work," writes Mrs. Townsend, "Lady Knightley stood bravely by us, and she had the help and countenance of one of the most eminent men of the day, Dr. Magee, Bishop of Peterborough. We met, as is shown by her Journal, in 1877, but my first distinct recollection of her was at the meeting of the Central Council held in May 1880, for drawing up the constitution and discussing proposed amendments. On this occasion Lady Knightley moved the first resolution. The importance of this meeting is quite unrealised now, but it laid the foundation of that which, humanly speaking, is the real strength of the Society's organisation, namely, its representative character. Without this, neither its number nor its expansion in the Empire and beyond would have secured any permanent hold on the national life. In these old days, it was no light matter to bring together an assembly of delegates from some twenty or thirty dioceses, but from north and south and east and west they came, and for six days they sat, to form a constitution for the Society more representative and less centralised than that which was at first put out. It was no easy task to preside over such an assembly, and one of the things the chairwoman most clearly remembers is the kind voice and winning words of encouragement given her at the end of the meeting by the Diocesan President of Peterborough."[1]

Lady Knightley on her part, in recording the prolonged meetings and lively discussions at which she assisted during that memorable week, speaks in the warmest terms of the President's (Mrs. Townsend) unvarying good temper and patience.

The opposition to the central rules of the Society was now overcome, and this chapter of its history was closed by the secession of the chief objectors. Lady Knightley gives the following account of the next General Meeting, which took place at Lambeth Palace:

"*June* 24.—The dear mother came up, and she and I, with Gertrude Henley and Mabel Montgomery, attended the General Meeting of the G.F.S. held in the library at Lambeth. The Archbishop himself presided and made

[1] *Associates' Journal*, G.F.S., January 1914.

a most able and thoughtful speech about our dear Society, speaking of it as an immense national influence for good in bringing classes together whom there is too great a tendency to set against each other. It was very interesting to hear of the sister Societies in Scotland, Ireland, and Australia, and of one to be started at the Cape, and Mrs. Townsend told us how the germ of it all was a little meeting of five—herself, Mrs. Tait, Mrs. Nassau Senior, Mrs. Harold Browne, and Mr. Fosbery—in the drawing-room of Lambeth Palace. Afterwards we went into more technical matters, and I made a little speech—quite short—about the girls being allowed to keep their cards when they marry respectably. It is wonderful how much improved women are in their way of carrying on business, and this meeting was the best we have ever had."

As Mrs. Townsend writes: " Lady Knightley had a great devotion for the G.F.S.: ' Our beloved Society,' she would call it, in these addresses of hers, which were so full of charm. A born speaker, simple and dignified, yet always with that childlike look in the blue eyes—she made people care because she cared herself, and they cared the more because she was a woman of affairs, and had so many other interests, town life and country life, politics and literature, as well as the great causes of womanhood, such as the Working Ladies' Guild and Protected Emigration, to which she devoted so much time in later years. The power of quite selfless encouragement of other workers was one of Lady Knightley's greatest gifts. She could rejoice in their work and yet be able to see quite clearly where they failed—always loyal and trusting, and yet always outspoken and straightforward. Yes, loyalty was indeed the keystone of her life—loyalty to Queen and country and Royal friends, loyalty in her home, in her outside work, and to that great thing, duty, which glows and shines before the eyes of men. Her motto might well have been, 'Loyal je serai durant ma vie.' "

The Working Ladies' Guild, which Mrs. Townsend

here mentions, was another institution with which Lady Knightley became connected in 1876 through Lady Mary Feilding, and in the management of which she took a very prominent part. About the same time she formed the Society for the Employment of Women and the Ladies' Sanitary Association, for which she wrote a pamphlet on *Dress* during one of her Homburg visits. In 1875 she became a regular visitor at St. George's hospital, and before long was elected a member of the Committee of Management.

In this, as in all her other philanthropic works, Lady Knightley showed those remarkable powers of organisation and that singular tact and sympathy which made her so admirable a chairman and president. Much of her success in this capacity was due no doubt to the personal charm, the winning voice and manner, the utter absence of self-consciousness, to which Mrs. Townsend alludes. But the true reason lay deeper still. It was to be found in the steadfast resolve to work for the welfare of others in the solemn consecration of her life, which lay at the root of all her manifold activities. As she wrote on her thirty-fourth birthday, a day spent happily in her old home at Richmond Park with "the dearest and best of husbands and mothers": "' To whom much is given, of him shall much be required.' How thankful I ought to be, and how much I ought to strive to love God and make the lives of others better and happier too!"

During these years of her life she was a regular attendant at St. Peter's, Eaton Square, where Mr. Wilkinson's[1] sermons and addresses produced a profound impression on her mind and made a vivid appeal to the higher side of her nature.

"To-day being Ascension Day," she writes in the middle of the prolonged sittings of the G.F.S. Central Council, "I went to St. Peter's and heard a fine sermon from Mr. Wilkinson on ' I saw and beheld a white horse, and He that sat on him had a bow, and a crown was given unto Him, and He went forth conquering and to

[1] Rev. G H. Wilkinson, afterwards Bishop of Truro and St. Andrews.

conquer.' It was a grand stirring address, saying that both as a Church and as individuals we want far more confidence in such promises as these. ' If ye had faith as a grain of mustard seed,' etc. And Mr. Wilkinson makes one feel as if he almost *saw* into that unseen world which lies so near us and is yet so far from our thoughts."

On Trinity Sunday she heard another famous preacher who also impressed her deeply.

"*May* 22, 1880.—Kind Rainald took me to the Guards' Chapel to see the window and inscription which dear mother and I have put up to my father's memory. It is a proud roll of services. We stayed for afternoon service, where, before the Prince and Princess of Wales and their two sons, and an immense congregation, including Mr. Gladstone, Canon Liddon preached an admirable sermon for the Guards' Institute. His text was, ' I know whom I have believed, and am persuaded that He is able to keep that which I have committed unto Him against that day.' Three answers, said the preacher, there are to the question, ' What shall I do with my life ? ' Either 1, ' Nothing—let it drift ; or 2, Get all the pleasure you can out of it ; or 3, Give it without reserve to Him from whom you have received it.' It was a grand and impressive service from its stately simplicity—the Guards' band leading the singing, and the whole congregation joining in singing ' Holy, holy, holy, Lord God Almighty ! ' "

CHAPTER XXIII

THE ROYAL TITLES BILL AND THE EASTERN QUESTION

1876–1877

"*Claridge's Hotel, February* 8, 1876.—I came up to town with much pleasure, being very glad of a little change. The Queen opened Parliament herself for the first time for several years, but I am sorry to say was not well received. In the afternoon I went to the House of Commons to hear Matt Ridley move the Address, which he did in a nicely prepared, well-delivered speech, without a spark of genius in it. Mr. Mulholland seconded him, and then came Lord Hartington, hammer, hammer on, for an hour—very good sense, but very dull to listen to. Dizzy was a great relief after that, although Rainald did not think he spoke as well as usual. However, he stuck his paws in his coat-tail pockets and talked freely to the House, and told us all about the Suez Canal, which was very amusing. Mr. Horsman came to ask Rainald if he would help to identify him as ' the superior person ' attacked in last week's *World*; but he declined to be mixed up with the affair.

"*February* 10.—I went down to Windsor, and spent a very pleasant day with Princess Christian at Cumberland Lodge. It is such a pretty place, and I enjoyed the drive through the grand old park in the winter sunshine.

"*Fawsley, February* 24.—The East Suffolk election ended in a majority of 951 for St. John Barne, which is, I think, very satisfactory, although it might have been larger. But I am most sincerely rejoiced to see him in what I think one of the proudest positions an Englishman can occupy, and one much to be coveted by everyone who loves his country and wishes to do good in his generation. In the evening I went in the brougham to Mrs. Rhodes' at Floore Fields—'dissipated Dot' being bent on a dance. It was very prettily done, only about 130 people there, and I danced a good deal, and had an interesting talk with a brother of Mr. Rhodes who has lately returned from Natal. He told me a good deal about South Africa, especially that the Prussians are great friends with the Transvaal Republic, and lately sent them a present of a large quantity of war ammunition. Mr. Rhodes fancies they wish to make settlements in South Africa, having lately employed two explorers to visit parts of the country, Petermann and Harmuck. He also thinks there is a great deal of gold to be found in the Transvaal, but says we were in the wrong about Griqualand, Delagoa Bay, and the Diamond Fields.

"*February* 28.—The hounds met at Adstone, and Lord Charles Fitzroy presented me to the ex-King of Naples—a dark man, with a long, narrow face, and to my mind not a pleasant expression; but then I am prejudiced. I do not care for the Bourbons, and ancient as their family may be, in all these centuries they have hardly produced an able or a good man. However, the said King was exceedingly polite, and being unused to hunting and very averse to jumping, placed himself under my wing. I was lucky, and able to show him a good deal of sport. We had a good gallop up to Warden Hill, and then round by Preston Church and Ashby, and back here, where the fox was killed and the brush duly presented to the King.

"*March* 6.—We hunted from Little Preston—an odious day, blowing a gale, frequent hailstorms, and no sport. The King and Queen of Naples were both out, and he presented me to her. She has fine dark eyes and a clear pale complexion, with brown hair; but her teeth spoil her. She is extraordinarily thin, and sits too high to look well on horseback. She spoke English very well, as far as I could judge from the few words which I exchanged with her. He galloped about with me all day again, but did not say much, and what he did say was difficult to hear, between the wind and his bad French.

"*March* 10.—Harry and I hunted from Floore. No particular sport, but a great crowd to see the Empress of Austria, who arrived at Easton Neston on Monday, and has hunted every day since, riding quite magnificently. That most factious party leader, Lord Hartington, was out to-day, and talked a great deal of the Queen's new title, Empress of India, about which Dizzy has made so much unnecessary fuss. Consequently the House of Commons feels affronted, and there are perpetual quarrels and wrangling, and I am sorry, for the Queen must be much annoyed. It is curious how strong the feeling of the country against the title of Empress seems to be.[1]

"*March* 17.—Yesterday Rainald had a very strong whip and a letter from Big Ben, begging him to come up and support the Government on the Royal Titles Bill; but he declined. Now we hear the division gave the Government a majority of 105—much more than we anticipated; but it has been thoroughly mismanaged, and both parties blame each other. The Opposition say they were not consulted, the Government say they were and that they broke faith. It all does so much harm. We hunted from Astwell Mill, and the King of Naples presented me to the Empress of Austria. She is wonderfully well preserved for forty, and is decidedly pretty, with charming manners—altogether far more attractive than the Queen of Naples. But what a leveller the hunting-field is! Empress, King, Queen, and courtiers go bumping along in the crowd and no one pays them any attention.

"*March* 24.—Another division last night on the Royal Titles Bill. Dizzy made a speech, which really

---

[1] The importance of this step has been amply proved by subsequent events.

deserved Mr. Lowe's unparliamentary epithets of
'drivelling and frivolous,' quoting children's geography-
books and Whitaker's Almanack as authorities for the
Queen being Empress, and finally winding up with the
astounding assertion that it is all intended as a threat
to the Russians in Central Asia! I really think he has
taken leave of his senses!

"*Northampton Races, March* 28.—A crowded meeting, and a good many London as well as county people,
which made it more amusing than usual. Prince
Christian was there, and he as well as everybody else
was talking about the Royal Titles Bill, which is to be
the subject of another great party fight in the Lords
on Monday. Mr. Gladstone is supposed to be at the
bottom of the insolent factious opposition, having over-
ruled Lord Hartington, who at first was disinclined to
move. There is a most extraordinary article in to-
day's *Times*, strongly objecting to the Queen's leaving England during the session, which she did this
morning, all her four sons being out of the country!
And a letter in the *Times* actually comments on
'the significant absence from the division of such men
as Mr. Henley, Sir Rainald Knightley, and Mr. Newdegate.' Flattering as it is to Rainald, I could have
dispensed with these remarks, and myself rather regret
his abstention.

"*April* 1.—Yesterday the King of Naples and
Prince Ruffano came to luncheon, and were very civil
and pleasant. The latter is a tall, fine-looking man, of
a very old Neapolitan family, and declares he remembers
seeing me at Cannes! To-day the hounds met at
Badby, and I thoroughly enjoyed my last day's hunting.
We had a capital run, and I really saw it all, and stuck
to the hounds closer than I ever did before. Rainald
led the field, and we both felt so keen. I am sorry it
is all over. I have hunted twenty-nine times this
season—fifteen with the Duke, nine with the Pytchley,
two with the Bicester and the Warwickshire, and once
with the Rufford, and never enjoyed a winter anything
like so much!

"*April* 6.—The King, Queen, and Prince Ruffano came to luncheon, and went over with us to Daventry steeplechases. We put four post-horses into the sociable, and went off with a splash, which, however, was rather marred by a trace breaking half-way up the hill. Daventry was on the *qui vive*, and received the ex-Royalties extremely well, which pleased them, and we were glad to do Daventry a good turn. But we heard afterwards that some of the people tried to hiss the King and Queen and raise shouts for Garibaldi—happily neither they nor we heard them. ' Bomba is coming ' was chalked up on several walls.

"*Richmond Park, April* 25.—Rainald came to join me here last week, and we found the dear mother looking very well and the little place in apple-pie order. Yesterday we went to Hampton Court, and wandered like children into the Maze, and roamed about the Palace together. It is very pleasant to look at the familiar scenes with another pair of eyes, and we examined with care which was the Tudor part of the building and which was William III.'s. Finally Mrs. Maude took us to tea at the Stud House, where we met Prince Teck, and had a nice walk home through the Home Park. To-day we walked over to luncheon at White Lodge with Princess Mary, Prince Teck, and their four nice children. They have made the house very pretty, and were particularly pleasant and friendly. Like everyone else, they regret extremely the mess that has been made of the Royal Title, and fear we have not yet seen the end of it.

" 4 *Grosvenor Crescent, April* 28.—We came to town, and Rainald went to the Duke of Edinburgh's levee, which I am glad of, as I am anxious he should show that his abstention from voting was against Dizzy—*not* the Queen. Many comments have been made on his action—more, he says, than he ever knew for merely staying away! Last night the Women's Suffrage Bill was thrown out by 87—double last year's majority. Bright turned round, and spoke and voted against us. I *am* sorry. London is singularly dull at present.

"*May* 8.—I dined with Nora and Sir Charles Trevelyan, and had a grand talk about Boarding Out, Charity Voting, etc. Afterwards, Nora and I went to hear *Tannhäuser* at Covent Garden, and were delighted with it. The story is beautiful, the music wonderfully fine, and the general effect splendidly dramatic. Albani acts and looks the character of the pure-minded Elizabeth to perfection. The house was a brilliant one. I saw well-known faces everywhere. The Duchess of Westminster was in a box, with her lovely little daughter, Lady Ormonde—a feast for the eyes.

"*May* 11.—Yesterday was taken up with the Drawing-room, at which I presented Nora Trevelyan and Nina St. Paul. It was bitterly cold, but not very full, as the public means to go on Friday and see our 'Wales.' I had a more gracious reception than I expected, considering Rainald's non-vote. To-day I spent the whole afternoon at Lady Stanhope's in Grosvenor Place, awaiting the Prince's arrival, on his return from India. The road was lined with troops, and most of the houses were decorated. He was very well received, and it did one's heart good to see the Princess's face—she is so glad to have him back. We dined with Nora, and I sat between Lord Eliot and Mr. Trevanion. Everyone talking of the extraordinary death by poisoning of a Mr. Bravo, the second husband of the Florence Campbell whom I used to know a thousand years ago at Coombe.

"*May* 31.—I, Louisa Mary Knightley, did go to the Derby, and this was the manner of it! I came down to Richmond Park with Charley as usual, and then drove over to Epsom through shady green lanes, finding no great crowd until we reached the race-course. We went into the Jockey Club Stand, and found the usual lot of racing ladies, together with a few others—Lady Spencer, Lady Dudley, etc. Certainly it is a wonderful sight—the immense sea of heads, reaching almost as far as the eye can see, and beyond quiet green fields and woods, and then the pandemonium of shouting. Petrarch, Lord Dupplin's horse, the winner of the Two

Thousand, was beaten, and Mr. Baltazzi's colt Kisber won at a canter. The race was a hollow one and the victory not popular, so there was no shouting, and what struck me most was the sea of suddenly uncovered heads below the Stand. After the race, Rainald and Charley came to help us out of the squash, and we came away with perfect ease. And so ends my first and last Derby day, but I have wished all my life to see the great national holiday.

"*June* 1.—William Honywood brought the Count d'Albany to luncheon. He is the grandson of Charles Edward's sister by her second husband, a Mr. Hay Allen, and fought as a boy at Leipzig with Napoleon, who himself gave him the Legion of Honour, which he wears, together with many lockets, rings, enamel buttons, and two long grey ringlets, a braided frock-coat, and quaintest of all—spurs! With all these absurdities, he has a fine head and dignified manners, and is a great naturalist, knowing all the notes of the different birds, and ekes out a modest income by making translations at the British Museum. His wife was a Miss Beresford, and his son, Colonel Stuart of 'Deerhound'[1] celebrity, married Lady Alice Hay.

"*4 Grosvenor Crescent, June* 21.—This afternoon I went with Mamma and Sophy to St. James's Hall to hear Père Hyacinthe. The Duke of Argyll introduced him to the densely crowded meeting in a few well-chosen sentences, and then he commenced an oration on the two requisites for reform in the Latin Church, *i.e.*'rupture avec la Papauté et maintien de l'ordre dans l'Église.' He is singularly eloquent; his language was forcible and elegant, especially in one passage in which he lamented the destruction of Lacordaire and Montalembert's great scheme of reform, and another in which he anticipated the day when Latin, Greek, and Anglican Churches shall all unite on the basis of the Apostles' Creed. Would God it might be so! Mr. Gladstone appeared on the platform, and was received with warm applause; but

---

[1] The yacht *Deerhound* was at hand when the *Alabama* was sunk off Cherbourg, on June 19, 1864.

the Protestant element was strongly represented, and the curious medley of people assembled was a sight to behold.

"*June* 24.—We went to see the Prince's Indian presents, the carpets and hangings struck me especially, also the gold filigree and a palanquin of inlaid ivory; but there was a great crowd, and we were glad to take shelter in the cool, quiet National Portrait Gallery—the best history lesson I know. We dined with dear old Lyveden, and went on to Dizzy's party at the Foreign Office, to meet the Prince and Princess of Wales. It was a great crowd, but a brilliant scene, and as Rainald came with me I enjoyed myself much, hearing him talking to different Ministers. He introduced me to Sir William Harcourt—'Historicus.' I wonder if that man has a great career before him? He has the talent, but as to principle! Sir Stafford Northcote told us a delightful story of some Yankee who remarked to a friend of his, ' Well, I guess you know how to manage your scandals! There's Sir Stafford Northcote, now! More public money passes through his hands than through those of any man in Europe, and he's never been found out yet!'

"*July* 8.—I went off by myself down to Cumberland Lodge, to have luncheon with Princess Christian, who is only now beginning to recover from the loss of her baby. She was very nice and dear, talked a good deal of the Royal Titles Bill and said she quite understood Rainald's vote from his point of view, but wished she could have seen me at the time to talk it over. Princess Amelia of Schleswig-Holstein was there—very pleasant as usual."

At the end of the month Sir Rainald and Lady Knightley again went to Homburg, with Mrs. Gage and her son Harry as their companions. They found plenty of friends, among them Prince Arenberg, whose gloomy views of the progress of Socialism and the downfall of Prussia once more impressed Lady Knightley deeply. The Bravo case then going on at home was the chief topic of conversation among the English visitors.

"*Homburg, August* 9.—We have found plenty of acquaintances here, among others Prince and Princess Colonna (the Thérèse Caracciolo of Lamington three years ago), the Clevelands, who are particularly pleasant and sociable, the Clancartys, Rosslyns, and Lord Warwick. Mr. Charles Russell [1] is the height of fashion, on account of his intimate knowledge of the Bravo case. Sir Montagu Smith, who has just arrived, takes a different view of it. Lord Henry Lennox's resignation, in consequence of his having been mixed up with Baron Grant over the Lisbon Tramways, is still the subject of much discussion. There is some idea of reinstating him, which would be disastrous both for him and the Government. But the money is of great importance to him, and Sir Montagu quotes the old adage, ' An empty sack cannot stand upright.' Mrs. Bravo stands revealed as a worthless, drunken wretch, still I do not see that the murder is clearly brought home to her. The Grand Duke of Mecklenburg and H.R.H. of Cambridge have arrived, and Mr. Knatchbull-Hugessen, whom I find very amusing. We dined on Saturday with the Sassoons and Macclesfields and the blind Grand Duke, with whom I have made friends at the Springs, and who is very cheerful and good-humoured. Dizzy's elevation to the peerage is generally approved. He is getting too old for House of Commons work.

"*Metz, August* 15.—We took leave of Sophy and Harry and left Homburg at 9 a.m., Lord Warwick and Lord Clancarty coming to see us off. We came here up the valley of Nahe, by Kreuznach and Forbach, through very pretty scenery; but what fills one with astonishment is that the French could ever have dreamt of invading Germany by a line every inch of which could be so easily defended. It is awful to think of the misery and bloodshed that has been concentrated on this smiling country. Would one could think it were all over! Lord Winmarleigh, who arrived yesterday, says the whole town has been *en fête* for the Assumption of

---

[1] Afterwards Sir Charles Russell and Lord Russell of Killowen, Attorney-General 1886, and Lord Chief Justice 1894.

the Virgin—really the fête-day of Napoleon—and going into the Cathedral he heard a violent sermon by a cardinal in abuse of the Prussians!

"*August* 16.—The anniversary of the battle of Vionville, and we spent it in a prolonged and most interesting examination of the field of Gravelotte. We drove first through a pretty wooded valley up to Amanvilliers, and then came out upon a vast tableland. Here the French were posted, and up this the Germans advanced to S. Privat, without an atom of shelter, and were mowed down like ripe corn; but in the meantime the Saxons got their artillery into position on the other side and took S. Privat in flank, thus deciding the battle. Our driver, a most intelligent man who had himself served in the French artillery on that day, told us that Canrobert, who commanded the Sixth Corps at the end of the line, telegraphed three times over to Bazaine for ammunition. Twice no answer came; the third time Bazaine telegraphed that he wanted all he had got for the defence of Metz, while at the same time he kept an immense reserve of cavalry doing nothing! If ever there was a traitor, it was that man! Our *cocher* was most indignant with Thiers for not having him shot, and said if ever Bazaine came to Metz, the women would be the death of him. From S. Privat we drove down the hill, passing numerous monuments and crosses to S. Marie-les-Chênes, and by a road which divided the two armies, past Verveville, where a fearful struggle raged round a farmhouse, to Gravelotte—a quiet, dirty village, now of bloody fame! Here two roads to Verdun come in, and along here the battles of Mars-la-Tour and Vionville were fought on the 16th. Turning east, we ascended a steep hill up which the Germans charged under Steinmetz, leaving the quarry half-way up full of their dead bodies. The farm of S. Hubert just above was taken and re-taken three times, but finally the Prussians remained in possession of it, and at this end also the battle was won, though at what an awful cost! There were monuments here at every step, and **at the** top of the hill I read upon one the name of Herr von Jasmund, whom I met at Potsdam eight years ago and had that dispute with about Frederic William I. of Prussia. It was a curious coincidence.[1]

"From the top of this hill we had a beautiful view of Metz and the surrounding country, and descending rapidly returned to 'La Pucelle,' as she ought still to be called, as but for treachery she never could have fallen! Our *cocher* showed us several villages where the Germans were posted, right under the guns of S. Quentin, and never a shot was fired at them.

"*Reims, Hôtel du Lion d'Or, August* 18.—Yesterday we travelled here by slow train—a very hot, tedious journey, changing at S. Hilaire and turning north past the camp of Châlons, the scene of Attila's great battle. We walked up from the station, and came suddenly upon the glorious west front of the Cathedral, which is indeed a thing of beauty—unequalled in grandeur of conception and richness of detail. The great rose-windows and the exquisite stained glass give it a peculiar charm. This morning we went back and studied the noble portals on the north side, with their quaint representations of the Last Judgment—the Devil leading kings and priests in chains to a blazing cauldron, and on the other side our Lord with children in His arms and angels bringing others to Him. We went back and back again to the wonderful west front and the glorious rose-windows, and tore ourselves reluctantly away, feeling we should probably never see it again. Reims is a very inaccessible place nowadays, and evidently few strangers go there. At the hotel they would not take a circular note, and the station-master refused both English banknotes and German gold, which Rainald says never happened to him before.

"*Fawsley, August* 22.—Ah! how delightful to find ourselves, after all our wanderings, safe in this dear

[1] It was of this brave officer that the Crown Prince of Germany wrote in his diary on September 8, 1870. "Rheims.—I am sorely grieved at Jasmund's death. Few were as gifted and very few as absolutely devoted as he was. I had hoped great things from him in the future" (*Deutsche Rundschau*, October 1888).

home, in this lovely summer weather. We settled down very easily and happily, and played croquet with Val. Rainald went beaking (*i.e.* electioneering), and I went to Badby and visited all my friends.

"The Eastern question becomes more and more anxious and complicated. I can quite feel with Rainald when he says he is thankful not to be in the Cabinet. The horrors in Bulgaria make one's blood boil, and the tide of feeling all over the country is rising rapidly. Meetings are being held everywhere. A good deal of the excitement is due to party, but everyone must share in it to a great extent and blame Sir Henry Elliot and Dizzy. Still, it is very embarrassing for the Government, and our position as a country is most painful and perplexing. Rainald and I talk Eastern question all day long, but never come to any satisfactory conclusion.

"*September* 10.—I read Mr. Gladstone's pamphlet on the Bulgarian atrocities. There is a great deal of truth in it, very damaging to the Government. His speech at Blackheath is much more moderate. Rainald went to Brackley for the Agricultural Show and dinner, at which he had to speak—I own to feeling anxious on the subject. Every utterance at this moment is of vital importance, especially with the Bucks election pending.

"*September* 16.—I think, as far as I can judge, I approve of Rainald's speech, but oh! I do wish that the *Right* and the *Expedient* for England did not appear at this moment to be two different things. Rainald fears a general war, with all its horrors and miseries. May God avert it.

"*September* 18.—A long, very prudent, and colourless speech from Sir Stafford Northcote. The other lot have quite broken out. Mr. Gladstone's letter and the Duke of Argyll's and Mr. Lowe's speeches betray such bitter spirit, I am quite disgusted. Mr. Baring's report is out at last, and fully confirms all the main outlines of the Bulgarian horrors. . . . Dizzy makes a very bold speech at Aylesbury, with a violent attack on Gladstone, passing over in total silence the crimes which have stirred the country so deeply. I fear it will do great harm."

During that autumn the Eastern question remained the one absorbing topic of thought and conversation, alike in Lady Knightley's quiet hours at Fawsley and in the Scottish country-houses — Blair Drummond, Lindertis, etc.—where the most of October was spent.

"The Eastern question," she writes on October 7, "has assumed a new phase, owing to Russia's proposal that she should occupy Bulgaria, and the public is beginning to come to its senses, and to see that what, as Lady Barrington told us to-day, Sir William Harcourt had said is but too true of the Liberals: 'We don't care a hang for the Bulgarians; we only want to turn the Government out.' Mr. Forster has not joined in this disgraceful agitation, and now Turkey has agreed to an armistice; but what Russia will say to this remains to be seen."

"*Raby Castle, Darlington, October* 18.—We made a careful and prolonged inspection of this magnificent old pile, and most bewildering it is—only the Duchess's clever handbook gives one any clue to the labyrinth. It has been sadly altered and spoiled, but the external walls, of enormous strength and thickness, have been here probably since Canute's time, and certainly since 1378. The kitchen is a wonderful sight, and the baron's hall also very fine. We walked round the outside of the castle, by far the most striking part, and went over the roof, which gives one a good idea of the different towers. Afterwards we walked down to the church at Staindrop, and saw the tombs of the Nevilles, Earls of Westmoreland, who lost Raby after the Rising of the North, when the then Earl was exiled. The Vanes bought it in 1639. The latest memories are of Mr. Gladstone's visit, when he inscribed himself in the visitors' book as 'anti-Bashi-bazouk,' and cut down an old tree. The Duke, however, was much annoyed at the speech which he made at Staindrop. Warlike rumours thicken every day. The funds have fallen more heavily than before the Crimea, and it seems almost impossible that war can be averted. The Duchess of Edinburgh, who has great influence with her father, is said to use it all in favour of Turkey, but the Princess Dolgorouki, to whom he is much attached, uses hers for Servia; so he vacillates between the two.

"*Winmarleigh, Garstang, Lancashire, October 22.*—We spent a very nice Sunday with old Lord Winmarleigh, a wonderful old man of seventy-five, who represented the whole of Lancashire with Lord Derby's grandfather before the Reform Bill, and was present at the Coronation of the Emperor Nicholas at Moscow in 1826. Yet he seems as hale and active as a boy, and fulfils every duty of life—serving his country, caring for his church and poor people, and is the best and kindest of fathers. Verily such men are the salt of the earth!

"*Fawsley, November 2.*—The papers brought very bad news. Just when the armistice was all but signed, Russia, maddened by Servia's defeat, presented an ultimatum demanding a six weeks' armistice and autonomy for the three provinces. Mercifully Turkey has given way, and we have a breathing space. Lord Hartington makes a capital speech, moderate and fair—wonderful to say, considering his position. Gladstone has completely discredited himself, although some—Lord Spencer, for instance—still go with him.

"*November 10.*—Dizzy made an excellent speech at the Mansion House—plucky, dignified, and statesmanlike. An admirable state paper of Lord Derby's is published, giving a résumé of all that has passed since August. Two especial points I note—one that Russia made her proposal of occupation to us as well as to Austria; the other, that we had to threaten to withdraw Sir Henry Elliot before Turkey would agree to the armistice. But it is a comfort to see England once more taking her proper place in the great European drama. And the best news of all is that Lord Salisbury goes as Plenipotentiary to the Conference at Constantinople. He is the very best man that could be chosen—bold, independent, a man of great powers, great position, and above all a Christian. God speed him! The Czar has pledged his word to Lord Augustus Loftus that he does not want Constantinople, and has desired the dispatch to be published. Meanwhile, he mobilises his army, makes preparations for war, and contracts a fresh loan.

"*January* 11, 1877.—Harry and I went to Gayton to stay with the Eykyns for the Northampton ball. We found the King of Naples paying a visit, with a little chevalier who spoke execrable French, and a very long time they sat there. Both he and the Queen are violently pro-Turkish. Colonel Burnaby ('Reindeer') and his wife were staying there as well as Lord and Lady Vane, Miss Mostyn, Edward Knatchbull-Hugessen, and Mr. Rupert Carington, the defeated candidate for Bucks, who talked a great deal of Radical rubbish. The ball was pretty and cheery, and I danced and enjoyed myself like an old goose.

"*Orwell Park, Ipswich, January* 15.—We came here to find Lady Cork, with three daughters, the Duke of Cambridge, Lord and Lady Dorchester, etc., an entertaining but not very harmonious party. *On dit*, that Mr. Delane retires from the *Times*, and probably Mr. Borthwick will succeed him. One story is that Russia has bought thirteen shares in the paper. It has certainly been playing Russia's game all the winter, and abusing the Government, who consequently give all their information to the *Daily Telegraph*. To-day it alone has the news that the Powers have abandoned all their points but one—the International Commission.

"*January* 20.—I came to town and lunched with Nora Trevelyan, where I met Mr. George Trevelyan, and heard as strong anti-Turk views as I have heard pro-Turk all the week, the said Turks having at a grand council refused to listen to any of the Powers' propositions and left them all *plantés là*. It remains to be seen if '*le revolver Russe a raté*,' as some people say, or whether it has only '*reculé pour mieux sauter*.'

"*Claridge's, February* 8.—The Queen opened Parliament, and was very well received. I went to see

Princess Christian at Buckingham Palace, and we talked almost entirely Eastern question. People say that Lady Salisbury made great mistakes at Constantinople, was *très liée* with Madame Ignatieff, and quarrelled with Lady Elliot and Madame Midhat. The truth is that undoubtedly both she and he are much more anti-Turkish than the rest of the Cabinet. However, Lord Salisbury speaks highly of the present Sultan, who has only one wife, and spends much less money than his predecessors. All the world that could, went to see ' the Earl of Beaconsfield ' take his seat ! "

CHAPTER XXIV

THE BALKAN WAR AND CONGRESS OF BERLIN

1877–1878

"4 *Grosvenor Crescent, April* 24.—The long, long suspense has come to an end, the Russians have crossed the Pruth, and their chargé d'affaires has left Constantinople. Where will it all end ? and what misery there will be first, although, as the *Times* says, we utterly fail to realise it, and were far more concerned about the five colliers who were dug out last week after being buried for ten days. To-morrow—or rather to-day, for it is past midnight—I am going to be thirty-five—half-way through my life.

"*April* 25.—I hope the said birthday is not to be an emblem of the coming year, for I have not had five minutes' pause from morning to night. Parliamentary papers, house-books, a visit to Mary Wheatley, then to Christie's to see Baron Grant's pictures. Oh, such a crowd ! Then to choose a bag which Rainald has given me. Mother gave me Turner and Ruskin's *Harbours of England.* Then to a capital rehearsal of *Hercules*—a cantata of Handel's never given in London before. Home to scurry over the papers, which, alas ! contain the formal declaration of war. Sir Thomas and Mary Wheatley to dinner, and a party at Mrs. Hardy's. Rather amusing this was—Colonel Burnaby of Khiva to look at, the Chinese Ambassadors, and poor Musurus Pacha, looking worn, ill, and aged. Rainald said to him, ' Moi, je suis Turc jusqu'au bout des doigts.' His face lighted up as he replied, ' Ah, que je vous remercie, tous les vrais Anglais sont comme-ça !' I could not have said it, and feel more and more that I hate the whole thing.

"*Windsor Castle, May* 16.—This afternoon we came down here, where I certainly had never expected to come again. I carried Rainald off at once to the library, where we spent a delightful hour looking at drawings by Raphael and Leonardo, etc. Nothing struck me more than some studies of sprays and leaves which are quite wonderfully drawn. Prince Leo joined us, and showed us some interesting miniatures of the Tudors and Stuarts, especially one of Mary Queen of Scots which belonged to Charles I. She has brown eyes, a pale face, and reddish hair, and altogether an attractive face, but which gives little clue to her extraordinary fascination. A miniature of Anna, sister of the Duchess of Kent and wife of the Grand-Duke Constantine, an elder brother of Czar Nicholas, led to the Prince telling me that she once told her niece, the Queen, that she was in the next room to the Emperor Paul when he was murdered, and heard the struggle. Our company at dinner consisted of the Queen, Princess Beatrice, Prince Leopold, Prince Christian, the Duchess of Edinburgh, Lord and Lady Elgin, Lord and Lady Ormonde, Lord Hawarden, Lady Gainsborough, and Sir Stafford Northcote, who amused us all with his ghost-stories. One curious story was about Howth Castle, near Dublin, where, until within the last twenty years, it was the custom to lay an extra knife and fork for dinner every day. Centuries ago, a powerful chieftainess came to the castle, and being refused admission because the family were at dinner, avenged herself by kidnapping the son and heir. From that time the hall door was never closed during meals, and an extra place was always laid.

"The Queen was most kind and gracious, and after talking to her some time after dinner we joined the Household and played a rubber with Prince Leo.

"*May* 17.—We spent another delightful morning in the library and armoury, where are trophies of every age and land. We saw the spoils of **Tippoo** Sahib, his standard with huge emeralds, the jewelled peacock from the top of his umbrella, the bullet which killed Nelson, and armour belonging to Columbus, Charles v., Marlborough, Charles I., etc., and finally tore ourselves away with great regret after a very pleasant and successful visit.

"4 *Grosvenor Crescent, June* 5.—I went to Lowther Lodge, to find heaps of people and amateur drawings, amongst others an excellent likeness by Princess Louise of my poor friend Mr. Motley, who died a few days ago. I came home with Hairy, and had a pleasant visit from Mr. Mackenzie Wallace, who seems to like Russia and the Russians much better than it is the fashion to do just now. We dined with the Archbishop of York, and I sat between Lord Clinton and Mr. Venables of the *Times* and *Saturday Review*. He told me that the real cause of the quarrel between Mr. Roebuck and J. S. Mill was not the respective merits of Wordsworth and Byron, but the fact that Mr. Roebuck remonstrated with Mill when he lost his head about Mrs. Taylor. He also talked of Maurice and Kingsley, and said that Maurice did not like to be told that Kingsley had imbibed his opinions from him, preferring to think that another original mind had arrived at the same conclusions, just as J. S. Mill's adoration of his wife was caused by her reflecting his opinions.

"*July* 12.—We went to an extremely pleasant and quite small garden-party at Marlborough House. Why we were asked I cannot imagine, as most of the Chiswick list were omitted, not only 'the Prince's mixture,' but many others with just as much claim to be asked as ourselves. However, there it was, and I found it very enjoyable. The Queen was most gracious and Princess Christian very nice. Rainald introduced me to John Bright, who has an honest, clever face and very good manners. But I cannot forgive him the mischief which he has done by saying that the Russian merchantmen may not pass the Dardanelles, and men like Lords Henley and Wolverton actually believe it! Meanwhile, the Russians are making alarming progress and are breaking through the Balkans in every direction—so one gathers from many contradictory telegrams. In all the wars I remember—and they have been many in the last twenty-three years—we have never been so utterly without reliable information.

"*July* 16.—Rainald very proud of himself because he beat the Government last night, speaking and voting against a job of Dizzy's in giving his rector's son, Mr. Pigott, a post[1] for which he was not properly qualified. They were only beat by four, so I dare say he turned the scale. He hears that the reason why the *Pall Mall* abuses Gladstone steadily is because he would not allow W. R. Greg (*Enigmas of Life*), who has just resigned this same office, to let the house belonging to it.

"*July* 21.—Dizzy made a capital speech last night in the House of Lords, putting the Pigott incident in a totally different light and proving it to be a *mistake*, not a *job*, which makes a great difference. The debate is to be reopened on Monday, and Rainald is sorely puzzled how to act, for still it is not a good appointment. We went to Holland House, which was crowded in spite of the apparent collapse of the season. The Prince was there, but not the Princess, owing to her eldest boy's illness of typhoid fever. We dined with the Hertfords, and Count Gleichen announced that the 26th and 13th sail for Malta on Wednesday. The news sent a thrill through us all, and both my neighbours, Colonel Lindsay and Lord Yarmouth, exclaimed, ' I wish I were going! ' like thorough Englishmen.

"*July* 23.—I spent all the afternoon and evening at the House of Commons, which was densely crowded at question time, everyone hoping to hear something about the troops ; but Sir Stafford only said they were going to Malta. Then came an Irish row, in which Parnell, Power, and O'Donnell made themselves more offensive one than another, and Mr. Chaplin told them they were no gentlemen, at which they naturally gibbered. ' Toute vérité n'est pas bonne à dire.' I rushed home to dress and dine, while the wretched Rainald remained,

[1] That of Comptroller of the Stationery Office.

and when I got back they were well into the Pigott incident. Sir Stafford made a very nice speech, so did Mr. W. H. Smith and Lord Hartington. Then Rainald and Sir George Bowyer rose together; but there was a roar of 'Knightley,' and he said a few generous words, after which Sir Walter Barttelot's resolution was agreed to without a division.

"Colonel B—— came to luncheon and stayed on afterwards. It is the first time I have seen him since some good while before I married. He was very friendly, and Rainald was very nice to him. It took me back to old times and to the episode in my life which I always remember with self-reproach. But oh! how can I be thankful enough for such a husband!"

August was spent as usual at Homburg, the Knightleys being once more accompanied by Mrs. Gage and her son, who had lately succeeded to the peerage on the death of his grandfather, Lord Gage.

"*Homburg,* 1 *Kisseliff Strasse, August* 3.—Here we are safe at bright little Homburg, 'quite at home,' as our excellent little landlord phrased it, in our old quarters, and have already begun drinking and walking as if we were not a year older! Plenty of people, including Captain Burnaby of Khiva fame, and plenty of books, and nothing to do but to enjoy both. It is a very jolly life, and I thoroughly enjoy the rest. The great excitement has been that last Tuesday, July 31, the House met at 3.45 and sat till 6.10 p.m. on Wednesday—twenty-six and a half hours! Such a thing not having been known since the days of the Long Parliament. All to carry the South Africa Bill against the determined obstruction of five Irish members — Parnell, Biggar, O'Donnell, etc. The Russians have been defeated both north and south of the Balkans. It remains to be seen if the Turks can follow up their success. Captain Burnaby says he would rather command Turkish than English troops—they fight as well, march better, and live on less. I wonder if he is as clever as he thinks himself! He is a desperate Radical, and has very little religion, but, like many others I know of little faith, seems to take pleasure in active good works. Well, our Lord says, ' Judge not, that ye be not judged.' Only we Christians ought to be a great deal better than they are, and I am not at all sure that we always are. Mr. W. H. Smith's appointment to succeed poor Mr. Ward Hunt, who died here last week, gives great satisfaction. We dined at the Kursaal to-night with the Tweeddales (she was a Miss Bartolozzi) and a large party, including Countess Usedom and her daughter, Countess Hildegarde, a gigantic, gushing German damsel, who amused me a good deal. I was busy writing my paper *Fetters and Follies of Fashion*, which interests me much.

" *Monday, August* 21.—Here is a week gone by, and not a line of Journal written—very like Homburg. I must try and make it up. There have not been many events except a very amusing expedition to Königstein, in company with Countess Bernstorff, the Usedoms, Miss Malcolm, Sir George Dallas, and Baron Lohe, a Prussian Ultramontane and great lover of England and things English. It was great fun to hear Baron Lohe and Countess Hildegarde dispute about the respective merits of England and Germany, all in perfect good temper, but with a vehemence perfectly startling to our ideas ! However, I agree with him in the main, and should not like to live under the paternal government of Bismarck, whom they are all greatly afraid of displeasing. Land in Germany often lets at twelve shillings an acre—a striking contrast to East Lothian, where Lord Tweeddale says it is often let at £6 or £7 ! Königstein is a fine old ruined castle, beautifully situated at the foot of the Feldberg, with lovely views over the Frankfort plains, and the spires of Worms in the far distance."

From Homburg the party went on to Heidelberg, the Lake of Geneva, and Chamonix, where Lady Knightley enjoyed the glories of Mont Blanc and saw wonderful sunsets over the Alpine snows, returning by Dijon, where she had stayed on her memorable journey sixteen years before.

At Ouchy the news of Thiers' death had reached

the travellers, and on arriving in Paris they found that his funeral was already over. " It was not a state funeral, Madame Thiers having chosen to insist that the 363 Deputies of the recently dissolved Chamber should immediately follow the family. This MacMahon refused to allow, so it took place very quietly, and a lot of troops were ordered out to prevent any disturbance. Sad! to perpetuate political squabbles over an open grave!"

The autumn and winter were spent as usual at Fawsley, where Lady Knightley devoted herself, with her wonted energy, to G.F.S. work, mothers' meetings, classes, and hunting, and watched the trend of Eastern affairs and the electoral struggle in France with keen interest.

"*Fawsley, Sunday, October* 14.— To-morrow the French elections begin. I wonder how they will turn? Our papers are so violently anti-MacMahon that it is difficult to judge, but it looks as if he or his Cabinet were carrying things with a very high hand. We walked to Badby after church, and were admiring the lovely autumn tints in the warm, bright sunshine, little dreaming of the awful night that was in store for us and that we should wake to a scene of the most frightful desolation. A violent hurricane sprang up in the night, and this morning the park is literally strewn with débris, and many, many magnificent trees are utterly destroyed. The elms opposite the front door, the fine chestnuts beyond, the cedar which was damaged by the snow two years ago, three or four fine ash outside the Dingle, a splendid oak near the road going to Badby Wood—in short, it is perfectly heart-breaking, and poor Rainald, who so loved and delighted in his trees, is quite overwhelmed. We went out to look at the *dégât*, and found that one hundred and thirty trees had been blown down, besides many which are entirely ruined, while there are but few which have not suffered in some degree.

"*October* 23.—The French elections cannot be said to be a triumph for either party, but the Republicans have a majority of over a hundred. ' Honours divided,' as a writer in the *Times* describes it, ' but the Republicans have the trick.' I think, as Gambetta has tersely expressed it, MacMahon ought either ' se soumettre ou se démettre.' He seems disposed to do neither. Neither party is strong enough to be generous, and bitter are the recriminations on both sides. A curious fact is that nearly two million voters did not go to the poll.

"*Sotterley, Suffolk, Sunday, November* 25.—The Sunday next before Advent, just the Sunday I have so often spent here! It seemed very nice to go to church here again, and see the dear old building, every line of which I know and love, and the changing lights which I have so often watched. But there were hardly more than two or three faces I knew, and the yews and cypresses round my dear father's grave remind me how the years have flown. One of my favourite Sunday-school boys, Harry Briggs, was ' asked ' in church. After service I roamed about with St. John, looking at their various improvements, which I like on the whole, and poked about among the books in the library, which, often as I have dusted them, I do not half know.

" *Claridge's Hotel, December* 3.—Rainald and I had a great treat in going to see the admirable collection of drawings at the Grosvenor Gallery, mostly belonging to Mr. Malcolm of Poltalloch or to the Queen. In the evening we went to the Opéra Comique, to see a very amusing bit of nonsense called *The Sorcerer*, by Gilbert, set to music by Sullivan. I have not laughed so much for long.

" *Fawsley, December* 11.—Plevna has fallen, after a most prolonged and gallant defence. What next? one asks anxiously. The country is divided and uneasy. I am reading with the deepest interest the third volume of the Prince Consort's Life just published, treating of the Crimean War, when some of our statesmen were as unpatriotic as they are now. Fancy a man of Lord Henley's intelligence saying that it won't hurt us if the Russians do get Constantinople! And Mr. Forster evidently is of the same opinion.

" *Claridge's Hotel, January* 17, 1878.—We came to town, and found everybody on the tiptoe of expectation as to what the Queen's speech might reveal. Between the opening of Parliament and the debate, everyone put different interpretations on the passage about supplies. Meanwhile the Russians are advancing rapidly, and unless peace is promptly signed, we must intervene.

"*Fawsley, January* 25.—Very exciting news! Lord Carnarvon has resigned, and important orders have been sent to the fleet. The Duke of Cambridge was summoned to town from Orwell last Wednesday. One cannot but rejoice that something is being done to arrest the onward march of the Russians, who are already perilously near Constantinople.

"*January* 27.—I had three letters presenting a curious contrast—one from Princess Christian praising Disraeli's wise, far-seeing conduct, and characterising Lord Derby (who resigned with Lord Carnarvon, and withdrew his resignation) as the worst Foreign Minister England has ever had; one from Big Ben saying, 'We must vote with the Government as the least of two evils'; and a third from Mr. Holthouse, the mouthpiece of many High Church clergy, begging Rainald to vote against the additional supplies, adding: 'I have never had any confidence in Lord Beaconsfield, and confess I shall not breathe easy as long as he is in office, and this war goes on.'

"*January* 29.—Our anxious suspense continues. The terms of peace are monstrous, and our fleet having gone up the Dardanelles, has returned to Besika Bay. All sorts of rumours are afloat as to what course Lord Hartington's mutinous crew will take, and how many Conservatives will vote with the Government.

"*February* 4.—A delightful hunting day. The meet was at Preston, and we were standing by Badby Wood when a telegram was brought to Rainald, begging him to come up at once for the division. This was most unexpected, but Rainald was off in little over half an hour. 'Dizzy has resigned,' was Sir Thomas Bateson's morning greeting—' the Privy Seal' was the end of his sentence. The Duke of Northumberland succeeds him,—plucky to join the Cabinet at such an anxious moment,—and Lord Spencer gives up the Pytchley, which means that he wants to save money to fight the county. But the armistice is signed at last. Altogether, a very exciting day.

"*February* 8.—Rainald need not have been hunted off so; they won't divide till I don't know when! Yesterday's rumour of the Russian advance on Constantinople was confirmed by Sir S. Northcote in the House on Mr. Layard's authority, and contradicted half an hour later on that of Prince Gortschakoff. The crisis is so momentous that one can hardly grasp its full meaning, and in the middle of it all the Pope is dead—*Pio Nono*. At any other time it would have made a great sensation, now we have no time to think of it, for the Russians have advanced to the lines of Tchataldja, twenty miles from Constantinople, and there is nothing to prevent them from taking the city whenever they please. This is what two years of vacillation have brought us to! Lord Hartington and Mr. Gladstone have apparently entirely broken with each other, and they say Schouvaloff is constantly with Lady Derby, and gets everything out of her. It is enough to make one think women had better know nothing about politics.

"*February* 15.—The fleet has gone up at last, and is anchored ten miles south of Scutari. What will be the next act in this wonderful drama? It would be a comedy if it were not a tragedy.

"*Wakefield Lodge, Stony Stratford, February* 19.—We drove over here this afternoon by Weedon and Towcester. Our party consists of the Prince Imperial, the Duc de Bassano, uncle to the Duchess of Grafton, Lord Strathnairn, Lady Elizabeth Biddulph, Mr. George Pennant, Colonel and Mrs. Stuart, and the Alfred Fitzroys. I sat by the Prince, who speaks English fluently, but with a strong French accent. He is a little man, not good-looking, and with the same melancholy expression as his father, whom Rainald says he much resembles. Poor little fellow! he has already been the innocent cause of a fearful war. What will be his history in the future?

"*February* 20.—The hounds met at Wakefield Lawn, and I could not help thinking, as I rode on to the ground beside the Prince Imperial, how many interesting people

I have come across—sitting at luncheon between the Crown Prince of Prussia and the Duke of Augustenburg, piloting the ex-King of Naples in the hunting field, and now riding to hounds with Napoleon III.'s only son. We had a good day's sport, and I did a little G.F.S. business, and told Mr. Praed about Clause 16 of the Factories and Workshops Act. Bismarck has spoken, and his speech resolves itself into, ' Bless you, my children. Fight it out as you like ; it pleases you and don't hurt me.' I hear that it is quite true that he proposed to us to take Egypt as long ago as last spring, and that the Queen was frantic at the idea !

"*February* 21.—We took a charming walk in the old Forest this morning, and after luncheon drove with the Prince and Lady Elizabeth to Stowe. It is an enormous palace of a place, standing well on a hill overlooking a lake and a fine arch with a three-mile avenue rivalling the Long Walk at Windsor. On every side you see temples, obelisks, statues, all laid out with great taste, but a melancholy picture of decadence, neglect, and ruin. The present Duke of Buckingham, ruined by his father's extravagance, is gone as Governor to Madras, and this great empty house remains forlorn and desolate. The Prince, who has hitherto been very shy and silent, talked a good deal and was very pleasant. He said that he was very fond of French Memoirs, and that Henri IV.. ' lui était très sympathique, que c'était un grand roi et un grand soldat,' and told us of the Dame Blanche who appears before the death of a member of the Prussian Royal Family, and of ' Le Grand Veneur,' of the Forest of Fontainebleau, whose voice used to be heard before the death of a King of France, crying ' M'attends-tu ? ' and of the lingering faith in touching for the king's evil, which made an old woman in the north of France ask to be touched by the Empress.

"*March* 29.—We were electrified by the news of Lord Derby's resignation, and the calling out of the Reserve forces. It seems as if war could not be averted. Rainald thinks it will, and that Russia, seeing we are in earnest, will cave in.

"*April* 9.—A most able State paper has been issued by Lord Salisbury, now Minister for Foreign Affairs, bringing out the whole bearing of this infamous Treaty of San Stefano, and its menace to our interests. It has already produced an immense effect abroad. Everyone is astonished and delighted to find that England can speak out as of yore. We drove to Northampton Races, taking a large party—Lady Stradbroke and her girls, the Carysforts, Sir Thomas Western, Harry, etc. The Prince and Princess of Wales brought the Crown Prince and Princess of Denmark. Our Princess looked prettier than ever, but I thought pale and sad. Rainald had to leave the races to go up for a division on calling out the Reserves. The majority was enormous—319 to 64. A very fine debate in the House of Lords. Lord Salisbury and Lord Beaconsfield both spoke admirably. Prince Gortschakoff's answer to Lord Salisbury's circular is more pacific than might have been expected.

" 4 *Grosvenor Crescent, May* 20.—This afternoon Rainald took me to the House of Lords to hear the debate on moving the Indian troops to Malta. Certainly a great debate in the Lords is a very stately thing. The House was crowded, the Peeresses' Gallery very full, the Crown Prince and Princess of Germany and the Princess of Wales being up there, and the Prince of Wales and Duke of Cambridge were in their places on the cross-benches, where I also saw Lords St. Germans, Strathnairn, Penrhyn, and old Lord Cottesloe. Lord Selborne spoke for two mortal hours, and was very dull; the only startling thing in his speech was the allusion to the fact of ' the balance of power in Europe ' not having been mentioned in the preamble to the Meeting Act since 1866—and this with the Crown Prince just over his head! The best point he made was when he quoted the words of a far higher authority than himself regarding Indian troops, a speaker who had once said ' that either India should not be denuded, or, if she can spare the men, she is unnecessarily taxed.' ' These, my Lords,' he added, ' were the words of Lord Cranborne, now Her Majesty's Foreign Secretary.' Lord Cairns followed, and Dizzy wound up the debate in a very able speech, after which I went on to the House of Commons and listened to Sir William Harcourt, who reminded me of Sir Robert Peel's remark that if there were any more lawyers in the House it would not be bearable, they were such bores! In the evening I went to Lady Norton's, where Sir Charles Mordaunt introduced me to his new wife, and my old Potsdam friend, Countess Brühl, who is in England with the Crown Princess, told me that the Duke of Connaught's fiancée is charming, very amiable, intelligent, and affectionate, and longing for love, which she has never had at home. Meanwhile there is great news. We are really going into congress, and Lord Beaconsfield is to represent England, which Rainald thinks looks well, as he would not care to imperil his reputation if he did not see some fair prospect of success. I am very curious to see if this Protectorate of the Christians in Asia Minor will mean anything!

"*June* 13.—To-day the Congress of Berlin meets for the first time. So important an assembly has hardly been known since the Congress of Vienna in 1815.

"*June* 29.—We dined with the Duke of Grafton, and I sat by Lord Dalkeith, who was very agreeable, talking of India. Travelling always makes people pleasant. On to an amusing party at Lady Cornelia Guest's house, where was that marvellous invention, the phonograph. Sir Stafford Northcote made us all laugh by shouting into it, ' Perhaps you are not aware that the British fleet has gone to the bottom of the Black Sea, where it has recovered the remains of the British Constitution, which was destroyed by the profligate government of Lord Beaconsfield.' This was distinctly repeated in a voice rather like a parrot's— except Baron Munchausen's horn, there never was anything like it. Lord Strathnairn laments the inclusion of Sofia in Bulgaria, which will, he fears, enable an enemy to turn the line of the Balkans. I don't think the flourish of trumpets with which the *Times* ushered in the week has been at all sustained.

"*July* 8.—I went to see the Art Embroideries Show

at Grosvenor House, which were most lovely in that grand house. Rainald came in at dressing-time with the startling news that we have guaranteed the Turkish possessions in Asia against Russia, and have got Cyprus for our pains—a fine coruscation of fireworks to wind up the Congress with! At least it ties the hands of any future Government, and Cyprus will be an excellent point from which to defend both roads to India. I went to a crowded party at Mrs. Portman's, being anxious to gather opinions on this great event. I think the general consensus of feeling is in favour of it. Of course the Radicals find fault, but they have no tangible objection to bring forward. The French, however, clearly do not like it, as I gathered from a long and earnest conversation which I overheard at the Queen's ball between Musurus and M. d'Harcourt.

"*July* 16.—I went to Whitehall with Mamma, and looked down from a window of the chapel as Lord Beaconsfield and Lord Salisbury drove by on the way from Charing Cross to Downing Street. There was no very enormous crowd, but the cheering was loud and continuous, and seemed to go on for a long time in Downing Street, where I believe Dizzy addressed a few words to the crowd. There were no troops and not much to see, but to me it was far more significant than many a stately pageant. For it means peace with honour, as the *Times* says to-day. It means the end of the long tension of two years of deep anxiety. And what a marvellous career is that of the man we acclaim to-day, who from a simple attorney's clerk has risen to the truly proud position which he now occupies, by the force of genius alone. And all one's heart goes out to the fine figure opposite, the grand, thoughtful head of the man who, putting aside all personal feeling, joined the Government from truly patriotic motives, and has stuck to it gallantly. Without Lord Salisbury, to-day's triumph would not have been possible, and England and Disraeli alike owe him a debt of profound gratitude."

CHAPTER XXV

AGRICULTURAL DEPRESSION AND CONSERVATIVE DEFEATS

1878-1880

LADY KNIGHTLEY and her husband spent September 1878 in Scotland, where they paid a succession of visits to Mr. and Lady Emily Hamilton at Dalzell, to Mrs. Ellice at Invergarry, to Sir Dudley Marjoribanks at Guisachan, to Sir Thomas Munro at Lindertis, and to Lady William Osborne at Tullyallan. Once more she thoroughly enjoyed the beauty of Highland scenery in glorious autumn weather, and rejoiced in this opportunity of increasing her knowledge of a country which she had loved from her early days at Balmoral. On the way south, a visit was paid to Mr. Sneyd at Keele, in Staffordshire, where she found a source of endless delight in the library, with its priceless store of illuminated missals, autograph letters of English sovereigns, miniatures, and county histories. She describes the famous gardens, with their unique holly hedge 26 feet high and 190 yards long, and a visit to Trentham, which she dismisses as one of the most odious places that she has ever seen, "like a bit " of Regent Street, with tin aloes at the top and the " Trent running close by and smelling—ugh! I would " not have it as a gift, and should hate having to live " there. Rainald says it reminds him of nothing so " much as of Pope's description of ' Timon's villa.'"

The remainder of the year was spent in her beloved home, where every year Lady Knightley became more absorbed in local affairs and in improving the condition of labourers and workmen on the Fawsley estates. Every good cause found a friend in her, and her kindness and sympathy were freely bestowed on men and women of all classes. A visit from the Bishop of Peterborough and a memorable sermon which he preached at a village church-opening were among the most noteworthy incidents of the autumn.

"*Fawsley, October 29.*—Rainald and I attended with great satisfaction the reopening of Woodford church, which has been completed with wonderful celerity in barely seven months since I laid the first stone of the new tower. It was a bright, hearty service, and our great Bishop preached a most admirable sermon, one of the finest I ever heard, on the text, ' Thy will be done in earth as it is in heaven.' He began with an eloquent description of the many places and ways in which that cry was going up to God, at this moment, in all parts of the world—by dying beds and unclosed graves, from hearts sick with disappointed hopes, worn out with vain and toilsome effort, or weary with that unutterable weariness of life which comes to so many in the present day. Then he went on to set forth three ways in which men answer God's will as revealed to each one of us in the circumstances of life. First, by open rebellion, saying, *Not Thy will, but my will*, setting up our own will against that of God, with that selfishness of the unsubdued nature which is the cause of all sin and crime, and the indulgence of which endangers the very existence of society. Secondly, by saying, *Thy will be done*—the submission which costs a hard struggle, the will yielded to God, lying crushed at His feet, as we say, *Not mine but Thine*. This is the answer we most of us try to make, with effort and sadness, but still saying it—the Christian surrender of the soul, a sacrifice in which there may be joy, but must be a degree of pain too. He bade us remember this, not only when crushed with an irremediable sorrow, but in all the petty details of everyday life, and strive ever more and more to realise this prayer both in doing and suffering. But thirdly, there is the answer that we shall make in heaven, and ought to aim at here, *Thy will and mine be done*—our wills being so perfectly in harmony with God's will that there is no longer any effort, any striving or pain, the blessed state to which we shall only fully attain in heaven, when it will be as easy and natural to do God's will as it is to live and breathe now. All these three stages are reflected in the Church's worship, in the confession where we deplore our past rebellion against God's will, in the prayers and communions where we seek for fresh grace to submit to God's will, and in the songs of praise in which the Church on earth rises out of herself, and in anticipation of a blessed future joins with angels and archangels in adoring the Divine Will as they do in heaven, in that rest which is not indolence, that quietude which is not indifference. But here on earth we can train ourselves by the discipline of daily life for that blessed future, here we can learn to lead the heavenly life, and in the little daily and hourly trials, by the repeated submission of our will to His, gather strength for the dark hours and great crises of life. Then the will of God will become no longer a law, but a guide to follow through all the difficulties and perplexities of life. In exact proportion as we are able to unite our wills with His, to say *Mine and Thine*, and rejoice in this union, our spiritual life will gain in power and beauty, and by thus imitating the example of Christ, whose work on earth was to do the will of His Father, we shall be preparing ourselves for the perfect worship of heaven, when we shall no more say, *Not my will but Thine*, as a hard and painful task, but *Mine and Thine*, ' now and for evermore.' The whole sermon, one felt, from beginning to end, was inspired by the chastened imagination of a great intellect and the loving sympathy of a great heart. And we who know, as the Bishop evidently did, the difficulties and hindrances which lay in the way of this church restoration, could not but admire with him the wonderful courage, perseverance, and patience shown by the Vicar, Mr. Minchin, in carrying out the work, in spite of poverty and ill-health. It is indeed an example to us all, and I am glad to feel that Rainald and I have been allowed to help in so good a work. It has all been so nicely and simply done by Mr. Hartshorne, keeping all of the old that could be kept, and the building now is just what a village church should be.

"*October* 31.—The Bishop came here to dine and sleep, and this morning I had the great pleasure of driving him to Charwelton to sign the deed annexing the new piece to the churchyard, after which he departed. I cannot say how much I have enjoyed his visit. I never felt his goodness so strongly before, his deep, earnest interest in all undertakings for his people, his real devotion. It strengthens and refreshes one, and encourages one to keep on ' pegging away ' in one's own small way. He read prayers this morning in the old hall very beautifully.

"*December* 6. — To-day a great gloom has been thrown over us all by our friend Major Whyte-Melville's death. His horse fell as he was galloping over a ploughed field and broke his neck. Only last night we were all singing his last hunting song, ' Drink, puppy, drink,' little dreaming the genial writer, the keen sportsman, was even then lying dead. Rainald and Mr. Angerstein both knew him so well, and feel it deeply.

"*December* 13.—The accounts of Princess Alice are very anxious. She is very dangerously ill of diphtheria, which she caught from her little boy. It is just seventeen years since her father died, and I have a superstitious feeling that if she lives over to-morrow, as the Prince of Wales did, she will recover.

"*December* 14. — By a most strange coincidence, on this very day she passed away. I cannot help feeling very deeply for the Queen and for them all at Windsor. How well I remember dear Princess Alice sitting in my little room at Osborne, listening to the wind howling, and saying how melancholy it made her feel. That was in April 1862, and after that I hardly saw her again to speak to till that day at Kranichstein in 1875, when she seemed so happy surrounded by her children. She was busy with her work, a large tablecover, and told me she was reading Hosack's *Mary Queen of Scots*. She talked of enjoying hunting, which both she and I began late in life, and then, when something was said about the Schloss at Homburg, remarked rather sadly, ' You know that would have been ours if the Prussians had not annexed it. Ah, well, it was the fortunes of war ! ' She looked worn and aged, I thought, and I was so sorry for the unlucky speech which I made, asking if that was her eldest boy ? Her answer sounded so sad : ' The only one I have left.' Two years had already elapsed since her eldest boy was killed by falling out of the window, but she had never recovered her spirits. How hard she worked at all good deeds, and what a noble example she has left behind ! May she indeed find her reward !

" 4 *Grosvenor Crescent, May* 3, 1879.—I enjoyed going with Rainald to the National Gallery, and looked at the Early Italian pictures, which are quite new to me. There is a Fra Angelico which struck me very much, and an Entombment by Francia, which I should like to look at again. The contrast between the Virgin, weeping over her dead Son, and the angels, who evidently see so much farther, is very remarkable. It is altogether a splendid collection, and not half enough appreciated. We dined with Sir Julian and Lady Goldsmid at 105 Piccadilly, a house built by the late Lord Hertford, but which he never saw. There were twenty-six people, and the company was pleasant enough, but our hostess was an Italian, and does not understand comfort. I sat between Harry Brand and Alfred Hardy, and we had some amusing political sparring. Miss Fitzclarence, our *compagnon de voyage* from Dalmally to Oban, was there too, and declared she should have known me anywhere, having a singular gift of remembering names and faces, evidently inherited from her grandfather the King. She has to a certain degree the large grey eyes and rather fat face of all the Royal Family. We went on to Lady Salisbury's, and walked upstairs with Lord Beaconsfield, who was particularly civil. Rainald had never spoken to him since the Pigott incident! We walked downstairs, to my surprise, with Mr. Gladstone, whom I did not expect to see after Lord Salisbury's bitter speech a day or two ago. And only the other evening Mr. Stratford Dugdale told me at Nora Trevelyan's that they had dined with M. Léon Say last autumn, and that he had remarked, ' Votre M. Gladstone — quelle chute inconcevable ! ' Party feeling to-day certainly runs high, but Rainald says not so high as in 1830–32 and the days of the Reform Bill."

This season Lady Knightley attended a course of ambulance lectures and joined in a series of Shakespeare readings at Mrs. Dugdale's, which, added to her hospital and workhouse visiting and the prolonged sittings of the G.F.S. Council, made her exceedingly busy, and it is not to be wondered at that she found little time for reading at home or for her favourite researches in the British Museum.

"*May* 9.—All my days seem long! Yesterday I had visitors all the morning, and spent the whole afternoon at the Academy. Mr. Gladstone by Millais is undoubtedly the picture of the year. It lives, and is a worthy representation of the ablest man of the day and the most incomprehensible of this or any other day. After tea Harriet Cartwright came to rehearse bandaging, rather a tiring process. To-day I did hope for a quiet morning, but it is now nearly 1 a.m., and I have been on the go all day. First Mrs. Magee came to talk G.F S., then I went to Ishbel Aberdeen, whom it is delightful to find so full of enthusiasm for all good works. It is nice to see those two young things in the heyday of youth and prosperity giving themselves entirely to the service of God and man. Then I rushed off to the Guild Committee, where I was in the chair. It is cheering to hear what good work is being done! I brought Miss Hubbard back with me to talk over her ' Perseverance Bands ' scheme, had a quarter of an hour's read of the *Times*, then a pleasant dinner at Nora Trevelyan's. I sat between Mr. W. H. Gladstone, who told me his father's portrait had been bought by the Duke of Westminster, and Baron Brinckmann of the Prussian Embassy. He says Bismarck did not see Busch's book before it was published, and is much annoyed by its indiscretions. Nora, Polly Ridley, and I went on to an amusing party at Mrs. John Dundas's charming new Queen Anne house on the Chelsea Embankment, built and furnished in the same quaint, picturesque style, with people dressed very much to match. Such is London life! very delightful, but it takes a good deal out of one.

"*May* 17.—I went to a concert at Lady Norton's, a cantata, *Christ and His Soldiers*, by Farmer, very well given by amateurs; sat next to Canon Farrar, to whom I was introduced. He remarked, apropos of the Duke of Argyll's envenomed attack on the Government last night, that the 'little red-headed brute is the greatest orator in the House of Lords.' In the evening to hear *Don Giovanni* at Covent Garden, with Patti, who, although thirty-five,—more's the pity!— is still the most charming of Zerlinas.

"*May* 21.—I walked with Rainald to see the Coaches' meet, a pretty sight. Had mother to luncheon, and took her to our Guild concert, at which I sang. We dined with the Manners, and I sat between Sir Michael Shaw Stewart and Lord Bury, who told me he was in Brest harbour in September 1870 when the German fleet came down the Channel and found the whole French fleet drawn up in line of battle ready to receive them. 'L'Amirault' told Lord Bury that he had not powder enough on board his ships to fire a royal salute, and not more than ten sailors on board several of them, every available man having been summoned to defend Paris. However, his brag answered, and the German fleet sailed away again without firing a shot. After dinner I talked hunting with the Duke of Buccleuch, who says he has been a master of hounds since 1827. Went on to Lady Salisbury's, where was the Empress of Germany—' my dear Augusta, we've had another awful buster,'—a wonderfully young-looking woman for her age, which is nearly seventy. The Edinburghs were there too, with the Crown Prince of Sweden, the Comte and Comtesse de Flandres—in short, the place was alive with Royalties and decorations. I ended up with a charming concert at Mr. Oppenheim's, cutting two other parties. In spite of 'hard times,' London *s'amuse*.

"*May* 24.—The Queen's sixtieth birthday, and she became a great-grandmother about ten days ago, Princess Charlotte of Saxe-Meiningen having given birth to her first child. I went to South Kensington Museum with Rainald, and spent some time in that bewildering, enchanting place. I was especially interested in the autographs bequeathed by Mr. Forster—'John Hampden to Sir John Eliot at his lodging in the Tower,' etc.—and in some of the Early Italian sculpture —Donatello; Niccolò Pisano, etc. We were much impressed by the preposterous prices given for some of the shrines, chalices, and other examples of gold and silver work, £2000 being no uncommon figure. In the evening to the Foreign Office party, which was gayer and more crowded than ever, with endless Royalties.

"*May* 29.—Yesterday, being Derby day, I went down to Richmond with Charley Newdegate, and desired him not to vote against the Government. I spent a happy day with dear mother, walked back to the station, and dined with the Carysforts. I sat between my old friend Bobby Gurdon and Sir Frederick Peel, that apparently most cautious of men, but really a bitter Radical. To-day I rejoiced in a quiet morning, the first for a fortnight. After luncheon to Mrs. Dugdale's, where, under Clifford Harrison's supervision, we read scenes from the *Merchant of Venice*, the 'Ode to the Passions,' and Browning's 'How they brought the good news from Ghent,' and very interesting it was. We dined with Lord Leven, where I sat next to Lord Selborne, and went on to a small party at Lady Stanhope's, where I met Princess Christian and Mr. Browning, who told me that the 'Ride from Ghent' was a pure invention, founded on no known incident, and merely composed when he was bored at sea.

"*Fawsley, Whitsun Eve, May* 31.—We came home yesterday with oh! such delight. I have been out and about all day, playing croquet with Val, and revelling in the beauty of the place. The weather was quite perfect, but quite a fortnight backward; primroses and marsh-marigolds are still to be found. The ash hardly shows leaf, the oak by no means fully out, and some of the elms still quite brown. It was delightful in Badby Wood, gathering primroses and bluebells, which spread a perfect carpet of blue under the vivid green of the spring foliage. It is quite impossible to describe the intense beauty of the colouring in this brilliant sunshine. But my poor Rainald is worried to death about money matters. Tuesday was the rent-audit, an anxious day in these times of agricultural depression. Most of the tenants paid, but there was much grumbling, which is scarcely justified, seeing how little arable land they have, and how low the land is let! I wish I could do more to help!

"4 *Grosvenor Crescent, June* 18.—We had our nursing examination on Monday, at the end of our course of ambulance lectures, at Lady Juliana Walker's. It was partly paper, partly viva voce, and two or three bandages to be done. I *hope* we are through! To-day Lord Shaftesbury presided at the meeting of our Employment of Women Association, and Miss Frances Power Cobbe spoke. It was a meeting of real earnest workers, and in that quiet room, with the sun streaming in on Lord Shaftesbury's honoured head, one felt what good work had been done since Jessie Boucherett first started her unpretending little Society twenty years ago. Sir Thomas and Sophy dined, and I went to a party at the Duchess of Northumberland's, the first since old Northumberland House is no more.

"*June* 20.—The very sad news of the poor little Prince Imperial's death in the papers. He was surprised and surrounded by Zulus. I much fear our people were greatly to blame. Everyone is filled with sorrow for the young life thus suddenly cut off, and the poor mother above all. Little I thought, when we met him at Wakefield the other day, that the end was to be so soon. I drove Uncle Frederick out in the afternoon, and listened with amusement to his reminiscences of Old London—a brick wall along the Green Park, small cottages on the south side of St. James's Square. All London is mad about the Comédie Française. We went last night to see *Le Demi-monde*. Certainly the acting is wonderful; there is a finish, a refinement, an ' at-homeness ' (to coin a word), which are quite unequalled by anything on our stage.

"*June* 26.—A strange mixture of a day, but I could not help it. Harriet Cartwright and I, with three of the maids, went to St. Paul's for the annual G.F.S. service. A crowded congregation assembled to hear a sermon from the Bishop of Winchester and attend the celebration, and I could not help thinking of the blessed change since the day when Paul's was a fashionable walk! When I came home I found stalls for the French play—*not* the day one would have chosen, but it could not be helped. First I had a pleasant drive round Hyde Park and Battersea Park with Lord Tollemache. I do enjoy bowling along behind those beautiful chestnuts, in spite of the cold and rain! This is actually the eighth month of temperature below the average. Then we had a real evening's enjoyment at the Comédie Française—first Racine's *Andromaque*, with Sarah Bernhardt in the chief part. She is wonderfully graceful, but hardly as fine an actress as I expected. After that *Les Plaideurs*, in which Got is exceedingly funny.

"*July* 3.—In the evening again to the French play—a pretty piece by George Sand, in which Mlle Barette, whom we saw last night at Mrs. Brassey's, did the *ingénue* wonderfully well. Then we roared over *Les Fourberies de Scapin*, in which Coquelin is quite inimitable. Had a little talk with Lord Granville, who agrees with us in not thinking Sarah Bernhardt so very wonderful, and told us Coquelin thinks Irving as tiresome as we do, but says we have one good actor in Charles Warner, now acting in *Drink*, a play that I have no wish to see.

"*July* 4.—A real drive! First with Nora to the Ladies' Dress Association Committee, which we have both joined, then mother to luncheon, and a long visit from an old Sotterley friend, Ellen Cundall. Afterwards to a party at Lady Listowel's, where the Duke of Connaught presented me, very prettily, to the Duchess as 'one of our oldest friends.' She has a nice little face and pleasant manners. The Prince-elect of Bulgaria, Alexander of Battenberg, is a singularly goodlooking man. Rainald went to the House to support Mr. Chaplin's motion for an inquiry into the causes of agricultural distress, which is indeed assuming alarming proportions. The incessant torrents of rain and extraordinarily low temperature have been most disastrous to the country. Little hope remains of a good harvest, so sorely needed by the farmers after four bad seasons, and what the effect will be upon rents and elections it is impossible to foresee. It makes Rainald and me very uneasy."

These anxious forebodings, as Lady Knightley remarks in the margin, were only too soon realised. After three weeks at Homburg, and a brief visit to Amsterdam, Haarlem, and the Hague, to explore the treasures of Dutch art in these fine old towns, Sir Rainald and Lady Knightley returned home to find a serious state of affairs. Five or six of the principal tenants gave up their farms, and all with one accord demanded large reductions of rent. The Fawsley estates, although considerable in extent, were already heavily mortgaged, and the rent-roll of some thirteen thousand a year represented a purely nominal income. It now became necessary to raise fresh sums to buy stock and employ bailiffs and labourers in order to farm the land given up by the different tenants. Lady Knightley set herself bravely to the task of practising needful economies, and the house in town, with the purchase of which she always reproached herself as a personal self-indulgence, was immediately put in an agent's hands and eventually sold. The prospect of farming their own land interested her greatly, and she took up agriculture with the same zest which she showed in every other department of country life.

"*Fawsley, January* 23, 1880.—I was occupied the whole morning in going over the Westcombe farm with Rainald and Waters (the agent), as we are going to take to it seriously and have engaged a bailiff at thirty shillings a week for himself and his wife. I shall delight in it, but I fear the heavy outlay required to put it in order will disgust Rainald. Its extent is 362 acres, of which 170 are arable. We are to leave 40 acres fallow this year, in order to clean it, buy 25 beasts, a few cows and 10 heifers, and a dozen cart-horses. Altogether, it is most interesting. But the sheep are dying by wholesale of ' rot ' or fluke, the result of the wet season.

"*March* 6.—I spent all the morning in walking over the farm with Waters, and settling various matters about turkeys, fowls, etc., and improving the dairy ! Fourteen horses are at work ploughing on the farm, including poor old Black Knight and the carriage horses that were bought when I married. The hedges have been trimmed, ditches cleaned, weeds burned, drains set in order, and on Monday we hope to begin putting in the beans. Happily, the weather is beautiful, and it is wonderful what it has done for the farm."

In the midst of these new interests and anxieties came the startling news of a Dissolution, bringing with it the fear of a contested election.

"*March* 9.—Rainald hunted from Thenford. I went farming, and watched the beans being put in with a drill and harrowing afterwards. When I came back I was startled by the news that Parliament was to be dissolved by the 24th. I do not think the Government could have chosen a better time, and hope and believe they will have a large majority, though I doubt if Dizzy's bombastic letter in to-day's *Times* will contribute much thereto. For ourselves, the next three weeks will be an anxious time, but I have every hope of escaping a contest, which would be ruin in the present state of affairs.

"*March* 12.—I helped copy Rainald's simple, straightforward, manly address. He has burnt his boats now, but one can't run away with no enemy in view, and the only really formidable opponent, Bob Spencer, is not going to stand here, as he has come forward for the North division. It is impossible not to feel very anxious about this election; humanly speaking, it seems as if the peace of Europe and the integrity of the Empire depended on the Conservatives gaining a decided victory.

"*March* 18.—We were greatly discomposed by the news that Sir Herewald Wake has convened a meeting at Northampton with a view to getting up a contest. It worried me all day. Nevertheless, *fais ce que dois, advienne que pourra*; and feeling as we do that the welfare of England depends on this election, we are doing right in trying our best to keep this seat for the Government, and come what may, we *will* do our best."

The threatened opposition fortunately collapsed, and on March 31 Sir Rainald and his old colleague, Major Cartwright, were duly returned members for South Northamptonshire. But this happy event was shortly followed by the loss of a large number of Conservative seats in all parts of the country.

"*April* 1.—I shall not soon forget my horror at this morning's papers. Fourteen seats lost by the balance of yesterday's elections, and it is quite clear that the current of public opinion is flowing as violently against the Conservative Government as it did against the Liberal one in 1874. It is a heavy blow, and a great encouragement to England's enemies.

"*Firle, April* 5.—Fifteen more seats lost yesterday! Mr. Gladstone returned for Midlothian by 211, over Lord Dalkeith. It is all of a piece; all comes of Dizzy's Reform Bill, putting the power in the hands of an uneducated, unreasoning mob. Bob Spencer is at the head of the poll in North Northants (well! anyhow, he can't stand for the South now!), and Edward Ridley is beaten in Northumberland. St. John has a majority of 114 in East Suffolk, but most of the county elections are going as badly as the boroughs, and Lord Yarmouth and Mr. Clare Read are both turned out—two of the safest seats in England, one would have thought.

"*April* 24.—Mr. Gladstone has been sent for, after Lord Hartington and Lord Granville had been down, and has undertaken to form a ministry. His task, however, proceeds slowly. . . . The Radical element, hitherto conspicuous by its absence, is now represented by Mr. Chamberlain (Board of Trade), Mr. Fawcett (Postmaster-General—a marvellous triumph of mind over body), Sir Charles Dilke (Under-Secretary for Foreign Affairs), and Mr. Mundella (President of the Council). Rainald is very unhappy about it all, and frightened to death, he says. But one looks back at 1832, and sees that the country has not yet 'gone to the dogs'; and one looks forward, and trusts for the future. But how any good Christian can get over Mr. Bradlaugh's return I cannot understand. Mr. Lowe said rather a good thing on being told of Monty Corry's peerage: 'Ah, well! people in all ages have had their favourites. Caligula made his horse a consul.'

"4 *Grosvenor Crescent, June* 29.—Nora Trevelyan and I went to look at a Rose show, and on to Brompton Cemetery, where she wished to visit her mother's grave. It seemed so quiet there under the trees and deep blue summer sky, carrying one away to another and a better world than this frantic London. Princess Christian came to tea, and asked me to take her a drive in the open carriage. We went to Marshall & Snelgrove's together, and she was very nice, as usual. Came home to a remarkably pleasant dinner—the Duke and Duchess of Somerset, Duke of Grafton, Clancartys, Hamiltons, Henleys, Trevelyans, Katherine Clive, Lady Lyveden, Bouveries, and Lord Strathnairn. All the old Whigs are terrified at the revolutionary measures proposed by the Government, and for the first time in my life I am really frightened at the mixture of tyranny and mob-worship; while as to the Bradlaugh business, it seems a national defiance of God to support a man who makes his living by blasphemy. Rainald is miserable about it, and Mr. Gladstone now proposes to move a resolution allowing everybody to affirm, which he thinks a horrible national sin. My last rags of belief in Mr. Gladstone's religion are rapidly disappearing !

"*July* 26.—I had a small tea, at which Mr. Browning very kindly read some of his poems to about thirty-five of my friends. I do not think that he reads well, but everyone seemed to like it. . . . This wicked Irish Bill occupies everybody. It is not only the man in the street, but the woman at home, who talks about it. It seems regular confiscation, as Lord George Hamilton showed in his speech, which demolished Mr. Gladstone's figures in the most wonderful way. To-day, after a busy morning at the British Museum, I went for a short time to the House, where Mr. Edward Clarke, the member for Plymouth, made an excellent speech. Harry Gage has a most significant whip for the Second Reading in the House of Lords, signed Somerset, Abercorn, Sligo, Dartrey, Aveland, Leconfield, Carysfort, Fitzwilliam, etc. The Lords are sure to throw it out, but the mischief is done by a responsible Government bringing in such a measure. So ends our season—not a remarkable one as far as we are concerned, but as usual a very busy and interesting time.

"*The Palace, Peterborough, July* 27.—I came down here by a fast train from town and presided at a well-attended and highly amicable Diocesan Meeting of the G.F.S. We passed Diocesan by-laws, signed Central Rules, and transacted much business. Mrs. Magee entertained us all at luncheon, and afterwards it was refreshing to sit in the gardens and go to the Cathedral service, and I was much pleased with a recreation room for G.F.S. members in business, which Mrs. Magee has lately opened. The Bishop was most agreeable as usual, and showed me his curious collection of autographs, including a letter from Mr. Bright, in which he tries to explain his sneer about ' consecrated ground,' but ends up with saying : ' I don't believe in holy ground any more than you do in holy water, and for the same reason—because there is nothing in it!'

"*Fawsley, July* 31.—We came home after, I think, the longest unbroken absence we have ever had. It is *triste* to hear Rainald say he does not care about coming home! The country looks green and luxuriant, and the crops are less laid than one might have expected, but there is a quantity of hay out still—a good deal of it has been damaged.

"*August* 2.—A worritsome day! In the first place, it opened with three hours' heavy rain, which entirely stopped all idea of hay-making. Then we had a long, tiresome interview with Waters, and, worst of all, inspected his accounts, which reveal the melancholy fact that all the various remissions of rent and losses amount to £2200 for the half-year, which is a very serious and heavy loss. No wonder my poor darling is low and out of heart! But we can but remember how many people are worse off and how much we have to be thankful for. I was busy reading the Report on Education and looking into *Hudibras*, about which I knew nothing, but which has suddenly become interesting since I read in Lady Aylesford's book that a Knightley is supposed to be portrayed in one of the characters. It is so pleasant to have a little time to read.

"*August* 13.—Glorious weather at last! I walked round Shepherd's farm, where the hay is being carried fast. The Irish Land Bill was thrown out in the House of Lords by a majority of 130, and even if all the Conservatives had stayed away, the Government would have been beaten, as 63 Liberal peers voted against them. Rainald went to town yesterday to vote against the Burials Bill. I wonder how often he has done that? But the parsons here are mad about it. I spent most of the afternoon with Val on the cricket ground, looking at a match between Fawsley and Towcester, which we won by 61 to 57. Dear Rainald returned. It is eleven years since the happy day when he asked me to be his wife, and he says he thought nice things of me in the train. God bless him! There have been shadows over us, but never *one* between us.

"*August* 24.—We spent the whole day—a most lovely one—in going to Julia Cartwright's wedding at Edgcote. A very pretty one it was, in the nice old church that stands between her old and her new home. The whole population of the villages on the edge of the park turned out to see her married, and women and children of all ages stood and sat on the grassy sward to watch the wedding procession. Solemn and reverent it was, too, so unlike the last marriage I attended at St. George's, Hanover Square, where everyone talked and laughed during the service, and the careless, giddy behaviour of the bride and bridegroom filled one with gloomy presentiments. To-day the bride's uncle, Dean Goulburn, read the service most impressively, and Mr. Scott Holland gave an address on the most approved Oxford lines, full of sweetness and light. But it was all very simple and touching. Dear Sophy Fremantle[1] was there, to my great pleasure, and Lord Cottesloe, sprightly as ever in spite of his eighty years, prepared to dance at his granddaughter's wedding, and Lord Midleton, who proposed the bride and bridegroom's health at the breakfast. I had pleasant talks with many people, as the long hours cast their shadows on the lawn, gay with tennis-players. I always think there is much of England's strength and solid goodness in the smaller country gentry, many of whom live round Edgcote, and were there to-day. Certainly the Edgcote Cartwrights themselves are fine specimens, both as regards intellect and goodness. It was a beautiful harvest day, and cutting was going on everywhere, although we saw the last loads of hay also being carried in the meadows near the Cherwell. There is good news from India, mercifully. 'Fighting Bobs' has accomplished his wonderful march from Cabul, and the mere news of his approach has caused Ayoob Khan to raise the siege of Candahar. A fortnight ago everyone was

[1] Sophia, daughter of Mr. Abel Smith of Woodhall, married Hon. Sir Charles Fremantle, 1865.

calling him mad for making such a desperate attempt, and now he has succeeded beyond all expectation.

"*Lindertis, Kirriemuir, October* 12.—To-day we have had very bad news from home. Five more tenants have given notice, and Rainald is in despair. We had a long talk over our affairs. It is much better to face the worst and arrange to live within our means, even if we have to leave home for a while. But it is no disgrace, and it is not irreparable, as long as we have each other. Sufficient for the day is the evil thereof.

"*November* 20.—The Queen has become patron of the G.F.S., to my great joy. We tried to hunt from Hellidon, but the ground is too hard, and we soon had to come home. There is every appearance of a long frost setting in. An admirable speech of Lord Salisbury's about Ireland. It is inconceivable to me how people in this country can sit still as they do and look on at the reign of terror which prevails in that hapless country, while nothing is done.

"*December* 31.—So ends another year. It has been in some respects a chequered one, yet how much one has to be thankful for. The prospects of this country, indeed, fill one with dismay. The state of things in Ireland would have been deemed, less than a year ago, utterly impossible and incredible."

CHAPTER XXVI

Lord Beaconsfield's Death—The Duke of Albany's Marriage

1881–1883

FORTUNATELY, the worst of the calamities which Sir Rainald and Lady Knightley anticipated at the close of 1880 were averted, in spite of the severe agricultural depression which affected them in common with other landowners during many years to come. They were able to live on at Fawsley and to spend the season in London, and did not find it necessary to alter their way of living in any important respect.

In politics the Irish question began to assume grave proportions, and Lady Knightley's Journal reflects the indignation and disgust of the Conservative party at the failure of the Government to take more active measures to restore order in Ireland, or to deal with the obstructionists in Parliament.

"*January* 19, 1881.—A memorable day, seeing that we are pretty well snowed up. No post came in or went out. Val started to drive to Daventry, but could not get past the Badby gate and finally walked in, and returned this afternoon to report a total block between Weedon and Daventry. No trains have passed since midnight. An ineffectual attempt was made to convey bread to the soldiers at Weedon, and several sheep had to be dug out in the park. Our only communication with the outer world was a telegram from Mr. Laurie, advising Harry to put off his shooting party at Firle to-morrow, saying, ' All the railways are blocked. It

FAWSLEY CHURCH.

has snowed all day, and now the moon is shining and the thermometer is down again at 20°.'

"*January* 20.—The letters arrived at 11 a.m., and the newspapers, which came by second post, are full of this fearful snowstorm, which seems to have raged over the whole kingdom. The sun shone and the winter landscape was lovely—bright sun and perfect calm. We walked to the Level and saw our ninety-nine sheep being fed. What between the scarcity of sheep, owing to the rot of last year, and the difficulty of moving them, mutton is at a premium. . . . Sir Thomas Munro returned yesterday, to our great joy, for, as Rainald remarked, we are reduced very much to the position of bears sucking their own paws—not for bodily but for mental food. Luckily, most of us have plenty of fat to fall back on in the way of reading. I live chiefly with Oliver Cromwell in the Commons Journals, where the active Mr. Knightley's name appears on almost every page, till Pride's Purge excluded him from the House. In the present House of Commons the Irish Home Rulers are obstructing the introduction of the Coercion Bill, and the House sat from 4 p.m. on Tuesday to 2 p.m. on Thursday!

"*Fawsley, February* 2.—The sitting of the House of Commons, which began at 4 p.m. on Monday, was terminated at 9 a.m. this morning, after forty-one hours, by the Speaker putting the question for the introduction of Mr. Forster's Coercion Bill, for which Parliament met on January 6, whereupon the Irish members left the House in a body. It is laughable and yet serious enough. Rainald had to go to London to attend a meeting of the party at the Carlton to choose a successor for poor Fairfax Cartwright—the best of colleagues—whose death has been a sorrow to us all.

"*February* 4.—More wonderful events than ever in the House. Thirty-six members, all Irish, suspended or broomed out by the Serjeant-at-Arms! After which, the orders placing new powers in the Speaker's hands were agreed to. Such a scene Rainald says he never saw, and I suppose never has been seen since Cromwell turned out the Long Parliament. He came home this evening with the satisfactory news that the country gentlemen have agreed to support Mr. Pickering Phipps, who has been unanimously chosen as Conservative candidate.

"4 *Grosvenor Crescent, February* 21.—I came up for a lark, combined with G.F.S. Council, spent the whole day on the committee, dined with the old Duchess, and went to a charming party at Nora's.

"*February* 22.—Again spent most of the day at the G.F.S. Council, dined with Lord Leven, and went to parties at Polly Ridley's and Mrs. Brand's. I sat between Lord Reay and Sir Stafford Northcote, who was particularly pleasant. He lamented, as Lord Strathnairn does, the failure to establish concurrent endowment in Ireland, when the Irish Church was disestablished, and declares that Parnell was really hiding in London when supposed to be in Paris, and only crossed the Channel when Biggar and Dillon went to fetch him back, upon which some strong language ensued. He does not like the new rules himself, and declares that Lord Beaconsfield gravely says, when asked a difficult question, that he shall look in Tancred. There was a great deal of snow in London, and it was bitterly cold, but I enjoyed the change after our quiet life here.

"*Firle, April* 7.—We came here yesterday from home. So ends another winter, the dullest we have ever spent. Rainald feels deeply the bad spirit shown among the tenants, who have been on the estate so many years. The east wind still rages, and Dizzy is very ill. But I delight in the change to this country, so different from Northamptonshire, and the forms of the Downs are a delight.

"*April* 19.—At midday we heard of Lord Beaconsfield's death early this morning. Certainly he was a great man in many ways, and few such careers are on record. . . . We met Lady Roberts, Bobs' mother, a cheery little old lady, who said her son was all the better for his double voyage to the Cape, but deeply disgusted, as well he may be, with this horrid peace and the cession of the Transvaal. And we hear, on very good authority, that Lord Beaconsfield's last words were, ' Are there any more disasters in the *Gazette* ? '

" 4 *Grosvenor Crescent, Sunday, May* 1.—I went to Westminster Abbey, which was crowded with a dense congregation, listening with rapt interest to an intellectual treat—a dissertation by Dean Stanley on Lord Beaconsfield. He selected a curious text : Judg. xvi. 30 : ' So the dead which he slew at his death were more than they which he slew in his life.' All the way through he coupled him with Gladstone, calling them the Great Twin Brethren. And I sat on the altar steps, at the foot of one of the columns, with the statues of the mightier rivals, Pitt and Fox, facing me, and listening to a magnificent anthem on King David, composed by Handel and finished by Goss, which had never been performed since the death of Wellington.

" Sir William Fraser told Rainald to-day that, when he entered Parliament in 1852, he asked Dizzy what he should take up. He recommended India as a coming subject, and added, ' Don't meddle with reform —we shall see great social changes within the next few years '; evidently showing that so far back as that he meditated to some extent the course which he afterwards took.

" *May* 4.—We went to a most amusing party at Lady Airlie's, full of Radicals. Mr. Gladstone was there, but we did not speak to him, as Rainald said that after calling him, as he had done that afternoon at Kettering, in words once applied to Bolingbroke, ' that magnificent but malignant genius,' he could not go up and shake hands ! Lord Dufferin was also there, *en route* from St. Petersburg to Constantinople ; Sir William Harcourt, full of his usual sledge-hammer chaff ; Sir Henry James and Mr. Bright, who talked to Rainald some time, saying the Land Bill was the only thing to prevent a general strike against rent, and his scheme of peasant-proprietorship the only thing to save the landlords. He has a very fine head and not at all a bad expression, which is more than can be said for ' Historicus.' He was very flattering to Rainald, telling him that if he made one of his racy little speeches on the Bill, it would have a great effect and be the best thing he could do for his order. The Duke of Somerset told us a charming story of Carlyle, who came to give evidence before a Committee to inquire into the management of the British Museum, of which he was chairman. ' I believe, Mr. Carlyle,' he began, ' that you make considerable use of this reading-room. Could you give us any suggestions for improving the arrangements ? ' ' My Lord,' replied Carlyle, ' the function of man is to go into Chaos and make it Kosmos.' ' I think, Mr. Carlyle,' said the Duke, ' we will leave Chaos and Kosmos for the present, and perhaps you will be so good as to tell us whether, when you ask for a book, you get it.'

" The political events of the week have been, first, the attempted assassination of President Garfield; secondly, the Duke of Argyll's most able speech, exposing in masterly fashion the injustice of the Land Bill, which has made a deep impression on all parties. Sir R. Cross told me he never saw a man so angry as Gladstone was that evening.

" *June* 1.—A long day. Went to Buckingham Palace to see Princess Christian, and with her and Lady Marian Alford to a Domestic Economy Congress meeting; brought her back to luncheon with Emmy Hamilton, Louisa Gordon, and Mr. Leveson, after which I drove with Nora and took her to a Derby tea at Mrs. Lloyd's. Iroquois, an American horse, won. We dined with Lady Lyveden, and went on to a pleasant party at Lady Salisbury's, where I was introduced to Sir Richard Temple, the author of *India in* 1880, and about the ugliest man whom I ever saw. But he is clever and agreeable, and I am pleased at the testimony he bears to the success of missions in India, which people are so ready to decry.

" *July* 16.—We had a most delightful drive to Wimbledon on Lord Tollemache's coach, taking with us Princess Mary's two nice boys. We came in for the

Lords and Commons match, and had tea with ' my beautiful lady,' Lady Brownlow, whose manners are as pretty as herself, which is saying a great deal. We met the Crown Prince of Germany to-night at Ishbel Aberdeen's, and Princess Frederica at Londonderry House. I was presented to her, and induced her to come to our bazaar for the Ladies' Guild. She is curiously like the old Royal Family, and very gracious and pleasing. Last night we went to a party given by the Spencers at South Kensington Museum, where were all the world and his wife, including the King of the Sandwich Islands, who walked about arm in arm with the Princess of Wales. The courts were lighted with electric light, which has a peculiar and not very becoming effect."

The summer was spent at Fawsley, where, in spite of another wet season, Lady Knightley found farming a most engrossing occupation. Visits to the Duke of Grafton at Euston, to Lord Penrhyn in North Wales, and to the Deanery at Worcester were paid in the course of the autumn, and the year ended with the usual Christmas family party and amateur theatricals.

The Duke of Albany's marriage was one of the chief events of the following winter. Lady Knightley was staying at the Bishop's Palace at Peterborough, to address a large gathering of G.F.S. Associates, when the news of the Prince's happy engagement reached her.

" *The Palace, Peterborough, November* 23. — I was greatly pleased with letters from the Duchess of Roxburghe and Mr. Collins, written by desire of the Queen and Prince Leopold, to announce the latter's betrothal to the Princess Hélène of Waldeck. May God bless his marriage, and give the dear boy every happiness. It was kind of the Queen to remember me.

" 4 *Grosvenor Crescent, February* 28, 1882.—I was much pleased with a pretty letter from the Duke of Albany, talking of old days and proposing that I should be one of the Duchess's honorary ladies-in-waiting. It is a pretty, gracious compliment to an old friend, and will please mother. I sat all day on the G.F.S. Council, held in our new office in Victoria Street. Mrs. Townsend announced her resignation, which fills us all with despair.

"*March* 2.—We were much shocked and horrified by the news of the attempt to shoot the Queen, which, thank God, did not succeed—to lose her would indeed be a calamity—and deeply disgusted to hear Bradlaugh had been returned again by a majority of 108. As Rainald says, it is enough to bring down a judgment on the country.

"*Fawsley, March* 7.—Sir Stafford has again carried his resolution to prevent Bradlaugh from taking his seat. The county magistrates are all desperately excited by Lord Spencer's proposal to add farmers and shopkeepers to the list of magistrates, a purely electioneering move on his part to secure Bobby's seat. They have protested violently, but he will do it all the same. I took a long farming walk. We are thrashing oats at Bull's Hill, which turn out much better than we expected—five quarters to the acre. Thirty-seven chickens out of fifty eggs have been hatched by the new incubator—better luck next time! The weather is heavenly. I never saw so early a spring. The hedges are bursting into leaf in every direction, elder and honeysuckle leaves have been out ages, the hazel catkins are nearly over, while the palm will certainly not last till Palm Sunday. Elms, ribes, mezerea are in full bloom, daffodils, hepaticas, celandines, primroses, marsh-marigolds, hellebore, and dog-mercury are all flowering, and to-day I actually saw a yellow butterfly. One cannot be too thankful for such a mild winter, and after the last three one really enjoys it.

"*4 Grosvenor Crescent, April* 19.—To-day was the first anniversary of Lord Beaconsfield's death. Quantities of people are walking about with primrose buttonholes to commemorate the day. I utterly decline. The Queen called it 'his favourite flower,' but I cannot stand this identification of the most simple and beautiful of flowers with one so artificial and stilted.

"*April* 26.—An amusing day. Off early to Windsor to be presented to my new mistress, accompanied by

Mrs. Bourke, who went down for the same purpose. I was really taken with the little I saw of Princess Helen. She is tall, with a good figure, and natural, engaging manners, not in the least stiff, very nice to her mother, and apparently very much in love. Prince' Leo, poor boy, is very lame. We saw all the presents, and were amused by Mr. Gladstone's gift of his own book, *Gleanings from Past Years*, not at all particularly well bound! Our first bit of waiting was to attend an audience, at which the Mayor and Corporation presented their bracelet; they looked such quaint relics of olden times with their robes and wigs, etc. Then we sat down to a Household luncheon in the Waterloo Chamber, and found several old friends, Count Seckendorf, Mr. Saḥl, etc. The King and Queen of the Netherlands arrived soon afterwards, and I returned to London. I must record that for the first, and I hope the last, time I saw an English lady smoking—Lady S—— M——, and of all places at Windsor! I was struck by Lady Charlotte Schreiber stopping me when I said, ' I wish,' and saying, ' No, my dear, don't *wish* for anything. God knows best.' How true it is!

" *April 27.*—It would be useless to try and describe the striking and stately ceremonial of to-day's Royal marriage, especially as the newspapers will do it much better than I can, but I own to having greatly enjoyed being present. It is so rare in these prosaic days to see anything of real grandeur, and to-day, with the trumpets and heralds and processions, the gorgeous dresses and trains of the Royal Princesses, and all the beauty and chivalry of England assembled in that grand old chapel, the whole thing seemed like a page of past history. The Queen was very gracious and winning, and with the grey hairs under her diamond crown appealed more strongly than ever to my feelings of loyalty. The bridegroom was very nervous, but walked better than I expected, and the bride looked very nice, and made her responses in the clearest of voices. The venerable Archbishop[1] gave a simple and impressive

[1] Dr. A. C. Tait, who died in the following December.

address, while the democratic age we live in was, to my mind, personified in Mr. Joseph Chamberlain, the acknowledged Republican, who would probably like, if he could, to sweep it all away. We went down and returned by special train, after luncheon in the Waterloo Chamber.

"*April* 29.—Mrs. Townsend came to luncheon and urged Rainald very strongly and persuasively to consent to my election as President of the G.F.S. in her place, this being the unanimous wish of the Council, as well as her own. But he says ' No,' quite decidedly, so my path is clear. I afterwards went to the British Museum, and hunted out all I could find about Edmund Knightley, who seems to have been a busy lawyer, and once got himself put into the Fleet Prison. Much excitement in the political world at the news that Lord Spencer succeeds Lord Cowper in Ireland, which is looked upon as a new departure in Irish policy. I was sorry to hear of the young Princess of Würtemberg's death. She was sister to the Duchess of Albany, and it is a sad blow for her in these early days of her wedded life. I had been wondering how they would spend their first Sunday, little thinking it would be in tears !

"*Sunday, May* 7.—I don't think I was ever more shocked in my life than, on coming down this morning, to learn from the *Observer* of the assassination of Lord Frederick Cavendish, who was only appointed on Thursday to succeed Mr. Forster, and his Under-Secretary, Mr. Burke, which took place yesterday evening in the Phœnix Park, Dublin. London is literally aghast. As to poor Lucy, my heart aches for her, and my thoughts go back to our time together at Osborne in 1864. May God comfort her, for no one else can. I went out on business in the morning, but could not get this dreadful news out of my head. I wonder how Mr. Gladstone feels now, at this result of his policy ?

"*May* 8.—I spent a long morning at the British Museum, and a long afternoon at home, receiving an endless stream of visitors, and ended by going to a party at Lady Jersey's. And still this awestruck feeling prevails, and there is a rising tide of indignation against the Government which in the event of a dissolution would make it go hard with them. But how are the Conservatives, if they did come in, to quench the flames which have been so recklessly fanned? If I live to be a hundred, I shall never forget these days in London.

"*May* 11.—The day was taken up with the Drawing-room, at which Lady Southampton presented me on my appointment. It seemed so funny to be presented for the *third* time, but I had the entrée, which is an immense advantage, and was pleased at the very cordial reception which the Queen gave me. We dined with the Clerks, where I sat between Lord Hertford and Sir George Warrender, both of whom were most agreeable; and went on to Mrs. Davenport's, and talked to Mr. W. H. Smith and Sir Richard Cross, who are both very unhappy at the alarming state of affairs in Egypt.

"*May* 21.—Last night we dined with the Bishop of Winchester, and I sat between Mr. Heywood Sumner, a grandson of the old Bishop's, an artist and etcher, and altogether a very pleasant and uncommon person, and Lord Selborne, who talked a great deal about the new romance, *John Inglesant*, which has been making such a sensation. He thinks it a very remarkable book, but Liddon condemns it as savouring of agnosticism, others say of Jesuitry. Lady Strangford was also there, and Prince Ghika, the Roumanian Minister, with his wife. I talked to him about the land question. He is all for the métayer system, as opposed to peasant proprietorship, and introduced it on his own estates, where it was very popular until political intrigues forced another system on the peasants. We were both very sad at hearing a bad account of the Duke of Grafton.

"*Sunday, May* 21.—Alas! even as I wrote these words, that true Christian and English gentleman entered into his rest. I cannot sum up his character better than in his sister Lady Penrhyn's words to me last autumn : ' Euston never thinks whether he likes a thing or not ; if it is right it has to be done, if it is wrong it has got to be let alone.' No man will be more deeply and universally lamented, especially in Northamptonshire, and Rainald's devotion to him has always been quite touching. I went to St. Paul's, Knightsbridge, this afternoon, and afterwards to Mrs. Munro's, where I met the Duke of Bedford, who told me that he and the Dukes of Sutherland and Argyll have all received threatening letters warning them that their houses will be blown up within the next three months, and one of his own agents in Bedfordshire has been warned that he will be shot. Such are the results of leaving crime unpunished ! Yet half the world believes in Mr. Gladstone's policy, and Lucy Cavendish telegraphs her congratulations to the Radical who has won the contest for her husband's seat. I cannot understand it ! They can't be all either knaves or fools, but talking to them on the Irish question has become quite impossible. Never since 1832 have parties been so bitterly divided. Meanwhile, Egyptian affairs drift, and no one knows what will happen there.

"*July* 11.—The day was heralded by the news of the bombardment of the forts at Alexandria by our ships. It is the necessary result of the Government policy, as expressed by Lord Granville's, ' We must dawdle a little,' last February, but when once guns are fired in the East, one never knows where it will end. At night to Lady Margaret Beaumont's, where I talked a good deal to Lord Houghton's daughter, Mrs. Fitzgerald, who has just come from Alexandria, where she was an actual eye-witness of the horrors of June 11.

"*July* 12.—I went to see Ristori in *Lady Macbeth*. She was atrociously supported, and played in English, which she cannot speak well ; but her gestures, walk, and, above all, her countenance with its extraordinary variety of expression are beyond all praise. She is a great actress and still an extremely handsome woman. Afterwards to Lady Waterford's, where Lord Salisbury and Sir Stafford were chuckling over Sir Wilfrid Lawson's speech to-night, in which he said that if *we* (the Conservatives) had bombarded Alexandria, the Prime Minister would have stopped his train at every wayside station to denounce the wickedness of the Tory Government.

" *July* 13.—We went to Christie's for the last part of the Hamilton sale. I am in despair to think that that charming lounge has come to an end! To-day there were tapestries, miniatures, china, an immense variety of beautiful oddments; and the money these things fetch is incredible! I should not like to give it, I must say. In the afternoon to a garden-party at Marlborough House, which I enjoyed as much as I always do. Nowhere else does one meet such a collection of distinguished men of every kind. Everyone was talking of the terrible news from Alexandria, which Arabi has given over to fire and pillage. The last rumour is that the Khedive and Dervish Pasha are both dead. It seemed such an awful contrast to think of these horrible scenes in the midst of that gay and brilliant assembly. And where it will all end, no human being can tell.

" *July* 14.—Mother and I had a most successful expedition to Claremont, and spent two hours very agreeably with these nice young people. *She* is a lively, merry, natural girl of twenty, *he* an extremely pleasant man of the world, and all he said pleased me greatly. There were only us four, no *gêne*, and I really enjoyed it. It is a good house, with pictures of Princess Charlotte all over the place, a wonderful Indian carpet, brought home by Lord Clive, and a lovely garden laid out by Capability Brown. The Duke and Duchess were very full of the Queen of Roumania's poems. Carmen Sylva is her *nom-de-plume*. She was Princess Elizabeth of Wied, and Prince Leo said, used to be so like me. We came back to find better news from Alexandria, the Khedive safe and order being restored. Chauncy Cartwright, who was chargé d'affaires at Cairo in Sir Edward Malet's absence through illness, seems to have done remarkably well. The *Times* says we are to send troops. Mr. Bright has resigned, but most people, except the extreme radicals, approve of what the Government has done. I am sorry, however, to see a tendency springing up to wish to take Egypt. Prince Leopold, Nora, and the St. James's *Gazette* are representatives of the more intelligent part of the community, and they all lean that way.

"*July* 22.—In the afternoon we went to Holland House, where the public made very merry over Mr. Childers' mistake of a million in the vote of credit to be asked for on Monday. If it had only been six million! But the parallel is curiously exact, only Lord Beaconsfield saved Constantinople, and Mr. Gladstone has destroyed Alexandria."

The next few weeks were spent at Homburg, which Lady Knightley describes as being given over to a crowd of third-rate English and Americans, in spite of the presence of H.R.H. the Prince of Wales and occasional visits from the Princess and her children who came over from Wiebaden. The progress of our troops in Egypt was anxiously watched, the Government, Lady Knightley remarks, doing every single thing which they denounced the late Government for doing, using Cyprus, bringing over our Indian troops, and making India pay for it.

"*Homburg, Kisseliff Strasse, September* 3.—The foreigners here all laugh in one's face if one says we shall not keep Egypt. I was amused with Sir George Bowen who, on someone saying, ' Why appoint that Irish fellow, Sir Garnet Wolseley, why not Sir F. Roberts ? ' replied, ' Why, he is an Irishman too, so with the exception of Lord Lorne are everyone of your Colonial Governors. You won't let Irishmen govern themselves at home, but you can't stop their governing English subjects all over the world !' He amused me with a *bon mot* of Gambetta's who, in speaking of the Revolution of 1848 and its origin in a public dinner, said it might be described as a ' revolution à la fourchette.' Mrs. Herbert, who is at the Windsor, tells me a very curious thing, that accidentally this year, through a servant, she became aware that a house in the best part of London, occupied by a rich merchant, was the headquarters of a secret society, as many as twenty men sleeping there at night, and being gone again in the morning. Among them were the murderers of Lord Frederick Cavendish and Mr. Burke, who spent a month in London early in the year. She informed the detectives of her suspicions, but was told the house had been on their list a long time, but they could do nothing. Yesterday (September 2) was the anniversary of Sedan, but beyond a few flags and a potpourri of patriotic music in the evening there were no manifestations. Only the ticket clerk at the station overwhelmed me with a torrent of German, saying there would shortly be another war with France, much worse than the last, adding that he had himself been a prisoner in 1870."

The return journey by Lady Knightley's favourite town of Brussels afforded an opportunity for a visit to the field of Waterloo, which she had always wished to see.

"*Hotel de Flandre, Brussels, September 6.*— We managed an expedition to Waterloo, going by train to Braine-la-Leude, and thence by omnibus to the centre of the field. Discarding all guides, we at once walked off to Hougomont, which is to me the most interesting place of all, since it was in the orchard there that my dear father was wounded. The farmhouse looked so quiet and peaceful, one could hardly believe that round it had waged the great battle on which the fate of Europe hung. The worthy *fermière* showed us the orchard with its loop-holed wall and the chapel where the fire, which burnt down the Château on that eventful day, stopped at the foot of the crucifix on the altar—a curious incidence which the peasants naturally hold to be a miracle. Then we tramped over the wet fields where the fury of the battle waged, looking in the damp mist very much as they must have done on that day. On the spot where the Prince of Orange fell, a large Belgian lion has been erected on the top of a huge mound, which alters the character of the place a good deal We returned to Brussels at four, and visited the

Palais d'Arenberg (the present Duke is the nephew of our Prince Antoine), which is interesting as having been once inhabited by Count Egmont, and has a good portrait of Roscius by Rubens, and several other Flemish pictures."

A series of G.F.S. meetings in different parts of the diocese filled much of Lady Knightley's time this autumn, and she thoroughly enjoyed a visit to Stoke Edith Park for the Hereford musical festival.

"*Fawsley, November* 10.—Rainald had to go up to town for a final division on the *clôture*, in which we were beat by 44. I hardly like to think how fateful a division it is—freedom of debate, our ancient privilege gone for ever ! The country little understands what is happening. All the rest of us, Cartwrights, Aldersons, Magees, etc., went in much pomp and state to Daventry, to attend the Bishop's visitation and conference. Most interesting it was, a real visitation, in which the case of each parish was carefully gone into. The Bishop gave an address, in which he summed up the statistics of the sixty parishes in four Rural Deaneries, cited to attend at this centre. He rejoiced that there were now only seven out of the sixty in which Holy Communion was celebrated less than once a month. I wish this were not one of them. At the conference which followed, the Bishop emphasised the importance of more definitely organised lay-help, and said he hoped to bring a scheme for aiding this before the diocese shortly. He was very pleasant as usual, talking a great deal of Northampton, where Bradlaugh had really been the cause of much good in bringing churchmen together. One new church he ascribed wholly to this spirit, while he ascribed much of the mischief to the terrible neglect in two large parishes for twenty-five years. One of his stories amused me, which Bishop Wilberforce himself told him. In his first visitation he put this question to the churchwardens : ' Is there anything you have to complain of in the walk and carriage of your minister ? ' The answer, in a number of instances, was, ' He don't keep a carriage.' Here is another of Mr. Gladstone, which was told him by a German professor who, dining there, got into an argument with Mr. G. and held his own. Upon which Mrs. Gladstone passed down a paper to him with the words : ' Please change the subject ; we never allow Mr. G. to be contradicted here.'

" *November* 24.—To-day there is a very clever, dashing speech by Lord Salisbury, in which he speaks of Mr. Gladstone as one who ' keeps the word of promise to our ear, and breaks it to our hope,' and then adds : ' You know of what kind of beings that was said.' The passage (from *Macbeth*) runs thus :

> ' And be there juggling fiends no more believed,
> That palter with us in a double sense,
> That keep the word of promise to our ear,
> And break it to our hope.'

The worst of it is, half the world won't know the context, or realise the cleverness and bitterness of the speech.

" *4 Grosvenor Crescent, December* 4 (for the last time !).—I was very busy making the final arrangements for moving furniture and giving up this house, which is really sold. I am heartily glad, for I am sure it is right, and will be a considerable economy. I went with Rainald to the Carlton, to see the Queen open the Law Courts. Pall Mall was hung with flags and lined with troops, and lit up with Queen's weather, as the Royal procession went by with an escort of Life Guards. At night, to the Monday Pop, which I had not done for years. Joachim played in a quartette of Beethoven quite splendidly. And now I am going to bed for the last time in this house. Thank God for many happy hours in it !

" *Claremont, Esher, December* 5.—We came down here and spent a very pleasant evening with the Duke and Duchess of Albany and Mr. and Mrs. Collins. They are most kind and friendly. Prince Leo entirely confirms the story of Mr. Gladstone's proffered resignation last summer, which we heard at Homburg, and which Lord Folkestone blurted out, indiscreetly enough, at Salisbury. He thinks it quite likely that he will shortly resign, if his colleagues will consent.

"*Windsor Castle, December* 6.—The Duke went off early to Salisbury, and Rainald later to Firle. How I wish he were here! I spent the day very pleasantly with the Duchess—all she says is so thoroughly good and sensible,—came on here this afternoon, and dined with the Household, always a grand and stately business. I enjoy it all the more from feeling free and independent, in a way I did not when here as a girl. Lady Abercromby, Miss Stopford, Miss Paget, Lord Dalhousie, Mr. (Bill) Carington, Sir John M'Neill, Sir John Cowell, etc., here.

"*Windsor Castle, December* 7.—A snowy day, but I can't imagine a more delightful place to pass it in! I spent most of the morning with the Maids of Honour in that ever enchanting library, where I found Sir John Eliot's letter-book with many letters to T. Knightley, who was tutor to his sons at Oxford. After an investiture of the Bath, which my Duchess did not attend, I stole down to service at St. George's, where we had a lovely anthem, ' How lovely are the feet.' We dined with the Queen, and had the Italian Ambassador and Madame Menabrea, Lord and Lady Selborne and Sir William and Lady Harcourt, and some of the Household—sixteen in all. Sir William Harcourt amused me by calling Rainald ' the stormy petrel of debate,' saying ' that he never spoke except when there was really some mischief up,' adding, ' he always tells me that he has great difficulty in making up his mind which of the two Governments is the biggest set of scoundrels!' I could not help thinking of what Dizzy once said of Sir William himself : ' He is sure to get on, he has an historic name, a commanding presence, considerable talent, and no principle!'

"*December* 8.—I walked with my Duchess in the morning, and drove with her after luncheon in one of these delicious phaetons with postilions and a pair of white ponies, which, if I were a swell, I would certainly set up! Besides, I found time to go and see the Albert

Memorial Chapel, which is all inlaid with fine coloured marbles. We dined with the Queen, who was kinder and more gracious to me than ever. Captain Edwards of the Mounted Infantry, who was wounded at Kassassin, was the only stranger. Prince Leo returned from attending Archbishop Tait's funeral, and I had some interesting talk with him. He has greatly improved in his politics, and takes a thoughtful and intelligent interest in great questions. He told me a witty remark made by a French statesman apropos of the Emperor and Empress of Austria : ' Ce n'est pas là un ménage, c'est un manège.' Terrible accounts of snow all over the country, trains blocked, telegraphic communication interrupted, etc.; and in the city, one of the biggest fires ever known.

"*Claridge Hotel, Easter Monday, March 26,* 1883.— On Maundy Thursday I was startled by a telegram from the Duchess of Albany, asking me to her baby's christening at Windsor on Monday, so I made an early start from home, leaving the dear place looking lovely in the bright sunshine, and caught the special at Paddington at 12.10. I travelled down with the Duchess of Roxburghe and Mrs. Moreton, and after waiting in the Red Drawing-room some minutes, we were all shown to our places in the private chapel, where the Queen and Royal Family were already assembled. The new Archbishop, Dr. Benson, performed the ceremony beautifully—he has such a fine head and spiritual face —and the Queen gave the names, Alice Mary Victoria Augusta Pauline, in her usual clear, distinct voice. Poor little mite! God bless her and make her grow up good and happy. Afterwards we were all received in the Red Drawing-room, the Queen being obliged to sit in a wheel-chair, owing to a sprain, and Prince Leopold was on crutches, but looked bright and happy. I had no particular conversation with any of them, excepting that the Prince of Wales talked of Ireland, and said how wonderfully well Lord Spencer had done there; and I was introduced to the Archbishop, who seemed very pleasant. After luncheon we returned to town, and Lady Emma Osborne told me in the train that she had just come back from Russia, where the Court is beginning to amuse itself, but that several arrests had been lately made among the upper classes, which produces an uncomfortable feeling, and shows that the mischief is still going on."

CHAPTER XXVII

Carlton House Terrace and Claremont

1883–1884

" 4 *Carlton House Terrace, May* 3.—Yesterday we took possession of this beautiful house, which we have rented for ten weeks, and where we shall hardly know ourselves. The view from the windows is something to remember all one's life, embracing as it does the Abbey and Houses of Parliament, St. Margaret's and Whitehall. On one side one looks down the Mall to Buckingham Palace, and on the other we catch sight of St. Paul's and of distant hills, and from our balcony at night we see the full moon rising above the towers of Westminster. This afternoon I went to Lowther Lodge, where the usual *embarras* of pretty things was to be seen, and at night to the House of Commons, where the Affirmation Bill was thrown out by three votes (292–289) amidst the greatest excitement. I thought our men would never have done cheering. Thank God indeed! I can never forget that scene. The Radicals met us coming out of the lobby, and as one recognised one face after another my heart sank, and Mrs. Gladstone, who sat next me, said, ' It will be better than we expected.' But a rumour flew along our benches before the tellers appeared and the cheering began, and when at last one saw the paper in Mr. Rowland Winn's hand, one could say from the bottom of one's heart, ' Thank God!' I was puzzled at seeing the Conservatives remain in their places, instead of pouring out, as they usually do after a division, but found afterwards that Rainald had warned them that

Bradlaugh might come and take the oath after every one was gone, so they waited till he had left, for the Speaker told us the other day that he would have no power to stop him. For Bradlaugh himself had been in the House, under the Strangers' Gallery, all the time. It was curious to watch his face while speaker after speaker said every sort of thing about him, he being muzzled and unable to answer. When it was over Lady Salisbury, who was sitting by me in the Speaker's Gallery, turned to Mrs. Gladstone and said, ' Now you know in your heart of hearts you are as glad as we are. We've got you out of a very nasty difficulty and deprived ourselves of a capital election cry.' But Mrs. Gladstone did not seem to see it, and I should think she saw it still less this afternoon, when the Government were beat by 106 in a full house, on attempting to support Mr. Labouchere's endeavour to shelve Sir Stafford's resolution to prevent Mr. Bradlaugh taking the oath.

" *May* 5.—In the evening we went to Lady Salisbury's, where Rainald employed himself in chaffing all the Radicals he could lay his hands upon, and asking them if they did not think it required a double-first man like Gladstone to turn a minority of 3 into one of 106 within twenty-four hours. It just shows what their men do when they are left free to act according to their convictions. Mr. Beresford Hope was full of his little joke that the Liberals held their dinner at the Aquarium because they were jelly-fish. Altogether an amusing evening.

" *May* 29.—A very long day ! We began by the trooping of the Colour, a brilliant and beautiful sight in this sunny weather. Then I went to luncheon with Mrs. Jeune to meet Princess Christian, who was her own most charming and agreeable self. But I am unhappy at her account of the Queen, who has never thoroughly got over her accident in the spring. She says the Duke of Albany was most anxious to go to Canada, and is much disappointed at Lord Lansdowne's appointment. It is hard, when so few careers are open to him. We dined with Mr. Petre, and I sat by Lord Greville whom I found pleasant and light in hand, although tremendously Radical. He told me that Mr. Gladstone's advice to speakers was : ' Never learn your speech by heart, except perhaps the peroration, but divide your subject into two or three heads and talk to yourself first about one, then another, and so on, out walking, or whenever you are alone.' On to the Queen's ball, where the electric light used in the ballroom for the first time made it much cooler. I have seldom seen more beauty, beginning with the Princess of Wales, Lady Dudley, Lady Garvagh, Lady De Clifford, etc. Well may Lord Dufferin, just returned from the East, exclaim, ' I do feel proud of my country-women.' Sir Hussey Vivian amused me by repeating the letter which Disraeli wrote to the Duke of Marlborough when Sir Ivor Guest wanted to be made a peer :

" ' My dear Duke, nothing would give me greater pleasure than to place a coronet on the brow of dear Cornelia, but—— What has he done?' Characteristic.

" *Thursday, June* 28.—This was quite the most successful thing in the way of Society which we have ever done—an exhibition of amateur sketches and work for the Ladies' Guild. I was hard at work all Tuesday arranging the pretty things that had been sent me—a really beautiful collection : sketches in India by Sir Richard Temple, by Miss Gordon-Cumming all over the world, clever sketches in Russia and Austria by General Crealock, a delicious little book of Scottish sketches by Mrs. Ellice, water-colour drawings by all manner of people—the Duke of Argyll, Louisa Lady Waterford, Mr. Clifford Harrison, Mr. Lutyens, etc.; lovely old embroideries lent by Mrs. Alfred Morison, Mrs. Denison, Lady Edward Cavendish, and Lady Margaret Majendie, besides the work of the English and Irish Working Ladies' Guild. I sent out 600 cards, and in the course of the two afternoons an enormous number of people came, and enough smart people to please even Rainald ! It has been hard work, but it succeeded, and has done the Working Guilds real good, I hope. I went out driving for a little air each morning, and to parties at Lady Margaret Beaumont's where were the Christians, and Mrs. Oppenheim's where I met Prince Leo. My Duchess has been laid up but is recovering, and he seemed bright and cheerful. On Wednesday we went to the Queen's concert, and on Thursday to Lady Moleworth's where we met the Connaughts—a kind of party I have not been at for years, very smart, very stiff, and very dull! Came home to see a splendid storm from my lovely balcony, the vivid flashes lighting up the Abbey and the Park trees most beautifully, and then the rain came rushing up.

"*Saturday, June* 30.—To-night we went to Lady Brand's, to meet the Prince and Princess of Wales— a brilliant and beautiful party on the terraces. It was a perfect summer's night and the lights were reflected in the water below. I walked about with Mr. Forster, whom I always like, and Sir Charles Dilke joined us. What would Val say? However, Lord Salisbury's daughter, Lady Maud Cecil, marries Lord Wolmer, the Lord Chancellor's son, which will shock him still more.

"*July* 4.—We spent the afternoon at the Fisheries, the International show which has excited such a sensation; met John Hamilton for the first time since poor Emmy's death. He looks very sad, and misses her terribly. Afterwards I spent a delightful hour with that charming old lady, Mrs. Duncan Stewart, in her Sloane Street house. She is full of life and intellect, and strikes me as the very picture of happy old age. Her career, as Mr. Augustus Hare has lately told me, seems to have been a most varied one. A Miss Gore, left an orphan early and brought up in a convent at Rouen, she afterwards lived with her guardian at Havre, where Washington Irving and his brother were both madly in love with her. However, she married neither of them, nor Lord Cecil Gordon, whom she liked, but whom her guardian sternly discouraged. Mr. Duncan Stewart, whom she did marry, was a rich Liverpool merchant of a strictly Presbyterian family, who was shocked at her French notions. On his death she was left very poor, with ten children to educate. She became intimate with the Disraelis, who were very fond of her, and her daughter was Lady-in-Waiting to the Queen of Hanover, and lived with her at the Court at Herrenhausen.[1] To an amusing party at Mrs. Tennant's, whom we met at Birnam years ago, and whose beautiful daughters Millais painted. Coquelin recited—his face is a comedy in itself—and Soria sang beautifully as he always does, and Oscar Wilde was amusing to contemplate with his curling locks, black stock, turned-back cuffs, and bunch of seals. Altogether a new world. I met him again at Mrs. Jeune's afterwards. There I found a strange mixture—Lady Brownlow, Lady Pembroke, Lady Jersey, Mr. Greenwood, Hamilton Aïde, the Bancrofts, etc.

"*July* 6.—To the G.F.S. Council in the morning, and to tea at Nora's. I rejoiced in a quiet evening, while they were debating Women's Suffrage in the House. We were beaten by 14—no large majority, but the matter does not gain ground. Only about 19 Conservatives voted with us. The rest of the 114 were chiefly ultra-Radicals. I begin to doubt if it will ever become law in my time. I called on Lady Dorothy Nevill, who is always amusing. She has taken up with Mr. Chamberlain now, *vice* Dizzy deceased, and told me what an atrocious speech he had been making, advocating universal suffrage."

Visits to Rushton, Mr. Clarke-Thornhill's fine old place in Northamptonshire, to Lady Willoughby d'Eresby at Grimsthorpe, and to Lamington, Tullyallan, and Lindertis were Lady Knightley's only diversion this autumn. In November she addressed several meetings of the G.F.S., and inaugurated a new branch at Finedon, where she stayed with Mrs. Mackworth Dolben, in the historic old Manor House of the Dolben family. A visit from Mr. Augustus Hare was among the chief events of the winter.

[1] Mrs. Duncan Stewart died in the following winter, and her *Recollections* were afterwards published.

"*January* 8, 1884.—Mr. Hare is certainly a very pleasant guest. He gives no sort of trouble, amuses himself in the library all the morning, and us all with accounts of his travels and ghost stories. Here are two good ones which he has just told us: Sir Thomas Watson once travelled from Euston with a young lady, who told him that she was going to Ulverstoke to meet her *fiancé* and be married there the next day. But at Rugby, to his surprise, she declared she had seen her lover on the platform, and that he had begged her to get out. The same thing happened at Stafford, and when at Crewe she told Sir Thomas that the same thing happened again, and, seeing her *fiancé* calling her to join him, she jumped out of the train. Another girl got in and took her place, and was killed in a railway accident which happened just afterwards. The other was about Lady Gwendoline Talbot, Marchesa Borghese, appearing after her death to one of her old pensioners who had gone to pray at her tomb in extreme distress at her pension having been stopped. She gave her a ring and told her to take it to her son, the Marchese, which the old woman did. It turned out to be a famous Borghese jewel which had been buried with the dead Marchesa."

But the most noteworthy record of Mr. Hare's visit is the following description of Fawsley and its inmates, which appeared in his *Story of My Life* a few years afterwards:

"*Fawsley, January* 8, 1884.—I came here from Lichfield to find a very large party in this large and most comfortable house with a hall of Henry VIII.'s time. Sir Rainald Knightley, its owner, is a splendid type of an English country gentleman, very Conservative, very courteous, very clever, and devoted to country sports and interests, which alternates with the politics in which his more serious moments are spent. The only blemish on his perfectly happy married life with Miss Bowater—who enters into all his pursuits, whether duties or pleasures, politics, country business, hunting, etc.—is that they have no children. He is surrounded by cousins, Charleses and Valentines, repeating in actual life the many Charleses and Valentines whose portraits hang on the walls, and to whom there are monuments in the fine old church near the house. In the autumn, rheumatism takes him to Homburg, but he refuses to learn German—'the grinding, guttural gibberish of the garrulous Goth.'

"The parish has a population of 58, and there is only one service on Sundays, performed by a cousin, who is in Orders. It is alternately in the morning and afternoon, the difference being that the morning service begins at noon, and the afternoon service at a quarter-past.

"Mr. Charles Knightley drove me to Canons Ashby, the beautiful and romantic old place of the impoverished and eccentric Sir Henry Dryden. I thought it looked like the background of a novel, and afterwards found that it was the background of *Sir Charles Grandison.*

"Lady Knightley took me to Shuckburgh, a pretty old place. When Charles 1. was going to the battle of Edgehill, he met the Sir Richard Shuckburgh of that day, merrily going out hunting. He had never heard that there was a civil war going on—such was the paucity of political news! But he turned about and followed the king into the battle, and was wounded there. At the beginning of this century a daughter of the house became engaged to be married to an officer quartered at Weedon, a *mésalliance* to which her family greatly objected. At last she was induced to break it off. But the officer persuaded her to grant him one last interview in a summer-house at the back of the hill that he might give her back her letters. He gave her the letters with one hand, while with the other he shot her dead, and then shot himself."

"*Claremont, Esher, March* 18.—I left home with great regret, travelling up with Rainald, and came on here to find only the Duchess, who, poor little woman, is shortly expecting a second child, and Mrs. Snow, mother of the Doctor's wife, Mrs. Royle. The Duke of Albany is at Cannes. The Queen telegraphs to me this evening, begging me to write every few days and let her know how H.R.H. is.

"*March* 21.—Life here passes very quietly, but not at all disagreeably. I drive out every morning with the Duchess. The country round Claremont is very pretty, with wild, breezy commons and many Scotch firs. The grounds are lovely, with long grassy glades and masses of rhododendrons and a great number of firs of rare varieties. It seems the place was originally built by Sir John Vanbrugh ; then the grounds were laid out for the Duke of Newcastle, the minister, then Lord Clive bought it and built the present house, and had the grounds laid out by Capability Brown, whose real name was Lancelot. There is a mausoleum to Princess Charlotte in the gardens, and a miniature fort made by the Orleans princes when they were here. One day the Rector of Esher came to talk ' boarding-out ' with the Duchess, as she is anxious to try the experiment. Another day a Mrs. Willis, who is devoted to farming, came to luncheon, and we spent an improving afternoon on the Home Farm. The Duchess seems to me very amiable, with plenty of good sound common sense and the best intentions, but does not seem to care much for reading. What she really likes, and does extremely well, is needlework. The little girl is a great darling. The Queen seems very anxious to have the Duke back from Cannes, saying she needs his help and advice in public affairs, especially the alarming situation of Egypt. She has telegraphed to him : ' Situation very critical, Gladstone ill, affairs in Egypt most difficult.' I hope he will return.

"*March* 26.—A few lines to record the remainder of my visit. On Sunday Mrs. Snow and I walked to Esher Church, the spire of which has been familiar to me for so many years from Richmond Park. On Monday we made a pleasant expedition to the lovely little church of Stoke d'Abernon, which has a very fine brass of 1277 to Sir John d'Abernon, and some curious monuments to the Norburys and Vincents. It is all beautifully kept and close to the ' squarsonage,' a large house with a handsome hall standing close to the river Mole. At tea, Princess Frederica of Hanover drove over from Hampton Court and stayed some time. She was certainly born to be an empress, she has such stately, gracious manners. Yesterday Princess Beatrice came to luncheon with Lady Biddulph and Mlle Norèle. The old servant who came with them told Batten, what touched me very much, that he remembered perfectly the Prince Consort saying to my father, as he took leave of Prince Leopold when they were starting for Cannes, ' You'll take care of the boy, won't you ? ' My father answered, ' I will, sir, as if he were my own.' And within six months both were dead. In the evening Princess Louise and Lord Lorne came to dine and sleep, and both made themselves very agreeable. ' Dear me,' she said as we came down to dinner, ' it seems so odd to come to Leopold's house and see Leopold's child ! ' I have been reading aloud to the Duchess Lord Macaulay's *Essays* on Lord Chatham, and now this morning before I left the Duke writes : ' I am so glad you are reading Macaulay's *Essays*, I am so fond of them.' And he sends me a charming message, rejoicing to think I am here and wishing he were with us. The Duchess told me how fond he always was of me, and that I was the first person outside his own family of whom he spoke to her, even before their engagement. He has never forgotten that winter at Cannes, when we were thrown so much together, and I felt so sorry for the poor fatherless boy away from home and mother and sisters. The Duchess told me all the details of their engagement, how he came to call on her mother, the Princess of Waldeck, at Soden, and how afterwards they met for two or three days at Frankfurt, soon after which it was all settled. I have really enjoyed my visit to Claremont very much, but was delighted to speed home and get back to my darling husband, after one of our longest separations."

Lady Knightley returned to Fawsley, as we see, on Wednesday, March 26. Three days afterwards she heard of the Duke of Albany's sudden death.

" *Saturday, March 29.*—Ah me ! how little I thought

when I described Claremont and the life there how soon it was all to be plunged in the deepest sorrow! The sudden death of the Duke of Albany at Cannes yesterday, Friday, at 2 a.m., was the awful news which greeted me this morning. God help that poor young widow and her fatherless baby! He alone can. I feel quite overwhelmed; having been there so lately, one realises it all so vividly. My mind goes back and back to the time at Cannes, and I think of the many tokens of faithful friendship since, and of the poor Duchess's affectionate words last Wednesday. Alas! I can think of nothing else.

"*April* 4.—All the details in the papers are most touching. I am thankful to have a fair account of the Duchess from Mrs. Snow this morning. Much to our surprise, Rainald has received orders to attend the funeral at Windsor, and went off to town this morning. I got out many of Prince Leo's pretty childish letters and read them over again with a sad heart.

"*Saturday, April* 5.—All day long my thoughts were at Windsor. It seems too melancholy to think of that mournful pageant on the very spot where, two short years ago, the joyous marriage ceremonial took place! Thank God there is a world beyond the grave.

"*Claremont, Esher, May* 8.—I left Rainald (I am always leaving him now) to come down here to my poor Duchess. The contrast between my last visit, when all was joyful expectation, and now is most melancholy, but the dear Duchess herself is so brave, so touching in her unselfish resignation, that it is less painful than I expected. Princess Christian too is here, which is of course a great pleasure to me.

"*May* 10.—To-day the Queen came over from Windsor with Princess Beatrice, Princess Alice's husband, the Grand Duke Louis of Hesse, and her second daughter, Princess Ella (Elizabeth of Hesse), who is quite beautiful, and is going to be married next month to the Grand Duke Sergius of Russia. I have never seen the Queen since the christening at Windsor, in March last year, and she struck me as being a good deal changed. They are all terribly worried at the Grand Duke Louis having contracted a so-called morganatic marriage with the divorced wife of a Russian diplomatist, and this while the Queen was at Darmstadt, on the very evening of his eldest daughter's marriage to Prince Louis of Battenburg ! What makes it seem all the worse is, that just at this moment the letters of his late wife, Princess Alice, which are so full of love and devotion for him, are being published. Princess Christian, who has edited and translated them, gave me a copy of the book to-night. As for the dear Duchess, she is too touching in her grief, so natural and unaffected, and often very cheerful, full of firm faith and patient, gentle, unmurmuring resignation. Above all, she lives and talks of her lost husband and of their brief spell of happy wedded life in the spirit of the beautiful lines :

' 'Tis better to have loved and lost
Than never to have loved at all.'

The weather is simply heavenly—an ideal May day.

" *May* 14.—A trying day for the Duchess, as Captain Perceval, in whose arms the Duke died, came to see her. Alec Yorke was here too. How little I thought we should first meet here in such sad circumstances. Princess Louise and Lady Sophia Macnamara came down from town this afternoon. Poor Princess Louise ! No one loved Prince Leo better, and to no one is he a greater loss. Yesterday we had Major Waller, and to-day Mlle Norèle, to whom I talked a good deal. I drove this afternoon with Princess Christian. I must say one always begins again with her exactly where one left off !

" *4 Carlton House Terrace, May 27.*—The whole day was taken up with receiving Princess Christian and the Duchess of Albany, who drove up from Claremont to see the Duchess of Cambridge, and had luncheon here, after which Princess Christian drove with me and we left the Duchess to rest. There is something very taking about her, and all my heart goes out to her in her widowhood and loneliness.

"*July* 25.—I went to the garden-party at Marlborough House, which was a good deal spoilt by the cold, dull weather. But I had a nice little talk with the Crown Prince of Germany, whose manners are as charming as ever, and who never forgets our meeting on the way to Primkenau. To-day he talked chiefly about the Duke of Albany, with real feeling and affection."

. . . .

The death of Prince Leopold, with whom Lady Knightley had been so closely associated in her youth, naturally moved her deeply, recalling as it did the great crisis of her early life, the death of her own father, and the sad winter at Cannes which she spent in the young Prince's company. The friendship which she formed at this time with her widowed mistress lasted to the end of her life, and the Duchess of Albany was her guest at Fawsley only ten days before her own death, twenty-nine years afterwards.

The ten following years (1884–94) were strenuous ones for Lady Knightley. Politics absorbed more and more of her time. Gordon's ill-fated expedition to Khartoum, the struggle for Home Rule, and the foundation of the Primrose League became prominent topics in her Journals. In the autumn of 1885, and again in the following summer, Sir Rainald was called upon to contest two hard-fought elections, and on both occasions his supporters and opponents alike recognised that his success was largely due to his wife's eloquence and popularity. When, at the dissolution of 1892, he finally took leave of his constituents, Lady Knightley had the satisfaction of seeing her husband's long parliamentary career crowned by a peerage. Two years later Lord and Lady Knightley celebrated their silver wedding, a fitting culmination to their singularly happy married life. But six months after this Lord Knightley had a paralytic stroke, and although he lived till the end of the year, he never fully recovered his former powers of body or mind. He died at Fawsley on the 19th of December 1895, to his wife's deep and lasting regret. But her strong faith and courage bore her

LADY KNIGHTLEY OF FAWSLEY.
1904.

[*To face p.* 374.

safely through the dark days of early widowhood, and she went back to work with fresh hope and ardour.

During the eighteen years of life that remained to her, Lady Knightley devoted herself more and more zealously to the good works of which she had been so long the moving spirit, while at the same time she found new channels for her untiring energy and benevolence. Her labours in the cause of British Emigration and of South African Colonisation are too recent and too widely known to need further description. In spite of trials and loneliness, she retained her power of enjoyment to the last. The Journals of these closing years are in some ways more full of variety and interest—even livelier and more amusing than the records of her earlier days. They abound in animated descriptions of public events and political controversies, of pleasant expeditions to Baireuth and Rome, and more distant journeys to South Africa and Greece, and of still happier months spent in the dear-loved home which, fortunately for her and for her dependants, she was never called to leave.

When Lady Knightley died, in September 1913, after a few days' illness, she was deeply lamented by a wide circle of relations and friends, who had felt the enduring spell of her goodness and charm. The unknown thousands whose lives she had helped to brighten by her unwearied efforts, the women and girls to whose welfare her activities had been more especially devoted, joined in paying her memory the same tribute. Their love and gratitude is to find permanent expression in the church which will soon be raised as a memorial to Lady Knightley at Regina, in the province of Saskatchewan, Canada, and which will be dedicated to St. Peter, in remembrance of the London church where her own wedding took place, and where she had so often listened to Bishop Wilkinson's sermons. So her name will live, alike in these far regions of Britain-beyond-the-seas and in the pleasant fields and familiar places of her old Northamptonshire home, where in days to come many will rise up and call her blessed.

APPENDIX

A CHRONICLE of Events kept by Thomas Lane, merchant, born at Tettenhall, Staffordshire, October 25, 1714, and great-grandfather of Lady Knightley. He went out to India as a young man, married Hannah Sanders at Bombay on September 19, 1750, returned from India in 1752, and went to his home in Staffordshire, where he began to write this record.

1753. This year my daughter, Louisa Lane, was born, on October 11.
1755. This year I moved to Stepney, and my son Thomas went to India.
1764. This year I went to live in Bedford Row, and dyed my dear, good mother.
1767. This year I purchased Cheshunt House.
1771. My son Henry left me for China.
1777. My son Richard left me for India, and died the same year in Bengal.
1779. This year I left Cheshunt and sold my house, and Miss Lane was married to George Edward Hawkins.
1780. This year was born Louisa Hawkins, on November 30, and baptized at St. George's, Hanover Square.
1781. This year I went to Ford Hook, and my son Henry came home from China.
1783. This year I left Bedford Row, and went to live in George Street, and dyed my dear wife. George Hawkins died at Acton, Middlesex, on September 29, aged thirty-two. His daughter, Laura Hawkins, was born in George Street on October 28, and baptized at Ealing Church.
1784. This year I rented a house at Hampton Court.
1785. This year was married my daughter, Louisa Hawkins, to Captain Bowater, on August 31.
1787. This year was born my Bowater grandson, on July 13, and baptized by the name of Edward at St. James's Palace.
1789. This year my son Henry returned from China.
1795. This year I surrendered the agency of the Ponsborne to my son Harry.

Mr. Thomas Lane died in September 1796, and was buried by the side of his wife in the vault of Abbots Langley Church, Herts. His grandson, Edward Bowater, continued the Chronicle as follows:

1794. This year, aged seven, I went to Warfield School, under Dr. Faithfull.

APPENDIX

1796. This year died my excellent grandfather, Mr. Lane, aged eighty-three.
1798. This year I went to Harrow School, under Dr. Drury.
1803. This year my sister, Laura Hawkins, married Sir Matthew White Ridley, Bart., on August 12.
1804. This year I entered the 3rd Regiment of Guards. Sarah Ridley was born.
1806. This year my sister, Louisa Hawkins, married Captain H. W. Wheatley.
1807. This year I went with the expedition to Copenhagen under Lord Cathcart. Georgiana Wheatley was born.
1808. This year I, Edward Bowater, embarked for Spain under General Sherbroke, and sailed for Cadiz and Lisbon.
1809. I was wounded at the battle of Talavera, appointed Lieutenant and Captain, and returned to England.
1810. This year I was appointed A.D.C. to General Turner by the Duke of Clarence.
1812. Laura Maria Wheatley was born. I returned to Spain, and was present at the battle of Salamanca and taking of Madrid.
1813. This year I was present at the battle of Vittoria and siege of S. Sebastian, and entered France, etc. General Bowater, my good uncle, died, aged seventy-two.
1814. This year I was present at the siege of Bayonne and taking of Bordeaux, appointed Captain and Lieut.-Colonel, returned to England and was sent to the Army at Brussels. Mary Wheatley was born.
1815. This year I was wounded at the battle of Waterloo, and received a year's pay and a medal for it, and entered Paris.
1816. I returned to England with a part of the Army.
1818. Sophia Wheatley was born.
1823. This year I was sent to Dublin with my regiment.
1826. This year I went to Portugal under Sir William Clinton, and was appointed Major and Colonel.
1827. I remained in Portugal in command of the 2nd Battalion of Guards.
1828. This year I returned to England with the Army.
1829. My dear father, Admiral Bowater, died, aged seventy-six.
1830. I went to Dublin with my battalion.
1832. This year I was appointed Equerry to the King.
1835. My kind, good mother, Mrs. Bowater, died, aged eighty-two.
1836. This year I was appointed Lieut.-Colonel of the 3rd Guards, and died my kind brother, Sir Matthew Ridley.
1837. This year I was appointed Major-General and Kt. Commander; died my kind master, King William IV.
1838. This year I proposed to Emilia Mary Barne on the 22nd November.
1839. This year I married my dearest wife, Emilia Mary Barne, on the 22nd May.
1840. This year died my niece Laura Wheatley, and I was appointed Equerry to H.R.H. Prince Albert.
1841. Her Majesty gave me the Lodge in Richmond Park.
1842. This year was born my daughter, Louisa Mary Bowater, on April 25.
1845. This year died my niece Cecilia, wife of Matthew White Ridley, April 2.

APPENDIX

1846. This year I was appointed Groom-in-Waiting to H.M. and Colonel of the 49th Regiment.
1849. This year died my niece, Alice Barne.
1852. This year died my kind brother-in-law, Major-General Sir Henry Wheatley, G.C.H., C.B., aged seventy-four.
1853. This year died my old schoolfellow and brother-officer, my kind friend and companion, Lord Charles Townsend.
1854. This year died my old friend Lord Colborne and his wife, a great loss to me.
1858. This year died my very dear sister, Louisa Wheatley, ever most kind and affectionate, on April 1, aged seventy-seven; and on December 11 my good mother-in-law, Mrs. Mary Barne, aged ninety-three.

Three years after this last entry, General Sir Edward Bowater died at Cannes, on December 14, 1861, and the record was continued by his daughter, Louisa.

1860. This year died my father's old and valued friend, the Duke of Richmond, on December 14.
1861. This year died my beloved father, aged seventy-four, and on the same day, within five hours, the Prince Consort, aged forty-two.
1862. We left the Lodge in Richmond Park, which was given by Her Majesty to Colonel Liddell, and on his resigning it, given back to my mother.
1864. This year died my cousin Edith Barne, aged nineteen, on January 11, during my visit to Osborne; also my cousin Sarah Cookson, aged sixty; my Aunt Laura, Lady Ridley, on July 23, aged eighty-one; and my cousin, Georgiana Wheatley, aged fifty-seven.
1865. This year I went to stay at Balmoral.
1866. I went to Windsor and Cliveden.
1868. My dear and good cousin Mr. Newdegate, and my cousin, General Sir William Ridley, both died, on January 21 and November 27. I went to Frogmore and to Germany, in July and September, with H.R.H. Princess Christian.
1869. On October 20, I was married to my dear husband, Rainald Knightley, at St. Peter's, Eaton Square.

INDEX

ABBOT, Mr., 135.
Abercromby, Lady, at Windsor Castle, 360.
Aberdeen, 90.
Aberdeen, Ishbel, 331.
Aberdeen, Lord, 263.
Abergeldie, 90, 94.
Aboyne, 90, 102.
Adderley, Sir Charles, his Unseaworthy Shipping Bill, 273.
Adderley, Mrs., 134.
Adstone, 297.
Affirmation Bill, 363.
Affric, 265.
Africa, South, Bill, 316.
Agricultural distress, causes of, 336.
Agricultural Holdings Bill, 280.
Agricultural labourers' strike, 228.
Agricultural Labourers' Union, notice from the, 240.
Aïde, Hamilton, 244, 367.
Airey, General, 260.
Airlie, Lady, her reception, 347.
Alabama question, 94, 226, 227, 234.
Albani, Mme, 280, 301.
Albany, Count d', 302.
Albany, Duchess of, her wedding, xvi, 351; death of her sister, 352; at Claremont, 355; birth of a daughter, 361; death of her husband, xvi, 371; at Carlton House Terrace, 373; friendship with Lady Knightley, 374; at Fawsley, xvi, 374.
Albany, H.R.H. Duke of, his engagement, 349; wedding, xvi, 351; at Claremont, 355; at the christening of his daughter, 361; at Cannes, 369; his affection for Lady Knightley, 371; death, xvi, 371. *See* Leopold.
Albany, Princess Alice of, her christening, 361.
Albert Hall, 246.
Albert Memorial Chapel, 361.
Albert, H.R.H. Prince, his surprise visit to Sir E. Bowater, 23; illness and death, xv, 30; inscription on his cairn, 93; his statue, 100; Life, 319.
Alderson, Lady, at Hatfield, 185.
Alexandra, H.R.H. Princess, her engagement, 40; arrival at Windsor, 48; appearance, 49; wedding, 50. *See* Wales, Princess of.
Alexandria, bombardment of, 354.
Alford, Lady Marian, 348; at Castle Ashby, 194; at Euston, 268.
Alfred, H.R.H. Prince, at Osborne, 32; his appearance, 32, 115; at Windsor Castle, 53; title of Duke of Edinburgh, 114. *See* Edinburgh.
Alice, H.R.H. Princess, at Windsor Castle, 25; her grief at the death of her father, 32. *See* Hesse.
Alington, Lady, at Crichel, 271.
Alington, Lord, at Osterley Park, 261.
Alsace Lorraine ceded to Germany, 214.
Alsen, taken, 84.
Althorp, 264; library, 264.
Alt-na-Guisach, 93.
Amanvilliers, 305.
Amberley, Lord, 38, 42, 82.
Ambulance lectures, course of, 331; examination, 334.
Amiens, 32.
Andermatt, 220.
Angerstein, Julia, 134; bridesmaid to Miss Bowater, 171.
Angerstein, Mrs., her ball, 166.
Annesley, Colonel, at Burghley House, 226; Ickworth, 252.
Aosta, Duke and Duchess of, at Wimbledon, 138.
Apponyi, Count, 126.
Apsley House, ball at, 248.
Arbury, 42, 106, 128, 139, 176, 205.
Aremberg, Prince d', 284.
Arenberg, Palais d', 358.
Arenberg, Prince, 303.

INDEX

Argyll, Duke of, 89; at Balmoral, 90–103; his mode of reciting poetry, 99, 101; at the marriage of Princess Helena, 126; Secretary for India, 163; at Lansdowne House, 247; member of the Metaphysical Society, 267; criticism on, 332; his speech on the Irish Land Bill, 348.
Arnim, Count, his arrest, 271; trial, 272.
Arnold, Adèle, 152, 172.
Art Embroideries Show, 324.
Arthur, H.R.H. Prince, his appearance, 26; at Dover, 32; Windsor Castle, 49, 142; Osborne, 64, 211; Balmoral, 92; expedition up Ben-na-Biurd, 98; at the marriage of Princess Helena, 126; attends the Waverley Ball, 220; at Sandringham, 223; at a party given by Lady Knightley, 235.
Arthur, Sir Frederick and Lady Elizabeth, at Knole Park, 201.
Ascot races, 81, 261.
Ashburton, Lady, at Euston, 269, 270.
Ashburton, Lord, 219.
Ashley, Lady Edith, 263.
Astley, 205.
Astley, Colonel, 44.
Astley, Thurlow, 139.
Astwell Mill, 298.
Atholl, Duchess of, 89; at Windsor Castle, 113, 141; Cliveden, 117; Osborne, 211.
Atlay, Mr., 27.
Augustenburg, Duke of, at Gotha, 148.
Augustenburg, Princess Augusta Victoria of, 148.
Augustenburg, Princess Caroline of, 148.
Augustenburg, Prince Ernst Günther, 148.
Augustenburg, Princess Feodora Louise, 148.
Austria, Empress of, at Easton Neston, 298; her appearance, 298.
Auvergne, M. le Prince de la Tour d', at Windsor Castle, 113.
Aveland, Lord and Lady, 231.
Avignon, 27.
Avricourt, 285.
Azeglio, Marquis d', 219.

B——, Captain, 44; his character, 45; attentions to Miss Bowater, 79–81; proposal of marriage, 85; illness, 235; meeting with Lady Knightley, 316.
B——, Sir R., his attentions to Miss Bowater, 80.
Babelsberg, 153.
Badby, 334; confirmation at, 191.
Baden, 285.
Bagot, Lord, 217; at Windsor Castle, 142, 144.
Baird, Sir David and Lady, 104.
Baker, Sir Samuel, 258, 275.
Bakewell, 236; church, 237.
Balkan War, 316.
Ballochbuie, Forest of, 92, 93.
Ballot Bill, 230, 232, 234.
Balmoral, 90–102.
Balston, Dr., Vicar of Bakewell, 236.
Banbury, 89, 251.
Baring, Colonel, 139.
Barker, Mr., his collection of *objets de luxe*, 259.
Barncleuth, 250.
Barne, Edith, her companionship with Louisa Bowater, 12; illness, 36, 62; death, 70.
Barne, Emilia Mary, her marriage, 2. *See* Bowater, Lady.
Barne, Frederick, at Sotterley, 12; at the wedding of his niece Louisa Bowater, 171, 172; his reminiscences of Old London, 335.
Barne, St. John, 12, 15, 25, 134, 139; at the wedding of his cousin Louisa, 172; his marriage, 236 *note*; member for Suffolk, 296, 339.
Barne, Colonel Michael, 2.
Barne, Philip, 12; death of his sister, 70.
Barne, Mrs., her appearance, 3; at Toulouse, 3; death, 10.
Barnes, Mr., his poems, 279.
Barrington, Augusta, 289; at Somerley, 272.
Barrington, Lady Caroline, at Windsor Castle, 25, 141; Osborne, 64, 65; her return from Berlin, 114.
Barrington, Dowager Lady, at Somerley, 272.
Barrington, Lord, 217.
Bartholomei, Herr, 284.
Bartolozzi, Miss, 317.
Bassano, Duc de, at Wakefield Lodge, 321.
Bath, Lady, 225.
Bathurst, Evelyn, bridesmaid to Miss Bowater, 171.
Battenberg, Prince Alexander of, Prince-elect of Bulgaria, 336.

INDEX

Battenberg, Prince Louis of, 146 *note*, 283 *note*, 373.
Battenberg, Princess Louis of, 146 *note*, 283 *note*.
Bauer, Fraulein, 67, 70, 120.
Bazaine, Marshal, defeated at Gravelotte, 205, 305.
Beaconsfield, Lady, story of, 162.
Beaconsfield, Lord, 311; his illness and death, 346; anniversary of his death, 350. *See* Disraeli.
Beatrice, H.R.H. Princess, at Windsor Castle, 25, 53, 313; attack of whooping-cough, 117; at Cliveden, 117, 120; at the marriage of Princess Helena, 126; at Claremont, 371.
Beauly, 266.
Beaumont, Lady Margaret, 190, 196, 231, 246.
Beaumont, Mr., 196, 231.
Bedford, Duke of, receives a threatening letter, 354.
Belgians, King Leopold, at the marriage of Princess Helena, 126, 127; his reception by Mr. Lowe, 230; at the Literary Fund dinner, 231.
Belgians, Queen of the, at the marriage of Princess Helena, 126, 127.
Belgium, 281.
Ben-na-Buird, 92, 97, 98, 102.
Benson, Archbishop, at the christening of Princess Alice of Albany, 361.
Bentinck, Baron, 74.
Bentinck, Lord George, his letter on his resigning the leadership of the Conservative party, 174.
Bentinck, George Cavendish, at Crichel, 271.
Berlin, 152; Congress of, 324.
Bernard, Montague, at Oxford, 278.
Bernhardt, Sarah, 335.
Bernstorff, Count, 126.
Bernstorff, Countess, at Homburg, 317.
Besika Bay, 320.
Beust, Count, at Highclere Castle, 251.
Biddulph, Lady, at Osborne, 67; Windsor Castle, 144.
Biddulph, Lady Elizabeth, at Wakefield Lodge, 321.
Biddulph, Sir Theodore, 128.
Biddulph, Sir Thomas, at Osborne, 64, 67; at Windsor Castle, 89, 113, 144.
Biggar, Mr., his motion in the House of Commons, 275.

Bingham, Lady Cuckoo, 247.
Bingham, Lord, at Crichel, 271.
Birch, Arthur, 15, 59.
Birk Hall, 94.
Birmingham, 205.
Bismarck, Prince, on the Treaty of 1867, 210; character of his policy, 274; his account of his interview with Thiers and Favre, 279.
Blair Atholl, 265.
Blanc, Mont, 220, 317.
Blandford, Lady, at Affric, 265.
Blantyre Priory, ruins of, 250.
Blisworth, 172.
Blücher, Countess, at Osborne, 64, 65.
Booth, Sclater, Secretary of the Local Government Board, 257.
Borough Franchise, debate on, 76.
Bost, Mlle, 148, 150.
Bothwell, 250.
Boucherett, Ayscoghe, 2.
Boucherett, Harry, 78, 82; at the opera, 110.
Boucherett, Jessie, 129.
Boucherett, Louisa, 129.
Boulogne, 26.
Bourbaki, General, 208.
Bourke, Mrs., honorary lady-in-waiting to the Duchess of Albany, 351.
Bowater, Admiral, 1, 2.
Bowater, General Sir Edward, his birth, 1; at Harrow, 1; his schoolfellows, 1; military career, 2, 6; marriage, 2; appointed Equerry to Prince Albert, 2; takes Prince Leopold abroad, 23; surprise visit from Prince Albert, 24; journey to Cannes, 26–29; his illness and death, xv, 30; funeral, 31.
Bowater, Lady, at Windsor Castle, 25; death of her husband, 30; interview with Queen Victoria, 33; at the wedding of her daughter Louisa, 172; at Fawsley, 176, 204, 209, 272; Firle, 192.
Bowater, Louisa Mary, her birth, 1; parents, 2; grandmother, 3; commences her Journal, xiv, xviii, 3; at a ball at Buckingham Palace, 4, 81, 135; her mode of life, 4; German governess, 4; visit to France, 5; strict bringing up, 5; present at the review of the Guards, 7; at the theatre, 8; at Sotterley, 9, 23, 39, 128, 139–141, 161; death of her

INDEX

grandmother, 10; her cousins, 12; first ball, 14; her connections the Ridleys, 15; at the National Rifle Association meeting, 17, 60, 138; the Crystal Palace, 17; first London season, 19; her appearance, xiv, 19; presentation at Court, 20; at a concert at Buckingham Palace, 21; at Harrow speech day, 22; leaves Sotterley, 23; at Windsor Castle, 25, 113–117; Paris, 26; Avignon, 27; Vidauban, 28; Cannes, xv, 29–32; death of her father, 30; at Osborne, 32–35, 145; interview with Queen Victoria, 33; her home at Richmond Park, 36, 40; presents from the Royal Family, 36; at the International Exhibition, 37; at Arbury, 42–45, 106, 128, 139; present at the wedding of the Prince of Wales, 47–52; proposals of marriage, 54, 63, 79, 85, 108; attends a Drawing-room, 55, 76, 104; at the Guildhall, 56; the opera, 57, 110, 137; the Guards' ball, 58; Hampton Court, 62, 78; Dunwich, 62; invited to dine with Queen Victoria, 65; death of her cousin Edith, 70; her interest in politics, xiii, 73, 121, 162; present at a debate in the House of Commons, 75, 121; at the South Kensington Museum, 77; Ascot, 81; death of her aunt, 87; journey to Balmoral, 89; life in the Highlands, 89–102; expedition up Ben-na-Biurd, 98; at Stoke Rochford, 105, 130; friendship with Edith Turnor, 105; bridesmaid to Bella Mainwaring, 108; at a reception at Buckingham Palace, 110; Cliveden, 117–120; Harefield Place, 122; meeting with Sir H. Jerningham, 124; at the marriage of Princess Helena, 125–128; her views on female franchise, 129; impressions of Mrs. Siddons, 131; at the Royal Academy, 133; death of her friend Mrs. Newdegate, 140; at Frogmore, 141–144; gift from Queen Victoria, 142; impressions of Disraeli, 146; on board the *Enchantress*, 146; at Cologne, 147; Gotha, 148–152; Berlin, 152; Potsdam, 153; Schloss Primkenau, 155–159; bridesmaid to Lady J. Melville, 163; first meeting with Sir R. Knightley, 164; at Fawsley, 167; engagement, 167; presents, 169; wedding, 171–173; bridesmaids, 171. *See* Knightley, Lady.

Bowen, Sir George, on the appointment of Irishmen, 356.
Bowment's Moss, 95.
Boyle, Mary, at Castle Ashby, 194.
Boyne, Lady, 134.
Brackley, 188; restoration of the Chapel, 188; Agricultural Show, 307.
Bradford, Lady, 247.
Bradford, Lord, 144.
Bradlaugh, Mr., returned to Parliament, 339; prevented from taking the oath, 350, 364.
Braemar Castle, 92.
Brand, Harry, 330.
Brand, Lady, her reception, 366.
Brandling, Mr., at Osterley Park, 261.
Bravo, Mr., his death by poisoning, 301.
Bravo, Mrs., 304.
Breton, Mme le, 209.
Bretton Park, 209.
Bridgewater House, 232; ball at, 248.
Bright, Rt. Hon. John, 314; his admission into the Cabinet, 163; views on consecrated ground, 340; on the Irish Land Bill, 347; his resignation, 355.
Brinckmann, Baron, 332.
Bristol, Lady, 217; at Ickworth, 210; her ball, 232.
Bristol, Lord, 217.
British Museum, 352.
Broglie, Duc de, 217.
Brooke, Lord, at Oxford, 278.
Brooke, Stopford, his sermons, 193, 199, 202.
Brougham, Lord, at Cannes, 32.
Broughton, Mr., 15.
Brown, John, 93.
Browning, Robert, 261; at Highclere Castle, 251; "Ride from Ghent," 333; his poems, 340.
Brownlow, Lady, 225, 367; her appearance, 231, 349.
Bruce, Lady Augusta, 25, 32.
Bruce, Lord Charles, at Ickworth, 252.
Bruce, Cumming, 134.
Bruce, Mr., Home Secretary, 163.
Bruce, Mrs., at Osborne, 64; Windsor Castle, 89, 113; Balmoral, 91–103.

INDEX

Brühl, Countess, 149, 151, 153, 324.
Brunnow, Baron, 126.
Brussels, 147, 281, 357.
Bruyère, La, his maxim, 248.
Buccleuch, Duke of, 332.
Buchanan, Sir Alexander, 45.
Buchwald, Fräulein von, 159.
Buckhurst, Lady, at Ickworth, 210.
Buckhurst, Lord, 201.
Buckingham, Duke of, Governor of Madras, 322.
Buckingham Palace, balls at, 4, 81, 135, 365; concerts at, 21, 260; Drawing-rooms, 110, 216, 301, 353; reception, 228.
Buff, Herr, tutor to Prince Leopold, 69, 76.
Bulgaria, atrocities, 307.
Bulwer, Colonel, 58.
Bulwer, Sir Henry, *Life of Lord Palmerston*, 210.
Burghley House, 212; political gatherings at, 226; the kitchen, 227; plate closet, 227.
Burghley, Lord, 236.
Burials Bill, 341.
Burke, Mr., his assassination, 352.
Burleigh, Lord, 213.
Burlington House, exhibition of Old Masters at, 238.
Burnaby, Colonel, 312; at Gayton, 310; Homburg, 316.
Burnham Beeches, 118.
Burns, Robert, lines from, 115.
Burrell, Lady, 122.
Burton, Helen, 108.
Burton, Captain and Mrs. Richard, 280.
Bury, Lord, 332.
Bury St. Edmunds, 210.
Bute, Lord, 246.
Buxton, 236.
Buxton, Sir Robert, 58.
Byng, Colonel and Mrs. Henry, at Somerley, 272.
Byron, Lady, separation from her husband, 139.
Byron, Lord, his nickname of "Hopping Dick," 1; escape from drowning, 92.

C——, Captain, his proposal of marriage to Miss Bowater, 108.
Cadzow Castle, 250; lines on, 250.
Caird, Dr., his sermons, 94.
Cairns, Lady, at Burghley House, 226.
Cairns, Lord, at Hatfield, 186; Burghley House, 226; on the Public Worship Bill, 260.

Cairns, Sir Henry, his speech on the Reform Bill, 109.
Caithness, Lord, at Windsor Castle, 113.
Caledon, Lady, 33.
Calthorpe, Lord, 232; at Somerley, 272.
Cambridge, Duchess of, at the marriage of Princess Helena, 126; at Wimbledon, 138.
Cambridge, H.R.H. Duke of, at Whitehall Gardens, 122; Osborne, 211; Euston, 268; Homburg, 304; Orwell Park, 310.
Cambridge, Princess Mary of, 20, 22; her engagement, 114; presents on view, 120. *See* Teck.
Campbell, Sir Colin, 8.
Campbell, Lady Muriel, bridesmaid to Princess Helena, 127.
Campbell, Nora, 79, 275.
Canné, the courier, 27.
Canon's Ashby, 173, 204.
Capel-Cure, Mrs., her concert, 79.
Cardigan, Lord, 8.
Cardwell, Mr., Secretary for War, 163; his scheme for reorganising the army, 259.
Carington, Hon. Rupert, at Gayton, 310.
Carington, Hon. Wm., at Windsor Castle, 360.
Carlisle, 90, 103.
Carlton House Terrace, view from, 363.
Carlyle, Thomas, *French Revolution*, 218; his definition of Disraeli and Gladstone, 267; story of, 348.
Carnarvon, Lord, 219; at Hatfield, 185, 186, 262; his article on the Lessons of the French Revolution, 254; resignation, 320.
Cartwright, Chauncey, chargé d'affaires at Cairo, 355.
Cartwright, Major Fairfax, member for South Northampton, 255, 338; his death, 345.
Cartwright, Harriet, 289, 290, 335.
Cartwright, Julia, her wedding, 342.
Castle Ashby, 194.
Cathcart, Miss, at Osborne, 64, 68.
Cavendish, Colonel, 31.
Cavendish, Lord Edward, his marriage, 96.
Cavendish, Lady Frederick, 247; at Guisachan, 265.
Cavendish, Lord Frederick, his marriage, 76; at Guisachan, 265; assassination, 352.

INDEX

Cavendish-Bentinck, Mrs., 200; her reception, 203.
Cawdor Castle, 266.
Cawdor, Lady, 217, 266.
Cawdor, Lord, 217; his book on *Housing*, 175.
Cecil, Lord and Lady Brownlow, at Burghley House, 213
Cecil, Lord and Lady Eustace, at Burghley House, 226.
Cecil, Lady Maud, her marriage, 366.
Chair, Dudley de, 48, 51.
Chamberlain, Rt. Hon. J., appointed to the Board of Trade, 339; at Windsor Castle, 352; his speech on universal suffrage, 367.
Chamonix, 317.
Chantrey, his monument of Lady Frederica Stanhope, 253.
Chaplin, Mr, at Burghley House, 226.
Charlton, Colonel, 14.
Charteris, Colonel, 139.
Charteris, Lady Margaret, her ball, 196.
Charwelton, 223; meet at, 273.
Chatham, Lord, at Chevening, 254.
Chelmsford, Lord, 122; at Homburg, 282, 283.
Cheney, Mr., 200, 219; at Fawsley, 190; Holmbury, 235.
Chesterfield, Lord, his death, 223.
Chetwynd, Sir George, 135.
Chevening, 253.
Childers, Rt. Hon. Hugh, 163.
Christian, H.R.H. Prince, his engagement, 106; marriage, 126; appearance, 126; at Frogmore, 141; his characteristics, 143; at Cologne, 147; Primkenau, 155–159; address of welcome, 156; his opinion of a journal, 160; at Osborne, 211; the French play, 258; Windsor Castle, 313. *See* Schleswig-Holstein.
Christian, H.R.H. Princess, birth of a son, 131, 163; at Frogmore, 141; Osborne, 145, 211, 212; Primkenau, 155–159; her appearance, 159; attack of illness, 216; meetings with Lady Knightley, 219, 339, 364; at the French play, 258; Darmstadt, 282; Cumberland Lodge, 296; death of her baby, 303; criticisms on Disraeli and Lord Derby, 320; at Claremont, 372; Carlton House Terrace, 373. *See* Helena, Princess.

Christian Year, lines from, 192.
Church of England, proposed disestablishment, debate on, 216.
Churchill, Lady, 122; at Osborne, 64, 65.
Churchill, Lady Cornelia, 143.
Clancarty, Lord, at Homburg, 304.
Claremont, 355, 359, 370; history of, 370.
Clarendon, Lady, at Windsor Castle, 113; her appearance, 113.
Clarendon, Lord, at Windsor Castle, 113; Secretary for Foreign Affairs, 163.
Clarke, Sir James, at Osborne, 64.
Clements, Mr., private secretary to Colonel Taylor, 135.
Clerk, Mr, 44
Clerkenwell Prison, attempt to blow up, 140.
Cleveland, Duchess of, 189, 261.
Clifden, Lady, 141; at Windsor Castle, 142, 144; Osborne, 145.
Clifford, Lady De, her appearance, 365.
Clifton, Colonel, at Osborne, 212.
Clinton, Lord, 314.
Cliveden, 117.
Clyde, the, 250.
Cobbe, Frances Power, 334.
Coburg, Duke of, 149.
Cochrane, Baillie, 211.
Cockerell, Mr., at Highclere Castle, 251.
Coercion Bill, 345.
Coleridge, Arthur, 43.
Coleridge, Sir John, 219.
Collins, Mr., at Osborne, 212; Claremont, 359.
Collins, Mrs., at Claremont, 359.
Collyns, Miss, 288.
Collyns, Mr., 289.
Cologne, 147; the Cathedral, 147.
Colonna, Prince and Princess, at Homburg, 304.
Commons, House of, 75; scene in, 275; debate on the motion to expel strangers, 275–278; length of a sitting, 316, 345; suspension of Irish members, 345; division on the *clôture*, 358.
Compton, Lady Alwyne, 190, 194, 203; at Holmbury, 235.
Connaught, H R.H. Duchess of, her appearance, 336.
Connaught, H.R.H. Duke of, his engagement, 324. *See* Arthur, Prince.
Conservatives, loss of seats, 338.
Conspiracy and Murder Bill, 10.
Cookson, Sarah, 87.

INDEX

Coquelin, his acting, 335; recitation, 367.
Corbet, Fanny, bridesmaid to Miss Bowater, 171.
Cork, Lady, 195, 217; her receptions, 187, 189; at Orwell Park, 237, 310; stories of her battles for precedence, 237.
Cork, Lord, 195.
Corry, Montagu, 190; at Burghley House, 213, 226.
Cottenham, Lord, 260.
Cottesloe, Lord, 181; at Edgcote, 342.
Coventry, 128.
Cowell, Sir John, at Windsor Castle, 113, 360.
Cowley, Lady, 27.
Cowper, Henry, at Highclere Castle, 251.
Cowper, Lady, 225.
Coyles, the, 93, 102.
Craig Gowan, 97, 102.
Craig-Lauriben, 93.
Cranborne, Lord, his letter on the Reform Bill, 175.
Cranborne Manor, 271.
Crathie, 94.
Crealock, General, his sketches, 365.
Crichel, 271.
Crimea, return of the Guards from the, 6.
Cross, Mr., his London Dwellings Bill, 273.
Cross, Sir Richard, 353.
Crystal Palace, meeting of the Rifle Association, 17; concert at, 87.
Cundall, Ellen, 336.
Custance, Mrs., her ball, 58.
Cyprus, annexation of, 325.

Dalhousie, Lord, 32; at Windsor Castle, 360.
Dalkeith, Lord, 324.
Dallas, Sir George, at Homburg, 317.
Dallas, Theo, 108.
Dalzell, 249, 326.
Darboy, Archbishop of Paris, murdered, 218.
Darmstadt, 282.
Dartmouth, Lady, her ball, 122.
Davenport, Alice, 15 *note*.
Daventry steeplechases, 190, 300; snowstorm at, 344.
De Grey, Lady, 122.
De Grey, Lord, at the meeting of the Rifle Association, 17.
Dee, the, 100; valley, 90.
Deininger, Herr, 283.
Delane, John, Editor of the *Times*, 175, 199; at Chevening, 253; Guisachan, 265.
Demi-monde, Le, performance of, 335.
Denbigh, Lord, 43; his congratulations to Miss Bowater, 172.
Denison, Lady Charlotte, her reception, 219.
Denison, Edward, 194.
Denmark, war with Germany, 74, 76; debate on, in the House of Commons, 85.
Denmark, Princess Alexandra of, her engagement, 40; marriage, 50. *See* Wales, Princess of.
Denmark, Princess Dagmar of, at the Albert Hall, 246; Lansdowne House, 247; Bridgewater House, 248.
Denmark, Prince Harald of, 148 *note*.
Denmark, Princess Helena of, 148 *note*.
Derby, the, races, 133, 301.
Derby, Lady, her reception at the Foreign Office, 258.
Derby, Lord, 122; at the marriage of Princess Helena, 126; criticism on his foreign policy, 320; resignation, 322.
Dhu Loch, 99.
Dieppe, 5.
Dijon, 317.
Dilke, Sir Charles, 228; Under-Secretary for Foreign Affairs, 339.
Disraeli, Rt. Hon. B., his speech on the Reform Bill, 109; at the wedding of Princess Helena, 125; his principles, 135; at Osborne, 145; resignation, 163; speech on Education, 196; his refusal to form a Government, 240; speech on Local Taxation, 243; on Ultramontanism, 252; antagonism to Lowe, 253; his speech on the county franchise, 259; Memoir of Lord George Bentinck, 268; at the Guildhall, 271; his motion to expel strangers from the House of Commons, 255, 277; on the Suez Canal, 296; the Royal Titles Bill, 298; peerage conferred, 304; at Aylesbury, 307; on the Eastern question, 309; the Pigott incident, 315; his career, 325; illness and death, 346; sermon on, 347; his criticism on Sir W. Harcourt, 360; letter to the Duke of Marlborough, 365. *See* Beaconsfield.

INDEX

Dixon, Mr., his speech on the Education Act of 1870, 227.
Dodford, 172.
Dolben, Mrs. Mackworth, 367.
Domestic Economy Congress Meeting, 348.
Don Giovanni, performance of, 57.
Donegall, Lord and Lady, 190.
Donoughmore, Lady, 231.
Donoughmore, Lord, 190.
Dorchester, 278.
Dorchester House, 261.
Dorchester, Lord and Lady, at Orwell Park, 310.
Dover, 32.
Drew, Mr. and Mrs., at Hatfield, 185.
Dropmore, 118.
Drummond, Alice, 108.
Drummond, Miss, at Burghley House, 213.
Drummond, Robert, 112.
Drumouchter, Pass of, 265.
Dryden, Sir Henry, 173.
Duckworth, Mr., at Frogmore, 141.
Dudley, Lady, her appearance, 116, 231, 365; at the opera, 137.
Dudley, Lord, 122.
Dufferin, Lord, 347.
Dugdale, Mrs., her Shakespeare readings, 331, 333.
Dun, Bridge of, 90.
Duncombe, Caroline, bridesmaid to Miss Bowater, 171.
Dundas, Mrs. John, 332.
Dunkeld, 265.
Dunmore, Lady, at the opera, 111.
Dunmore, Lord, 258.
Dunwich, 36, 39, 236.
Dupplin, Lord, 247.
Dyke, Lady Emily, 283.

E——, Mr., his attentions to Miss Bowater, 53, 79; proposal of marriage, 54.
Eastbourne, 146.
Eastern question, 307.
Easton Neston, 298.
Eaton, Mrs., housekeeper at Fawsley, 173.
Edgcote, 342.
Edgcumbe, Lady Ernestine, bridesmaid to Princess Helena, 127.
Edgell, Capt., his account of the siege of Lucknow, 10.
Edgell, Mr, 190.
Edinburgh, Duchess of, her appearance, 260; at Windsor Castle, 313.
Edinburgh, H R.H, Duke of, at Cliveden, 119; at the wedding of Princess Helena, 126; at Sandringham, 223; his marriage, 269. *See* Alfred, Prince.
Education Bill, 188, 214; debates on, 196, 227.
Edwards, Capt., at Windsor Castle, 361.
Elcho, Lady, 18.
Elcho, Lord, President of the Rifle Association, 17; at the Crystal Palace, 17, 18.
Election, General, 255.
Elgin, Lord and Lady, at Windsor Castle, 313.
Elijah, performance of, 205.
Eliot, George, her novels, 42; *Felix Holt*, 125.
Eliot, Lord, 246, 301.
Ellesmere, Lady, 195.
Ellesmere, Lord, 188, 195.
Ellice, Sir Charles and Lady, at Ickworth, 252.
Ellice, Helen, bridesmaid to Miss Bowater, 171.
Ellice, Mrs., 326; her Scottish sketches, 365.
Elphinstone, Sir Howard, 25, 32; at Osborne, 64, 65, 212; Balmoral, 93, 97; at the wedding of Princess Helena, 127; at Windsor Castle, 142; his return from the East, 274.
Elphinstone, Mercer, 20 *note*.
Ely, Lady, 122.
Employment of Women Society, 294, 334.
Enchantress, the yacht, 146
Enfield, Lord, 218.
Epsom races, 301.
Erfurt, fortress of, 151.
Esmarch, Dr. Jean d', 156 *note*.
Esterelles, the, 29.
Eton and Harrow cricket match, 200.
Eugenie, Empress, her flight from Paris, 209.
Eulenburg, Count, 149; at Holland House, 220.
Euston, 268, 349.
Evans, Dr., 209.
Eversley, Mr., 125.
Exeter Hall, meeting at, 46.
Exeter, Lady, at Burghley House, 213, 227.
Exeter, Lord, at Burghley House, 212.
Exhibition galleries, Guards' ball at, 58.
Exhibition, International, 37.
Eyder, the, 74.

INDEX   389

Falbe, Captain de, 38.
Fane, Lady Rose, 38.
Fane, Mr., 112.
Fanshawe, Miss, 12.
Fantees, their characteristics, 259.
Farmer, his cantata *Christ and His Soldiers*, 332.
Farquhar, Lady, her ball, 112.
Farrar, Canon, 332.
Farre, Dr., 68, 190.
Favre, Jules, his interview with Bismarck, 279.
Fawcett, Mr., appointed Postmaster-General, 339.
Fawcett, Prof., 228.
Fawsley, 166, 173, 179, 188, 266, 272, 290, 306, 318, 326, 334, 341; improvements, 181; church services, 183; hurricane, 318; result of the agricultural depression, 336, 341.
Feilding, Lady Mary, 294.
Felagie-Forest, 100; glen of, 93.
Felixstowe, 237.
Fenian outrage, 140.
Fenwick, Jeanie, 58.
Fergusson, Mr., at Hatfield, 185, 186.
Fillongley, 129.
Finch, Colonel, 145.
Finch, Mrs., at Burghley House, 227.
Findhorn, the, 266.
Finedon, G.F.S., branch at, 367.
Firle, 164, 192, 242, 346.
Fisher, the Misses, 5, 13.
Fisheries exhibition, 366.
Fitzclarence, Miss, 330.
Fitzgerald, Lady Otho, 200.
Fitzgerald, Mrs., her return from Alexandria, 354.
Fitzroy, Lord Charles, 217, 297; in charge of Prince Leopold, 31; at Balmoral, 96; Windsor Castle, 113; Cliveden, 118. *See* Grafton.
FitzWilliam, Lady Mary, bridesmaid to Princess Helena, 127.
Flahault, Auguste, Comte de, 20 *note*.
Flahault, Madame de, 20.
Flandres, Comte and Comtesse de, 333.
Fletcher, Colonel, 274.
Forbes, Atholl, 107.
Forbes, Mrs., at Ickworth, 210; death of her father, 210.
Foreign Office, receptions at, 274, 303, 333.
Forres, 265.
Forster, Mr., 366; his character, 214; speech on Education, 228.

Four-in-hand Club, meet of the, 244.
Fox, Marie, her wedding, 233; appearance, 233.
Frampton Court, 278.
France, alleged *Projet de Traité* with Prussia, 203; terms of peace with Germany, 214; result of the elections, 318.
Franchise Bill, 121; the county, 259.
Francis, Colonel, 83.
Franco-German War, 202, 204.
Frankland, Dr., at Hatfield, 185.
Fraser, Sir William, 347.
Frederick the Great, portrait of, 153.
Fréjus, 29.
Fremantle, Hon. Sir Charles, private secretary to Disraeli, 135.
Fremantle, Lady, her concert, 79.
Fremantle, Sophy, at Edgcote, 342.
French plays, 258, 335.
Friendly Societies Bill, 273.
Frogmore, 115, 116, 141.
Froude, J. A., at Hatfield, 185; his views on political economy, 244; member of the Metaphysical Society, 267.
Froude, Mrs., at Hatfield, 185.

G——, Colonel, his attentions to Miss Bowater, 136, 139.
Gage, Harry, 180, 248; at Fawsley, 204, 272; Gayton, 310; succeeds to the title, 316.
Gage, Henry, 164, 172; at Fawsley, 177, 204, 272; his illness and death, 286.
Gage, Sophy, 164, 166, 168; at Fawsley, 177, 204, 272.
Gainsborough, Lady, at Windsor Castle, 313.
Gambetta, *bon mot* of, 356.
Gaol Bill, 82.
Gardiner, Col. and Mrs., 161.
Gardoni, Signor, 21.
Garfield, President, attempt on his life, 348.
Garibaldi, in London, 75.
Garry, the, 265.
Garvagh, Lady, her appearance, 365.
Gathorne-Hardy, Mr., at Burghley House, 226; his refusal to take office under Disraeli, 239.
Gathorne-Hardy, Mrs., 144; at Hatfield, 185, 186; Burghley House, 226.
Gavant Minard, performance of, 258.
Gayton, 310.

Geneva, 220, 317.
George v., King, his birth, 97.
Germany, Augusta Victoria, Empress of, 148 *note*.
Germany, Frederick, Crown Prince of, at Holland House, 220; on the death of Jasmund, 306 *note*; in London, 349; at Marlborough House, 374. See Prussia.
Germany, war with Denmark, 74, 76; annexation of Schleswig-Holstein, 158; war with France, 202, 204; terms of peace, 214; system of education, 284.
Gharb-allt, Falls of, 92.
Ghika, Prince, 353.
Gibson, Milner, at Orwell Park, 237.
Giessen, 147.
Girls' Friendly Society, xii, 287; meetings, 289, 290, 291, 292, 340, 349, 367; constitution drawn up, 292; service at St. Paul's Cathedral, 335; Council, 346, 367.
Girls' Public Day School at Chelsea, 247.
Giuglini, Signor, 21.
Gladstone, Lady, her ball, 58.
Gladstone, Rt. Hon. W. E., his speech on the repeal of the malt tax, 75; on universal suffrage, 77; the Reform Bill, 109; the Irish Church Bill, 165; his opinion of Sir R. Knightley, 182; introduction to Lady Knightley, 189; on the Irish Land Bill, 189; on Education, 196; on the merits of tea, 229; his ignorance of rural life, 238; on the Irish University Bill, 239; character of his electoral address, 255; his resignation, 257, 273; criticisms on, 258, 331, 347, 359; his speech on the Public Worship Bill, 264; his pamphlet *The Vatican Decrees in their Bearing on Civil Allegiance*, 270; on the Bulgarian atrocities, 307; portrait, 331; elected member for Midlothian, 338; his ministry, 339; story of, 359; advice to speakers, 365.
Gladstone, W. H., 331.
Glamis Castle, 208.
Glassalt, the, 96.
Gleichen, Count, 315.
Glen Ferness, 266.
Glen Gelder, 95.
Glen Muick, 93.
Glienike, 154.
Goethe, statue of, at Weimar, 151.

Gold Coast, debate on, 258.
Goldschmidt, Mme, 47, 48; at the wedding of the Prince of Wales, 51; her views on the characteristics of German, American, and Swedish women, 61.
Goldschmidt, Walter, 48.
Goldsmid, Sir Julian and Lady, 330.
Gomshall, 235.
Gordon, Colonel, at Frogmore, 141, 142.
Gordon, Duchess of, story of, 134.
Gordon, Lady Francis, 196, 220, 248; at Fawsley, 190.
Gordon, General, at Balmoral, 90–103.
Gordon, General, 274; his expedition to Khartoum, 374.
Gordon, Mrs., at Balmoral, 91–103; expedition up Ben-na-Biurd, 98; at Windsor Castle, 142.
Gordon - Cumming, Miss, her sketches, 365.
Gore, Col. and Lady Emily, at Guisachan, 265.
Gortschakoff, Prince, his circular on the Treaty of 1856, 209.
Goschen, Rt. Hon. G., 163; his appointment at the Admiralty, 215; elected member for the City, 256.
Gotha, 148.
Goulburn, Dean, his *Personal Religion*, 75, 101; sermon, 197; at the wedding of Julia Cartwright, 342.
Gourramma, Princess, 49.
Grafton, Charles Fitzroy, seventh Duke of, 31. See Fitzroy.
Grafton, Duchess of, 269.
Grafton, Duke of, 188, 349; his illness and death, 353; character, 354.
Graham, Cyril, at Hatfield, 186.
Graham, Mr. and Mrs., at Chevening, 253.
Graney, Fräulein von, 145.
Grant, Sir Francis, 122.
Grant, Sir Hope, 134.
Grant, John, 93.
Grant, Miss, 122, 135.
Granville, Lady, 66.
Granville, Lord, at Osborne, 66; Colonial Secretary, 163; at Fawsley, 257.
Gravelotte, battle at, 205, 305.
Graves, Mr., at Burghley House, 226.
Greece, Ionian Islands, ceded to, 44, 46.

INDEX 391

Greenwood, Mr., 367.
Greg, W. R., member of the Metaphysical Society, 267; *Enigmas of Life*, 315.
Greville, Lord, on Mr. Gladstone's advice to speakers, 365.
Greville Memoirs, 268.
Grey, General Charles, at Osborne, 33; private secretary to Queen Victoria, 52 *note*; at Windsor Castle, 89, 113, 115; at Balmoral, 91-101; recites poetry, 99, 101; at Cliveden, 118.
Grey, Sir George, at Osborne, 66.
Grey, Sybil, 52, 126.
Grimsel Hospice, 220.
Grisi, Mme, 79.
Grosvenor Crescent, sale of, 359.
Grosvenor Gallery, collection of drawings at the, 319.
Grosvenor, Lady Constance, at the opera, 111.
Grosvenor, Lord, his marriage, 260.
Guards, their return from the Crimea, 6; review in Hyde Park, 7.
Guest, Lady Cornelia, 324.
Guest, Montague, at Somerley, 272.
Guildhall, balls at the, 56, 245.
Guisachan, 264, 326.
Günther, Dr. Albert, medical attendant to Prince Leopold, 26; his scientific researches, 26 *note*; at Richmond, 249.
Gurdon, Mr. and Mrs., 58, 161.
Gurdon, Robert, 134, 333.
Gurdon, Willy, 112, 123.

H——, Mr., his attentions to Miss Bowater, 80.
Haag, Carl, 94.
Hall, Sir Benjamin, 8.
Hallé, 232.
Ham House, 248.
Hamilton, Lady Albertha, bridesmaid to Princess Helena, 127.
Hamilton, Lady Emily, at Dalzell, 326; her death, 366.
Hamilton, John, at Dalzell, 250, 326; death of his wife, 366.
Hamilton Palace, 250.
Hampton Court, 78, 300; dance at, 62.
Hanbury, Mr., his resolution on the Gold Coast, 258.
Hanover, Princess Frederica of, at Londonderry House, 349; Claremont, 371.
Happy Land, performance of, 246.

Harberton, Lady, her ball, 131.
Harcourt, Lady, at Windsor Castle, 360.
Harcourt, Mlle d', 149.
Harcourt, Sir William, 303, 347; criticism on, 324, 360; at Windsor Castle, 360.
Hardinge, Mr., 111.
Hardy, Alfred, 330.
Hardy, Thomas, *Far from the Madding Crowd*, 279.
Hare, Augustus, *Memorials of a Quiet Life*, 242; at Fawsley, 368; his stories, 368; description of Fawsley, 368.
Hare, Julius and Marcus, their graves, 242.
Hare, Maria, inscription on her grave, 242.
Harefield Place, 122.
Harris, Lord, 25.
Harrogate, 206.
Harrow School, speech day, 21.
Hartington, Lord, 163, 239; his speech on expelling strangers from the House of Commons, 275, 276; on the Address, 296; on the Eastern question, 309.
Hartshorne, Mr., 329.
Harvey, Mrs., 43.
Hastings, Lady, at the opera, 111.
Hastings, Lord, his marriage, 86.
Hatfield, 185; fête at, 262.
Hatherley, Lord, 249.
Hatherton, Lord and Lady, at Burghley House, 213.
Havel, the, 153.
Hawarden, Lord, at Windsor Castle, 313.
Hawkins, George, 15.
Hay, Sir John, at Burghley House, 226.
Hayward, Mr., 233.
Heathcote, Mr., 130, 198.
Hedsor Park, 120.
Heidelberg, 317.
Helena, H.R.H. Princess, at Osborne, 33, 64; her appearance, 50; development of her character, 53; at Balmoral, 90-103; expedition up Ben-na-Biurd, 98; her engagement, 106; at Windsor Castle, 113; her bust, 115; at Cliveden, 117, 120; marriage, 125-127; bridesmaids, 127. *See* Christian, Princess.
Hellidon, 288.
Helmingham, 238.

INDEX

Helps, Sir A., *Friends in Council*, 66; *Companions of my Solitude*, 75.
Henley, Gertrude, 292.
Henley, Lord, 161.
Henniker, Lady, 263.
Henniker, Lord, 82.
Herbert, Mrs., 356.
Hercules, performance of, 312.
Hertford, Lord, 261, 353.
Hervey, Lord John, at Ickworth, 252.
Hervey, Lady Mary, 128; at Ickworth, 210.
Hesse, Princess Alix of, 283 *note*.
Hesse, Princess Elizabeth of, 146, 283 *note*, 372. See Russia.
Hesse, Ernst Louis, Grand Duke of, 283 *note*.
Hesse, Princess Irene of, 146, 283 *note*. See Prussia.
Hesse, Prince Louis of, at Buckingham Palace, 21; Windsor Castle, 48, 53, 56; joins the Austrian army, 115; his morganatic marriage, 373.
Hesse, Princess Louis of, at Buckingham Palace, 135; her children, 146, 283 *note*; Palace at Darmstadt, 282; her illness and death, 329; publication of her letters, 373. See Alice, Princess.
Hesse, Princess Marie Victoria of, 283 *note*.
Hesse, Princess Victoria of, 146, 283 *note*, 373. See Battenberg
Hewett, James, his marriage, 136.
Hibbert, Mrs., 111.
Higgins, Matthew James, 122 *note*.
Highclere Castle, 251.
Hildegarde, Countess, at Homburg, 317.
Hildyard, Miss, 53.
Hill, Lady Alice, 135.
Hodgson, Miss, her marriage, 136.
Hohenlohe, Princess, at Osborne, 64, 69; at Gotha, 148.
Holford, Mr. and Mrs., at Highclere Castle, 251.
Holford, Miss, at Highclere Castle, 251, 252.
Holland House, 199, 200, 202, 220, 234, 315, 356; the garden, 199.
Holland, Lady, 198, 252.
Holland, Canon Scott, 342.
Holmbury, 235.
Holthouse, Mr., Rural Dean, 288; his distrust of Lord Beaconsfield, 320.
Holzendorff, Herr von, 150.
Holzmann, Dr., at Osborne, 64, 68.

Homburg, 281, 303, 316, 336, 356; the Schloss, 282.
Honeywood, William, 302.
Hood, Lady Mary, 127.
Hotham, Lord, 189.
Hough, Mr., 16; his opinion of Kingsley and Spurgeon, 16.
Houghton, Lord, 187.
Howard, Mr., 104.
Howth Castle, 313.
Hubbard, Miss, her "Perseverance Bands" scheme, 331.
Hudson's Bay territory, native Indians of the, 186.
Hughes, Mr. and Miss, at Guisachan, 265.
Huguenots, The, performance of, 110.
Humboldt, Wilhelm von, his opinion of old letters, 40.
Hunt, Ward, at Burghley House, 226; his death, 317.
Huntingfield, Lady, 22.
Hurstmonceaux, 242.
Hyacinthe, Père, his oration on reform in the Latin Church, 302.

Ickworth, 210, 252.
Ightham Mote, 201.
Ilchester, Lady, her appearance, 231.
Imperial, Prince, at Wakefield Lodge, 321; his death, 334.
Indian troops moved to Malta, debate on, in Parliament, 323.
Inkermann, anniversary of, 269.
Inselberg, 151.
Interlaken, 220.
Invercauld, 101; bridge of, 91.
Invergarry, 326.
Ionian Islands, ceded to Greece, 44, 46.
Ireland, condition of, 343.
Irish Church Bill, 165.
Irish Land Bill, 189, 340, 341, 348.
Irish University Bill, 239.
Ixelheim, Countess, 282.

Jackson, Dr., Bishop of London, story of, 264.
James, Sir Henry, 347.
Jameson, Mrs., her opinion of old letters, 40.
Jasmund, Herr von, 306.
Jenner, Dr., at Windsor Castle, 113.
Jerningham, Sir Hubert, 124; his career, 124 *note*.
Jersey, Lady, 367; at Osterley Park, 261.
Jersey, Lord, at Osterley Park, 261.

INDEX 393

Jeune, Rt. Hon. Sir F., at Harrow, 22. *See* St. Helier.
Jeune, Mrs., 364; her reception, 367.
Jew Bill of 1848, 174.
Jungfrau, 220.

Kalckreuth, Count, 149, 151.
Kalckreuth, Countess Anne, 149, 151.
Kean, Mr. and Mrs., 8.
Keane, Captain, 23.
Keble, Rev. John, criticisms on his *Christian Year*, 16.
Keele, 326; the library and gardens, 326.
Keen, Mount, 102.
Kenlies, Lord, 135.
Kennaway, Sir John and Lady, 284.
Kent, Duchess of, 4; her death, 19.
Kerr, Miss, 33.
Killiecrankie, Pass of, 265.
Kingsley, Rev. Charles, criticisms on, 16; at Cliveden, 119; his sermon, 119.
Kirkcaldy, Lord, 45, 47, 51.
Knatchbull-Hugessen, Edward, at Homburg, 304; Gayton, 310.
Knightley, Sir Charles, 178; his life at Fawsley, 179; method of canvassing, 180; death, 181.
Knightley, Charlie, 251.
Knightley, Edmund, 352.
Knightley, Harry, 251.
Knightley, Louisa, Lady, her wedding, 171-173; arrival at Fawsley, 173; letter and present from Queen Victoria, 174; interest in cottage improvements, 175, 183; at Arbury, 176, 205; happiness in her married life, 177; her interest in politics, xiii, 178, 374; influence on her neighbours, 183; improvement of the church services, 184; at Hatfield, 185-187, 262; her life at Fawsley, 188, 209, 241, 266, 272, 318, 326, 334, 341; introduction to Mr. Gladstone, 189; friendship with Dr. Magee, 191, 267; at Firle, 192, 242, 346; houses in London, 192-194, 215, 228, 243, 257; taken over the House of Lords, 193; affection for her husband, 194; at Castle Ashby, 194; her dinner-parties, 195, 231, 235, 245, 248, 260, 339; at the House of Commons, 196, 227, 275, 277, 315, 324, 363; at Windsor Castle, 197, 313, 360; Holland House, 199, 200, 202, 220, 234; Knole Park, 200-202; Harrogate, 206-208; Lindertis, 208; her meeting with Mr. Motley, 209, 248; at Ickworth, 210, 252; her friendship with Lord Stanhope, 211; at Osborne, 211; Burgbley House, 212, 226; at the National Portrait Gallery, 215; attends a Drawing-room, 216, 231, 301, 353; her dream, 217; attends Mass, 218; at the Tichborne trial, 219; tour in Switzerland, 220; at Paris, 221, 285; her anxiety on the illness of the Prince of Wales, 223; at the thanksgiving service, 224; at Buckingham Palace, 228; her conversation with Lord Salisbury, 231; at Bridgewater House, 232, 248; attends the wedding of Prince Lichtenstein, 233; at Holmbury, 235; entertains Prince Arthur, 235; at Dunwich, 236; Sotterley, 236, 319; Buxton, 236; Orwell Park, 237, 310; her impressions of the Shah of Persia, 245; at the Albert Hall, 246; Dalzell, 250; Highclere Castle, 251; Chevening, 253; at Grosvenor Crescent, 257, 274; at the French pla , 258; meeting with Sir G. Wolseley, 259; impressions of Disraeli, 260; at Osterley Park, 261; Althorp, 264; tour in Scotland, 264-266, 326; at Guisachan, 264, 326; Euston, 268, 349; Crichel, 271; Somerley, 271; Richmond Park, 274, 308; Oxford, 278; Frampton Court, 278; Homburg, 281-284, 303, 316, 336, 356; Darmstadt, 282; Wildbad, 284; member of the Girls' Friendly Society, 287; her interest in the work, 287-293, 358, 367; speech at Northampton, 291; characteristics, xix, 293, 294; loyalty, 293; interest in the Working Ladies' Guild, 293; and other philanthropic works, xii, 294; presented to the King and Queen of Naples, 297; at the Derby, 301; Metz, 304; Gravelotte, 305; impressions of Reims Cathedral, 306; interest in the Eastern question, 307; at Raby Castle, 308; Winmarleigh, 309; her conversation with Mr. Venables,

314; meeting with Col. B——, 316; at Wakefield Lodge, 321; meeting with Prince Imperial, 321; at the House of Lords, 323; at the reopening of Woodford church, 327–329; attends ambulance lectures, 331; presented to the Duchess of Connaught, 336; sale of her house in town, 337, 359; interest in farming, 337, 349; entertains Princess Christian, 339, 348, 373; at Edgcote, 342; meeting with Sir R. Temple, 348; honorary lady-in-waiting to the Duchess of Albany, xvi, 349; at the wedding of the Duke of Albany, 351; at Claremont, 355, 359, 369–371, 372; Brussels, 357; expedition to Waterloo, 357; at the christening of Princess Alice of Albany, 361; at Carlton House Terrace, 363; Finedon, 367; her grief at the death of the Duke of Albany, 372, 374; friendship with the Duchess of Albany, 374; illness and death of her husband, 374; her death, 375; tribute to her memory, 375.

Knightley, Sir Rainald, his first meeting with Miss Bowater, 164; engagement, 167; presents, 169; wedding, 171; arrival at Fawsley, 173; refuses the Under-Secretaryship of Foreign Affairs, 174; member for South Northamptonshire, 178, 255, 256, 338; his parents, 179; character, 181; appearance, 181; abilities, 182; devotion to Lord Salisbury, 182; distrust of Disraeli, 182, 240; at Hatfield, 185; his affection for his wife, 194; at Knole Park, 200–202; Osborne, 211; on the Ballot Bill, 232, 234; at Chevening, 253; his conversation with Dr. Smith, 253; electoral address, 256; decision on the debate on the Gold Coast, 258; declines an invitation from Disraeli, 258; his political views, 269; his speech on expelling strangers from the House of Commons, 277; attacks of gout, 281; at Homburg, 281; abstains from voting on the Royal Titles Bill, 298–300; his speech at Brackley, 307; views on the Eastern question, 312; at Windsor Castle, 313; views on the Pigott incident, 315, 316; losses from agricultural depression, 336, 341; criticism on Gladstone, 347; peerage conferred, 374; illness and death, 374.

Knightley, Sir Richard, 178.
Knightley, Selina Hervey, 179.
Knightley, Sophy, 179. *See* Gage.
Knightley, Rev. Valentine, 172; at Fawsley, 179.
Knightleys, history of, 177.
Knole Park, 200.
Königstein, 317.
Kranichstein, 282, 329.
Krogh, Fräulein von, 159.

Ladies' Dress Association Committee, 336.
Ladies' Guild Exhibition, 365.
Ladies' Sanitary Association, 294.
Lambeth Palace, G.F.S. meeting at, 292.
Lamington, 250, 264, 367.
Lane, Louisa, 15; her portrait, 15 *note*.
Lane, Thomas, portrait of, 15 *note*.
Langton, Bennett, 12.
Langton, Miss, 12.
Lansdowne House, ball at, 247.
Lansdowne, Lord, appointed Governor of Canada, 364.
Lascelles, Gerald, 233.
Lascelles, Miss, at Windsor Castle, 89; her marriage, 96.
Lascelles, Mr., 153.
Law Courts, opening of the, 359.
Lawley, Lady Constance, 245.
Lawson, Sir Wilfrid, on withdrawal from the Gold Coast, 258; on the bombardment of Alexandria, 354.
Layard, Mr., 74.
Leamington, 89, 103; concert at, 43.
Lecky, Mr., 217.
Leconfield, Lady, 219.
Leigh, Boughton, 128.
Leiningen, Prince, 64.
Leiningen, Princess of, at the marriage of Princess Helena, 126.
Lennox, Lady Caroline Gordon, bridesmaid to Princess Helena, 127.
Lennox, Constance, 45.
Lennox, Lord Henry, 304; at Crichel, 271.
Lentz, Agnes, governess to Miss Bowater, 4; her visit to Lady Knightley, 197.
Leopold, H.R.H. Prince, ordered abroad, 23; his journey to

INDEX

Cannes, 26-29; death of his father, 30; return home, 32; accident, 40; at Windsor Castle, 49, 114, 313; Osborne, 64, 146, 211; his tutor, 69; at Cliveden, 117; attack of faintness, 120; at the wedding of Princess Helena, 126; his delicate appearance, 142; Confirmation, 163; illness, 198; development, 212; at the thanksgiving service, 225; at Buckingham Palace, 229; Oxford, 278; engagement, 349; wedding, 351. *See* Albany.
Leven, Lady, 47, 49, 234, 246.
Leven, Lord, 45, 47, 266, 274, 346.
Leveson-Gower, Mr., at Holmbury, 235.
Lichtenstein, Prince Louis of, 201; his wedding, 233; appearance, 233.
Liddell, Alice, 278.
Liddell, Colonel, declines offer of Thatched House Lodge, 2, 36; at Windsor Castle, 113.
Liddon, Canon, his sermons, 198, 295.
Lind, Jenny, 47. *See* Goldschmidt.
Lindertis, 208, 326, 343, 367.
Lindsay, Mrs. Loyd, 232.
Linley, Miss, portrait of, 238.
Linn of Dee, 92.
Listowel, Lady, 167, 247.
Listowel, Lord, 167.
Lochnagar, 91, 93, 97, 102.
Loftus, Lord Augustus, British Minister at Berlin, 152, 153.
Lohe, Baron, at Homburg, 317.
Lohengrin, performance of, 280.
Lohgau, Count, 158.
Lohlein, valet to Prince Albert, 117.
Londesborough Lodge, drains of, 223.
London, financial panic, 111.
London dwellings, Bill for the improvement of, 273.
Longleat, 176.
Lords, House of, 193; attendance of Peers, 267.
Lorne, Lord, his marriage, 208; at Claremont, 371.
Louise, H.R.H. Princess, at Osborne, 33, 64, 68, 69, 211; Balmoral, 93; Windsor Castle, 114, 142; Cliveden, 117, 120; at the wedding of Princess Helena, 126; Buckingham Palace, 135; her marriage, 208; at Sandringham, 223; her reception, 233; at Claremont, 371, 373.

Lowe, Mr., his speech on the Reform Bill, 109; Chancellor of the Exchequer, 163; his criticism of Mr. Disraeli's speech, 187; reception of the King of the Belgians, 230; political views, 230; antagonism to Disraeli, 253; on the fall of the Cabinet 258.
Lowell, Mr. and Lady Rose, at Somerley, 272.
Lowther Lodge, 363.
Lowther, Mr. and Mrs., 248.
Lucan, Lord, 8.
Lucerne, 220.
Lucknow, siege of, 10.
Lumley, Lady Sybil, her marriage, 260.
Lunden, Baron, 230.
Lyons, 32.
Lyttelton, Hon. Lucy, at Osborne, 68; her characteristics, 69; marriage, 76. *See* Cavendish.
Lytton, Lord, 219.
Lytton, Sir Edward Bulwer, his speech on the Reform Bill, 109.
Lyveden, Lord and Lady, at Harrogate, 207.

Macclesfield, Lady, 68; at Windsor Castle, 116.
Macdonald, Colonel, at Euston, 268.
Macdonald, Miss, at Windsor Castle, 25, 113; Cliveden, 117.
MacGregor, Sir Malcolm, 62.
MacGregor, Miss, at Osborne, 212.
Mackenzie, Sir Kenneth, 104.
Mackenzie, Mrs. Stewart, 3.
Mackenzie, Susan Mary, 22 *note*.
Macleod, Dr., at Balmoral, 99; his sermon, 100.
MacMahon, Marshal, his defeat at Weissenburg, 204; at Sedan, 206.
Macnamara, Lady Sophia, 373.
Macon, 32.
Maffei, Count, 161.
Magdeburg, Lieut. von, 154.
Magee, Dr., Bishop of Peterborough, 183; his speech on the Irish Church Bill, 165; criticism on his speech, 187; his address at Brackley, 188; at Fawsley, 191, 266, 327, 329; friendship with Lady Knightley, 191; at Burghley House, 213; on the proposed alterations in the Rubric, 266; his stories, 267, 358; at the G.F.S. meeting at Northampton, 291; his sermon

INDEX

at the reopening of Woodford church, 327; his collection of autographs, 340; visitation at Daventry, 358.
Magee, Mrs., at Burghley House, 213; Fawsley, 266; her interest in the G.F.S., 331, 340.
Mahon, Lord and Lady, at Chevening, 253.
Mahon, Pakenham, at Burghley House, 213.
Maine, Sir Henry, Professor of Jurisprudence, 278.
Mainwaring, Bella, her engagement, 107; wedding, 108. *See* Milman.
Malcolm, Miss, at Homburg, 317.
Malet, Sir Edward, his illness, 355.
Malt tax, debate on the repeal of the, 75.
Manchester, Duchess of, her appearance, 78; at the opera, 111.
Manners, Lady, 236, 260.
Manners, Lord, 260.
Manners, Lord and Lady John, at Burghley House, 226.
Manners, Mr., at Ickworth, 252.
Manning, Archbishop, his address at the marriage of Prince Lichtenstein, 233; member of the Metaphysical Society, 267.
Mar Lodge, 97.
Marburg, 147.
Mario, 87.
Marjoribanks, Sir Dudley, 198, 264, 326.
Marjoribanks, Lady Fanny, at Affric, 265.
Marjoribanks, Hon. Mary, 15 *note*.
Marlborough, Duchess of, at Frogmore, 143; at Burghley House, 226.
Marlborough, Duke of, 74; at Burghley House, 226.
Marlborough House, garden-parties at, 314, 355, 374.
Marseilles, 32.
Mars-la-Tour, battle of, 305.
"Martin Marprelate" tracts, issue of, 178.
Mary, Queen, her visit to Fawsley, xvi.
Mary Queen of Scots, miniature of, 313.
Masaniello, performance of, 137.
Massey, Lady, 288.
Maude, Miss, at the wedding of Princess Helena, 125.
Maude, Mrs., 300.
Maurice, Mrs. Frederick, her grave, 242.

Mecklenburg, Grand Duchess of, at Wimbledon, 138.
Mecklenburg, Grand Duke of, at Homburg, 304.
Melville, Lady Anna, 49.
Melville, Lady Emily, 49.
Melville, Lady Florence, 47.
Melville, Lady Julia, her marriage, 163.
Melville, the Hon. Ronald, 112.
Melville, Sophy, 47, 49, 108, 266; at Fawsley, 190.
Menabrea, Mme, at Windsor Castle, 360.
Merchant Shipping Bill, abandonment of the, 281.
Mérimée, prosper, his *Letters*, 270.
Metaphysical Society, meetings, 267; members, 267.
Metz, 304.
Mexico, Maximilian, Emperor of, deposed and executed, 135.
Meynell, Mrs. Hugo, 111.
Meynell-Ingram, Hugo, 111.
Miall, Mr., his proposed disestablishment of the Church of England, 216.
Midleton, Lord, at Edgcote, 342.
Mikkelsen, Herr, 158.
Mill, J. S., Autobiography of, 254; causes of his quarrel with Mr. Roebuck, 314.
Milman, Bella, birth of a son, 131.
Milman, General, his engagement, 107; wedding, 108.
Minchin, Mr., 328.
M'Neill, Sir John, at Windsor Castle, 360.
Molesworth, Lady, her dinner-party, 219; reception, 366.
Monck, Arthur, 112.
Monk, Mrs., her concert, 57.
Montgomerie, Tina, at Astley Castle, 44; Arbury, 128; bridesmaid to Miss Bowater, 171.
Montgomery, Mabel, 292.
Montpensier, Duke of, 7.
Montrose, Duchess of, at Knole Park, 201; Homburg, 282.
Montrose, Duke of, at Homburg, 282.
Moray Firth, 266.
Mordaunt, Sir Charles, 84, 112, 123, 324.
Mordaunt, Lady, 82; her ball, 83.
Moreton, Mrs., at the christening of Princess Alice of Albany, 361.
Morier, Mr., at Highclere Castle, 251.
Morris, Mr., Solicitor-General for Ireland, anecdote of, 226.

INDEX

Mostyn, Miss, at Gayton, 310.
Motley, Mr., 244 ; his meeting with Lady Knightley, 209 ; style of his conversation, 248 ; death, 314.
Mulck, Loch, 96, 99.
Müller, Prof. Max, his lecture on the "Origin of Language," 64.
Mundella, Mr., President of the Council, 339.
Munro, Sir Thomas, 164, 248, 326 ; at the wedding of Louisa Bowater, 172 ; at Fawsley, 177, 179, 204, 345 ; his illness, 272.
Murchison, Sir Roderick, 187.
Murray, Lady Alexandrina, bridesmaid to Princess Helena, 127.
Murray, John, at Hatfield, 185, 186 ; his opinion on publishing the Maintenon letters, 197.
Muskerry, Lord, 77.
Musurus, Madame, at the opera, 137 ; death, 137 *note*.
Musurus Pacha, 312.

Nahe, valley of, 304.
Napier, Sir Charles, 7.
Napier, Miss, 135.
Naples, King of, his appearance, 297 ; at Gayton, 310.
Naples, Queen of, 297.
Napoleon III., Emperor, his surrender, 206.
Napoule, 32.
National Gallery, pictures, 330.
National Portrait Gallery, 215.
Nemours, Duke of, 7.
Neruda, Mm Norman, 233.
Netherlands, King and Queen of the, at Windsor Castle, 351.
Nevill, Lady Dorothy, 367 ; at Highclere Castle, 251.
Newdegate, Charles, his home at Arbury, 42 ; parliamentary career, 55 ; on the Schleswig-Holstein question, 74 ; on the Borough Franchise, 76 ; his political views, 83 ; character, 83 ; his views on Roman Catholics and Jesuits, 124, 129 ; at Fawsley, 167 ; at the wedding of Louisa Bowater, 172 ; at Astley, 205 ; Richmond, 333.
Newdegate, Mrs., 55 ; her friendship with Louisa Bowater, 73 ; at the opera, 110 ; her death, 140.
Newnham, 172.
Newton, Sir Isaac, his birthplace, 106.
Newton, Mr., at Guisachan, 265.
Nilsson, Mlle, 200, 203.

Noel, Roden, member of the Metaphysical Society, 267.
Norèle, Mlle, at Balmoral, 96 ; Claremont, 373.
Normanton, Lady, at Somerley, 271.
Northampton, races, 191, 299, 323 ; new cattle market opened, 247 ; Agricultural Show, 264 ; meeting of the G.F.S., 291 ; election, 338.
Northampton, Lord, at Castle Ashby, 194 ; his drawings, 195.
Northcote, Sir Stafford, at Burghley House 213 ; his Friendly Societies Bill, 273 ; on the Bulgarian atrocities, 307 ; at Windsor Castle, 313 ; his ghost stories, 313 ; use of the phonograph, 324 ; his conversation with Lady Knightley, 346.
Northumberland House, ball at, 235.
Norton, Lady, her concert, 332.
Norton, Mr, 122.
Norton, Mrs., 208, 217.
Nugent, Nina, bridesmaid to Miss Bowater, 172.

Observer, article in, 206.
O'Grady, Annabel, 108.
Olliffe, Sir Joseph, 153.
Omnium, Jacob, 122.
Oppenheim, Mr., his concert, 333.
Ormonde, Lady, her appearance, 301 ; at Windsor Castle, 313.
Ormonde, Lord, at Windsor Castle, 313.
Orwell Park, 237, 310.
Osborn, Sir George, at Fawsley, 167.
Osborne, 32, 64, 145, 211 ; Privy Council at, 66.
Osborne, Lady Emma, her return from Russia, 362.
Osborne, Lady William, 231, 248, 326.
Osborne, Lord William, 190, 198, 231, 248.
Ostend, 147.
Osterley Park, 261.
Ouchy, 317.
Ouse, the, 161.
Overend and Gurney, their failure 111.
Owen, Prof. and Mrs., 42.
Oxenham, Miss, 290.
Oxford, 89, 103, 251, 278.
Oxford, Bishop of, 122.

Packe, Nina, 198.
Packe, Mrs., her ball, 123.

INDEX

Paget, Lord Alfred, 125; at Osborne, 212.
Paget, Lord Ernest, 7.
Paget, Lady Florence, her marriage, 86.
Paget, Miss, at Windsor Castle, 360.
Pakington, Sir John, at Burghley House, 226.
Palk, Sir Lawrence, at Burghley House, 213.
Palmer, Sir Roundell, 187.
Palmerston, Lady, 8.
Palmerston, Lord, 8; defeat of his "Conspiracy and Murder" Bill, 10; his resignation, 10.
Panmure, Lord, 7.
Paris, 5, 26, 32, 285; measures for the defence, 205; siege, 209; capitulation, 214; condition, 217, 218; result of the destruction, 221.
Parker, Cecil, 139
Parliament, dissolution of, 255, 337.
Patti, Adelina, 21, 332.
Patti, Carlotta, 57.
Paynter, Major, 58, 59.
Peace Preservation Bill, 275.
Peel, Lady Alice, 162.
Peel, Lady Emily, 122.
Peel, Sir Frederick, 333.
Peel, General, 42; at the wedding of Princess Helena, 126, 127.
Peel, Sir Robert, 122.
Pembroke, Lady, 367.
Pembroke Lodge, 38, 42.
Pennant, George, at Wakefield Lodge, 321.
Pennant, Lady Louisa, her ball, 104.
Pennant, Miss, at Burghley House, 213.
Pennington, Mr, 123.
Penrhyn, Lady, at Burghley House, 213; her ball, 236; on the character of the Duke of Grafton, 353.
Penzance, Lord and Lady, at Ickworth, 252.
Peper Harow, 14.
Perceval, Captain, 373.
Percy, Lord, at Hatfield, 185.
Persia, Shah of, in London, 244; at the Albert Hall, 246.
Persigny, M. de, 27.
Perth, 90, 102.
Peterborough, number of G.F.S. branches started, 291.
Peterborough, the Palace, 340, 349.
Peyronnet, Mlle de la, at Holmbury, 235.
Phipps, Sir Charles, 24; at Osborne, 64.

Phipps, Lady Laura, bridesmaid to Princess Helena, 127.
Phipps, Miss, at Osborne, 64.
Phipps, Pickering, chosen member for South Northampton, 346.
Phonograph, invention of the, 324.
Pigott, Mr., debate in Parliament on his appointment of Comptroller of the Stationery Office, 315, 316.
Pius IX., Pope, his death, 321.
Plat, Colonel Du, 56.
Playfair, Dr. Lyon, 228.
Plevna, fall of, 319.
Plimsoll, Mr., 262; on the abandonment of the Merchant Shipping Bill, 281.
Plunkett, Mr., 153.
Political Economy, lecture on, 247.
Ponsonby, Colonel, at Osborne, 65, 68, 212; Windsor Castle, 89; Balmoral, 91–96; his "Rhyme of Lochnagar," 96; leaves Balmoral, 96.
Ponsonby, Lady Emily, her verses, 71.
Ponsonby, Mrs., at Osborne, 69.
Poore, Dr., at Osborne, 212.
Portal, Miss, her lecture on Political Economy, 247.
Portsmouth, Lady, 251.
Potsdam, 153.
Powerscourt, Lord and Lady, at Burghley House, 213.
Preston, meet at, 320.
Primkenau Schloss, 155–159.
Primrose League, foundation of the, xiii, 374.
Primrose, Mr., 201.
Prince's, roller skating at, 262.
Princess Theatre, fire at, 8.
Prothero, Canon, at Osborne, 146.
Prussia, alleged *Projet de Traité* with France, 203.
Prussia, Alexandra, Princess Augustus of, 148 *note*.
Prussia, Prince Augustus of, 148 *note*.
Prussia, Crown Prince Frederick of, his appearance, 7, 154; marriage, 10; at Windsor Castle, 47; in command in Silesia, 115; at Rheinhardtsbrunnen, 148; at Berlin, 152; Potsdam, 154. *See* Germany.
Prussia, Crown Princess Frederick of, at Windsor Castle, 47; Rheinhardtsbrunnen, 148; Potsdam, 154; her appearance, 154.
Prussia, Prince Henry of, 146 *note*, 283 *note*.

INDEX

Prussia, Princess Henry of, 146 *note*, 283 *note*.
Public Worship Bill, 260, 262, 263.
Punch, parody in, 67 *note*.
Purvis, Colonel Home, 115.

Queensberry, Lord and Lady, 122.

R——, Mr., his attentions to Miss Bowater, 79.
R——, Sir J., his proposal of marriage to Miss Bowater, 63.
Raby Castle, 308
Raglan, Lord, at Burghley House, 213.
Railways, State-control of, 227.
Ramsden, Mr. and Lady Harriet, 123.
Ranfurly, Lord, at Burghley House, 213.
Ranzow, Count, 159.
Reading, 251.
Reay, Lord, 346.
Redesdale, Lord, 237.
Redistribution Bill, 112.
Reform Bill, debates on the, 109; third reading passed, 137.
Regina, memorial to Lady Knightley, 375.
Reims Cathedral, 306.
Rendlesham, Lord, 19.
Reserve forces called out, 322.
Reventlow, Countess, 149.
Reydon Hall, 13.
Rheinhardtsbrunnen, 148, 151.
Rhine, the, 147.
Rhodes, Mr., 297.
Rhodes, Mrs., her dance, 297.
Ricardo, Mr. and Mrs., 14.
Richards, Mr., his speech on Education, 228.
Richmond Park, 36, 274, 300.
Ridley, Charles, 8, 15.
Ridley, Edward, 15; at Harrow, 22; Oxford, 278.
Ridley, George, on household suffrage, 133.
Ridley, Harriet, 15.
Ridley, Laura, Lady, 15, 62; her death, 87.
Ridley, Mary, at Guisachan, 265.
Ridley, Sir Matthew, 15; his sons, 15.
Ridley, Matthew, 15, 88, 231; at Harrow, 22; his clever opinions, 112; at Osterley Park, 261; Guisachan, 264; his speech on the Address, 296.
Rifle Association, National, first meeting at Wimbledon, 17.
Righi, the, 159.

Ristori, Mme, her acting, 354.
Roberts, Lady, 346.
Roberts, Lord, his march from Cabul, 342.
Robertson, Dr., at Windsor Castle, 144.
Robertson, General, his marriage, 163.
Roebuck, Mr., cause of his quarrel with J S. Mill, 314.
Roehampton, 234, 246, 274.
Rokeby, Lord, 32.
Rosebery, Lord, his opinion of Lady Knightley, xiv.
Ross, Sir William, 217.
Rothschild, Baron Ferdinand, 239.
Rothschild, Leopold, 200, 232.
Rouen, 5.
Roumania, Queen of, her poems, 355.
Rowley, Captain, 128.
Rowley, Susan, bridesmaid to Miss Bowater, 171.
Rowsell, Mr., 142.
Roxburghe, Duchess of, at the christening of Princess Alice of Albany, 361.
Royal Academy, 111, 133, 331.
Royal, H.R.H. Victoria, Princess, 7; her marriage, 9. *See* Prussia.
Royal Titles Bill, 298.
Royston, Lord and Lady, at the opera, 111.
Rubric, proposed alterations in the, 266.
Ruffano, Prince, 299.
Rushton, 367.
Russell, Lord Arthur, at Holmbury, 235.
Russell, Sir Charles, member for Westminster, 256; at Homburg, 304.
Russell, Lady, 274.
Russell, Lord, 274; his interest in the Colonies, 274.
Russell, Lord Odo, his *mot* on the Shah of Persia, 245.
Russia, Alexander, Czar of, murdered, 270 *note*.
Russia, Alix, Empress of, 283 *note*.
Russia, Anna, Grand Duchess of, miniature of 313.
Russia, Grand Duchess Sergius of, 146 *note*, 283 *note*.
Russia, Grand Duke Sergius of, 146 *note*, 283 *note*.
Russia, Nicholas II, Czar of, 283 *note*.
Russia, proposal to occupy Bulgaria, 308, 309; war declared

against Turkey, 312 ; advance on Constantinople, 321.
Ruthven, Lord and Lady, at Ickworth, 252.
Ruthven, Mr., 49.
Rutland, Duke of, 219.

Saarbrück, victory at, 204.
Sahl, Mr., at Windsor Castle, 89, 351 ; Frogmore, 141 ; Cologne, 147.
Salisbury, Lady, 231 ; her receptions, 259, 332 ; at Constantinople, 311.
Salisbury, Lord, entertains a party at Hatfield, 185 ; on the state of religion, 186 ; his conversation with Lady Knightley, 231 ; joins the Conservative Ministry, 257 ; Plenipotentiary to the Conference at Constantinople, 309 ; Minister for Foreign Affairs, 323 ; his patriotism, 325 ; his speech on Ireland, 343 ; criticism on Gladstone, 359.
San Stefano, Treaty of, 323.
Sand, George, 335.
Sandringham, 223.
Sandwich Islands, King of the, 349.
Santley, Mr., 21.
Savaria, General, 13.
Saxe-Coburg, Charles Edward, Duke of, 148 note.
Saxe-Coburg, Duke of, 115.
Saxe-Coburg, Princess Dorothea of, 148 note.
Saxe-Coburg, Victoria, Duchess of, 148 note.
Saxe-Coburg, Princess Victoria of, 283 note
Saxe-Meiningen, Princess Charlotte of, birth of a child, 333.
Say, Léon, his criticism on Mr. Gladstone, 331.
Scharf, Mr., keeper of the National Portrait Gallery, 216.
Schiller, statue of, at Weimar, 151.
Schleswig-Holstein question, 74, 125 ; annexation of, 158.
Schleswig-Holstein, Duke of, 155 ; his death. 162.
Schleswig-Holstein, Prince Christian of, his engagement, 106. See Christian.
Schleswig-Holstein, Princess Amelia of, 156, 303.
Schleswig-Holstein, Princess Augusta of, 156.
Schleswig-Holstein, Princess Henriette of, 156.
Schleswig - Holstein - Glüchsburg, Duchess of, her daughters, 148 note.
Schleswig - Holstein - Glüchsburg, Frederick, Duke of, 148 note.
Schreiber, Lady Charlotte, her collection of china, 263.
Schwalbach, 220.
Scott, General, at Highclere Castle, 251
Scott, Lady Margaret, bridesmaid to Princess Helena, 127.
Scott, Sir Walter, his lines on Cadzow Castle, 250.
Scutari, 321.
Sebright, Sir John and Lady, 248.
Seckendorf, Count, 149 ; at Windsor Castle, 351.
Sedan, battle of, 206 ; anniversary, 357.
Sefton, Lord, 236.
Selborne, Lady, at Windsor Castle, 360.
Selborne, Lord, on the Public Worship Bill, 263 ; on moving the Indian troops to Malta, 323 ; his opinion of *John Inglesant*, 353 ; at Windsor Castle, 360.
Senneau, Marquis de, 3.
Sevenoaks, 200.
Seymour, Captain, 54.
Seymour, Colonel Lee, at Burghley House. 213.
Seymour, General, 48.
Seymour, Lady Constance, 236 note.
Seymour, Miss, 18, 126.
Shaftesbury, Lord, at the meeting of the Employment of Women Association, 334.
Shaw Stewart, Sir Michael, 332.
Sherborne, Lady, 134.
Sheridan, Mr., at Frampton Court, 279.
Shuckburgh, 369 ; meet at, 190.
Siddons, Mrs. Scott, 131.
Sieveking, Dr , 67.
Skelmersdale, Lord, 144.
Sligo, Lord, 196.
Sluggan, the, 97.
Smith, Emily, 78.
Smith, Lady, her critique of Queen Victoria's book, 141.
Smith, Martin, 14, 171.
Smith, Dr. William, editor of the *Quarterly Review*, at Chevening, 253 ; his conversation with Sir R. Knightley, 253 ; article on Grote, 254.
Smith, Rt. Hon. W. H., his resolution on Local Taxation, 243 ; member for Westminster, 256.

INDEX 401

Smollett, Mr., his attack on Gladstone, 258.
Sneyd, Mr., 326.
Snow, Mrs., at Claremont, 369, 370.
Somerley, 271.
Somerset, Duke of, at Orwell Park, 237; his criticism of Gladstone, 258; story of Carlyle, 348.
Sonderburg, ruin of, 78.
Sorcerer, The, performance of, 319.
Soria, his singing, 367.
Sotterley, 2, 9, 23, 39, 128, 139–141, 161, 319.
South Kensington Museum, 333; reception at, 77, 349.
Southampton, Lord, his funeral, 236.
Spencer, Robert, 338.
Spencer, Lady, 18, 49.
Spencer, Lord, 350; Chairman of the National Rifle Association, 138.
Spiers, Mrs., 45.
Spurgeon, Rev. C., character of his preaching, 16.
St. Helier, Lord, 22 *note*. *See* Jeune.
St. Paul, Nina, 301.
St. Paul's Cathedral, thanksgiving service at, 224.
St. Privat, 305.
Stafford, 89.
Stallingborough, 3.
Stamford, 212, 227.
Stanhope, Mr. and Mrs. Edward, 216.
Stanhope, Lady Frederica, monument of, 253.
Stanhope, James Banks, 216, 253.
Stanhope, Lady, 231; her dinner-party, 244.
Stanhope, Lord, 231; his friendship with Lady Knightley, 211; at the National Portrait Gallery, 215; his reception, 217; dinner-party, 219; collection of autographs, 253.
Stanhope, Hon. Philip, at Chevening, 254.
Stanley, Lady Augusta, 125; at Osborne, 145.
Stanley, Dean, 187; his sermon on Disraeli, 347.
Stanley, Colonel and Mrs. John, at Chevening, 253.
Stanley, Miss, 25.
Stanley, Mr., at Euston, 268.
Stewart, Mrs. Duncan, 366; her career, 366; *Recollections*, 367.
Stirling, Mr., 117, 127, 135; at Cliveden, 120.
Stirling-Maxwell, Lady Anna, 228.

Stirling-Maxwell, Sir William, 228.
Stoke d'Abernon, church, 370.
Stoke Edith Park, 358.
Stoke Rochford, 105, 130.
Stopford, Miss, 141; at Windsor Castle, 360.
Story, Rev. W., Rector of Fawsley, 172, 179; his manner of conducting the services, 184.
Stowe, 322.
Strangford, Lady, 353.
Strathallan, Lord, 58; at Burghley House, 213.
Strathnairn, Lord, 259; at Hatfield, 262; Wakefield Lodge, 321.
Strathspey, 265.
Strawberry Hill, ball at, 84.
Streleczki, Count, at Hatfield, 185.
Strickland, Miss Agnes, 13; *Bachelor Kings*, 13.
Stuart, Colonel and Mrs., at Wakefield Lodge, 321.
Suffolk election, 296, 339.
Suffrage, household, 133; universal, views on, 77.
Sumner, Heywood, 353.
Sutherland, Duke of, at the opera, 111.
Sweden, Crown Prince of, 333.
Sydney, Lady, at Euston, 268, 269.
Sydney, Lord, at Euston, 268; his visit to St. Petersburg, 269.

Tabley, Lord De, 89.
Tait, Archbishop, his address to Prince Leopold on his Confirmation, 163; criticism on, 187; his address at the G.F.S. meeting, 292; at the wedding of the Duke of Albany, 351; his funeral, 361.
Talbot, Lady Adelaide, 135.
Tankerville, Lord and Lady, at Windsor Castle, 142.
Tannhäuser, performance of, 301.
Taxation, Local, debate on, 243.
Tchataldja, 321.
Teck, Duke of, 115, 245.
Teck, Princess Mary, Duchess of, 245, 247; at Wimbledon, 138; White Lodge, 300; her children, 300.
Teesdale, Colonel, 111, 258.
Teleki, Janie, her death, 280.
Temple, Sir Richard, *India in 1880*, 348; his sketches, 365.
Tennant, Mrs., her reception, 367.
Thames Embankment, opening of the, 200.
Thames valley, 118.
Thatched House Lodge, Richmond Park, 2, 36.

INDEX

Theed, Mr., his statue of Prince Albert, 100.
Thetford, 268.
Thicknesse, Canon, his sermon at Brackley, 188.
Thiers, M., his interview with Bismarck, 279; death, 317; funeral, 318.
Thomas, Mr., 217; at Firle, 164.
Thorneycroft, Mr., his bust of Princess Helena, 115.
Thornton, Clare, 47.
Thüringerwald, 148, 151.
Tichborne trial, 219.
Titiens, Mlle, 21.
Tollemache, Lord, 335, 348.
Tollemache, Mr., 238, 248.
Tomline, Colonel, 231, 233, 237.
Tower, Mrs. Henry, 139.
Townsend, editor of the *Spectator*, at Highclere Castle, 251.
Townsend, Mrs., founds the Girls' Friendly Society, 287, 289; on the characteristics of Lady Knightley, 293; her resignation, 350.
Transvaal, cession of the, 347.
Trebelli, 83.
Trentham, 326.
Trevanion, Mr., 301.
Trevelyan, Sir Charles, 301.
Trevelyan, George, 310.
Trevelyan, Nora, 301, 310, 339.
Trianon, 222.
Trochu, General, 205, 207.
Tryon, Mr., at Burghley House, 213.
Tullyallan, 208, 326, 367.
Turkey, Sultan of, in London, 136; at the opera, 137; his appearance, 137; at the National Rifle Association, Wimbledon, 138.
Turkey, war declared against Russia, 312.
Turnor, Edith, her friendship with Miss Bowater, 105; at a ball at Buckingham Palace, 135.
Turnor, Lady Mary, 130.

United States, system of education, 248.
Unseaworthy Shipping Bill, 273.
Usedom, Countess, at Homburg, 317.

Vallette, M. de la, 208.
Vane, Lord and Lady, at Gayton, 310.
Vanneck, Frances, bridesmaid to Miss Bowater, 171.
Venables, Mr., his conversation with Lady Knightley, 314.
Ventoux, Mont, 28.

Vernon, Lord, at Guisachan, 265.
Versailles, 222; peace signed at, 214.
Verulam, Lord, at Hatfield, 185.
Victoria, Queen, her review of the Guards, 7; at the National Rifle Association meeting, Wimbledon, 17; at the Crystal Palace, 17; death of Prince Consort, 30; her interview with Lady Bowater, 33; present at the wedding of the Prince of Wales, 51; at Osborne, 64, 211; receives Miss Bowater, 65; drives in the Park, 83; her journey to Balmoral, 89; life at Balmoral, 90–103; attends the Kirk, 100 *note*; her reception at Buckingham Palace, 110; at Cliveden, 117; at the wedding of Princess Helena, 127; Fenian plot against, 140; her ascent of the Righi, 159; her letter to Louisa Bowater on her marriage, 174 *note*; at Sandringham, 223; attends the Thanksgiving Service, 225; opens Parliament, 296, 310; her title of Empress of India, 298; at Windsor Castle, 313, 360; patron of the G.F.S., 343; attempt on her life, 350; at the wedding of Prince Leopold, 351; opens the Law Courts, 359; at the christening of Princess Alice of Albany, 361; at Claremont, 372.
Vidauban, 28.
Villiers, Lady Elizabeth, 217.
Villiers, Fred, 78.
Villiers, Mr., 217; at Osborne, 66.
Villiers, Reggie, at Osterley Park, 261.
Vionville, battle of, 305.
Virginia Water, 113, 114.
Vivian, Mrs., her concert, 78.
Volunteer Review at Wimbledon, 60, 137 *note*, 138.

Wake, Sir Herewald, 338.
Wakefield Lodge, 321.
Waldeck, Princess Hélène of, her engagement, 349; appearance, 351; wedding, xvi, 351. *See* Albany.
Waldegrave, Lady, 74, 122; her influence on the Duc d'Aumale, 233.
Walden, Lady Howard de, at Ickworth, 252.
Wales, H.R.H. Albert Edward, Prince of, his engagement, 40; wedding, 50; at the Guildhall,

INDEX

56; at the Guards' ball, 58; the reception at South Kensington Museum, 77; at the opera, 111; at the wedding of Princess Helena, 127; his illness, 223, 224; attends the Thanksgiving Service, 224; at Lansdowne House, 247; Bridgewater House, 248; his return from India, 301; presents, 303; at Holland House, 315; Homburg, 356.
Wales, H.R.H. Alexandra, Princess of, her first Drawing-room, 55; at the Guildhall, 56; birth of a son, 67, 97; at the opera, 111; at the wedding of Princess Helena, 126; her illness, 131; at the Albert Hall, 246; Lansdowne House, 247; Bridgewater House, 248; the French play, 258; her appearance, 365.
Wallace, Mackenzie, 314.
Waller, Major, 373.
Walpole, Horace, his description of Osterley, 261.
Walrond, Mr., at Burghley House, 213.
Waltersdorf, 155.
Ward, Dudley, his death, 210.
Warrender, Sir George 353.
Warwick, Lord, at Homburg, 304.
Waterford, Lady, 22.
Waterloo, 357.
Weedon, 172; snowstorm at, 344.
Week in a French Country House, 272.
Weguelin, Mr., at Chevening, 253.
Weguelin, Mrs., her ball, 134.
Weimar, 151.
Weissenburg, victory at, 204.
Wellesley, Lady C., at Burghley House, 213.
Wellington, Duchess of, 7, 18; at Windsor Castle, 144.
Wellington, Duke of, his campaigns, 6.
Wentworth, Lady, her appearance, 189; escapade, 234.
Wentworth, Lord, 189.
West, Cornwallis, 201.
West, Mr., 89; at Holmbury, 235.
West, Mrs., at Holmbury, 235.
Westminster, Duchess of, 301.
Westmoreland, Lady, at the opera, 111.
Weyer, Mme Van de, 45.
Wheatley, Mary, 87, 165, 198, 312; at Fawsley, 176.
Wheatley, Sir Thomas, 312.
White Lodge, 300.

White, Louisa, her illness, 14; death, 14 *note.*
Whyte-Melville, Major, 194, 248; his death, 329.
Wied, Princess Elizabeth of, 355. *See* Roumania.
Wilberforce, Bishop, his sermon, 243; sudden death, 249.
Wilbraham, Miss, 135.
Wildbad, 284.
Wilde, Oscar, 367.
Wilkinson, Rev. G. H., his sermons, 229, 294.
William II, Emperor of Germany, 148 *note.*
William IV., King, 2; stories of, 268.
Willingham, 2, 129.
Wimbledon, 348; Volunteer Reviews at, 17, 60, 137 *note,* 138.
Winchilsea, Lord, at Crichel, 271.
Windsor Castle, 25, 47, 113, 197, 313, 350, 360; the Chapel, 47; dance at, 117.
Winmarleigh, 309.
Winmarleigh, Lord, 309; at Metz, 304.
Wolff, Sir Henry Drummond, at Hatfield, 185, 186.
Wolmer, Lord, his marriage, 366.
Wolseley, Sir Garnet, his opinion of the Fantees and Chinese, 259.
Women, enfranchisement of, views of, 129.
Women Workers, National Union of, Congress at Hull, xii.
Women's Franchise Bill, 227, 230, 300; debate on, 367.
Wood, Hon. Emily, 111 *note.*
Wood, Miss, 126.
Wood, Sir W. Page, Lord Chancellor, 163.
Woodford church, reopening of, 327–329.
Woodward, Mr., at Frogmore, 141.
Woolsthorpe, 106.
Working Ladies' Guild, xii, 293, 365.
Wormald, Lucy, 172.
Wotton, 235.
Wurtemberg, Princess of, her death, 352.
Wynne-Finch, Colonel, 128.

York, Archbishop of, 314; at Buckingham Palace, 228.
Yorke, Alec, 373.
Yorke, Eliot, 119.

Zanzibar, Seyyid of, 279.
Zouche, Lord, at Osterley Park, 261.

Printed by
MORRISON & GIBB LIMITED
Edinburgh, Scotland

WS - #0050 - 240225 - C0 - 229/152/24 [26] - CB - 9780266397540 - Gloss Lamination